Public Services in EU Law

In the EU public services, both utilities and welfare services can be seen not only as building blocks for the internal market but also as a persistent irritant in the integration process. This book provides a comprehensive overview of the EU law on public services within the context of European integration. It brings together important analysis of the primary Treaty law, mainly on the internal market and competition, and of the secondary legislation at EU level, including different sector-specific regimes. Particular attention is given to case law of the EU Courts. This will be essential reading for those looking to have a broader understanding of the subject.

Wolf Sauter is Professor of Healthcare Regulation at Tilburg University, senior member of Tilburg Law and Economics Center (TILEC) and competition expert at the Dutch Healthcare Authority (NZa). Apart from previous academic appointments in Bremen and Groningen, Wolf has worked in telecommunications and financial markets regulation, as well as in private practice and with the DG Competition of the European Commission in Brussels.

The Law in Context Series

Editors: William Twining (University College London), Christopher McCrudden (Queen's University Belfast) and Bronwen Morgan (University of Bristol).

Since 1970 the Law in Context series has been at the forefront of the movement to broaden the study of law. It has been a vehicle for the publication of innovative scholarly books that treat law and legal phenomena critically in their social, political and economic contexts from a variety of perspectives. The series particularly aims to publish scholarly legal writing that brings fresh perspectives to bear on new and existing areas of law taught in universities. A contextual approach involves treating legal subjects broadly, using materials from other social sciences, and from any other discipline that helps to explain the operation in practice of the subject under discussion. It is hoped that this orientation is at once more stimulating and more realistic than the bare exposition of legal rules. The series includes original books that have a different emphasis from traditional legal textbooks, while maintaining the same high standards of scholarship. They are written primarily for undergraduate and graduate students of law and of other disciplines, but will also appeal to a wider readership. In the past, most books in the series have focused on English law, but recent publications include books on European law, globalization, transnational legal processes and comparative law.

Books in the Series

Anderson, Schum & Twining: *Analysis of Evidence*
Ashworth: *Sentencing and Criminal Justice*
Barton & Douglas: *Law and Parenthood*
Beecher-Monas: *Evaluating Scientific Evidence: An Interdisciplinary Framework for Intellectual Due Process*
Bell: *French Legal Cultures*
Bercusson: *European Labour Law*
Birkinshaw: *European Public Law*
Birkinshaw: *Freedom of Information: The Law, the Practice and the Ideal*
Brownsword & Goodwin: *Law and the Technologies of the Twenty-First Century*
Cane: *Atiyah's Accidents, Compensation and the Law*
Clarke & Kohler: *Property Law: Commentary and Materials*
Collins: *The Law of Contract*
Collins, Ewing & McColgan: *Labour Law*
Cowan: *Housing Law and Policy*
Cranston: *Legal Foundations of the Welfare State*
Darian-Smith: *Laws and Societies in Global Contexts: Contemporary Approaches*
Dauvergne: *Making People Illegal: What Globalisation Means for Immigration and Law*
Davies: *Perspectives on Labour Law*
Dembour: *Who Believes in Human Rights? The European Convention in Question*
de Sousa Santos: *Toward a New Legal Common Sense*

Diduck: *Law's Families*
Fortin: *Children's Rights and the Developing Law*
Ghai & Woodham: *Practising Self-Government: A Comparative Study of Autonomous Regions*
Glover-Thomas: *Reconstructing Mental Health Law and Policy*
Gobert & Punch: *Rethinking Corporate Crime*
Goldman: *Globalisation and the Western Legal Tradition: Recurring Patterns of Law and Authority*
Harlow & Rawlings: *Law and Administration*
Harris: *An Introduction to Law*
Harris, Campbell & Halson: *Remedies in Contract and Tort*
Harvey: *Seeking Asylum in the UK: Problems and Prospects*
Hervey & McHale: *Health Law and the European Union*
Holder & Lee: *Environmental Protection, Law and Policy*
Jackson & Summers: *The Internationalisation of Criminal Evidence*
Kostakopoulou: *The Future Governance of Citizenship*
Lewis: *Choice and the Legal Order: Rising above Politics*
Likosky: *Transnational Legal Processes*
Likosky: *Law, Infrastructure and Human Rights*
Maughan & Webb: *Lawyering Skills and the Legal Process*
McGlynn: *Families and the European Union: Law, Politics and Pluralism*
Moffat: *Trusts Law: Text and Materials*
Monti: *EC Competition Law*
Morgan: *Contract Law Minimalism*
Morgan & Yeung: *An Introduction to Law and Regulation: Text and Materials*
Norrie: *Crime, Reason and History*
O'Dair: *Legal Ethics*
Oliver: *Common Values and the Public–Private Divide*
Oliver & Drewry: *The Law and Parliament*
Picciotto: *International Business Taxation*
Probert: *The Changing Legal Regulation of Cohabitation, 1600–2010*
Reed: *Internet Law: Text and Materials*
Richardson: *Law, Process and Custody*
Roberts & Palmer: *Dispute Processes: ADR and the Primary Forms of Decision-Making*
Rowbottom: *Democracy Distorted: Wealth, Influence and Democratic Politics*
Sauter: *Public Services in EU Law*
Scott & Black: *Cranston's Consumers and the Law*
Seneviratne: *Ombudsmen: Public Services and Administrative Justice*
Siems: *Comparative Law*
Stapleton: *Product Liability*
Stewart: *Gender, Law and Justice in a Global Market*
Tamanaha: *Law as a Means to an End: Threat to the Rule of Law*
Turpin & Tomkins: *British Government and the Constitution: Text and Materials*
Twining: *Globalisation and Legal Theory*
Twining: *Rethinking Evidence*
Twining: *General Jurisprudence: Understanding Law from a Global Perspective*

Twining: *Human Rights, Southern Voices: Francis Deng, Abdullahi An-Na'im, Yash Ghai and Upendra Baxi*
Twining & Miers: *How to Do Things with Rules*
Ward: *A Critical Introduction to European Law*
Ward: *Law, Text, Terror*
Ward: *Shakespeare and Legal Imagination*
Wells and Quick: *Lacey, Wells and Quick: Reconstructing Criminal Law*
Zander: *Cases and Materials on the English Legal System*
Zander: *The Law-Making Process*

International Journal of Law in Context: A Global Forum for Interdisciplinary Legal Studies

The *International Journal of Law in Context* is the companion journal to the Law in Context book series and provides a forum for interdisciplinary legal studies and offers intellectual space for ground-breaking critical research. It publishes contextual work about law and its relationship with other disciplines including but not limited to science, literature, humanities, philosophy, sociology, psychology, ethics, history and geography. More information about the journal and how to submit an article can be found at http://journals.cambridge.org/ijc.

Public Services in EU Law

WOLF SAUTER

CAMBRIDGE
UNIVERSITY PRESS

CAMBRIDGE
UNIVERSITY PRESS

University Printing House, Cambridge CB2 8BS, United Kingdom

Cambridge University Press is part of the University of Cambridge.

It furthers the University's mission by disseminating knowledge in the pursuit of education, learning and research at the highest international levels of excellence.

www.cambridge.org
Information on this title: www.cambridge.org/9781107066120

First published 2015

Printed in the United Kingdom by Clays, St Ives plc

A catalogue record for this publication is available from the British Library

Library of Congress Cataloguing in Publication Data
Sauter, Wolf, author.
Public services in EU law / Wolf Sauter.
pages cm. – (Law in context)
ISBN 978-1-107-06612-0 (hardback)
1. Public utilities – Law and legislation – European Union countries. 2. Public welfare – Law and legislation – European Union countries. 3. Municipal services – Law and legislation – European Union countries. 4. Trade regulation – European Union countries. I. Title. II. Title: Public services in European Union law.
KJE6848.S28 2014
343.2409–dc23

2014023807

ISBN 978-1-107-06612-0 Hardback

Contents

Preface

This book is the result of an attempt to impose a structure on my reading and thinking about services of general economic interest (SGEI). This is one of the key categories in which public services are addressed in EU law. SGEI is a theme that I have been interested in since I prepared my PhD thesis on EU competition law and industrial policy at the European University Institute in Florence in 1991–6. Although it was not the topic of that thesis, I did use the telecommunications sector as a case study, which has remained a source of inspiration regarding the categories of SGEI and universal service in the context of liberalization of public services. Since then, as I argue in this book, SGEI have only become more pertinent with the growing impact of EU law, and the increasing market orientation of public services (including not just the utilities but welfare services as well), within the constraints of the rules and exceptions of EU law. At the same time a citizenship dimension is emerging, although its shape remains indistinct.

Evidently, I could not have completed this book without the generous help of others. I am particularly grateful to José Luis Buendia Sierra, Jim Davies, Leigh Hancher, Dairmuid Rossa Phelan and Nicolas Rennuy who have freely provided their time and expertise, suggested materials, as well as read and commented on the text as a whole. I am grateful to them for this essential contribution even though I realize that I may not always have done full justice to their remarks. Able and timely research assistance was provided by Tilburg law students Charlotte Aardoom and Rina Verbakel. Evidently I alone am responsible for any remaining flaws in the text.

TILEC has provided me with an academic home over the past seven years and it would be difficult to overstate the benefits that I have derived from this academic community of lawyers and economists. I greatly appreciate the inspiring exchanges there that have helped shape the present book. In addition, TILEC staff Ilse Streng and Maartje van Genk, as well as Marijke van Schijndel and Femke Bijleveld at the secretariat of the Tilburg department of European and international public law, have organized welcome assistance in a time of constrained budgets. My daytime employer, the Dutch Healthcare Authority (NZa), has not just provided a stimulating working environment but facilitated my academic pursuits where they overlapped with issues of healthcare regulation. I thank especially Misja Mikkers and Annemiek van der Laan for their support in this regard.

The staff at Cambridge University Press, Sinead Moloney, Rebecca Roberts, Rachel Cox and Helen Francis, have both been highly professional and a pleasure to work with. The Law in Context series editors, especially William Twining and Bronwen Morgan, have kindly encouraged this project from the beginning, which was a great boost to its momentum. I feel particularly honoured that my book will become a part of the venerable Law in Context series. As a student, I first came across this series in the form of Francis Snyder's *New Directions in Community Law*, 2nd edn 1990, which since then has remained a standard of scholarship for me to strive towards. Although he may find much to disagree with in the present work, the past guidance by Christian Joerges likewise continues to inspire me.

Finally I would like to thank my children, Zachary (also for help with the proofs), Aäron and Zoë, for cheerfully enduring and thereby enabling my academic pursuits. This book is dedicated to my parents.

Table of legislation

Regulations

Directives

Commission Decisions

Commission Notices

Commission communications

Commission staff working documents

Commission staff working document, Third biennial Report on social services of general interest, SWD(2013) 40 28
Commission staff working document, Guide to the application of the European Union rules on state aid, public procurement and the internal market to services of general economic interest, and in particular to social services of general interest, SWD(2013) 53 14, 16, 28, 49, 144

Commission Interpretative Communications

Commission Interpretative Communication on the Community law applicable to contract awards not or not fully subject to the provisions of the Public Procurement Directives, [2006] OJ C179/2 167

Guidelines

Guidelines on the application of EEC competition rules in the telecommunications sector, [1991] OJ C233/2 136
Guidelines on the assessment of horizontal mergers under the Council Regulation on the control of concentrations between undertakings, [2004] OJ C31/5 119
Guidelines on the application of Article 81 of the EC Treaty to maritime transport services, [2008] OJ C245/2 133
Community Guidelines for the application of state aid rules in relation to the rapid deployment of broadband networks, [2009] OJ C235/7 151, 187
EU Guidelines for the application of state aid rules in relation to the rapid deployment of broadband networks, [2013] OJ C25/01 187

Council Resolutions

Council Resolution of 7 February 1994 on universal service principles in the telecommunications sector, [1994] OJ C48/1 184

Commission Recommendation

Commission Recommendation 2011/442/EU of 18 July 2011 on access to a basic payment account, [2011] OJ L190/87 182

Table of cases

Court of Justice

General Court

1

Questions, concepts and context

1.1 Outline

Public services: building blocks or persistent irritant?

Public services are frequently a source of friction in the course of European integration. In the words of former Internal Market and Competition Commissioner Mario Monti: 'Since the nineties, the place of public services within the single market has been a persistent irritant in the European public debate.'[1] Yet just a few pages earlier in his report on the single market he states that these services form building blocks for reconciling the single market and the social and citizenship dimensions as components of the highly competitive social market economy that the 2007 Lisbon Treaty has introduced as one of the main objectives of European integration.[2] These contrasting observations coming from such a well-placed and respected commentator will require some explanation. In addition, the topic of public services in EU law is salient today not only because of the liberalization and (re)regulation trend of the past two decades but also given the increasing financial constraints on public budgets that are partly due to the ongoing international financial crisis. As a consequence the preference for private provision prevalent in the utilities may be spilling over into the sphere of welfare services. More generally, changes are now being made in the scope and delivery of a broad range of public services along a trajectory that is shaped at least in part by EU law.

In this book I aim to provide an overview of the EU law on public services within the context of the process of European integration and what appears to be the concomitant transformation of the welfare state into a regulatory state. This account is intended for an audience of lawyers, social scientists and others interested in these processes and in identifying building blocks for transforming society in a European context.

The law covered will include the internal market as well as the state aid and competition law, both the primary (Treaty) and secondary (largely

[1] M. Monti, *A new strategy for the single market: At the service of Europe's economy and society.* Report to the President of the European Commission, José Manuel Barroso, 9 May 2010, 73.

[2] Ibid., 68.

harmonization) rules, with emphasis on the case law of the EU Courts on services of general economic interest (SGEI). Apart from universal service obligations (USO), SGEI are the most important specific concept of EU law with regard to public services.[3] Hence these two concepts will form the key elements of my account of the EU law on public services. This book forms part of a series called 'law in context'. This context will be provided by the integration process and the transformation of economic regulation mentioned above. In addition, the context of the legal issues discussed will be provided by dealing with all public services jointly, instead of just one or several of them: apart from providing a comparative perspective this is intended to reveal the broader EU policy setting and trends. In this setting the balance between positive (market correcting) and negative (unleashing the market) integration will also be examined. In turn this may mean shedding light not just on public services but also on the course of EU integration.

Utilities versus welfare services

Introducing this topic raises an obvious preliminary question that is easier to ask than to answer: what are public services? This question is addressed in more legal and metaphysical detail in the third section of this introductory chapter. For practical purposes I can say here that I will use the term public services as comprising, on the one hand, infrastructure-based utilities such as electronic communications, energy and transport, and, on the other hand, welfare services directed at the individual, such as healthcare, education and pensions.[4] Although not all public services are covered neatly by this two-part distinction – for instance basic banking services and public broadcasting services are not covered – such exceptions can be accommodated within the overall discussion. In economic terms public services carry weight not just because of their social function (of which the usefulness may be debated) but because, jointly, public services account for a significant percentage of GDP (with healthcare alone having a growing share in excess of 10 per cent). Finally they are also intertwined with the post-Second World War Western state – the welfare state.

In EU law public services must be distinguished from public policy exceptions and overriding reasons related to the public interest in the internal market context: public policy may likewise be accommodated in EU state aid and competition law in pursuit of a wide range of (efficiency and equity) objectives. In both cases the existence of legitimate public objectives and the proportionality and coherence of the manner in which they are pursued are of central

[3] The overarching EU law concept of services of general interest (SGI) and that of social services of general interest (SSGI) are also noteworthy but used less frequently; all four concepts are discussed in section 1.3.

[4] Cf. L. Hancher and W. Sauter, 'Public services and state aid', in C. Barnard and S. Peers (eds.), *European Union law* (Oxford University Press, 2014), 539–66. This two-part distinction is also made by the Commission in its 2012 *Altmark* package. See note 11, below.

importance. As we will see below, exceptions claimed for public services similarly require legitimate objectives and have to meet a proportionality test. Public services, however, are concerned foremost with the actual provision of specific services to the public, which is different from public policies dedicated to regulating beer purity, the safety of inland watercraft, driving with motorcycle trailers or bottle recycling.[5]

There are no EU-level public services that are designed and carried out by the EU – although a minimum set of USO may be established in EU legislation this can generally be topped up by the Member States who are also responsible for their provision. This is logical also given the limited spending power of the EU compared to the Member States: national governments generally spend some 40 per cent of GDP; whereas the EU budget is stuck at 1 per cent of GDP and is largely dedicated to the Common Agricultural Policy. Hence the EU is focused on rule-making – strengthened by the agenda-setting powers and the monopoly on proposing EU legislation of the Commission – rather than on spending to promote the public good. Consequently the EU has been described as a 'regulatory state'.[6] In the context of public services this means the EU is involved in setting the standards and coordinating the national regulators but not in providing the services to EU citizens and consumers.

Focus on exceptions and on access

The manner in which public services are organized and indeed whether the services concerned are organized as public services at national level differs between the Member States according to national preferences and conditions. Although this is more an ex post justification than a deliberate ex ante method of organization it is in line with the principle of subsidiarity which requires that decisions should be taken at the lowest effective level.[7] Nevertheless when viewed through the prism of EU law there are significant similarities regarding public services. On the one hand, these concern the scope provided for national public services under exceptions to EU rules and, on the other hand, they reflect the emergence of increasing EU-level regulation of such activities.

Here again the distinction between utilities and welfare services surfaces. In part due to the impact of European integration and EU law, utilities are now

5 Case 178/84 *Commission* v. *Germany* [1987] ECR I-1227; Case C-142/05 *Åklagaren* v. *Percy Mickelsson and Joakim Roos* [2009] ECR I-4273; Case C-110/05 *Commission* v. *Italy* [2009] ECR I-519; Case 302/86 *Commission* v. *Denmark* [1988] ECR 4607.

6 Cf. G. Majone, 'The rise of the regulatory state in Europe', *West European Politics*, 17 (1994), 77–101; F. McGowan and H. Wallace, 'Towards a European regulatory state', *Journal of European Public Policy*, 3 (1996), 560–76.

7 The first part of Article 5(3) TEU reads: 'Under the principle of subsidiarity, in areas which do not fall within its exclusive competence, the Union shall act only if and in so far as the objectives of the proposed action cannot be sufficiently achieved by the Member States, either at central level or at regional and local level, but can rather, by reason of the scale or effects of the proposed action, be better achieved at Union level.'

generally subject to liberalization under the competition rules and harmonized secondary law frameworks. From a more general and contextual framework we also see:

(i) a demise of public provision (privatization);
(ii) the emergence of third-party (competitor) access rights; and
(iii) the rise of specialized sectoral authorities at national level who coordinate their actions under the guidance of the EU Commission.[8]

These are three topics that deserve (and have received) specialized treatment in their own right. Instead my focus will be on SGEI and USO, which means a focus on exceptions to competition and free movement on the one hand, and on consumer access rights on the other. These other trends will only also be reviewed to the extent that they provide the context to the rise of SGEI and USO. The welfare services in large part remain subject only to the primary Treaty rules, notably those on free movement and possibly citizenship. In all cases the injunction of Article 18 TFEU on non-discrimination applies.[9] The impact has been more at the level of the rights of individuals to services of which the reach and nature are decided at the level of the Member State. Hence, so far welfare services have failed for instance to give rise to SGEI and USO.

In addition, I will deal with some of the main recent and ongoing changes regarding public services in secondary law such as the Services Directive,[10] the framework for the application of state aid to SGEI[11] and the proposals for a new

[8] Cf. M. de Visser, *Network-based governance in EC law: The example of EC competition and EC communications law* (Hart Publishing, Oxford, 2009); L. Hancher and S. A. C. M. Lavrijssen, 'Networks on track: From European regulatory networks to European regulatory "network agencies"', *Legal Issues of Economic Integration*, 36 (2009), 23–55.

[9] There appear to be three potential legal bases for such non-discrimination obligations, a general one and two more specific (and limited) ones. The first (i) is citizenship. Article 18 TFEU first para. reads: 'Within the scope of application of the Treaties, and without prejudice to any special provisions contained therein, any discrimination on grounds of nationality shall be prohibited.' Case C-413/99 *Baumbast and R* v. *Secretary of State for the Home Department* [2002] ECR I-7091; E. Spaventa, 'Seeing the wood despite the trees? On the scope of Union citizenship and its constitutional effects', *Common Market Law Review*, 45 (2008), 13–45. Second (ii) there are general obligations set out in Article 20 of the Services Directive 2006/123/EC. Third (iii) similarly in the field of public procurement general obligations of non-discrimination, equal treatment and transparency have been derived directly from the Treaty. Case C-458/03 *Parking Brixen GmbH* v. *Gemeinde Brixen and Stadtwerke Brixen AG* [2005] ECR I-8585.

[10] Directive 2006/123/EC of the European Parliament and of the Council of 12 December 2006 on services in the internal market, OJ 2006, L376/36. Cf. C. Barnard, 'Unravelling the Services Directive', *Common Market Law Review*, 45 (2008), 323–94.

[11] I refer only to the package published in 2012 (which replaced the 2005 one): Commission Decision of 20 December 2011 on the application of Article 106(2) of the Treaty on the Functioning of the European Union to state aid in the form of public service compensation granted to certain undertakings entrusted with the operation of services of general economic interest, OJ 2012, L7/3; Communication from the Commission on a European Union framework for state aid in the form of public service compensation, OJ 2012, C8/15; Communication from the Commission on the application of the European Union state aid rules to compensation granted for the provision of services of general economic interest, OJ 2012, C8/4; Commission

public procurement regime.[12] Another relevant aspect are a number of changes in the primary law that were wrought by the 2007 Lisbon Treaty which came into force on 1 December 2009:

- its introduction of the objective of a 'highly competitive social market economy, aiming at full employment and social progress' in Article 3(3) TEU;
- the addition of a legal basis for legislation on SGEI in Article 14 TFEU and of a Protocol 26 on SGI and SGEI;
- giving the Charter of Fundamental Rights, including its Article 36 on SGEI, the same legal value as the Treaties by force of Article 6(1) TEU;
- instead of making competition policy a Treaty objective (as had been mooted under the Draft Constitution), linking it with the internal market in Article 3(1)b TFEU and in Protocol 27.[13]

These developments illustrate well how new the legal framework for public services is and the degree to which the relevant law is still in flux. To this I should add contrasting developments with, on the one hand, competitive provision of public services and, on the other hand, a bottom-line regime that applies when the entities involved are non-economic in nature and hence fall outside the scope of the competition rules and most secondary law. These various aspects will be discussed in detail in the following chapters. Before moving on to the research questions and the issues that will be addressed in the body of this chapter I will first say a few words about the relevant literature.

The literature

There is a significant body of literature on public services in the EU on which I am grateful to draw and to which I cannot do justice in this short section. It serves merely as a suggestion for further reading and as an indication of the type of literature which I have used.

Regulation (EU) No 360/2012 of 25 April 2012 on the application of Articles 107 and 108 of the Treaty on the Functioning of the European Union to de minimis aid to undertakings providing SGEI, OJ 2012, L114/8. Cf. E. Szyszczak, 'Modernising state aid and the financing of SGEI', *Journal of European Competition Law and Practice*, 3 (2012), 332–43; W. Sauter, 'The *Altmark* package mark II: New rules for state aid and the compensation of services of general economic interest' *European Competition Law Review*, 33 (2012), 307–13.

12 In December 2011 the Commission proposed reviewing the two existing procurement directives (Directive 2004/17/EC of the European Parliament and of the Council of 31 March 2004 coordinating the procurement procedures of entities operating in the water, energy, transport and postal services sectors, OJ 2004, L134/1; Directive 2004/18/EC of the European Parliament and of the Council of 31 March 2004 on the coordination of procedures for the award of public works contracts, public supply contracts and public service contracts, OJ 2004, L134/114) and adding a new Procurement Directive on concessions: http://ec.europa.eu/internal_market/publicprocurement/modernising_rules/reform_proposals_en.htm.

13 See N. Fiedziuk, 'Services of general economic interest and the Treaty of Lisbon: Opening doors to a whole new approach or maintaining the "status quo"?' *European Law Review*, 36 (2011), 226–42.

The monograph that provides the earliest comprehensive treatment of the main issues regarding SGEI is that by José Luis Buendia Sierra in 1999.[14] More recently Erika Szyszczak and Tony Prosser likewise produced essential volumes on the relationship between state and market in EU law.[15] However, all three of these books also deal with the *effet utile* dimension of state action (useful effect, based on the Member States' good faith obligations under the Treaty to respect the competition rules), which I will not cover. In turn they do not cover welfare services, which I will do, so our texts may in this respect be regarded as complementary. Among edited volumes those in the TMC Asser/Springer Verlag series on legal issues of services of general interest by Johan van de Gronden, Markus Krajewski, Ulla Neergaard and Erika Szyszczak (in various constellations) stand out,[16] as does that edited by Marise Cremona.[17] There are too many individual articles and contributions to edited volumes to mention here except the incisive chapter on SGEI in the utilities sector by my Tilburg colleagues Leigh Hancher and Pierre Larouche.[18]

On EU law and the welfare state, and on social services and EU law, there is again a rich literature that is largely based on edited volumes. Worth mentioning are the collections edited by Gráinne de Búrca,[19] by Michael Dougan and Eleanor Spaventa[20] and by Beatrice Cantillon and others.[21] By definition there are too many contextual books to mention individually, but I benefited especially from the integration-oriented works of the political scientists Fritz

[14] J. L. Buendia Sierra, *Exclusive rights and state monopolies under EC law: Article 86 (former Article 90) of the EC Treaty* (Oxford University Press, 2000).

[15] E. Szyszczak, *The regulation of the state in competitive markets in the EU* (Hart Publishing, Oxford, 2007); T. Prosser, *The limits of competition law: Markets and public services* (Oxford University Press, 2005). Cf. W. Sauter and H. Schepel, *State and market in European Union law: The public and private spheres of the internal market before the EU Courts* (Cambridge University Press, 2009).

[16] Such as: E. Szyszczak and J. W. van de Gronden (eds.), *Financing services of general economic interest: Reform and modernization* (TMC Asser Press, The Hague, 2013); U. Neergaard et al. (eds.), *Social services of general interest in the EU* (TMC Asser Press, The Hague, 2013); M. Krajewski, U. Neergaard and J. van de Gronden (eds.), *The changing framework for services of general interest in Europe: Between competition and solidarity* (TMC Asser Press, The Hague, 2009); E. Szyszczak et al. (eds.), *Developments in services of general interest* (TMC Asser Press, The Hague, 2011). Also in this series: L. Nistor, *Public services and the European Union: Healthcare, health insurance and education services* (TMC Asser Press, The Hague, 2011).

[17] M. Cremona (ed.), *Market integration and public services in the European Union* (Oxford University Press, 2011).

[18] L. Hancher and P. Larouche, 'The coming of age of EU regulation of network industries and services of general economic interest', in P. Craig and G. de Búrca (eds.), *The evolution of EU law*, 2nd edn (Oxford University Press, 2011), 743–81.

[19] G. de Búrca (ed.), *EU law and the welfare state: In search of solidarity* (Oxford University Press, 2005).

[20] M. Dougan and E. Spaventa (eds.), *Social welfare and EU law: Essays in European law* (Hart Publishing, Oxford, 2005).

[21] B. Cantillon, H. Verschueren and P. Ploscar (eds.), *Social inclusion and social protection in the EU: Interactions between law and policy* (Intersentia, Antwerp, 2012).

Scharpf[22] and Giandomenico Majone.[23] I have used, perhaps not obviously, Maurizo Ferrara,[24] Julian Le Grand[25] and Anton Hemerijck's[26] works on the future of welfare states. On regulation I have referred mainly to the works by Anthony Ogus,[27] and by Robert Baldwin, Martin Cave and Martin Lodge,[28] as well as several more legal texts (edited) by Dawn Oliver, Bronwen Morgan and others.[29] Regarding the economics of welfare states, where I am less well qualified, I have relied on the standard work by Nicholas Barr.[30]

The reasons that I thought the present book might have something to add to the above-mentioned works are: (i) as an update; (ii) because of its contextual nature; (iii) because it covers not only the utilities but also welfare services; and (iv) given its approach combining a discussion of primary and secondary law in their horizontal and vertical dimensions. To this I could add the current topicality of reviewing the welfare state at a time of global economic hardship which however forms only a very general background.

Purpose of the chapter

As its title shows, in the remainder of this first and introductory chapter I want to do the following three things: first, introduce the research *questions* that I intend to address in the course of this book as a whole; second, discuss the *concept* of public services and introduce the various related categories that are relevant to this concept in EU law in more detail; and third, provide a broader *context* in terms of the debate on the changing role of the state and of the shape and merits of EU integration in relation to public services. These three tasks will be intermingled to some extent. In addition, I will set out the way the book is

[22] F. W. Scharpf, *Community and autonomy: Institutions, policies and legitimacy in multilevel Europe* (Campus, Frankfurt am Main, 2010). Earlier: F. W. Scharpf, *Governing in Europe: Effective and democratic?* (Oxford University Press, 1999).

[23] G. Majone, *Dilemmas of European integration: The ambiguities and pitfalls of integration by stealth* (Oxford University Press, 2009).

[24] M. Ferrara, 'Towards an "open" social citizenship? The new boundaries of welfare in the European Union', in de Búrca (2005), above n. 19, 11–38; M. Ferrara, 'Modest beginnings, timid progress: What's next for social Europe?' in Cantillon, Verschueren and Ploscar, above n. 21, 17–40; M. Ferrara, *The boundaries of welfare: European integration and the new spatial politics of social protection* (Oxford University Press, 2005).

[25] J. Le Grand, *The other invisible hand: Delivering public services through choice and competition* (Princeton University Press, 2007).

[26] A. Hemerijck, *Changing welfare states* (Oxford University Press, 2013).

[27] A. I. Ogus, *Regulation: Legal form and economic theory* (Hart Publishing, Oxford, 2004).

[28] R. Baldwin, M. Cave and M. Lodge, *Understanding regulation: Theory, strategy and practice*, 2nd edn (Oxford University Press, 2013); and R. Baldwin, M. Cave and M. Lodge (eds.), *The Oxford handbook of regulation* (Oxford University Press, 2010).

[29] D. Oliver, T. Prosser and R. Rawlings (eds.), *The regulatory state: Constitutional implications* (Oxford University Press, 2010); B. Morgan and K. Yeung, *An introduction to law and regulation: Text and materials* (Cambridge University Press, 2009).

[30] N. Barr, *Economics of the welfare state*, 5th edn (Oxford University Press, 2012).

structured and introduce the approach of the various chapters. First we will look at the research questions.

1.2 The research questions

More detailed issues will be raised on a chapter by chapter basis. However, the overarching research questions that I will address can be grouped under the following three sets of issues.

The first set of issues revolves around the question of what are the rules of EU law on public services, using the traditional triad of EU law as regards the legal basis, the applicable legal rules and the exceptions to these rules.

1. What is the relevant primary and secondary EU law?
2. What are the limits that EU law imposes on public services?
3. What scope is left for national policies regarding public services under EU law exceptions?

The second set of questions regard the dynamics in the case law and the legislative process. This will involve looking at the balance between positive and negative integration.

4. What are the common elements regarding public services in the case law?
5. Are EU standards emerging and what is their role?
6. How does this affect legislation?

The final set of questions regards the role and development of the main EU-level concepts.

7. What is the role of the concept of service of general (economic) interest?
8. What is the role of universal service in this context?
9. Is there an EU citizenship dimension?

In the present chapter I aim to give a provisional answer on the role of the concepts of USO and SGEI, as well as what constitutes the EU law on public services, providing themes that will be revisited and explored more fully in the subsequent chapters. The European integration process and the multi-level system of governance of the EU provide the context for this analysis, as does a short section on the economic context.[31] At a general level these political and economic contextual aspects will be dealt with mainly in the current chapter. Specific applications will follow in the later chapters.

[31] Cf. G. Marks, L. Hooghe and K. Blank, 'European integration from the 1980s: State-centric v. multi-level governance', *Journal of Common Market Studies*, 34 (1996), 341–78; F. W. Scharpf, 'The joint-decision trap: Lessons from German federalism and European integration', *Public Administration*, 66 (1998) 239–78.

1.3 The concept of public services in EU law

Public services in EU law: terminology

Throughout this book I will use the term public services as a convenient form of shorthand for the utilities and the welfare services sectors combined (which also includes basic banking services and public broadcasting even though these are more difficult to group in either of these two categories). At the same time the usage of the vernacular term public services underlines the contextual nature of my approach where the starting point is the more traditional general (and/or national) concept that is gradually being colonized by EU law and its technical terminology – or argot. For instance, as over time Member States may want to rely more frequently on the SGEI exception of Article 106(2) TFEU they will more frequently explicitly define their services – or at least: the relevant part of their services – thus.[32] Likewise liberalization tends to lead to the definition of USO. Strictly speaking, however, there is no such thing as an EU law concept called public service. The concept of services of general interest (SGI) that will be discussed later in this section comes closest as a functional equivalent but has so far rarely been used in a legal context – although in a policy context it dates back to 1996 (see section 1.4).

This does not mean the term public services is not used in EU law: it is used relating to transport (as it appears in the text of Article 93 TFEU) and as public services compensation in the state aid setting. The much-quoted *Altmark* case (2003) is a prominent example of such usage.[33] In general the term 'public services' is used in EU legal texts interchangeably with SGI and SGEI just like USO is frequently used interchangeably with the term 'public service obligations' (PSO).[34] Also there is legislation with regard to 'public' undertakings (the Transparency Directive),[35] and with regard to public services in the public

[32] Although the existence of an SGEI can be derived from its legislative and regulatory context, for instance in the state aids context (see e.g. Case T-289/03 *British United Provident Association Ltd (BUPA), BUPA Insurance Ltd and BUPA Ireland Ltd* v. *Commission* [2008] ECR II-81, para. 181ff, noted by W. Sauter in *Common Market Law Review*, 46 (2009), 269–86), emphasis is increasingly placed clearly on an explicit act of entrustment. See para. 3.3 'Entrustment act' in SGEI compensation Communication (2012), above n. 11.

[33] This usage appears to originate from the reference to public services in the transport provisions of the TFEU. Cf. N. Fiedziuk, 'Putting services of general economic interest up for tender: Reflections on applicable EU rules', *Common Market Law Review*, 50 (2013), 87–114. Case C-280/00 *Altmark Trans GmbH and Regierungspräsidium Magdeburg* v. *Nahverkehrsgesellschaft Altmark GmbH, and Oberbundesanwalt beim Bundesverwaltungsgericht* [2003] ECR I-7747.

[34] On the universality requirement see especially Case T-289/03 *BUPA*, above n. 32, at para. 172. However, the General Court in *BUPA* also frequently uses the terms PSO and public service requirements.

[35] Commission Directive 2006/111/EC of 16 November 2006 on the transparency of financial relations between Member States and public undertakings as well as on financial transparency with certain undertakings, OJ 2006, L318/17. The legal basis is Article 106(3) TFEU. Public undertakings are undertakings over which public authorities exercise dominant influence by virtue of ownership, financial participation or rules that govern them.

procurement context,[36] alongside rules for water, energy, transport and telecommunications.[37] Nevertheless, as noted, there is a tendency to revert to SGEI and USO.

As an indication of the complications involved it should be noted that the concept of public services is fundamentally wider than SGEI because it generally refers to the services as a whole – postal services, healthcare services or transport services – not just that element that is part of or required to ensure a public service obligation or USO that will constitute an SGEI. Nor are public services (such as general education or statutory social insurance) necessarily economic in nature, which all services of general *economic* interest (SGEI) by definition must be. It is worth highlighting that in my view it is not the public service concerned as a whole that forms an SGEI. Rather the SGEI forms part of a public service (or SGI), and in turn a PSO is part of an SGEI, of which PSO if it contains universal service requirements a USO can form part. I will return to this point below with the help of more formal definitions and some visual aids.

Public services in the national context

It should be added that there is no ready general concept of public services at national level to rely on either, at least not one that is widely shared across the different national jurisdictions of the Member States. In the literature a comparative analysis of the various national concepts of public service is sometimes provided.[38] However, because I am adopting an EU law perspective, and to some extent a forward looking one, there does not appear to be a pressing need to attempt to disentangle up to twenty-eight national definitions (assuming there would be just one per Member State). This reluctance is even stronger because, as we will see, SGEI are an open-ended category, and Member States are free to claim SGEI status for any set of services which they wish to be universally available within proportionate constraints on the applicability of the Treaty rules. According to the Commission's 2012 Communication on SGEI and state aid:

> Since the distinction between economic and non-economic services depends on political and economic specificities in a given Member State, it is not possible to draw up an exhaustive list of activities that a priori would never be economic. Such a list would not provide genuine legal certainty and would thus be of little use.[39]

[36] Directive 2004/18/EC, above n. 12. [37] Directive 2004/17/EC, above n. 12.

[38] Thus, Heike Schweitzer has referred to the French administrative law category of *service public* and contrasted this with the German concept of *Daseinsvorsorge* in her chapter 'Services of general economic interest: European law's impact on the role of markets and of Member States', in Cremona, above n. 17, 11–62. Likewise Tony Prosser has looked at UK versus French and Italian approaches to the concept of public service, above n. 15.

[39] Above, n. 11, para. 14.

National preferences and differences can therefore be accommodated, so the precise definitions at that level are not crucial. What is crucial is the scope for national policies that remains available within the constraints of EU law. At the same time, in spite of national differences, modern welfare states (more specifically: the Member States of the EU) generally reserve special treatment to what is broadly the same set or a highly similar set of public services – which makes it possible to refer to public services without indicating a specific legal category.

In general terms the notion of public services seems to cover services that are provided

(i) to the public, and/or in the public interest;
(ii) in some uniform or regulated manner;
(iii) by entities in public ownership.

Or do we really (perhaps at different times) mean all three?[40] What we will see is that whereas the first and the second categories are promoted and to an increasing extent shaped by EU law, the third dimension is gradually being eroded by European integration. However, there are many other reasons why public ownership is no longer a preferred modus operandi in the modern welfare state and its erosion in itself does not signify that the welfare state is under serious threat.[41] The increased focus on what it is that constitutes the public interest and what regulation this requires is in my view part of a process of rationalization of public policy in terms of both means and ends (that is to say it would increase output legitimacy). It is accompanied by a demise of public ownership because, as a result of the rationalization process, this form of property is perceived as largely obsolete and rarely cost-effective in terms of promoting the public interest. However, in this book I am not interested in the issue of public ownership per se, as represented in EU law primarily by Articles 106(1) and 345 TFEU, which will be discussed in the second chapter.[42] Instead I am interested in the first two dimensions of public services set out above: the public interest and regulatory aspects that inform the rationalization process.

The asymmetric impact of EU law on public services

Finally, note that the impact of EU law in the utilities and the welfare services is asymmetrical. That is because for EU law it is decisive whether the services

[40] M. Cremona, 'Introduction', in Cremona, above n. 17, 1–10. Cf. Communication from the Commission, Services of general interest in Europe, OJ 1996, C281/03, p. 3.

[41] Cf. C. Hay and D. Wincott, *The political economy of European welfare capitalism* (Palgrave Macmillan, Basingstoke, 2012); M. P. Smith, *States of liberalisation: Redefining the public sector in integrated Europe* (SUNY Press, Albany, 2005).

[42] 'In the case of public undertakings and undertakings to which Member States grant special or exclusive rights, Member States shall neither enact nor maintain in force any measure contrary to the rules contained in the Treaties, in particular to those rules provided for in Article 18 and Articles 101 to 109.' See further Chapter 2.1 on primary law/the Treaty framework.

concerned are economic in nature (and therefore qualify as SGEI). Social services may frequently constitute non-economic services of general interest (non-economic SGI) which remain outside the scope of the Treaties altogether apart from the application of some general principles like non-discrimination (see below). As I have mentioned above, for each utility sector (electronic communications, gas, electricity, posts and transport) a distinctive EU law regulatory framework has been created where the USO logic is used to legitimize and thereby leverage and promote liberalization (although in some sectors, such as energy, public service obligations that do not concern USO also exist). The welfare services have started coming under the influence of non-discrimination and free movement as well as the competition rules much more recently and there is no comparable uniform pattern of liberalization discernible. Aside from this basic distinction, the degree to which EU law has influenced public services also differs considerably between the various types of services within the two categories, as we will see in the following chapters. I now move on to the EU level by discussing the key EU law concepts.

The key EU law concepts: SGEI and USO

Instead of a single concept of public services at EU level there are several related concepts which in part overlap and are relevant both to the utilities and the social service dimension. The most important of these are the following two: SGEI and USO.[43]

Services of general economic interest (SGEI), which are found in Articles 14 and 106(2) TFEU as well as Protocol 26 to the TFEU and Article 36 of the Charter of Fundamental Rights of the EU. As mentioned above, a specific secondary law framework for SGEI in the context of state aid was introduced in 2005 and updated in 2012, alongside changes to the Treaty basis for SGEI itself.[44] In the Commission's policy documents SGEI have been defined as follows:

> SGEI are economic activities which deliver outcomes in the overall public good which would not be supplied (or would be supplied under different conditions in terms of quality, safety, affordability, equal treatment or universal access) by the market without public intervention. The PSO [public service obligation] is imposed on the provider by an act of entrustment and on the basis of a general interest criterion which ensures that the service is provided under conditions allowing it to fulfil its mission.[45]

[43] Cf. W. Sauter, 'Services of general economic interest and universal service in EU law', *European Law Review*, 33 (2008), 167–92.

[44] Cf. Szyszczak, above n. 11; and Sauter, above n. 11.

[45] Communication from the Commission, A quality framework for services of general interest in Europe, COM(2011) 900, p. 3.

Here the economic nature and the public service obligation (PSO) stand out as the material elements of the definition.[46] The EU law definition of economic activity is functional in nature. Economic activity is defined as: 'any activity consisting in offering goods and services on a given market is an economic activity'.[47] Being economic in nature means being provided by undertakings, which are again defined according to their function – these are entities that provide goods or services, in principle (or at least potentially) under conditions of competition.[48] (The purpose of the SGEI need not be economic: it can be efficiency or equity related.) Article 57 TFEU defines services as follows:

> Services shall be considered to be 'services' within the meaning of the Treaties where they are normally provided for remuneration, in so far as they are not governed by the provisions relating to freedom of movement for goods, capital and persons.

More formal aspects are the act of entrustment and the general interest criterion. Under the state aid rules concerning SGEI, for instance, an entrustment act must set out the content and duration of the PSO alongside the identity of the undertaking involved, any special and exclusive rights as well as the parameters for compensation and the arrangements for avoiding and recovering overcompensation. In practice, the entrustment and PSO are frequently derived from the legal and regulatory context. It is not immediately clear whether universality is always required (which is key to the distinction between a PSO and a USO; see further below). Therefore it is not clear either whether the PSO (the overarching category) should always be a USO (the subset focusing on universality of the service). In the 2008 *BUPA* case the General Court stated:

> It must be made clear that in Community law and for the purposes of applying the EC Treaty competition rules, there is no clear and precise regulatory definition of the concept of an SGEI mission and no established legal concept definitively fixing the conditions that must be satisfied before a Member State can properly invoke the existence and protection of an SGEI mission, either within the meaning of the first *Altmark* condition or within the meaning of Article 86(2) EC [now Article 106(2) TFEU].[49]

For the same reason it is also not clear quite what the scope of an SGEI is apart from the fact it is carried out by an undertaking – because of the economic

[46] In Protocol 26 on SGI, Article 1, third indent, refers to: 'a high level of quality, safety and affordability, equal treatment and the promotion of universal access and of user rights' as shared values of SGEI.

[47] Joined cases C-180/98 to C-184/98 *Pavel Pavlov et al.* v. *Stichting Pensioenfonds Medische Specialisten* [2000] ECR I-6451, para. 75.

[48] Case C-475/99 *Firma Ambulanz Glöckner* v. *Landkreis Südwestpfalz* [2001] ECR I-8089, para. 20.

[49] Case T-289/03 *BUPA*, above n. 32, para. 165. Cited also in U. Neergaard, 'Services of general economic interest: The nature of the beast', in Krajewski, Neergaard and van de Gronden, above n. 16, 17–50.

nature of the activity – and delivers PSO. In the past I have argued that an SGEI consists of three elements:

(i) the PSO and/or USO obligations (USO being a specific type of PSO concerned with universality which may be involved but need not be);
(ii) any related elements of the service needed to provide these PSO and/or USO – which could be regarded as ancillary restraints; and
(iii) if necessary, the aspects needed to make this provision affordable – that is to say the funding regime to which much attention has been paid in the state aid context.[50]

Today I am still convinced that this approach makes sense. That is also because it helps to distinguish public services – the activities such as providing transport services or social housing – as a whole from their socialized component or the mission with which an undertaking is in this context charged with an SGEI. This restrictive definition is useful also in order to satisfy the proportionality requirement in EU law that it is necessary that any restrictions are limited to what is necessary to provide the PSO/USO concerned.

Over the past decades a significant body of case law on SGEI has developed predominantly in the utilities sectors. It ranges from *Sacchi* (1974) on broadcasting transmission and *British Telecom* (1985) on telecommunications services to *Corbeau* (1993) on posts, *Almelo* (1994) on electricity and *Altmark* (2003) concerning transport services. I would also note the *BUPA* (2008) case on health insurance that I have already cited.[51] All these cases will be discussed in some more detail below. Typically they emerged as competitive provision became a contested issue in the wake of (partial) liberalization and/or technological change, raising issues of legal interpretation. Technical change is one reason why over time the view of whether a certain public service is an SGEI can change on the merits: for instance the emergence of broadband, e-mail and social

[50] Sauter, above n. 43. Also according to the Commission staff working document, Guide to the application of the European Union rules on state aid, public procurement and the internal market to services of general economic interest, and in particular to social services of general interest, SWD(2013) 53, at p. 22 the content of an SGEI is equivalent to a PSO. V. Hatzopoulos, *Regulating services in the European Union* (Oxford University Press, 2012) at 43, relies on para. 162 of Case T-289/03 *BUPA* for the observation that PSO and SGEI are identical. However, the General Court here only states that it is common ground between the parties that this is so and does not express its own view let alone a decisive view. In any event there is much indistinct usage of the various terms.

[51] Case 155–73 *Giuseppe Sacchi* [1974] ECR 40; Case 41/83 *Italy* v. *Commission (British Telecom)* [1985] ECR 873; Case C-320/91 *Criminal proceedings against Paul Corbeau* [1993] ECR I-2533; Case C-393/92 *Municipality of Almelo and Others* v. *NV Energiebedrijf Ijsselmij* [1994] ECR I-1477; Case C-280/00 *Altmark*, above n. 33. For an overview see J. L. Buendia Sierra, 'Chapter 6: Article 86 – exclusive rights and other anticompetitive state measures', in J. Faull and A. Nikpay (eds.), *The EC law on competition*, 2nd edn (Oxford University Press, 2007), 593–655; updated in J. L. Buendia Sierra, 'Chapter 6: Article 106 – exclusive or special rights and other anti-competitive state measures', in J. Faull and A. Nikpay (eds.), *The EU Law of Competition*, 3rd edn (Oxford University Press, 2014), 809–79. For a thematic discussion comparing parallel internal market developments, see Sauter and Schepel, above n. 15.

media services arguably decrease the relevance of traditional postal and broadcasting services.[52] The existence of this case law therefore does not mean there is now a fixed list of SGEI even Member State by Member State: any list will be open-ended as change may occur when services are liberalized.[53] We now move on to the second key EU law category.

Universal service obligations (USO): the Commission has defined this term as follows:

> USO are a type of PSO which sets the requirements designed to ensure that certain services are made available to all consumers and users in a Member State, regardless of their geographical location, at a specified quality and, taking account of specific national circumstances, at an affordable price.[54]

There are two distinct meanings of the term USO. First, in the broad sense USO are relevant as a specific form of PSO that is focused on providing a universal service, which PSO is a requirement for a finding of SGEI. Although in this context sometimes the term PSO is used interchangeably with USO, it is then not clear whether PSO must always cover a universal service or whether they could cover other types of services. I believe PSO do not always involve USO: security of supply and environmental objectives in the context of the

[52] Cf. Case C-18/88 *Régie des télégraphes et des téléphones* v. *GB-Inno-BM SA* [1991] ECR I-5941, para. 16.

[53] It is possible to list the sectors where the Court or the Commission have accepted the existence of an SGEI in past cases. These include river port operations; establishing and operating a public telecommunications network; water distribution; the operation of television services; electricity distribution; the operation of particular transport lines; employment recruitment; basic postal services; maintaining a postal service network in rural areas; regional policy; port services; waste management; ambulance services; and basic health insurance. However, this does not mean these services are to be regarded as SGEI in all Member States, at all times. Buendia Sierra (2007), above n. 51, 629–30; cited in Sauter, above n. 43, at note 22.

[54] COM(2011) 900 final, above n. 45, p. 4. Cf. Green paper on services of general interest, COM(2003) 270 final, p. 16, with reference to Article 3(1) of Directive 2002/22/EC of the European Parliament and of the Council of 7 March 2002 on universal service and users' rights relating to electronic communications networks and services (Universal Service Directive), OJ 2002, L108/51. Cf. Directive 97/67/EC of the European Parliament and of the Council of 15 December 1997 on common rules for the development of the internal market of Community postal services and the improvement of quality of service, OJ 1998, L15/14; Directive 2003/54/EC of the European Parliament and of the Council of 26 June 2003 concerning common rules for the internal market in electricity and repealing Directive 96/92/EC, OJ 2003, L176/37; Directive 2003/55/EC of the European Parliament and of the Council of 26 June 2003 concerning common rules for the internal market in natural gas and repealing Directive 98/30/EC, OJ 2003, L176/57; Regulation (EC) No 1370/2007 of the European Parliament and of the Council of 23 October 2007 on public passenger transport services by rail and by road and repealing Council Regulations (EEC) Nos 1191/69 and 1107/70, OJ 2007, L315/1; Council Regulation (EEC) No 3577/92 of 7 December 1992 applying the principle of freedom to provide services to maritime transport within Member States (maritime cabotage), OJ 1992, L364/7; Regulation (EC) No 1008/2008 of the European Parliament and of the Council of 24 September 2008 on common rules for the operation of air services in the Community (recast), OJ 2008, L293/3; Commission Recommendation 2011/442/EU of 18 July 2011 on access to a basic payment account, OJ 2011, L190/97; Communication from the Commission on the application of State aid rules to public service broadcasting, OJ 2009, L257/1.

energy legislation of the EU provide a clear example of this. Hence to use the term PSO where a USO is meant is confusing.[55]

Second, in the narrow sense the term USO is also used to identify a limited set of services where USO have been defined at least in part at EU level. This applies to electronic communications and posts as well as electricity – and in terms of content if not terminology to gas where the term used is PSO, whereas for basic banking services the term 'access' is used. 'Defined in part at EU level' here means that Member States can top up the basic EU-level USO with more stringent national requirements. For example the basic voice telephony and internet connection at an affordable price under the current EU universal service definition[56] could by national authorities be extended to include a faster and technically more advanced (high speed or ultra-high speed) broadband connection. This type of EU-standardized USO (the specialized category) can be seen as a subset of USO at large (the overarching category).

Conceptually we can see this as a set of five nested categories that rank from most inclusive to least inclusive as follows: (i) public service/service of general interest (SGI); (ii) service of general economic interest (SGEI); (iii) public service obligation (PSO); (iv) universal service obligation (USO); (v) EU-defined USO (see Figure 1.1). Not all stages need to be present in a particular case.

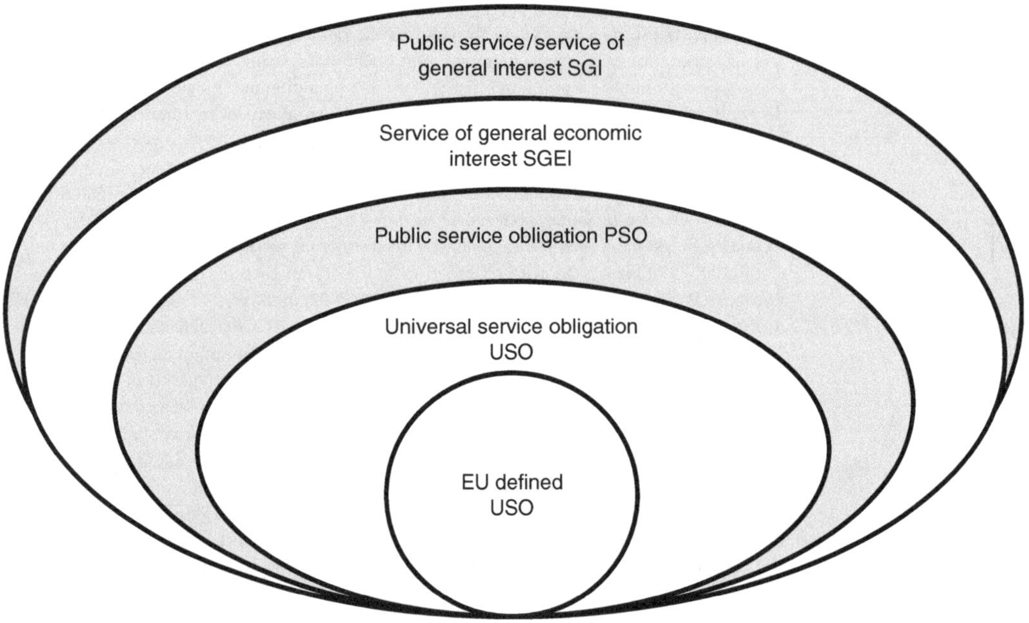

Figure 1.1 Nested model of the content of public services/services of general interest

55 In its staff working document SWD(2013) 53, above n. 50, the Commission staff speak of 'the content of an SGI – i.e. public service obligations' (at p. 22).

56 Article 4 of Directive 2002/22/EC, above n. 54,

In the preceding visualization the universal service obligation defined at EU level forms the pearl that sits at the centre of the public services oyster shell. However, of these five levels only the two shaded areas, public service and public service obligation, must always coexist. The unshaded areas, that of the SGEI level and the two USO levels, are optional: in principle it is possible to have a public service which has a PSO but does not rely on an SGEI, for instance where the service is not economic, as in the case of general education or statutory social services. Also it is possible to have an SGEI of which the PSO do not involve a USO at retail level but a wholesale access obligation. Below we will see an example of the latter in the area of broadband. In banking services we see an access obligation at retail level that (as mentioned) is not called a USO but materially does constitute one.

Moreover in principle Member States are free to add new SGEI and to top up EU-defined USO as they see fit – making these open-ended categories. SGEI may be assigned to monopolists including undertakings enjoying special and exclusive rights as well as to several undertakings engaged in competitive provision or to a specific undertaking as provider of last resort. I will now turn to the definitions of the remaining concepts.

Related EU concepts: SGI and SSGI

Services of General Interest (SGI) are defined as follows:

> Services that public authorities of the Member States classify as being of general interest and, therefore, subject to specific public service obligations (PSO). The terms covers both economic activities . . . and non-economic services.[57]

Conceptually services of general interest or SGI are therefore the overarching concept in EU law in relation to SGEI as well as social services of general interest (SSGI) that will be discussed next.[58] They are services classified as being of general interest and therefore as subject to specific PSO. This means that SGI are the closest functional equivalent in EU law to the general notion of public services. In practice, however, the concept is both still relatively new and rarely used. Although already mentioned in a Commission Communication of 1996, it was only introduced as a legal category with Protocol 26 when the Lisbon Treaty came into force in 2009.[59] To avoid the risk of drowning in an alphabet soup of acronyms identifying overlapping types of public services in the course of my explanation I will use the diagram below (Figure 1.2) to illustrate the relationship between SGI, SSGI and SGEI.

[57] COM(2011) 900, above n. 45, p. 4.

[58] Communication from the Commission, Reform of the EU state aid rules on services of general economic interest, COM(2011) 146, p. 4. Note that at the time the Services Directive was adopted these distinctions were still unclear. In its recital 17 SGI are regarded as by definition non-economic and contrasted with SGEI. Directive 2006/123/EC, above n. 10.

[59] Services of general interest in Europe, above n. 40.

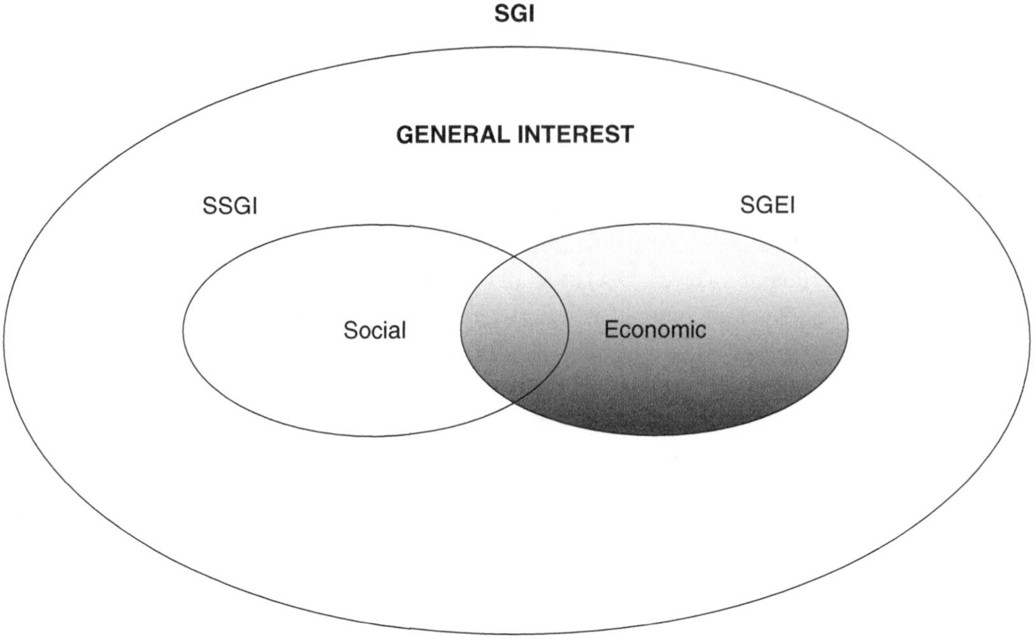

Figure 1.2 Visualizing SGI, SSGI and SGEI (source COM(2011) 146)[60]

The shaded oval located centre-right in this diagram indicates the types of public services that are primarily relevant in EU law: SGEI. I will now discuss their relationship with SSGI. Social services of general interest, or SSGI

> include social security schemes covering the main risks of life and a range of other services provided directly to the person that play a preventive and socially cohesive role.[61]

Social services (or SSGI) are relevant in EU law primarily to the extent that they are also economic in nature and hence are at the same time SGEI: that is the shaded area where the two smaller ovals overlap in the centre of the diagram. The same applies to SGI in general terms: in principle they are caught by EU law only if they are economic in nature. There are two main categories of SGI that are non-economic:

- State provision that does not involve (potential) competition remains outside the scope of the Treaty. An example concerning welfare services would be statutory social security or general education and healthcare provided in a national healthcare system.

[60] Communication from the Commission, Social services of general Interest, COM(2006) 177; Communication from the Commission, Services of general Interest including social services of general interest, COM(2007) 725.

[61] COM(2011) 900, above n. 45, p. 3.

- Services where the 'intrinsic prerogatives of the state' are at stake. For instance, airspace management and pollution control even when carried out by private parties have been regarded as the exercise of powers which are typically those of a public authority.[62] In this case the question would be whether a PSO for a service provided to the public is concerned.

These categories are less watertight than they may appear: they apply only if the Member State concerned has decided to introduce market mechanisms – which will often be the case if private parties have been involved (even if they are monopolists, the service may have been tendered so there was competition for the market). On the other hand, the concept of undertaking is also functional in nature, meaning that the legal status of a private party is not decisive – but again whether the services concerned can in principle be provided in competition. I propose to make the distinctions outlined above based on the application of the following three cumulative criteria.[63] Is the service provided:

(i) in the public interest?
(ii) a service to the public (subject to a PSO)?
(iii) economic (that is, provided by an undertaking)?

As we can see, an SGEI meets all three of these criteria, a non-economic SGI meets only the criteria of being a service to the public and being in the public interest and the function of a public authority meets only the criterion of being in the public interest but not the other two. Finally, even where they are economic, public services may not have an effect on trade – that is to say, they lack an EU dimension – or be de minimis: so small as to pass under the radar of EU law scrutiny.[64]

With the development of the concept of EU citizenship (from the 1992 Maastricht Treaty onwards) the view has emerged that some general principles of EU law, such as non-discrimination, should apply in such cases as well.[65] In the framework of EU law the category of public services could be seen as co-extensive with SGI. Because so far the expression SGI has played a very limited

[62] Communication from the Commission, Services of general interest in Europe, OJ 2001, C17/4, para. 28. Case C-364/92 *SAT Fluggesellschaft GmbH* v. *Eurocontrol* [1994] ECR I-43; Case C-343/95 *Diego Calì & Figli Srl* v. *Servizi ecologici porto di Genova SpA (SEPG)* [1997] ECR I-1547. Cf. Sauter and Schepel, above n. 15.

[63] Neergaard, above n. 49, adds the categories of market services that are not as such in the public interest. They may be regulated in general terms such as relating to health and safety and consumer protection.

[64] Commission Regulation (EU) No 360/2012, above n. 11.

[65] COM(2011) 900, above n. 45, p. 3; Communication from the Commission, Services of general interest including social services of general interest, COM(2007) 725, p. 4. In the TFEU Part 2, non-discrimination and citizenship, Article 18 TFEU provides: 'Within the scope of application of the Treaties, and without prejudice to any special provisions contained therein, any discrimination on grounds of nationality shall be prohibited.'

role we will persist with the usage of public services unless a specific SGI aspect is involved (such as with reference to Article 2 of the Protocol on SGI).[66]

In the subsequent chapters we will move on to examine some questions that are too complex for present purposes: to what extent is the EU regime applicable to SGI, notably how are social services covered? What is the role for citizenship? What are the rights of consumers? Are the two linked? Here I will first provide some general context.

1.4 A potted history of EU law on public services

The purpose of adopting a contextual approach is to promote a broader understanding of the legal issues involved. Here I will first briefly discuss the development of EU law on public services and some of the main cases to develop a general background. This is intended as an introduction and not to replace the more extensive discussion in the subsequent chapters. In the next section I will examine public services in the context of economic regulation and the role of the state, and in a further section against the background of some theories of European integration. Finally some current issues relating to the scope of USO and competitive provision will be examined.

The development of the Treaty framework

The second chapter is dedicated to taking a closer look at the primary law on public services – the Treaty basis. The purpose of the present section is just to set the scene by providing a very general outline. The 1957 Rome Treaty contained three provisions that are pertinent to public services:

- Article 37 EEC (now Article 37 TFEU) on state monopolies of a commercial character;
- Article 90 EEC (now Article 106 TFEU) on public enterprises and undertakings benefiting from special and exclusive rights; as well as on services of general economic interest;
- Article 222 EEC (now Article 345 TFEU) on the neutrality of the Treaty with regard to the national systems of (public or private) ownership.

These provisions have often been seen as part of an early grand economic policy compromise whereby the liberal provisions concerning the internal market freedoms and the competition rules (traditionally seen as championed by Germany and the Benelux countries) were traded off against allowing a certain degree of protection for public enterprises (at this stage traditionally associated

[66] Protocol 26 on SGI, Article 2, provides: 'The provisions of the Treaties do not affect in any way the competence of Member States to provide, commission and organise non-economic services of general interest.'

with France and Italy), perhaps more than for public services as such.[67] The general idea behind this arrangement is that public ownership, state monopolies, special and exclusive rights as well as SGI are compatible with EU law to the extent that they only involve proportionate restraints with regard to the internal market and the competition rules. This is an attempt to balance the EU interest in free markets with the national public interest as it was tied in with the public sector in a broad variety of arrangements.

Article 106(3) TFEU allows the Commission to legislate with regard to the provisions on public undertakings, special and exclusive rights and SGEI without having to rely on the European Parliament and the Council, who are jointly the normal legislator in the EU. (Apart from Decisions, the Commission can adopt Directives, which, however, normally need to be transposed into national law to gain their intended binding effect.) Expanding the Treaty with a provision on SGEI that would allow legislation to be adopted by the European Parliament and the Council had long been under discussion before it was introduced by the Lisbon Treaty. The 1993 Maastricht Treaty had cleared the way for Economic and Monetary Union, giving off contradictory signals on its economic orientation by also introducing for the first time a Community competence on industrial policy, a social policy protocol and EU citizenship. A fairly general Article 16 EC on SGEI without a legislative competence was eventually introduced by the 1997 Amsterdam Treaty.[68] This provision was complemented by the Lisbon Treaty with an additional text to (now) Article 14 TFEU that allows the adoption of Regulations (which, unlike Directives, do not require transposition and are directly applicable) in accordance with the normal legislative procedure: that is to say by the European Parliament and Council acting jointly.[69]

The Charter of Fundamental Rights of the European Union that was adopted in 2000 included an Article 36 on access to SGEI (in its chapter on solidarity, and not, notably, under citizenship rights). This Charter became binding with equal effect to the Treaties when the Lisbon Treaty came into force in 2009 and may provide an additional albeit indirect link between public services and citizenship. Finally, as I have mentioned in the preceding section, the Lisbon Treaty added a

[67] Cf. regarding in particular Article 90 EEC (Article 106 TFEU) A. C. Page, 'Member States, public undertakings and Article 90', *European Law Review*, 7 (1982), 19–35.

[68] Article 16 EC read: 'Without prejudice to Articles 73, 86 and 87, and given the place occupied by services of general economic interest in the shared values of the Union as well as their role in promoting social and territorial cohesion, the Community and the Member States, each within their respective powers and within the scope of application of this Treaty, shall take care that such services operate on the basis of principles and conditions which enable them to fulfil their missions.'

[69] The text that was added to Article 14 TFEU (apart from minor modifications) reads: 'The European Parliament and the Council, acting by means of regulations in accordance with the ordinary legislative procedure, shall establish these principles and set these conditions without prejudice to the competence of Member States, in compliance with the Treaties, to provide, to commission and to fund such services.'

Protocol 26 on SGI to the TFEU, thereby introducing for the first time non-economic and social services of general interest at the level of primary law. This has coincided with the adoption of the social market economy as an objective of the TEU and the relegation of competition policy to a Protocol 27.[70]

By setting out these developments I have tried to provide a thumbnail sketch of the background to the current Treaty setting. We will now briefly look at the case law, the secondary law and the development of the general (horizontal) policy context in the various documents produced by the European Commission.

Case law and secondary law

The case law on public services[71] developed from a discussion that initially focused on the scope for legal monopolies and exclusive and special rights under Article(s) (37 and) 106(1) TFEU in cases such as *Costa* (1964)[72] and *Sacchi* (1974).[73] In the latter case the Court found that Italian restrictions on broadcast advertising were exempted from the free movement of services under Article 106(2) TFEU – but only to the extent necessary to fulfil legitimate public tasks. This was followed by cases on the scope and direct effect of Article 106(2) TFEU – such as *Corbeau* (1993).[74] In this case, concerning an alternative operator of postal services in the Belgian city of Liège, the Court drew a careful (but not ultimately very illuminating) balance between on the one hand the right of providers of a 'service of general interest' to cross-subsidize its services in the interest of operating in a financial equilibrium, and on the other hand the right of competitors to offer new services that were severable from the service of general interest and that were not offered by the incumbent – in so far as those services did not compromise the aforementioned financial equilibrium. In *Almelo* (1994) a regional electricity distributor with universal service obligations in the Netherlands was held to fall within the scope of the SGEI exception of Article 106(2) TFEU.[75] In sum, in the early cases, the principle of direct effect of Article 106 TFEU was established (or discovered) without much material effect or major incursions into the Member States' jurisdictions.

[70] As paraphrased in my introduction above, Monti in his report on the internal market refers to social services of general interest as one of the 'building blocks for a reconciliation between the single market and the social and citizens' dimension in the Treaty logic of a "highly competitive social market economy"': above n. 1, at 68. Highly critical of these aspirations: F. W. Scharpf, 'The asymmetry of European integration, or why the EU cannot be a "social market economy"', *Socio-Economic Review*, 8 (2010), 211–50.

[71] For a discussion of the case law regarding public authorities see Sauter and Schepel, above n. 15.

[72] Case 4/64 *Flaminio Costa* v. *ENEL* (1964) ECR (English special edition) 585.

[73] Case 155/73 *Sacchi*, above n. 51.

[74] Case C-320/91 *Corbeau*, above n. 51. Cf. Case C-260/89 *Elliniki Radiophonia Tiléorassi AE and Panellinia Omospondia Syllogon Prossopikou* v. *Dimotiki Etairia Pliroforissis and Sotirios Kouvelas and Nicolaos Avdellas et al.* [1991] ECR I-2925; Case C-41/90 *Klaus Höfner and Fritz Elser* v. *Macrotron GmbH* [1991] ECR I-1979.

[75] Case C-393/92 *Almelo*, above n. 51.

This relatively peaceful state of affairs changed rather spectacularly with the emergence of sector-specific legislation based on Article 106(3) TFEU and cases brought by the Member States to contest the Commission's powers to use this legal basis to legislate single-handedly (without giving the European Parliament and the Council a say – although they were eventually consulted on subsequent add-on Article 106(3) TFEU Directives). Such legislation was first adopted in the form of a Directive to promote transparency of financial relations (1980) between Member States and public enterprises (the Transparency Directive).[76] That is to say this legal basis was first used almost twenty-five years after it had been created. The objective of the Transparency Directive was inter alia to impose accounting separation in order to allow the state aid rules (and the competition rules) to be applied equally to public and private undertakings.

Once the legality of the Transparency Directive had been confirmed by the Court in 1982,[77] it was followed by a more invasive approach when the Commission used Article 106(3) TFEU to adopt two Directives abolishing legal monopolies in the electronic communications terminal equipment (1988)[78] and electronic communications services (1990)[79] sectors respectively. The Court subsequently confirmed the Commission's power to do so in the *Terminal equipment* (1990) and the *Telecommunications services* (1992) cases.[80] The reasoning was that exclusive rights constituted restraints on free movement that could be abolished because Article 106(3) TFEU gave the Commission the power to supervise the exercise of such rights. These rulings led to the complete liberalization of telecommunications networks and services in the EU by 1 January 1998.[81] This in turn set the scene for liberalization elsewhere, particularly in the energy sector (gas and electricity). As regards the energy sector however, the Court made clear that abolishing special and exclusive rights in the absence of further Community legislation was

[76] Now Commission Directive 2006/111/EC, above n. 35. Formerly Commission Directive 80/723/EEC of 25 June 1980 on the transparency of financial relations between Member States and public undertakings, OJ 1980, L195/35.

[77] Joined cases 188 to 190/80 *France, Italy and United Kingdom* v. *Commission* [1982] ECR 2545.

[78] Commission Directive 88/301/EEC of 16 May 1988 on competition in the markets in telecommunications terminal equipment, OJ 1988, L131/73.

[79] Commission Directive 90/388/EEC of 28 June 1990 on competition in the markets for telecommunications services, OJ 1990, L192/10.

[80] Case C-202/88 *France* v. *Commission* [1991] ECR I-1223; (except in relation to abolishing special rights) in Joined cases C-271/90, C-281/90 and C-289/90 *Spain, Belgium and Italy* v. *Commission* [1992] ECR I-5833.

[81] An additional factor was the leverage provided over regulatory reform in France and Germany due to the Commission's review of the *Atlas* and *GlobalOne* merger cases in which the incumbent operators of these two key Member States were involved. Cf. P. Larouche, *Competition law and regulation in European telecommunications* (Hart Publishing, Oxford, 2000).

unacceptable.[82] Hence the Commission was directed towards extensive and eventually successful harmonization efforts.

It is worth noting here that USO have played a particular role in the context of telecommunications liberalization: formulating USO meant defining more clearly the public interest in terms of individual rights and thereby allowing market provision of the remainder of services.[83] Hence, defining a common minimum standard of protection forms part of a trade-off. Such USO can be topped up by national law – but increasingly only in so far as competitive provision fails to satisfy demand at acceptable prices. Moreover, as we will see in the *BUPA* case (2008),[84] it is even possible for a general USO to be supplemented by a more selective secondary form of USO. In this context it is worth quoting the 2010 Monti report again:

> In order to be able to effectively participate in the single market citizens need access to a number of basic services of general economic interest, in particular in the area of the network industries, such as postal services, transport services or telecommunications services. In the network industries, market opening at EU level has therefore always been accompanied by measures ensuring that a universal service continued to be provided.[85]

As regards welfare services there is neither a comparable liberalization trend nor a comparable EU-level definition of USO. Instead two lines of case law stand out. The first is to do with the classification of welfare services as either solidarity based (and hence outside the scope of the competition and free movement rules) or economic (and hence in principle caught). An early example is the 1993 *Poucet* case,[86] where the conditions for a finding of solidarity (such as the compulsory nature of the scheme and its non-profit nature) were set out. Its counterpart is *FFSA* in 1995 where a supplementary social insurance scheme was found to be economic, inter alia because entitlements were based on contributions and financial results.[87] This distinction is important with regard to

[82] C-157/94 *Commission* v. *Netherlands* [1997] ECR I-5699; C-158/94 *Commission* v. *Italy* [1997] ECR I-5789; C-159/94 *Commission* v. *France* [1997] ECR I-5815; C-160/94 *Commission* v. *Spain* [1997] ECR I-5851.

[83] H.-W. Micklitz, 'Universal services: Nucleus for a social European private law', in Cremona, above n. 17, 63–102; W. Sauter, 'Universal service obligations and the emergence of citizens' rights in European telecommunications liberalization', in M. Freedland and S. Sciarra (eds.), *Public services and citizenship in European law: Public and labour law perspectives* (Oxford University Press, 1998), 117–43.

[84] Case T-289/03 *BUPA*, above n. 32.

[85] Above, n. 1, at 73. Also cited by J. Davies and E. Szyszczak in their chapter 'Universal service obligations: Fulfilling new generations of services of general economic interest', in Szyszczak et al. (2011), above n. 16, 155–77, at 157.

[86] Joined cases C-159/91 and C-160/91 *Christian Poucet* v. *Assurances Générales de France and Caisse Mutuelle Régionale du Languedoc-Roussillon* [1993] ECR I-637.

[87] Case C-244/94 *Fédération Française des Sociétés d'Assurance, Société Paternelle-Vie, Union des Assurances de Paris-Vie and Caisse d'Assurance et de Prévoyance Mutuelle des Agriculteurs* v. *Ministère de l'Agriculture et de la Pêche* [1995] ECR I-4013.

boundary issues: whether the schemes in question are caught and/or, if they are, subject to an SGEI exception (as in *Albany*, 1999).[88]

The second line of case law concerns the scope of solidarity in the context of citizenship. This may require extending welfare services (such as a subsistence allowance) to EU citizens based on the general non-discrimination principle in Articles 18 and 20 TEU in *Grzelczyk* (2001).[89] It may also require a personalized assessment of proportionality, such as regarding residency requirements in *Baumbast* (2002)[90] and concerning the right to reimbursement for medical treatment in another Member State in *Watts* (2006).[91] The relevance of this case law to public services remains to be examined – in particular as regards SGEI and USO. I regard this as a boundary issue: what is the scope of the services concerned with regard to the persons who are covered?

More recently (in 2005 and 2012) the legislative basis of Article 106(3) TFEU was used to provide a framework for the use of Article 106(2) TFEU to enable exemptions of public service compensation in the context of state aid.[92] This development concerns both utilities and welfare services. Here the Commission again built on the case law of the Court, in this case on public transport (regional bus services) in *Altmark* (2003).[93] There the Court decided a long-standing debate on the (compatible) state aid versus the compensation approach by opting decisively for compensation. The state aid approach meant that compensation would be regarded as aid, but could be declared compatible with the internal market. Instead the Court held that compensation and not state aid was involved where: (i) an SGEI had been attributed; (ii) costs were controlled by establishing parameters in advance; (iii) compensation was limited to costs plus a reasonable rate of return; and (iv) costs were either based on a public tender, or fixed at those of an efficient undertaking. In such cases the advantage requirement that is necessary for a finding of state aid was not met and they were therefore outside the scope of the state aid rules. Two years later the Commission consolidated this approach in its *Altmark* package of 2005, renewed in 2012.[94] This 2012 package now forms the most complete statement of SGEI that is available in EU law.

In broad strokes I believe this represents three different stages of development (individual cases; a sector-specific approach; and a horizontal approach) which culminate in a regime that is in principle applicable to all public services that are carried out by undertakings, that is to say actually or potentially in competition. Moreover it is worth noting that under the Article 106(2) TFEU

[88] Case C-67/96 *Albany International BV* v. *Stichting Bedrijfspensioenfonds Textielindustrie* [1999] ECR I-5751.

[89] Case C-184/99 *Rudy Grzelczyk* v. *Centre public d'aide sociale d'Ottignies-Louvain-la-Neuve* [2001] ECR I-6193.

[90] Case C-413/99 *Baumbast*, above n. 9.

[91] Case C-372/04 *The Queen, on the application of Yvonne Watts* v. *Bedford Primary Care Trust and Secretary of State for Health* [2006] ECR I-4325.

[92] See above, note 11. [93] Case C-280/00 *Altmark*, above n. 33.

[94] Cf. Szyszczak, above n. 11; Sauter, above n. 11.

regime for state aids our broad division of public service in two parts pertains as well: for state aid welfare services by and large benefit from a (collective) block exemption and the utilities are examined for exemption on an individual basis. This reflects both the relative stage of development of SGEI and USO in these two areas of public services and the corresponding degree to which they remain within the sway of the Member States.

The general policy context

EU policy with regard to public services is largely dominated by the European Commission. This institution combines a number of different roles. These include exclusive responsibility for initiating proposals for EU legislation (although the Parliament and Council may request it to do so, it need not oblige), guardianship of the Treaties by (inter alia) opening infringement proceedings against Member States that it considers to be in contravention of EU law, and acting as a competition authority in the areas of state aid, antitrust and mergers. All these roles are pertinent to our topic. (I am leaving aside other roles that are not relevant here such as representing the EU in certain international organizations and planning medium-term strategies for the EU.)

The Commission tends to prepare its policies by issuing Communications, which are non-binding soft-law documents.[95] Such texts also often accompany binding instruments: Decisions, Directives and Regulations. A good example is provided by the 2005 and 2012 *Altmark* frameworks which were accompanied by two explanatory Communications of which one also set out the standard for the Commission's review in individual cases.[96] The first such Communication that is relevant to public services was issued in 1996 and coincided with preparations for the Treaty of Amsterdam. It concerned services of general interest (SGI) and in fact pioneered this concept.[97] This first Communication set out the relationship between the different concepts much as was discussed above, claiming inter alia the EU origins of the USO concept:

> Universal service is the expression in Europe of the requirements and special features of the European model of society in a policy which combines a dynamic market, cohesion and solidarity.[98]

This looks like a clear expression of the social market economy *avant la lettre*. The same Communication also proposed adding the promotion of SGI simply as one of the tasks of the EU listed in Article 3 EEC in what can be seen as an attempt to forestall more interventionist ambitions favouring SGI. Instead, as we have seen, Article 16 EC was added by the 1997 Amsterdam Treaty.

The next Communication was requested by the European Council of Lisbon in 2000, and appeared early in 2001. Here the context was that of the run-up to

[95] L. Senden, *Soft law in European Community law* (Hart Publishing, Oxford, 2004).
[96] Above, n. 11. [97] Services of general interest in Europe, above n. 40. [98] Ibid., para. 32.

the 2001 Nice Treaty that enabled enlargement. This Communication set out three general principles with regard to the application of the internal market and competition rules: (i) neutrality with regard to public ownership; (ii) Member States' freedom to define SGI subject to control for manifest error; and (iii) proportionality.[99] In addition, it attempted to link access to SGI and citizenship ('a core common concept of such general interest may be necessary to sustain allegiance to the Union').[100] It claimed this was supported by the text on access to SGEI in the 2000 Charter of Fundamental Rights – although this appeared in the chapter on solidarity, and not that on citizenship (which was more concerned with political rights).

A second Communication at the end of 2001 provided a report to the Laeken European Council, including an economic underpinning for SGI.[101] It also signalled the need for more certainty, in particular concerning state aid and public service compensation (at a time before the *Altmark* case (2003) was decided,[102] when the 'state aid' and 'compensation' approaches were still competing views), as well as the need to apply the public procurement rules where possible. However, the Commission argued against the need for a single framework Directive (for which a specific legal basis did not exist, with the exception of Article 106(3) TFEU) to consolidate the various principles. Instead it repeated its 1996 proposal by offering the (somewhat hollow) alternative of adding SGI to the activities of the Union in Article 4(2) TFEU (then Article 3 EC).

Not all the Communications on SGI were equally significant.[103] Drowning discord in a stream of Communications is one way of describing the Commission's containment strategy on this topic.[104] Such discord was not in short supply, fuelled by demands from primarily France, the European trade unions (ETUC) and the left-wing party grouping (PES) in the European Parliament that SGEI be used to enforce a wide range of exceptions to the internal market. The Commission's Communications followed the familiar pattern of providing an overview of SGI principles and practice, and continued a holding pattern with regard to providing a Treaty basis for SGI framework legislation, albeit ultimately without success: as we have seen the Lisbon Treaty added such a legal basis in Article 14 TFEU. It has not been used, however, and, because using it requires the Commission (which remains opposed, or of the view that such legislation is not necessary) to prepare a proposal, it is unlikely to be used soon.

[99] Communication from the Commission on SGEI, above n. 61. [100] Ibid., para. 64.

[101] Communication from the Commission, Report to the Laeken European Council, Services of general interest, COM(2001) 598.

[102] Case C-280/00 *Altmark*, above n. 33.

[103] Communication from the Commission, Green paper on services of general interest, COM(2003) 270; Communication from the Commission, White paper on services of general interest, COM(2004) 374.

[104] Cf. Sauter, above n. 43.

An innovation was the 2006 Communication on SSGI which introduced welfare services into the SGI context, explaining that 'social policy objectives are overriding reasons of general interest which may justify the application of measures intended to regulate the market'.[105] Here the setting was that of the difficult adoption of the Services Directive,[106] with its eventual exceptions for SGEI, which I will discuss in Chapter 5 on horizontal secondary law on public services. Also it reflected the European social model that was promoted by the 2005 Social Agenda and Lisbon programme, following on from the Lisbon European Council in March 2000 that established socio-economic goals for 2010.[107] Protocol 26 and the new Article 14 TEU were interpreted in a 2008 Communication which presented the Protocol, somewhat disingenuously, as the clarification all parties had been waiting for, making framework legislation – that would be in the hands of the European Parliament and the Council – superfluous.[108]

From 2008 onwards the Commission services have presented biennial reports,[109] as well as guides to the application of SGEI, that answer many practical questions that might arise at national – including regional and municipal – level.[110] Both achieve a level of detail which goes well beyond what can be summarized for purposes of the present discussion. More specific are the Communications in the context of the 2005 and 2012 *Altmark* framework that I have already referred to in the preceding section. Most recently (2013) the Commission issued a Communication on a quality framework for SGI.[111] As a response to the President's political guidelines of 2009[112] aimed at promoting the European social model, and Europe 2020,[113] it mainly sets out what is already being done (setting USO in various sectors).

105 Communication from the Commission, Implementing the Lisbon programme: Social services of general interest in the European Union, COM(2006) 177, at p. 9.

106 Directive 2006/123/EC, above n. 10.

107 Ibid., p. 3. Cf. Communication from the Commission, Social policy agenda, COM(2000) 379; Communication from the Commission on the Social agenda, COM(2005) 33; Communication from the Commission, Common actions for growth and employment, the Community Lisbon programme, COM(2005) 330.

108 Communication from the Commission, Accompanying the Communication on 'A single market for 21st century Europe' – Services of general interest, including social services of general interest: A new European commitment, COM(2007) 725.

109 Commission staff working document, Biennial report on social services of general interest, SEC(2008) 2179; Commission staff working document, Second biennial report on social services of general interest, SEC(2012) 1284; Commission staff working document, Third biennial report on social services of general interest, SWD(2013) 40.

110 Commission staff working document, Guide to the application of the European Union rules on state aid, public procurement and the internal market to services of general economic interest, and in particular to social services of general interest, SEC(2010) 1545; SWD(2013) 53, above n. 50.

111 COM(2011) 900, above n. 45.

112 Political guidelines for the next Commission, Brussels, 3 September 2009: http://ec.europa.eu/commission_2010-2014/president/pdf/press_20090903_en.pdf.

113 Communication from the Commission, Europe 2020: A strategy for smart, sustainable and inclusive growth, COM(2010) 2020.

Where are we now?

At present the Commission's agenda on public services appears to focus more on specific areas like state aid and procurement, which are also general concerns (or horizontal policies) outside the area of public services, rather than on SGI, SGEI or SSGI as such. Hence aside from the sectoral regulatory regimes for the utilities there does not appear to be a coherent EU programme other than a relatively loose set of legal principles and a so far limited set of USO that is likewise restricted to the individual utilities. In principle, however, the scope of SGEI is vast. Whether or not an effect on trade is at stake is therefore likely to become crucial. We will test this thesis in the following chapters. SSGI are now within the purview of EU law when they are SGEI, but there is not much experience with this yet. Looking at the different levels of government at which SGEI may play a role, the same is true for SGEI and public services provided or regulated by regional or local government. Keeping in mind the in all likelihood minimal effect on trade of municipal swimming pools or libraries and local music academies it appears that this limit to the applicability of the EU free movement and competition as well as state aid rules is equally key to the European model of society – or the social market economy – as is the SGEI concept itself. My examination will, however, focus on the latter.

1.5 Economic regulation and the role of the state

Market failure and state intervention

Here I will mainly look at the economic context of public services and EU integration. The role of the state in a market economy is a contentious issue that continues to fuel the political as well as the academic debate. This debate is evidently complicated if the role of European integration is added in. Increasingly, however, it is accepted that the market mechanism where it works well is an efficient way of connecting supply and demand with beneficial effects for the welfare of consumers and that of the economy at large (total welfare). Effective competition between undertakings provides benefits to consumers. State intervention in private markets can nevertheless be justified in cases where markets do not deliver goods and services at desirable levels from either an efficiency (economic) or from an equity (social) perspective, or from a combination of both. These cases are usually described as instances of 'market failure'. At the same time this does not mean that public intervention to remedy market failure will always lead to superior results: 'government failure' (for instance due to a lack of information or the absence of an efficient allocation mechanism) may lead to even worse results, in which cases intervention is not warranted.[114]

[114] Cf. C. Veljanowski, 'Economic approaches to regulation', in Baldwin, Cave and Lodge (2010), above n. 28, 17–38.

I will first look briefly at two instances where the issue of market failure was raised by the Commission and its economic advisers in relation to justifying EU policy with regard to SGEI. Next I will discuss the sources of public intervention and why the EU predominantly selects regulation, before going into more detail about what regulation entails with respect to public services.

In its 2001 report on SGI to the Laeken European Council mentioned above,[115] the Commission set out three types of market failure leading to underprovision of services, which are: externalities; merit and club goods; and solidarity. It did so in order to provide an ex post economic justification of the provisions on SGEI in Article 16 EEC, adopted by the Treaty of Amsterdam in 1997, and Article 36 of the Charter of Fundamental Rights of the European Union, which had then recently been proclaimed by the 2000 European Council in Nice.

Spelling out these three categories in relation to SGI in some more detail, this means that public intervention can be justified by:

(i) externalities, where the parties fail to value all the benefits to society as a whole, such as in the case of education, or where there are network effects (where each member of a network adds utility to the existing members) such as in the case of electronic communications or postal services;
(ii) public goods such as merit goods, that benefit all those who receive them to a degree that exceeds their private information, such as health services; and club goods of which the use does not decrease their usefulness to others (such as parks or museums);
(iii) solidarity, where access to specific services is deemed necessary for all citizens, including those who cannot independently afford it.

An Opinion on SGEI by the Commission's economic advisory group of academic experts issued in 2006 against the backdrop of the 2005 *Altmark* package provides a specific view with regard to the concepts of SGEI and USO.[116] It states that state aid policy should be guided by three principles:

(i) state aid may be a legitimate response to market failure – notably relating to externalities or public goods – or a legitimate response to equity concerns;
(ii) however, this state aid should not unduly distort the market: hence the first principle should be pursued in a cost-effective manner. In particular,

[115] COM(2001) 598, above n. 100, para. 3.

[116] Services of general economic interest. Opinion prepared by the State aid group of the Economic advisory ground on competition policy, 29 June 2006. Cf. more broadly the Common principles for an economic assessment of the compatibility of state aid under Article 87.3 (now Article 107(3) TFEU), at http://ec.europa.eu/competition/state_aid/reform/economic_assessment_en.pdf.

competition on the market or competition for the market in a public procurement setting should not be excluded;

(iii) state aid should be subject to a cost–benefit analysis.

In addition, according to the advisory group, there should be a clear effect on trade. These are useful insights into the reasons why public services in the EU may require public intervention and what some of the limits on this intervention might be. Categories that may be relevant from an efficiency perspective which are not listed include consumption smoothing (maximizing utility by redistributing income over a life cycle) and risk sharing (social insurance, or risk equalization schemes in health insurance).[117] This adds strength to the observation that public intervention and public services need not just or predominantly be motivated by equity concerns.[118]

Potentially state intervention to address market failure on efficiency and equity grounds can take four forms: regulation, financing, public production and income transfers. Regulation (the setting and enforcing of rules, often in a sector-specific context) may affect both the quality and the quantity produced as well as prices; finance involves subsidies or taxes applied to the prices of the services produced; production means that the state takes over the supply side (bringing it into the public sector); and income transfers can be tied either to specific expenditure (such as housing benefits) or generic expenditure (such as social security benefits that can be freely spent).[119]

To some extent these methods of intervention are substitutes: this means public authorities can choose which method they prefer in the light of their institutional resources. At national level all four of these forms of intervention are found at various times and frequently applied simultaneously with regard to public services. As far as EU-level policies with regard to public services are concerned however, the form of intervention that is applied most, if not almost exclusively, is regulation.[120]

The reasons for this are simple: first, the EU does not dispose of the powers to tax public services or any other sector, nor of the funds to subsidize them to a meaningful degree (the Common Agricultural Policy being the exception that proves the rule) or to engage in redistributive politics by means of income transfers. Whereas the Member States typically dispose of around 40 per cent of GDP the EU is stuck at around 1 per cent. This severely limits its possibility to use financial instruments. Second, the EU could not conceivably engage in public production. It simply does not command the authority to do so. Third, given the manner in which it has developed and been interpreted over time, the

117 Barr, above n. 30, p. 76.

118 Cf. N. Fiedziuk, 'Towards a more refined economic approach to services of general economic interest', *European Public Law*, 16 (2010), 271–88.

119 Ibid., p. 50.

120 On regulation cf. e.g. Ogus, above n. 27; Baldwin, Cave and Lodge (2013), above n. 28; on regulation in the EU Majone, above n. 6; McGowan and Wallace, above n. 6.

system of the Treaties as a whole is predominantly oriented towards free trade and competition in open markets. This means that for reasons of effectiveness and consistency the pursuit of public services by the EU would have to be consistent with that overarching approach.

Regulation and reregulation

Here regulation fits the bill. In addition, since the 1990s regulation has become a favoured indirect form of governance for the EU. Regarding the utilities, the natural monopoly argument (especially prevalent in the network sectors) that a single-provider model was the most efficient was rejected and defeated first in telecommunications and then (largely) in energy. This led to the privatization and liberalization trends of the past decades. Regulation (or reregulation) often follows in the wake of liberalization because in order to function well markets in fact need more rules than the internal processes of public provision by state monopolists do. One reason why this is the case is that liberalization in the first instance replaces public monopolies with fledgling markets dominated by incumbent operators (private near-monopolies). The necessary rules tend to be enforced by professional technocrats at one step removed from politics and democratic control – for instance because the state still holds a financial stake in the incumbent. In practice the new regulators serve primarily to police not USO but third-party access (which is defensible from an effect on trade perspective).

According to Francis McGowan and Helen Wallace: 'While national regulation focuses on firms and citizens, the European level increasingly focuses on regulating the regulators.'[121] This reflects the coordination mechanisms that the European Commission has created. These tend to give it a pivotal role where transnational issues are concerned, while at the same time relying on the staffing and manpower supplied at national level to do the legwork. Regulating the regulators primarily requires coordination. In this setting the emergence of expertise-based networks of national regulators has occurred for instance in electronic communications and posts, but also in the energy sector, and under the decentralization of antitrust in 2004 even with regard to general competition policy.[122] Worth noting here is that the actual cross-border trade affected is generally minimal, whereas the effects of EU coordination efforts on promoting competition at national level are highly significant – another EU law paradox. This development fits with Majone's analysis that following privatization the dirigiste or economic interventionist state of the past is not followed by the end of regulation but on the contrary is being replaced by the regulatory state.[123] Hence

[121] McGowan and Wallace, above n. 6, at 561.

[122] S. A. C. M. Lavrijssen and L. Hancher, 'Networks of regulatory agencies in Europe', in P. Larouche and P. Cserne (eds.), *National legal systems and globalization: New role, continuing relevance* (TMC Asser Press, The Hague, 2013), 183–220.

[123] Majone, above n. 6, at 97. Critical, K. Yeung, 'The regulatory state', in Baldwin, Cave and Lodge (2010), above n. 28, 64–85.

in this view it is not, as is often thought, the welfare state that is (primarily) being displaced, but discretionary state intervention in the economy.[124] This also fits with the rationalization thesis that I will try to develop.

The welfare state

However, the link between liberalization, regulation and the welfare state is contentious. First of all, academic commentators hold different views on the scope of regulation. Again according to Majone, 'regulation has a single normative justification: improving the efficiency of the economy by correcting specific forms of market failure'.[125] Prosser, however, sees no fewer than three such justifications: 'those based on economic principles, those based on individual rights and those based on social solidarity'.[126] I will get back to individual rights at a later stage although I note that the Charter of Fundamental Rights of the European Union includes a section on solidarity – or social rights – so the two categories are at least in part contiguous. For now I will focus briefly on solidarity, a principle which has many defenders.[127] Nina Boeger for instance seeks to explain the case law on SGEI by reference to a 'public ethos' that is respected by the CJEU.[128] However, the principle of solidarity is not a panacea. Nor is it clear whether solidarity-based mechanisms of provision of welfare services, even if they are sheltered from the impact of EU law, will survive in practice as they are placed under stress not only by the economic crisis but also by rising demand, ageing societies and increasing costs.

Moreover, modern accounts of welfare in the context of European integration as provided by social policy experts like Ferrara[129] and Hemerijck[130] do not present a straightforward account of a struggle or choice between national solidarity and EU-generated liberalization. Instead this is a tale of gradually shifting boundaries: welfare, or indeed solidarity, is based on drawing boundaries between those who are included and excluded as beneficiaries and contributors. Against this backdrop regions, for example, are emerging as a new focus for welfare organization at the expense of nation states. The scope of EU involvement in this area has also widened with the new Regulation on the coordination

124 On the resilience of the welfare state see Hay and Wincott, above n. 41.

125 Majone, above n. 6, at 79.

126 T. Prosser, 'Regulation and social solidarity', *Journal of Law and Society*, 33 (2006), 364–87, at 365; Prosser, above n. 15, Chapter 2: 'Competition law, citizenship rights and social solidarity'. Earlier: T. Prosser, 'Theorising utility regulation', *Modern Law Review*, 62 (1999), 196–217.

127 Cf. C. Barnard, 'EU citizenship and the principle of solidarity', in Dougan and Spaventa, above n. 20, 157–180; N. Boeger, 'Solidarity and EC competition law', *European Law Review*, 32 (2007), 319–40; de Búrca, above n. 19; Prosser (2006), above n. 126; T. Prosser, 'Competition law and public services: From single market to citizenship rights', *European Public Law*, 11 (2005), 543–63; M. Ross, 'Article 16 EC and services of general interest: From derogation to obligation', *European Law Review*, 25 (2000), 22–38; M. Ross, 'Promoting solidarity: From public services to a European model of competition', *Common Market Law Review*, 44 (2007), 1057–80.

128 Boeger, above n. 127. 129 Above, n. 24. 130 Above, n. 26.

of social security regimes 883/2004.[131] Although contrasts between competition and solidarity remain useful to clarify opposing positions and will be used below, they do not necessarily reflect reality. Nevertheless even among specialists there is a general sense that there may not be enough EU-level solidarity, or in any event that it may so far have been insufficiently institutionalized:

> The EU's original sin of pushing for rapid market and currency integration, to let the social-political-institutional underpinnings of European integration catch up later, is in need of correction.[132]

With this observation, whether or not it is realistic in view of the existence or absence of popular support for such measures, I want to move on to look at public services in the context of the integration debate.

1.6 The context of the integration debate

It would be a tall order to reproduce in this section the integration debate and the theories explaining European economic integration – which, starting from their functionalist origins in the 1950s, have expanded to intergovernmentalism, institutionalism and pluralism as well as various theories of choice and, especially among political scientists, have long since become an academic cottage industry in their own right.[133] Instead I will be highly selective and first focus on Ordoliberalism (on the right of the political spectre) and the writings of the pre-eminent German political scientist Fritz Scharpf (on the left). These two perspectives are relevant both to the basic economic orientation of EU law, and to its capacity to pursue social policy goals. I will attempt to connect this discussion with the preceding section on regulation.

Ordoliberalism versus the mixed economy

Rescued from relative obscurity in recent years for a broader audience especially by scholars of EU competition law,[134] Ordoliberalism is a German school of liberal economic thought that originated at the University of Freiburg between

131 Regulation (EC) No 883/2004 of the European Parliament and of the Council of 29 April 2004 on the coordination of social security systems, OJ 2004, L166/1; Regulation (EC) No 987/2009 of the European Parliament and of the Council of 16 September 2009 laying down the procedure for implementing Regulation (EC) No 883/2004 on the coordination of social security systems, OJ 2009, L284/1. Cf. F. Pennings, *European social security law* (Intersentia, Antwerp, 2010); F. Pennings, 'Inclusion and exclusion of persons and benefits in the new coordination Regulation', in Dougan and Spaventa, above n. 20, 241–60.

132 Hemerijck, above n. 26.

133 Cf. P. Craig, 'Integration, democracy and legitimacy', in Craig and de Búrca, above n. 18, 13–40.

134 Cf. D. J. Gerber, *Law and competition in twentieth century Europe: Protecting Prometheus* (Oxford University Press, 1998). It has now become a standard category in competition law. Cf. G. Monti, *EC competition law* (Cambridge University Press, 2007).

the World Wars. It long embraced European integration as propagating a system based on free markets and individual freedom of property grounded in the rule of law which the Ordoliberals thought at national level had been compromised by social policy goals of the welfare state (especially the German social market economy). Consequently they hailed liberalization due to (or mediated by) the application of EU law and saw the Rome Treaty (1957) as an *economic* constitution that did not require democratic legitimacy.[135] As Christian Joerges has pointed out, the emergence of reregulation instead of deregulation that I have signalled above is also a negation of the expectations that Ordoliberals harboured with respect to European integration.[136] Similar negations were the extension of EU integration to industrial policy, social policy and economic policy coordination.[137]

Although proposals to revert to little more than a free-trade area may still occasionally surface in current national politics this is not regarded as a serious option at European level. To borrow the Ordoliberal terminology, the EU now has a mixed economic constitution: neither totally free-market oriented, nor fully solidarity based. This is reflected well by the objective of pursuing a highly competitive social market economy set out in Article 3(3) TEU. I will return to the theme of the mixed economic constitution in the next chapter. One reason why this category remains relevant is that, after the constitutional charter was voted down in France and the Netherlands in 2005, the EU still does not have a formal constitution: instead it is the case law of the Court of Justice of the European Union (CJEU) which has 'constitutionalized' the Treaties, creating a functional equivalent to a constitution, but not a democratically legitimized framework.[138] How change will develop, in particular along the vector of citizenship, will most likely in large part depend on the EU Courts – and their national counterparts.

Positive versus negative integration

Since this distinction was introduced by Tinbergen theories of European integration have often focused on the tension between positive and negative integration.[139] Especially Scharpf has developed the idea that discriminatory regulation is habitually struck down by the European Courts – therefore

135 C. Joerges, '*Rechtsstaat* and social Europe: How a classical tension resurfaces in the European integration process', *Comparative Sociology*, 9 (2010), 65–85, at 69.

136 C. Joerges, 'Law, economics and politics in the constitutionalisation of Europe', *Cambridge Yearbook of European Legal Studies*, 5 (2002–3), 123–50. Cf. Sauter and Schepel, above n. 15.

137 Cf. M. E. Streit and W. Mussler, 'The economic constitution of the European Community: From "Rome" to "Maastricht"', *European Law Journal*, 1 (1995), 5–30; W. Sauter, *Competition law and industrial policy in the EU* (Oxford University Press, 1997).

138 G. de Búrca and J. H. H. Weiler, *The worlds of European constitutionalism* (Cambridge University Press, 2011); J. Habermas, *The crisis of the European Union: A response* (Polity Press, Cambridge, 2012).

139 J. Tinbergen, *International economic integration*, 2nd edn (Elsevier, Amsterdam 1965).

promoting negative integration – whereas positive measures fail to be adopted by the EU legislature. As a consequence Scharpf is deeply pessimistic about the prospects of redistributive public policy and thereby implicitly public services: he sees multi-level governance in the EU as a threat to solidarity-based national systems and lacking in legitimacy.[140] More precisely he sees the EU as providing mainly output legitimacy in terms of results (but also the protection of individual rights) and lacking input legitimacy, not so much based on procedure as on majoritarian politics. With regard to the 2007 *Viking* and *Laval* judgments of the CJEU on the limits on the right to collective action (strikes) Scharpf even advocates resorting to civil disobedience in response to justice that has in his view run amok.[141] Unsurprisingly therefore Scharpf also doubts the potential of the EU to live up to its newly constitutionalized goal of becoming a social market economy.[142]

For present purposes it would go too far to attempt to produce a rebuttal of Scharpf's views, which are obviously on the whole more detailed and sophisticated than summarized above. However, I do want to note that in his analysis Scharpf neglects important mitigating factors such as:

- the exception for SGEI;
- (other) public policy exceptions and overriding reasons;
- the trade-off between liberalization and harmonization, and the paradox of liberalization requiring more regulation, not less;
- the emergence of mutually supportive technical expertise-based interlocking networks of national regulatory authorities.

The first two are standard legal solutions for balancing the interest at the different levels of governance in the EU. The latter two have already been discussed to some extent in the preceding section. In particular the exceptions regime (including SGEI) will be examined in depth in the following chapters. Some observers like Prosser and Hans-W. Micklitz see yet another avenue for legitimacy at EU level: the emergence of USO as linked to citizenship.[143] Yet much as this might be desirable in principle for evident reasons of enhancing legitimacy there is so far not really much evidence of this in practice – unless it is sought in the linking of SGI and non-discrimination.[144] Both this

[140] F. W. Scharpf, 'The European social model: Coping with the challenges of diversity', *Journal of Common Market Studies*, 40 (2002), 645–70.

[141] Case C-438/05 *International Transport Workers' Federation and Finnish Seamen's Union* v. *Viking Line ABP and OÜ Viking Line Eesti* [2007] ECR I-10779; Case C-341/05 *Laval un Partneri Ltd* v. *Svenska Byggnadsarbetareförbundet, Svenska Byggnadsarbetareförbundets avdelning 1, Byggettan and Svenska Elektrikerförbundet* [2007] ECR I-11767; F. W. Scharpf, 'Der einzige Weg ist, dem EuGH nicht zu folgen', Interview in *Mitbestimmung*, 7/8 (2008), 18–23. Cf. the introduction by C. Barnard and the contributions to *The Cambridge Yearbook of European Legal Studies*, 10 (2007–2008).

[142] Scharpf (2010), above n. 22. [143] Prosser, above n. 15; Micklitz, above n. 82.

[144] S. O'Leary, 'Solidarity and citizenship rights in the Charter of Fundamental Rights of the European Union', in de Búrca, above n. 19, 39–88.

angle and the link with access to SGEI in Article 36 of the Charter of Fundamental Rights of the EU likewise remain to be examined in the following chapters.[145]

1.7 Conclusion

What is the appropriate conclusion of an introduction? I will sum up some of the findings so far and finish by setting out the contents of the next chapters.

Findings and issues raised

First, I have identified what I believe to be the key legal concepts with regard to public services in EU law, that is to say, in declining order of importance, SGEI, USO, SGI and SSGI. I have postulated that these can all be ranked as successive subsets of public services and of each other, or nested categories, with EU-defined USO as the final nugget of public services law in the EU, albeit so far with a fairly limited scope of application (mainly, the utilities sectors).

Second, I have claimed that an SGEI in EU law is much narrower than the public service concerned as a whole. An SGEI consists of: (i) a PSO or USO; (ii) any ancillary restraints (such as special and exclusive rights); and (iii) a funding regime. In addition, the latter two factors have to be proportional to the legitimate needs of the former. Especially funding, or compensation, has been the subject of much recent interest in the context of state aid. To me the application of the proportionality requirement is proof that such a restrictive definition of SGEI is logical. In addition, it is a matter of common observation that public services as a whole are not normally subject to exceptions and obligations under EU law: not the entire postal service, but letter mail up to 50 grams; not all of electronic communications, but public voice communications services and a basic internet connection at a fixed location, etc. I believe this too supports my position which will be tested in the chapters to come.

Third, I have tried to place public services in the EU in context. Their provision can be consistent with economic notions of market failure. The historical overview sees a reluctant Commission elaborating an SGEI instrument step by step in interaction with the CJEU in a manner that is broadly consistent. At the same time it refuses to provide the European Parliament and Council with a platform to adopt framework legislation in this area. Distinguishing the service provided from the public status of the entity providing it enabled liberalization – in spite of the formal neutrality of the Treaty on the national regimes of property ownership (Article 345 TFEU). SGEI have played a role in the liberalization of public services, notably electronic communications, which came to provide a template of sorts. However,

[145] COM(2001) 598, above n. 100, para. 2.

the result has been not deregulation but reregulation, as markets require a stable legal environment to function and former monopolies had to be contained. In the process a new type of public servant emerged: the national regulatory authorities. These are coordinated at EU level to an extent that raises the question whether it is still legitimized by the actual cross-border effects involved.

Examining the scope for public services in EU law also means looking at the future shape of the EU project, especially regarding the balance between competition and solidarity, respectively equity and efficiency. The pursuit of USO is increasingly a matter of competitive provision, and it turns out that universality can mean covering only part of the population, even the wealthier half. Also, citizenship may play a role in the EU rules on public services, and may constitute a new source of legitimacy. With universality, citizenship, competition and solidarity we clearly have sufficiently demanding themes to examine in the chapters to follow, at least those aspects that pertain to public services.

Structure of the book

The remaining chapters are structured as follows:

- The primary law framework is the topic of the second chapter. It contains a discussion of the relevant Treaty provisions and Protocol on SGEI, the Charter, on the goal of a social market economy and the instrument of free competition in open markets. Citizenship will also be covered. In addition, this chapter provides a concise overview of the other relevant primary law provisions (free movement, state aid and competition) to be fleshed out in the subsequent chapters.
- The third chapter concerns free movement. It gives an overview of the relevant case law at EU level, which so far mainly involves healthcare, education and social security services (including the citizenship dimension).
- The fourth chapter deals with state aid and competition: state aid is the focus for much of the development (and hence of the case law) on SGEI. In this chapter again primarily the case law is reviewed.
- The fifth chapter is the first of two chapters that deal with secondary law, in this case with the horizontal rules that are of general application across different sectors (the following chapter deals with vertical or sectoral rules). The first part of this chapter concerns the Services Directive: this will be a relatively short section as SGEI are generally exempted. In addition, the public procurement rules are covered (the Utilities Directive). The Commission's 2005/2011 SGEI package (state-aid oriented) and related decisional practice is also dealt with here.
- The sixth chapter regards vertical rules in secondary law. The vertical rules concern harmonization, liberalization and coordination. This will be a lengthy chapter because in particular the utilities (and to a lesser extent the

social services) have extensive sector-specific EU legal frameworks. However, the focus will be on the public service characteristics rather than, for example, the detailed regulatory regime for significant market power (SMP) and third-party access in communications.

- The concluding seventh chapter summarizes the research findings, in particular regarding the answers to the research questions outlined above.

2

The Treaty framework and the mixed economic constitution

2.1 Introduction

In this chapter I intend to discuss the primary law on public services, that is to say the relevant provisions of the EU Treaties themselves. This discussion will focus on their scope and content as well as any relevant exceptions. What I will not do, at least not systematically, is examine the case law and/or the secondary law (implementing legislation at EU level) because I will deal with these in separate chapters. The aim of the current text is to help set the stage for the more detailed discussion in these subsequent chapters.

From Rome to Lisbon

Rome and Lisbon are shorthand for the founding treaty of the EU and its most recent version. Here I will focus only on the elements pertinent to public services. Hence I will not, for instance, dwell on the rules on economic and monetary union.[1] Since the Lisbon Treaty came into force on 1 December 2009 the basis for EU law is formed by the Treaty on European Union (TEU) and the Treaty on the Functioning of the European Union (TFEU), as well as the Charter of Fundamental Rights of the European Union (CFREU), as interpreted by the General Court and in the final instance by the Court of Justice of the EU. In a material sense (that is aside from the institutional rules on competences and voting procedures, etc.) the original 1957 Rome Treaty focused on economic governance with rules intended to create a free internal market (free movement of goods, services, persons – including the freedom of establishment – and of capital: removing barriers to market access) with free competition, guaranteed by the rules on competition and state aid. By means of successive Treaty amendments these rules have been supplemented with sector-specific provisions, for instance on healthcare, social policy and culture. Moreover, EU citizenship was created by the Treaty of Maastricht in 1992 (and subsequently extended) and in 2000 the above-mentioned CFREU was

[1] See F. Snyder, 'EMU – integration and differentiation: Metaphor for European Union', in P. Craig and G. de Búrca (eds.), *The evolution of EU law*, 2nd edn (Oxford University Press, 2011), 687–716.

adopted, which, due to the Lisbon Treaty, obtained binding force based on Article 6(1) TEU.

Last but not least the Lisbon Treaty contained a number of specific provisions that are relevant to public services. These presently concern Articles 14, 37, 93 and 106 TFEU, as well as Protocol 26 on SGI and SGEI. Articles 37, 93 and 106 TFEU, which were part of the original Rome Treaty, can be seen as resulting from a compromise between, on the one hand, more market-oriented Member States – who obtained the four freedoms and competition law – and, on the other, Member States with a large public sector – who obtained the above-mentioned provisions that contain proportional exceptions to these liberal rules. Article 14 and Protocol 26, as well as Article 36 CFREU, were added later as the result of a tug of war. On the one hand, this involved the Commission, which tried to protect a liberal vision of the internal market and held that the existing rules were sufficient to accommodate public services where needed. On the other hand, it involved certain Member States (especially France, but also Belgium and Italy), backed by the European organization of trade unions (ETUC) as well as the left-wing party in the European Parliament (PES), which held that the European model of society required extensive exceptions to protect the provision of public services. The mixed result, as we shall see, is texts that try to balance these two opposing forces. We will examine whether they follow the established pattern in EU law of sweeping prohibitions modified by extensive exceptions subject to a proportionality test.

Research questions

In the first chapter I have formulated a number of research questions with regard to the position of public services in EU law that apply to this book as a whole. Several of these questions will be addressed here:

- What is the relevant primary EU law?
- What are the limits that EU law imposes on public services?
- What scope do EU law exceptions leave for national policies on public services?
- What is the role of the concept of service of general (economic) interest: SGI and SGEI?

The methodology of this chapter is simple. First I will discuss the specific legal basis for public services in the Treaties (including the CFREU and Protocol 26) article by article. This is followed by a short general introduction to the material rules on free movement and competition as well as state aid: it is not my intention to provide a primer on these issues but just some pegs on which to hang the subsequent discussion. Next I will discuss the mixed economic constitution and the highly competitive social market economy, also in relation to the status of competition policy under the Treaties. I will round off this chapter by a short section on citizenship and legitimacy, followed by some concluding remarks.

2.2 The legal basis for public services in the Treaties

We will here deal with the provisions that are directly relevant to public services in the order in which they appear in the Treaties.[2] Because this is not the chronological sequence in which they were introduced the discussion in some parts will refer backwards and forwards in time.

Article 14 TFEU: SGEI principles and conditions

This article on SGEI was introduced by the 1998 Amsterdam Treaty and – without having seen much practical use in the meantime – expanded some ten years later with a basis for framework legislation by the European Parliament and Council by the 2007 Lisbon Treaty.[3] Article 14 TFEU reads as follows:

> Without prejudice to Article 4 of the Treaty on European Union or to Articles 93, 106 and 107 of this Treaty, and given the place occupied by services of general economic interest in the shared values of the Union as well as their role in promoting social and territorial cohesion, the Union and the Member States, each within their respective powers and within the scope of application of the Treaties, shall take care that such services operate on the basis of principles and conditions, particularly economic and financial conditions, which enable them to fulfil their missions. The European Parliament and the Council, acting by means of regulations in accordance with the ordinary legislative procedure, shall establish these principles and set these conditions without prejudice to the competence of Member States, in compliance with the Treaties, to provide, to commission and to fund such services.

This article starts with assurances that it will not impinge on the established division of competencies in the Treaties nor on the specific provisions regarding public services in transport (Article 93 TFEU), on SGEI and concerning state aid (Articles 106 and 107 TFEU). Next it emphasizes the solidarity dimension (social and territorial cohesion) and the requirement that within the framework provided by EU law the Union and the Member States must enable operators of SGEI to fulfil their mission. One important precondition (economic and financial conditions) is of course funding. It is indeed in this area that we see the most elaborate horizontal secondary law framework, albeit adopted based not on Article 14 TFEU but on Article 106(3) TFEU.[4] As I have already mentioned a basis for legislation according to the ordinary legislative procedure (the

[2] On the Lisbon innovations in particular see N. Fiedziuk, 'Services of general economic interest and the Treaty of Lisbon: Opening doors to a whole new approach or maintaining the "status quo"?' *European Law Review*, 36 (2011), 226–42.

[3] On the earlier text see M. Ross, 'Promoting solidarity: From public services to a European model of competition', *Common Market Law Review*, 44 (2007), 1057–80.

[4] Commission Decision of 20 December 2011 on the application of Article 106(2) of the Treaty on the Functioning of the European Union to state aid in the form of public service compensation granted to certain undertakings entrusted with the operation of services of general economic interest, OJ 2012, L7/3; Communication from the Commission on a European Union framework

standard procedure in EU law) in the second part of Article 14 TFEU was added at a later stage and has so far not been used.[5] According to the Commission, this is because Protocol 26 on SGI, which was adopted at the same time, already provided all the clarification needed.[6] This stance is not so much logical – why then at the same time introduce a specific legal basis for clarifying legislation? – as understandable because the Commission is trying to contain the use that is made of the SGEI exception under Article 106(2) TFEU, which provides a potential threat to the internal market. I now move on to examine a *lex specialis* in relation to the provision on SGEI.

Article 37 TFEU: commercial monopolies

This provision deals with commercial monopolies and dates back to the 1957 Rome Treaty. It is a throwback to earlier times when such state monopolies played an important economic role in several Member States, for instance with regard to electricity imports. However, it was also significant with regard to socially motivated monopolies such as the production and distribution of tobacco (originally in France and Italy) as well as matches and cigarette lighters (in Italy), and with regard to alcohol in the Nordic Member States even today. As will become clear from the examples provided below, Article 37 TFEU is not concerned with public services as such, nor with universal service obligations (USO) or public service obligations (PSO), or in fact even with services – except those that can justifiably be considered goods, such as electricity. The reason that I will briefly deal with this provision nevertheless is its link with Article 106(2) TFEU on SGEI.

Article 37 TFEU reads as follows:

1. Member States shall adjust any State monopolies of a commercial character so as to ensure that no discrimination regarding the conditions under which goods are procured and marketed exists between nationals of Member States. The provisions of this Article shall apply to any body through which a

for state aid in the form of public service compensation, OJ 2012, C8/15; Communication from the Commission on the application of the European Union state aid rules to compensation granted for the provision of services of general economic interest, OJ 2012, C8/4; Commission Regulation on de minimis aid to undertakings providing SGEI, OJ 2012, L114/8. Cf. E. Szyszczak, 'Modernising state aid and the financing of SGEI', *Journal of European Competition Law and Practice*, 3 (2012), 332–43; W. Sauter, 'The *Altmark* package mark II: New rules for state aid and the compensation of services of general economic interest', *European Competition Law Review*, 33 (2012), 307–13.

5 An example: the 2010 Monti report on the internal market at p. 75 included a proposal 'extending, possibly on the basis of Article 14 TFEU, universal service in electronic communications to the provision of broadband access' which has not been adopted. M. Monti, *A new strategy for the single market: At the service of Europe's economy and society.* Report to the President of the European Commission, José Manuel Barroso, 9 May 2010.

6 Communication from the Commission, Accompanying the Communication on 'A single market for 21st century Europe' – Services of general interest, including social services of general interest: A new European commitment, COM(2007) 725.

Member State, in law or in fact, either directly or indirectly supervises, determines or appreciably influences imports or exports between Member States. These provisions shall likewise apply to monopolies delegated by the State to others.

2. Member States shall refrain from introducing any new measure which is contrary to the principles laid down in paragraph 1 or which restricts the scope of the articles dealing with the prohibition of customs duties and quantitative restrictions between Member States.
3. If a State monopoly of a commercial character has rules which are designed to make it easier to dispose of agricultural products or obtain for them the best return, steps should be taken in applying the rules contained in this Article to ensure equivalent safeguards for the employment and standard of living of the producers concerned.

Article 37 TFEU forms a *lex specialis* with regard to Article 106(1) TFEU and essentially contains an explicit non-discrimination clause with regard to a particular undertaking that is granted exclusive rights. It has probably so far seen more practical application than the preceding Article 14 TFEU because it was introduced into the Treaty to deal with a specific pre-existing problem: that of the conformity of commercial monopolies with EU law. More particularly this provision has been invoked a number of times by Member States that wished to protect their commercial monopolies for particular products, and/or their modes of regulation based on such monopolies, against challenges by competitors. Although Article 37 TFEU does not spell out a particular form of exemption the mere fact that it exists and treats commercial monopolies as a given can be regarded as an implicit assumption that commercial monopolies should be acceptable within certain bounds, notably a strict prohibition on discrimination. This is noteworthy because non-discrimination requirements are normally imposed on the Member States, not on undertakings, with the exception of the ex post prohibition for abuse of dominance under Article 102 TFEU. Admittedly monopolies are in the absence of countervailing market power and/or regulatory control almost by definition dominant. The legality of public monopolies can be regarded as being in line with the freedom of Member States to choose their system of property ownership, guaranteed by Article 345 TFEU.

Article 37 TFEU covers not just true monopolies but all situations where an undertaking appreciably affects the flow of imports or exports.[7] One of the issues that arises in this context is whether it includes only production and distribution monopolies with regard to goods or also monopolies with regard to services. The latter do not appear to be covered. In the 1997 *Electricity* cases

[7] J. L. Buendia Sierra, 'Chapter 6: Article 106 – exclusive or special rights and other anti-competitive state measures', in J. Faull and A. Nikpay (eds.), *The EU Law of Competition*, 3rd edn (Oxford University Press, 2014), 809–79, 839, with reference to Case C-347/88 *Commission* v. *Greece* [1990] ECR I-4747, para. 41. Cf. J. L. Buendia Sierra, *Exclusive rights and state monopolies under EC law: Article 86 (former Article 90) of the EC Treaty* (Oxford University Press, 2000).

where the Commission contested the existence of import monopolies in the Netherlands, Italy, France and Spain, the Court held that such monopolies were covered by Article 37 TFEU even if they did not relate to all imports, as long as they covered a proportion of imports that had an appreciable influence on such imports.[8] As far as the question of whether services are covered is concerned, electricity in this context was considered to be a good.

> Article 37 of the Treaty applies to situations in which the national authorities are in a position to control, direct or appreciably influence trade between Member States through a body established for that purpose or a delegated monopoly ... By their nature, exclusive import rights give rise to such a situation.[9]

The Court held that by its very nature an import monopoly infringes Article 37 TFEU.[10] Because Article 37 TFEU was held to be infringed, an examination of the effects on free movement of goods or the exceptions to that regime was no longer held to be necessary. However, although Article 37 TFEU was held to be infringed, the import monopolies were saved by Article 106(2) TFEU as they concerned the pursuit of a legitimate public policy objective by means of an SGEI in an area that had not been harmonized by EU law. The Court also specified that the norm for reliance on Article 106(2) TFEU was not whether the survival of the undertaking concerned was at issue, but its ability to perform its SGEI task. These cases seem to suggest that the degree to which the EU has pre-empted a policy area is relevant to the type of test applied – in particular under the proportionality heading.[11]

Another significant case on Article 37 TFEU in the same year (1997) was *Franzén*, which regarded the Swedish monopoly on the retail distribution of alcohol.[12] Here it was Article 37 TFEU itself which was held to provide a proportional exception to free movement that could be justified by the public interest. Higher investment and licensing costs for products from other Member States could only be accepted if necessary to attain the public interest invoked. The effect on trade of potential restrictions that are not related to the existence of the monopoly must however be examined under the free movement rules.[13] This line was confirmed in *Rosengren* (2007), a case likewise regarding the scope of the Swedish alcohol distribution monopoly with regard to exclusive import rights.[14]

[8] C-157/94 *Commission* v. *Netherlands* [1997] ECR I-5699; C-158/94 *Commission* v. *Italy* [1997] ECR I-5789; C-159/94 *Commission* v. *France* [1997] ECR I-5815; C-160/94 *Commission* v. *Spain* [1997] ECR I-5851.

[9] Case C-157/94 *Commission* v. *Netherlands*, above n. 8, para. 20; with reference to Case C-387/93 *Criminal proceedings against Giorgio Domingo Banchero* [1995] ECR I-4663, para. 26.

[10] Ibid., citing Case 59/75 *Pubblico Ministero* v. *Manghera* [1976] ECR 91, paras. 9–10.

[11] W. Sauter and H. Schepel, *State and market in European Union law: The public and private spheres of the internal market before the EU Courts* (Cambridge University Press, 2009).

[12] Case C-189/95 *Criminal proceedings against Harry Franzén* [1997] ECR I-5909.

[13] Ibid., para. 36.

[14] Case 170/04 *Klas Rosengren et al.* v. *Riksåklagaren* [2007] ECR I-4071.

A more recent example of this approach is provided by the 2012 *ANETT* case,[15] concerning the Spanish tobacco monopoly. Here the Court addressed the relationship between the general application of the free movement rules and the scope for the implicit Article 37 TFEU exemption as follows:

> [T]he effect on trade within the Union of the other provisions of the domestic legislation, which are separable from the operation of the monopoly although they have a bearing upon it, must be examined in the light of Article 34 TFEU . . .
>
> In those circumstances, it is necessary to check whether the prohibition at issue in the main proceedings amounts to a rule relating to the existence or the operation of the monopoly.
>
> In this regard, it must be borne in mind that, firstly, the specific purpose of the monopoly in question is to reserve the exclusive right of sale of tobacco products at retail level to authorised retailers, which does not imply that they should be prohibited from importing such products.
>
> Hence, by preventing tobacco retailers from importing those products on to the Spanish territory, the prohibition at issue in the main proceedings affects the free movement of goods within the European Union, and does not govern the exercise of the exclusive right relating to the monopoly in question.
>
> Consequently, this prohibition does not concern the exercise of the specific purpose of the monopoly in question and thus cannot be considered as relating to the very existence of the monopoly.[16]

Hence the exceptions in Articles 37 and 106(2) TFEU were irrelevant to the existence of import restrictions as violations of EU law per se, and the outcome was that the restrictions involved could not be saved under the regime of Article 34 TFEU either. This result is effectively the opposite of that which was reached in the *Electricity* cases fifteen years earlier: a prohibition on tobacco retailers from importing tobacco products from other Member States was illegal. Because the difference cannot be explained by the harmonization context (which was virtually non-existent in both cases) we must assume that either the rule has become stricter over time, or that politically sensitive sectors like energy merit a more circumspect approach.

The lessons from this goods-oriented provision for public services, with the exception of electricity which appeared here doubling as a good (as could gas and water, presumably), are threefold. First, we see monopolies being accepted and the development from what appears to be a presumption of legality given the existence of a provision on commercial monopolies, as long as strict non-discrimination is adhered to. Second, we see its justification under Article 106(2) TFEU when discrimination is held to be necessary to attain the objective of an SGEI. Third, any other restrictions that are ancillary or even unrelated to the specific purpose of the monopoly and hence to the existence of the

[15] Case C-456/10 *Asociación Nacional de Expendedores de Tabaco y Timbre (ANETT) v. Administración del Estado*, Judgment of 26 April 2012.

[16] Ibid., paras. 23–7.

monopoly are subject to the strictures of Article 34 TFEU and must be proportionate to their purpose. I will now move on to another provision that is somewhat outside the mainstream of EU law.

Article 93 TFEU: aid for public service in transport

This provision, which is not widely known outside the circles of EU lawyers working in the transport sector, reads as follows:

> Aids shall be compatible with the Treaties if they meet the needs of coordination of transport or if they represent reimbursement for the discharge of certain obligations inherent in the concept of a public service.

Article 93 TFEU is thus a sector-specific provision with regard to state aid for transport, and it happens to be the only instance in the Treaties where the concept of public service is used in so many words.[17] In effect it is a *lex specialis* with regard to the exemption for SGEI in Article 106(2) TFEU.

This provision came to the fore in the well-known 2003 *Altmark* case concerning the award of a regional public bus service concession in Germany. Here the Court ruled that the compensation of such services did not constitute aid provided four conditions were met: (i) entrustment with a public service obligation; (ii) cost parameters set out in advance; (iii) reimbursement at the level of cost plus a reasonable rate of return; and (iv) cost based on the result of a public tender or of an efficient operator.[18] The *Altmark* test is now widely applied in practice, at least in the decisional practice of the Commission. Concerning state aid for public services in general – outside the transport context – the alternatives to this route are a declaration of compatibility with the internal market either based on the application of the Article 106(2) TFEU exemption for SGEI or under the general provision in Article 107(3) TFEU. In the case of transport the alternative to the *Altmark* test is the application of Article 93 TFEU. If the *Altmark* conditions were met no aid would be involved. Hence, there would not be any need to refer to Article 93 TFEU.

In the *Altmark* case the Court also ruled that Article 93 TFEU cannot be applied to public subsidies that compensate for the costs of a PSO without taking into account the specific provisions of secondary legislation provided for in Regulation 1191/69.[19] The latter summed up the circumstances where aid may be warranted and is considered to be compatible based on this Regulation.

[17] The reference to employment in the public service in Article 45(4) TFEU on the free movement of workers has a different meaning, analogous to public administration, that is not related to our topic of the provision of public services. See Sauter and Schepel, above n. 11. Public service broadcasting in Protocol 29 is closer in meaning and will be briefly covered below.

[18] Case C-280/00 *Altmark Trans GmbH and Regierungspräsidium Magdeburg v. Nahverkehrsgesellschaft Altmark GmbH, and Oberbundesanwalt beim Bundesverwaltungsgericht* [2003] ECR I-7747.

[19] Regulation (EEC) No 1191/69 of the Council of 26 June 1969 on action by Member States concerning the obligations inherent in the concept of a public service in transport by rail, road

Hence the system with regard to public services compensation in the transport sector is that compensation either:

(i) is cleared under the *Altmark* criteria as not constituting aid; or
(ii) is found to constitute aid but covered by the Regulation; or
(iii) constitutes aid not covered by the Regulation but covered by Article 93 TFEU.

Regulation 1191/69 has been replaced by Regulation 1370/2007 which serves the same purpose.[20] It states that compatible aid for public service in the third category listed above that is subject to Article 93 TFEU mainly covers infrastructure costs and research and development. This regulation is also the main piece of sector-specific SGEI legislation that exists today, complementing the generally applicable *Altmark* packages of 2005 and 2012 introduced by the Commission on the application of the state aid rules in the context of SGEI.[21]

Article 106 TFEU: public undertakings, special and exclusive rights; SGEI; enforcement and legislation

This is the main article with regard to public services in the Treaty. Given its central importance, I will deal separately with its three paragraphs. Article 106 TFEU reads as follows:

1. In the case of public undertakings and undertakings to which Member States grant special or exclusive rights, Member States shall neither enact nor maintain in force any measure contrary to the rules contained in the Treaties, in particular to those rules provided for in Article 18 and Articles 101 to 109.
2. Undertakings entrusted with the operation of services of general economic interest or having the character of a revenue-producing monopoly shall be subject to the rules contained in the Treaties, in particular to the rules on competition, in so far as the application of such rules does not obstruct the performance, in law or in fact, of the particular tasks assigned to them. The development of trade must not be affected to such an extent as would be contrary to the interests of the Union.
3. The Commission shall ensure the application of the provisions of this Article and shall, where necessary, address appropriate directives or decisions to Member States.

I will now deal with each paragraph in turn.

and inland waterway, OJ 1969, L156/1, as last amended by Regulation (EEC) No 1893/91 (OJ 1991, L169/1).

[20] Regulation (EC) No 1370/2007 of the European Parliament and of the Council of 23 October 2007 on public passenger transport services by rail and by road and repealing Council Regulations (EEC) Nos 1191/69 and 1107/70, OJ 2007, L315/1.

[21] Above, n. 4.

Article 106(1) TFEU: public undertakings, special and exclusive rights

This provision, once hotly contested, has become less debated in recent years, because attention has shifted to SGEI and Article 106(2) TFEU. The purpose of Article 106(1) TFEU is balancing, on the one hand, the existence of public undertakings and undertakings enjoying special and exclusive rights (similarly to the existence of commercial monopolies under Article 37 TFEU) with, on the other hand, the need to have them respect the internal market rules (non-discrimination), as well as the rules on competition and on state aid.

The focal point in this provision is formed by the state measures to which it refers. Article 106(1) TFEU is invoked against the relevant authorities of the Member States, not (at least not directly) against the undertakings concerned. Such measures may be taken by public authorities at national, regional or local level.[22] It is implicit that these measures concern economic activities on account of the undertakings concerned: in fact the EU law definition of undertaking is an entity that engages in economic activities, notably the provision of goods or services on a market,[23] that is (potentially) under conditions of competition. This is important in particular as regards the impact of the state measures concerned on the state aid and competition rules. In the 1991 *Höfner* case regarding a German monopoly on job placement services the Court stated:

> It must be observed in the context of competition law, first that the concept of an undertaking encompasses every entity engaged in an economic activity, regardless of the legal status of the entity and the way in which it is financed and, secondly, that employment procurement is an economic activity.
>
> The fact that employment procurement activities are normally entrusted to public agencies cannot affect the economic nature of such activities. Employment procurement has not always been, and is not necessarily, carried out by public entities. That finding applies in particular to executive recruitment.
>
> It follows that an entity such as a public employment agency engaged in the business of employment procurement may be classified as an undertaking for the purpose of applying the Community competition rules.[24]

Hence it will suffice that the services can be provided, even in theory, in competition. It is worth contrasting this position with that of the

[22] Buendia Sierra (2014), above n. 7, at 814, with reference to Case 30/87 *Corinne Bodson* v. *SA Pompes funèbres des régions libérées* [1988] ECR 2479, concerning local concessions for funeral services; and Case C-323 *Société Civile Agricole du Centre d'Insémination de la Crespelle* v. *Coopérative d'Elevage et d'Insémination Artificielle du Département de la Mayenne* [1994] ECR I-5077, concerning regional concessions for bovine artificial insemination services. See also Commission Staff working document, Guide to the application of the European Union rules on state aid, public procurement and the internal market to services of general economic interest, and in particular to social services of general interest, SWD(2013) 53.

[23] Thus concerning medical doctors in Joined cases C-180/98 to C-184/98 *Pavel Pavlov et al.* v. *Stichting Pensioenfonds Medische Specialisten* [2000] ECR I-6451 the Court ruled that 'any activity consisting in offering goods and services on a given market is an economic activity'. Ibid., para. 75.

[24] Case C-41/90 *Klaus Höfner and Fritz Elser* v. *Macrotron GmbH* [1991] ECR I-1979, paras. 21–3.

Commission under the 2012 *Altmark* package, where it holds that only a test of manifest disproportionality is applied to the entrustment of PSO with public service compensation – in which case it is not allowed to read across jurisdictions in order to determine whether elsewhere similar services are successfully provided in competition with comparable conditions in terms of cost, access and quality.[25] This suggests that a very different standard is applied for deciding whether the competition rules, at least in principle, apply (a boundary issue), and for deciding whether recourse to an SGEI in a particular instance in itself (short of the manner in which it is applied) is manifestly disproportionate.[26]

Of the three categories of undertakings that are listed in Article 106(1) TFEU, public undertakings and special rights are relatively unproblematic. Exclusive rights are the most contested. All three are defined in the 2007 Transparency Directive. There, the category of public undertaking is defined as follows:

> '[P]ublic undertakings' means any undertaking over which the public authorities may exercise directly or indirectly a dominant influence by virtue of their ownership of it, their financial participation therein, or the rules which govern it.[27]

The provision does not imply that public undertakings are as such illegal in EU law. As I have mentioned above, there is even a specific provision of the Treaty, Article 345 TFEU, which underlines that EU law is neutral with respect to the property regime (public or private) at national level. By definition therefore, public undertakings are acceptable at least in principle. In practice, however, the effect of European integration may well undermine their role and their existence. (We will look at Article 345 TFEU in the section on the economic orientation of the Treaties below.) As we shall see, this presumption of legality is different for special and exclusive rights. Special rights are defined in the Transparency Directive as follows:

> '[S]pecial rights' means rights that are granted by a Member State to a limited number of undertakings, through any legislative, regulatory or administrative instrument, which, within a given geographical area:
>
> (i) limits to two or more the number of such undertakings, authorised to provide a service or undertake an activity, otherwise than according to objective, proportional and non-discriminatory criteria; or
> (ii) designates, otherwise than according to such criteria, several competing undertakings, as being authorised to provide a service or undertake an activity; or

[25] SGEI compensation Communication (2012), above n. 4, paras. 12 and 48.

[26] This restrictive approach can also be observed in relation to the freedom of establishment. See L. Hancher and W. Sauter, 'One step beyond? From *Sodemare* to *Docmorris*: The EU's freedom of establishment case law concerning healthcare', *Common Market Law Review*, 47 (2010), 117–46.

[27] Commission Directive 2006/111/EC of 16 November 2006 on the transparency of financial relations between Member States and public undertakings as well as on financial transparency within certain undertakings, OJ 2006, L318/17, Article 2(b).

(iii) confers on any undertaking or undertakings, otherwise than according to such criteria, any legal or regulatory advantages which substantially affect the ability of any other undertaking to provide the same service or to operate the same activity in the same geographical area under substantially equivalent conditions.[28]

In my view special rights could well instead have been conceived as any limited set of rights that are awarded by a Member State to the exclusion of other interested parties without requiring in addition that this limitation had been carried out in a discretionary and discriminatory manner. For instance, licence awards for the use or frequency spectrum for purposes of providing mobile telephony services would then have been caught. Now they are not. The fact that the present definition was chosen implies that special rights, where they do exist, are by definition in infringement of the internal market rules unless they can be saved by a proportionate public interest defence. Because these special rights are by definition to a significant extent arbitrary in nature, defending them will be a tall order.

I now move on to the most complex category under Article 106(1) TFEU, which is also the most important in practice: that of exclusive rights. The Transparency Directive defines exclusive rights as follows:

'[E]xclusive rights' means rights that are granted by a Member State to one undertaking through any legislative, regulatory or administrative instrument, reserving it the right to provide a service or undertake an activity within a given geographical area.[29]

Exclusive rights are more problematic than the other two categories. This is so not for reasons of definitional complexity but because their existence itself can be at issue. Just as is the case for commercial monopolies under Article 37 TFEU, it is not entirely clear whether awarding an exclusive right forms under Article 106(1) TFEU an infringement of EU law unless it is covered by an exemption – notably that on SGEI provided by Article 106(2) TFEU. In my view the 1991 *Corbeau* case suggests that this is not so:

[T]he Court has consistently held that an undertaking having a statutory monopoly over a substantial part of the common market may be regarded as having a dominant position within the meaning of Article 86 of the Treaty [now Article 106 TFEU] . . .

However, Article 86 applies only to anti-competitive conduct engaged in by undertakings on their own initiative, not to measures adopted by States . . .

[28] Ibid., Article 2(g). Cf. earlier Commission Directive 94/46/EC of 13 October 1994 amending Directive 88/301/EEC and Directive 90/388/EEC in particular with regard to satellite communications, OJ 1994, L268/15. Another type of special rights in EU law was the golden shares by which several Member States retained control over partially or largely privatized undertakings. Cf. for instance case C-58/99 *Commission* v. *Italy* [2000] ECR I-3811; Case C-212/09 *Commission* v. *Portugal*, Judgment of 10 November 2011.

[29] Commission Directive 2006/111/EC, above n. 27, Article 2(f).

> The Court has had occasion to state in this respect that although the mere fact that a Member State has created a dominant position by the grant of exclusive rights is not as such incompatible with Article 86, the Treaty none the less requires the Member States not to adopt or maintain in force any measure which might deprive those provisions of their effectiveness.[30]

Hence, in my view, granting an exclusive right as such is not illegal unless its creation already entails certain infringements of the Treaty. Thus in various cases the Court has held not the exclusive right, but its extension,[31] its combination with regulatory responsibility,[32] the innate conflict of interest involved,[33] the inability to meet demand,[34] or various pricing abuses[35] to lead to infringements of EU law. These involved notably infringements of Article 102 TFEU on abuse of dominant position that, if committed by undertakings enjoying an exclusive right, can lead to an infringement of Article 106(1) and 102 TFEU jointly. In the more recent *DEI* case (2012),[36] the General Court held that for an infringement of Articles 106(1) and 102 TFEU to occur, it did not suffice that the Member State concerned had created an inequality of opportunities between economic operators (electricity generators) in an adjacent market (in this case by awarding a monopoly on the exploitation of lignite in Greece) but that additionally a related or resulting abuse by the undertaking concerned had to be shown. The General Court held:

> [T]he abuse of a dominant position by the undertaking enjoying an exclusive or special right may either result from the possibility of exercising that right in an abusive way or be a direct consequence of that right. However, it does not follow from that case-law that the mere fact that the undertaking in question finds itself in an advantageous situation in comparison with its competitors, by reason of a State measure, in itself constitutes an abuse of a dominant position.[37]

According to José Luis Buendia Sierra, a leading commentator in this field, the jury is still out on the question whether the Court looks at effects (and therefore at the granting of the exclusive rights) or at behaviour (and therefore at the

[30] Notably Case C-320/91 *Criminal proceedings against Paul Corbeau* [1993] ECR I-2533, para. 11, with reference to Case C-260/89 *Elliniki Radiophonia Tiléorassi AE and Panellinia Omospondia Syllogon Prossopikou* v. *Dimotiki Etairia Pliroforissis and Sotirios Kouvelas and Nicolaos Avdellas et al.* [1991] ECR I-2925. Cf. Case C-203/96 *Chemische Afvalstoffen Dusseldorp BV et al.* v. *Minister van Volkshuisvesting, Ruimtelijke Ordening en Milieubeheer* [1998] ECR I-4075, para. 61.

[31] Case C-475/99 *Firma Ambulanz Glöckner* v. *Landkreis Südwestpfalz* [2001] ECR I-8089.

[32] Case C-18/88 *Régie des télégraphes et des téléphones* v. *GB-Inno-BM SA* [1991] ECR I-5941.

[33] Buendia Sierra (2014), above n. 7, at 828, with reference to Case 260/89.

[34] Case C-41/90 *Höfner*, above n. 24.

[35] Case C-179/90 *Merci convenzionali porto di Genova SpA* v. *Siderurgica Gabrielli SpA* [1991] ECR I-5889.

[36] Case T-169/08 *Dimosia Epicheirisi Ilektrismou AE (DEI)* v. *Commission*, Judgment of 20 September 2012.

[37] Ibid., para. 103.

infringement of the dominance abuse prohibition), although he believes that in actual practice this may not make much of a difference.[38] My own view is that the importance of Article 106(1) TFEU on public undertakings, special and exclusive rights has decreased with a corresponding increase of the relevance of Article 106(2) TFEU on SGEI. This means that the purpose of the restrictions related to the exclusive rights and its proportionality as an instrument in pursuit of the relevant public interest objectives are key to the legality of any exclusivity. This will be discussed in the next section.

Apart from Article 102 TFEU infringements that are related to dominance abuse, at least in theory the anti-cartel provision Article 101 TFEU could also be at issue. So far there do not appear to be many significant examples of such cases, with the exception of bilateral landing slots (airlines) and the acquisition and sharing of sports broadcasting rights.[39] This is unsurprising as it is almost logically precluded that dominant operators would need each other's assistance – or could even coexist (in which case joint dominance may be involved), unless cartels are organized between them across different jurisdictions. Likewise the application of the internal market rules, notably the non-discrimination provision of Article 18 TFEU, does not appear to be of much practical significance in this context, although it is mentioned expressly in the text of Article 106(1) TFEU.[40] I now move on to deal with the next paragraph of Article 106 TFEU which is the most important provision with regard to public services in the Treaties.

Article 106(2) TFEU: the exception for SGEI

SGEI have already been discussed as part of the family of EU law concepts regarding public services in the first chapter. Here they will be discussed primarily in terms of their legal implications. Article 106(2) TFEU has been described by the Court as designed to

> reconcile the Member States' interest in using certain undertakings, in particular in the public sector, as an instrument of economic or fiscal policy with the

[38] Buendia Sierra (2014), above n. 7, at 833.

[39] Buendia Sierra, ibid., at 835 cites Case 66/86 *Ahmed Saeed Flugreisen and Silver Line Reisebüro GmbH* v. *Zentrale zur Bekämpfung unlauteren Wettbewerbs e.V.* [1989] ECR 803. The next closest example appears to be Joined cases T-185/00, T-216/00, T-299/00 and T-300/00 *Métropole Télévision SA (M6), Antena 3 de Televisión SA, Gestevisión Telecinco SA and SIC – Sociedade Independente de Comunicação SA* v. *Commission* [2002] ECR II-3805. Another example could have been roaming agreements in mobile telephony but this problem was ultimately addressed by regulation instead. Regulation (EU) No 531/2012 of the European Parliament and of the Council of 13 June 2012 on roaming on public mobile communications networks within the Union, OJ 2012, L172/10.

[40] However, as I have observed earlier, it seems that given its predefined arbitrary nature, the grant of special rights in itself, by definition, might provide such a (possibly justifiable) breach of Article 18 TFEU.

> Community's interest in ensuring compliance with the rules on competition and preservation of the unity of the common market.[41]

This provision forms the counterpoint to the presumption that publicly assigned monopolies may exist, which is found both in Article 106(1) TFEU as just discussed and in Article 37 TFEU as discussed earlier. This is not to say that the provision on SGEI legalizes restrictions of competition or of free movement by commercial monopolies and/or (public) undertakings benefitting from special and exclusive rights as such, but it does provide an exception to the internal market and competition rules as well as to state aid rules on which these undertakings can rely – provided the relevant requirements are met.[42] This does not mean that the application of Article 106(2) TFEU is limited to cases where Article 106(1) and/or Article 37 TFEU are involved. Rather Article 106(2) TFEU has its own category of services to which this exception applies, which is the same as that which we have already come across in the context of Article 14 TFEU: that of services of general economic interest (SGEI). As their name testifies, this means we are leaving the realm of privileges (even although they may have public policy objectives) and are entering the realm of public services, ultimately to the benefit of consumers, or market citizens.

In a provocative contribution to the debate on SGEI, Gareth Davies has argued that Article 106 TFEU is superfluous because other Treaty provisions, in particular those regarding free movement, already provide standard exceptions with sufficient scope to enable public services.[43] I disagree, especially with regard to Article 106(2) TFEU. First, as we have already discussed, there were historic motives to create additional certainty for public services as part of a fundamental compromise on the mixed economic constitution. Second, at a more technical legal level, the comparison is flawed. The provisions on free movement and competition do provide for exceptions, but these do not have an equal or equivalent scope to that provided by Article 106(2) TFEU. This is so because in free movement public policy exceptions and overriding reasons of public interest are allowed, but at least in principle not on economic grounds.[44] Vice versa, the exceptions allowed in competition policy are on the whole

[41] Case C-67/96 *Albany International BV* v. *Stichting Bedrijfspensioenfonds Textielindustrie* [1999] ECR I-5751, para. 103; Case C-265/08 *Federutility et al.* v. *Autorità per lénergia elettrica e il gas* [2010] ECR I-3377, para. 28.

[42] An example concerning the application of the Article 106(2) TFEU exemption to the freedom to provide services in Article 56 TFEU is formed by Joined Cases C-147/97 and 148/97 *Deutsche Post AG* v. *Gesellschaft für Zahlungssysteme mbH (GZS) and Citicorp Kartenservice GmbH* [2000] ECR I-825.

[43] G. Davies, 'What does Article 86 actually do?' in M. Krajewski, U. Neergaard and J. van de Gronden (eds.), *The changing legal framework for services of general interest in Europe: Between competition and solidarity* (TMC Asser Press, The Hague, 2009), 51–67.

[44] An exception is found with regard to planning in healthcare. Cf. Case C-385/99 *V. G. Müller-Fauré* v. *Onderlinge Waarborgmaatschappij OZ Zorgverzekeringen UA and E. E. M. van Riet* v. *Onderlinge Waarborgmaatschappij ZAO Zorgverzekeringen* [2003] ECR I-4509, codified in Directive 2011/24/EU of the European Parliament and of the Council of 9 March 2011 on the application of patients' rights in cross-border healthcare, OJ 2011, L88/45.

economic, so efficiency-, but not equity-based, and the benefits must accrue at least in part to consumers. Finally, in state aid Article 107(3) TFEU allows both efficiency and equity grounds for exception but these have to be in the general interest as established at EU level and not at that of the Member States. Article 106(2) TFEU not only allows both efficiency and equity reasons but does so at the level of the Member State involved. In my view this difference in scope goes hand in hand with a degree of deference – a manifestly disproportionate test, at least in the absence of specific harmonization legislation – that indicates a qualitative difference in kind as well. Hence I do believe that Article 106(2) TFEU serves a purpose, and an important one at that.

The exception to the Treaty rules for SGEI applies if four conditions are met that can be derived directly from the text of Article 106(2) TFEU:[45]

(i) an undertaking must be involved;
(ii) that is charged with a public service obligation (PSO);
(iii) any resulting restrictions of competition or of the internal market freedoms must be necessary and proportionate to pursuit of the PSO; and
(iv) the development of trade is not affected to an extent that is contrary to the EU's interests.

Because it is an exception to the general rules of the Treaty, as a general matter of EU law Article 106(2) TFEU should be interpreted strictly, at least in theory.[46] In practice this does not appear the case, or rather there is a graded approach which tends to favour the status quo. I will now examine each of the above-mentioned four criteria in turn, in relation to this practice.

Undertaking

Article 106(2) TFEU applies to undertakings – a category which also functions as a filter with respect to the application of the rules on competition and on state aid – that are entrusted with the operation of services of general economic interest. The category of undertaking is defined relatively straightforwardly. In *Pavlov* (2000), a case that revolved around mandatory subscriptions to a supplementary pension scheme, but with regard to the qualification of self-employed medical doctors who were subject to the scheme, the Court stated the following:

> The Court has consistently held that, in the context of competition law, the concept of an undertaking covers any entity engaged in an economic activity, regardless of the legal status of the entity or the way in which it is financed . . .
>
> It has also been consistently held that any activity consisting in offering goods and services on a given market is an economic activity.[47]

[45] Cf. J. Holmes, 'Fixing the limits of EC competition law: State action and the accommodation of the public services', *Current Legal Problems*, 57 (2004), 149–74, at 168–9.

[46] Case 127/73 *BRT* v. *SABAM and NV Fonior* [1974] ECR 313, para. 19.

[47] Joined cases C-180/98 to C-184/98 *Pavlov*, above n. 23, paras. 74–5. Cf. Case C-41/90 *Höfner*, above n. 24.

This appears clear enough. However, in practice a greater degree of complexity and detail is involved regarding the qualification as undertaking with regard to the provision of particular types of services. For instance, in the Commission's 2012 Communication concerning compensation for SGEI and state aid, somewhat confusingly, no fewer than four different sets of criteria are given to decide whether undertakings are concerned in respect of the relevant types of public services:[48]

(i) Exercise of public powers: 'activities that intrinsically form part of the prerogatives of official authority and are performed by the state' such as police powers and air traffic control – but also pollution control services carried out by a private entity in this instance are exercises of public authority.[49]
(ii) Social services: these are predominantly based on expressions of solidarity such as compulsory affiliation, an exclusively social purpose and the non-profit nature of a scheme. Other factors are rights to claims that are not proportional to individual contributions and the existence of state supervision.[50]
(iii) Health services: it has been claimed that public hospitals that are part of a national health service (NHS) and provide a tax-funded universal service free of charge at point of delivery are not individual undertakings.[51]
(iv) Education: here the Court has held that a system of public education financed entirely or mainly by public funds and not by pupils or parents is non-economic in nature.[52]

The 2014 Draft Commission Notice on the notion of state aid (which regarding the other categories repeats the 2012 Communication practically verbatim) adds a fifth category: that of infrastructure.[53]

Evidently, the above criteria can be difficult to interpret in particular cases and, in addition, their validity may be contested. Hence the issue of what constitutes an undertaking can become a vexed one.[54] Moving on from the

[48] SGEI compensation Communication, above n. 4, pp. 6–8.

[49] Case C-343/95 *Diego Calì & Figli Srl* v. *Servizi ecologici porto di Genova SpA (SEPG)* [1997] ECR I-1547.

[50] Joined cases C-159/91 and C-160/91 *Christian Poucet* v. *Assurances Générales de France and Caisse Mutuelle Régionale du Languedoc-Roussillon* [1993] ECR I-637.

[51] Based on Case C-205/03 P *Federación Española de Empresas de Tecnología Sanitaria (FENIN)* v. *Commission* [2006] ECR I-6295. Contrary: O. Odudu, 'Are state-owned health-care providers undertakings subject to competition law?' *European Competition Law Review*, 32 (2011), 231–41.

[52] Case C-318/05 *Commission* v. *Germany* [2007] ECR I-6957.

[53] Communication from the Commission, Draft Commission Notice on the notion of state aid pursuant to Article 107(1) TFEU. Cf. Case T-128/98 *Aéroports de Paris* v. *Commission* [2000] ECR II-3929; Case T-196/04 *Ryanair* v. *Commission* [2008] II-3643.

[54] Cf. for instance, just in the case of healthcare services, Case C-205/03, *FENIN*, above n. 51; Joined cases C-264/01, C-306/01, C-354/01 and C-355/01 *AOK Bundesverband, Bundesverband der Betriebskrankenkassen (BKK) et al.* v. *Ichthyol-Gesellschaft Cordes et al.* [2004] ECR I-2493; and Case C-437/09 *AG2R Prévoyance* v. *Beaudout Père et Fils SARL* [2011] ECR I-973.

issue of what constitutes an undertaking, which is after all a general question of EU law, or at least of EU competition law, I now want to look at another component of the term SGEI. In what sense is the term 'economic' used here? It appears there are now two main answers to this question:

- The qualification economic is generally assumed to relate to the concept of undertaking: that is to say concerning services provided, at least in principle, in competition. This does not mean that objectives that are non-economic are not justified: the SGEI provision can cover both economic (efficiency) and non-economic (equity) justifications.
- In addition (as an ex post but systematically valid justification for its use), the qualification economic now serves (at least since the introduction of Protocol 26 by the Lisbon Treaty) to distinguish the overall general category of public services as SGI from the subcategory of such services as provided by undertakings at least in principle in competition.

This 2014 Draft Notice also covers the approach that activities that are public authority based and activities that are carried out by an undertaking are severable.[55] This means that the latter, but not the former, will be addressed by the rules on competition and state aid. This approach is still in its infancy but could rationalize the treatment under EU law of entities with mixed tasks.

Consistent with what I have said above regarding the fact that SGEI can cover both economic and non-economic justifications, it is up to the Member States to decide what services they wish to define as SGEI. Or rather, it is up to them to define the relevant public service obligations (PSO) and, to the extent necessary and proportionate to these legitimate objectives, entrust particular undertakings with the task of carrying out the respective SGEI. As discussed in the first chapter, this does not mean that the national postal service as a whole is an SGEI even if the net is cast widely. Thus the amended Postal Services Directive (2008) states:

> Member States shall ensure that users enjoy the right to a universal service involving the permanent provision of a postal service of specified quality at all points in their territory at affordable prices for all users . . . Member States shall take steps to ensure that the universal service is guaranteed not less than five working days a week.[56]

[55] Cf. Joined Cases T-443/08 and T-455/08 *Freistaat Sachsen and Land Sachsen-Anhalt and Mitteldeutsche Flughafen AG and Flughafen Leipzig-Halle GmbH* v. *Commission* [2011] ECR II-1319, paras. 99–100; Case C-138/11 *Compass-Datenbank GmbH* v. *Republik Österreich*, judgment of 12 July 2012, para. 38, with reference to Case C-113/07 P *SELEX Sistemi Integrati* v. *Commission* [2009] ECR I-2207, paras. 72ff.

[56] Articles 3(1) and 3(3) of Directive 97/67/EC of the European Parliament and of the Council of 15 December 1997 on common rules for the development of the internal market of Community postal services and the improvement of quality of service, OJ 1998, L15/14, as amended by Directive 2008/6/EC of the European Parliament and of the Council of 20 February 2008 amending Directive 97/67/EC with regard to the full accomplishment of the internal market of Community postal services, OJ 2008, L52/3.

Hence one or more postal operators in a Member State may be entrusted with an SGEI, such as for instance the duty to deliver letter mail up to 50 grams at a minimum frequency of at least five days a week and at standard rates, possibly under a compensation regime under terms which are specified by the Postal Services Directive. This involves either compensation from public funds or cost sharing based on a universal service fund, both under conditions of transparency, non-discrimination and proportionality. It does not mean that the Postal Service or a postal service as such form an SGEI.

Public service obligation

The second criterion, the PSO, is the substance of the SGEI. The PSO contains its purpose, to which the necessity and proportionality requirements are relative. At the same time, a PSO is different from a normal service because it involves a task or set of tasks that an undertaking would not normally take on under the same conditions, especially in view of the financial terms provided. In the context of public services in the transport sector (rail, road and water), this is set out as follows:

> '[P]ublic service obligation' means a requirement defined or determined by a competent authority in order to ensure public passenger transport services in the general interest that an operator, if it were considering its own commercial interests, would not assume or would not assume to the same extent or under the same conditions without reward.[57]

It is left largely up to the Member States to define PSO (although in the *Deutsche Post* case of 2000, uniquely, the Court assumed that with regard to the most rapid possible delivery of international mail within the national territory this had been done by the Universal Postal Convention by which the Member States were bound).[58] In principle only a manifest error test is applied to the question whether a public service is involved.[59] This allows excesses to be curtailed. Hence in *Merci convenzionali* (1991) the CJEU found, concerning docking services in the harbour of Genoa, that

> it does not appear ... that dock work is of a general economic interest exhibiting special characteristics as compared with the general economic interest of other economic activities or, even if it were, that the application of the rules of the Treaty, in particular those relating to competition and

[57] Regulation (EC) No 1370/2007 of the European Parliament and of the Council of 23 October 2007 on public passenger transport services by rail and by road and repealing Council Regulations (EEC) Nos 1191/69 and 1107/70, OJ 2007, L315/1, Article 2(e).

[58] Joined Cases C-147/97 and C-148/97 *Deutsche Post*, above n. 42, para. 44: 'For the postal services of the Member States, performance of the obligations of the UPC is thus in itself a service of general economic interest within the meaning of Article 90(2) of the Treaty.'

[59] Case T-17/02 *Fred Olsen SA* v. *Commission* [2005] ECR II-2031, para. 216 (regarding maritime cabotage).

> freedom of movement, would be such as to obstruct the performance of such a task.[60]

Whether an activity is already provided or can be provided satisfactorily under market conditions is likewise a matter that is subject only to control for manifest error. It is highly unlikely that on this basis comparisons between Member States where different systems of supplying the public services involved are in place could ever play a significant role in deciding on the legality of the particular choice made in a given Member State. Where public services are in flux, however, it may be possible for the Commission to provide guidance in advance of public intervention. This can be based on objective criteria, such as the presence of one or more effective competitors in the market providing services to a given standard. This approach, which was spelled out in Commission Guidelines in 2009 and 2013,[61] is already being applied by the Commission in the rapidly developing broadband sector. It was recently confirmed by the General Court in the *Colt* case (2013).[62]

In the *BUPA* case (2008), concerning private medical insurance (PMI) services, the General Court distinguished general regulatory obligations from the entrustment of a PSO. The criterion applied was the degree to which commercial freedom is restricted:

> [T]he Health Insurance Act and also the ... Health Insurance Regulations ... define in detail the PMI obligations, such as community rating, open enrolment, lifetime cover and minimum benefits, to which all PMI insurers ... are subject. Furthermore, with the stated object of serving the general interest by allowing what is at present approximately half of the Irish population to benefit from alternative cover for certain health care, in particular hospital care, the above-mentioned PMI obligations restrict the commercial freedom of the PMI insurers to an extent going considerably beyond ordinary conditions of authorisation to exercise an activity in a specific sector.[63]

Moreover, the above-mentioned PMI obligations all reflect dimensions of the universality requirement which, based on the case law, can be seen as being inherent in a PSO but are not spelled out in Article 106(2) TFEU itself. Subsequently the General Court confronts this issue directly:

[60] Case C-179/90 *Merci convenzionali*, above n. 35, para. 27. Cf. also Case C-242/95 *GT-Link A/S* v. *De Danske Statsbaner* (DSB) [1997] ECR I-4449 and Joined cases C-34/01 to C-38/01 *Enirisorse SpA* v. *Ministero delle Finanze* [2003] ECR I-14243.

[61] Cf. SGEI compensation Communication, above n. 4, paras. 48–9. Communication from the Commission, EU Guidelines for the application of state aid rules in relation to the rapid deployment of broadband networks (2013/C 25/01), OJ 2013 C25/1. A. Kliemann and O. Stehmann, 'EU state aid control in the broadband sector – The 2013 broadband guidelines and recent case practice', *European State Aid Law Quarterly*, 12 (2013), 493–515.

[62] Case T-79/10 *Colt Télécommunications France* v. *Commission*, Judgment of 16 September 2013.

[63] Case T-289/03 *British United Provident Association Ltd (BUPA), BUPA Insurance Ltd and BUPA Ireland Ltd* v. *Commission* [2008] ECR II-81, para. 182.

> [T]he universality criterion does not require that the service in question be free of charge or that it be offered without consideration of economic profitability. The fact that certain potential users do not have the necessary financial resources to take advantage of all the PMI cover available on the market, in particular 'luxury' cover, does not undermine its universal nature provided that the service in question is offered at uniform and non-discriminatory rates and on similar quality conditions for all customers.[64]

As this reference illustrates, the distinctive criterion regarding universality is open access, or an obligation to deal on publicly predefined terms, even if in practice not the entire population would be able to afford the services concerned. It is therefore not necessary for every citizen to take up the service as long as the service would be offered to them. In addition, offering the PSO must also be mandatory. This too was specified in *BUPA*, and connected to the above-mentioned universality requirement:

> [I]n the absence of an exclusive or special right, it is sufficient, in order to conclude that a service is compulsory, that the operator entrusted with a particular mission is under an obligation to provide that service to any user requesting it. In other words, the compulsory nature of the service and, accordingly, the existence of an SGEI mission are established if the service-provider is obliged to contract, on consistent conditions, without being able to reject the other contracting party. That element makes it possible to distinguish a service forming part of an SGEI mission from any other service provided on the market.[65]

Given these criteria as set out in the case law, it would be vastly preferable if, in the context of SGEI, undertakings were always entrusted with a PSO by an explicit legal act. This has advantages concerning legal certainty, regarding the scope for competition, and it facilitates an effective proportionality test: if the objectives pursued are vague, improvised or to be guessed at, how can related restrictions be found necessary and proportionate?[66] In practice, however, the EU Courts as well as the Commission are prepared to accept situations where, in the absence of a specific act, the entrustment must be derived from the legal and regulatory context. Thus, with regard to the Dutch import monopoly for electricity, the CJEU held:

> The Member States . . . cannot be precluded, when defining the services of general economic interest which they entrust to certain undertakings, from taking account of objectives pertaining to their national policy or from endeavouring

[64] Ibid., para. 203. Cf. on the same argument with regard to electricity provision Case C-393/92 *Municipality of Almelo and Others* v. *NV Energiebedrijf Ijsselmij* [1994] ECR I-1477, para. 48.

[65] Case T-289/03 *BUPA*, above n. 63, para. 190.

[66] Cf. Case C-567/07 *Minister voor Wonen, Wijken en Integratie* v. *Woningstichting Sint Servatius* [2009] ECR I-9021, where the Court refused to entertain the applicability of Article 106(2) TFEU in relation to a naked restriction which was not based on objective, non-discriminatory criteria known in advance and which were capable of adequately circumscribing the exercise by the national authorities of their discretion. Ibid., para. 57.

to attain them by means of obligations and constraints which they impose on such undertakings.[67]

Hence the existence of obligations and constraints which do not constitute a formal act of entrustment can suffice. Likewise an act of assignment can be substituted by means of a public service concession.[68] The Commission's *Altmark* package is also neutral on the precise format that is used, stating that an act may take the form of a legislative or regulatory instrument or a contract, or conditions may be laid down in several acts. It does, however, require that this act(s) must specify the content and duration of the PSO; the undertaking and (if applicable) territory concerned; the nature of any special and exclusive rights; the parameters for compensation; and the arrangements regarding over-compensation.[69] On balance therefore, the regime concerning the assignment of a PSO is a flexible one that appears to be easily met for genuine SGEI, that is to say those which meet the requirements of being universal and mandatory.

Necessity and proportionality

Proportionality is a key principle of EU law that legitimizes its supremacy and direct effect and sets limits to both levels of governance. There are different tests of proportionality in EU law. These range from the least challenging form, manifest disproportionality (a type of sanity check), to a stringent least restrictive means test (no less restrictive equally effective means are available) and finally to balancing the public interest invoked by the Member State against that of the EU (which is often and somewhat confusingly called 'strict balancing' in the literature).[70] In earlier publications, I have defended the thesis that the nature of the test that the CJEU applies is determined in large part by the degree to which the field has been occupied by EU law: where there is extensive harmonization there is less scope for an invasive intervention on behalf of public services as defined at national level (so a strict test applies) than where no such harmonization exists (so a mild test is applied).[71]

Evidence on this count is provided for instance by the 1997 *Electricity* cases.[72] Here the CJEU not only held that the Commission could not revoke the exclusive rights granted to national operators by the Member States concerned but also refused to consider the scope for alternative (less restrictive) regulatory

[67] Case C-157/94 *Commission* v. *Netherlands*, above n. 8, para. 40.

[68] Case T-17/02 *Olsen*, above n. 59, para. 188; Case C-393/92 *Almelo*, above n. 64, para. 47.

[69] SGEI compensation Communication, above n. 4, para. 52.

[70] Cf. for instance G. de Búrca, 'The principle of proportionality and its application in EC law', *Yearbook of European Law*, 13 (1993), 105–50; J. Jans, 'Proportionality revisited', *Legal Issues of Economic Integration*, 27 (2000), 239–65; T. I. Harbo, 'The function of the proportionality principle in EU law', *European Law Journal*, 16 (2010), 158–85.

[71] W. Sauter, 'Proportionality in EU law: A balancing act?' *Cambridge Yearbook of European Legal Studies*, 15 (2012–13), 439–66; Sauter and Schepel, above n. 11; W. Sauter, 'Services of general economic interest and universal service in EU law', *European Law Review*, 33 (2008), 167–92.

[72] C-157/94 *Commission* v. *Netherlands*, above n. 8; C-158/94 *Commission* v. *Italy*, above n. 8; C-159/94 *Commission* v. *France*, above n. 8; C-160/94 *Commission* v. *Spain*, above n. 8.

solutions in the absence of a common EU policy. A contrario therefore, if such a common policy or closely harmonized regime had existed, alternatives would have been considered in a least restrictive means format. Other cases such as *FFSA* (1997) with regard to postal services also indicate that Commission powers and those of the Member States are corresponding vessels in this respect. The Commission simply lacks the legal competence to second-guess political choices that were made at national level until some form of pre-emption has taken place:

> [I]n the absence of Community rules governing the matter, the Commission has no power to take a position on the organization and scale of the public service tasks assigned to a public undertaking or on the expediency of political choices made in this regard by the competent national authorities, provided that the aid in question does not benefit the activities pursued in competitive sectors or exceed what is necessary to enable the undertaking concerned to perform the particular task assigned to it.[73]

In sum, I still believe this argument regarding the relative or contextual nature of proportionality is plausible with regard to EU law as a whole as well as concerning public services in particular. However, I must admit that I can find no cases yet specifically regarding Article 106(2) TFEU where the Court applies a strict test explicitly on account of the degree to which the field has been harmonized. The reverse, however, has already been illustrated,[74] and there are also some cases where a least restrictive means test is applied even in the absence of common rules.[75] Normally, however, the Court uses a manifest disproportionality test – and therefore the exception of Article 106(2) TFEU is not applied in a restrictive manner. Here it examines whether the application of the Treaty rules would obstruct the performance, in law or in fact, of the particular tasks assigned to an undertaking entrusted with the operation of SGEI. Seen from another angle, it examines whether the restrictions involved are necessary.[76]

In this setting the financial compensation involved is important. As we have seen, SGEI are by definition services that require non-market funding of some sort – otherwise they would normally have been provided at a sufficient level at market rates. To have recourse to Article 106(2) TFEU it is not necessary that the financial balance or the economic survival of the undertaking concerned

[73] Cf. Case T-106/95 *Fédération française des sociétés d'assurances (FFSA) et al.* v. *Commission* [1997] ECR II-229, paras. 99, 108 and 192.

[74] Cf. Case C-179/90 *Merci convenzionali*, above n. 35, para. 26; Case T-260/94 *Air Inter SA* v. *Commission* [1997] ECR II-997, paras. 134ff.

[75] Cf. Case C-203/96 *Dusseldorp*, above n. 30, para. 67.

[76] Case C-1/12 *Ordem dos Técnicos Oficiais de Contas* v. *Autoridade da Concorrência*, Judgment of 28 February 2013, para. 106. With reference to Case C-203/96 *Dusseldorp*, above n. 30, para. 65; Case C-320/91 *Corbeau*, above n. 30, para. 14; and Case C-393/92 *Almelo*, above n. 64, para. 46.

should otherwise be threatened.[77] At the same time, the funding provided must not exceed what is necessary. As regards efficiency, however,

> in the absence ... of Community rules governing the matter, the Commission is not entitled to rule on the basis of public service tasks assigned to the public operator, such as the level of costs linked to that service, or the expediency of the political choices made in this regard by the national authorities, or the economic efficiency of the public operator.[78]

In early cases like *Corbeau* (1994), the CJEU had held the test (in this case for cross-subsidization of the Belgian universal postal service) to be whether the conditions compromised the economic equilibrium of the service of general economic interest concerned.[79] The subsequent case law has culminated in the 2003 *Altmark* case on regional public transport services. Here the CJEU adopted the compensation approach, holding that a quid pro quo for providing a public service was not a state aid.[80] This meant rejecting the competing state aid approach which held that such payments should be regarded as compatible state aid that could be exempted under Article 107(3) TFEU.[81] The CJEU set out the following four criteria which, if met, meant that the compensation involved did not constitute aid and remained outside the boundaries of the state aid realm:

> first, the recipient undertaking must actually have public service obligations to discharge and the obligations must be clearly defined;
>
> second, the parameters on the basis of which the compensation is calculated must be established in advance in an objective and transparent manner to avoid it conferring an economic advantage which may favour the recipient undertaking over competing undertakings ...;
>
> third, the compensation cannot exceed what is necessary to cover all or part of the costs incurred in the discharge of public service obligations, taking into account the relevant receipts and a reasonable profit for discharging those obligations;
>
> fourth, where the undertaking which is to discharge public service obligations is not chosen pursuant to a public procurement procedure, the level of compensation needed must be determined on the basis of an analysis of the costs which a typical undertaking, well run and adequately provided with means of transport so as to be able to meet the public service requirements, would have incurred in discharging those obligations, taking into account the relevant receipts and a reasonable profit for discharging the obligations.[82]

[77] Joined cases T-568/08 and T-573/08 *Métropole télévision (M6) and Télévision française 1 SA (TF1)* v. *Commission* [2010] ECR II-3397, para. 138.

[78] Ibid., para. 139. [79] Case C-320/91 *Corbeau*, above n. 30, para. 19.

[80] The first case in which it did so was Case C-53/00 *Ferring SA* v. *Agence centrale des organismes de sécurité sociale (ACOSS)* [2001] ECR I-9067.

[81] Cf. Case C-387/92 *Banco de Crédito Industrial SA, now Banco Exterior de España SA* v. *Ayuntamiento de Valencia* [1994] ECR I-877.

[82] Case C-280/00 *Altmark*, above n. 18, paras. 89–93.

These criteria have given rise to ample discussion, especially the fourth – or efficiency – criterion.[83] This does not mean that Article 106(2) TFEU no longer plays a role: if in a particular case not all the *Altmark* criteria are met so aid is found to exist, then the Article 106(2) TFEU test can be applied to determine whether this aid is compatible.[84] However, the similarities between the two tests as they have now evolved are significant. As I have already mentioned, the Commission has used the first three criteria set out in the *Altmark* case as a platform for a series of measures dealing with state aid and compensation.[85] The case law and the Article 106(3) TFEU powers of the Commission thus complement each other to provide a complex but comprehensive framework that represents the state of the art in the area of financing of public services in EU law.

Effect on trade not contrary to Community interest

This is the fourth and final criterion summed up in Article 106(2) TFEU. In the 1997 *Electricity* cases the Court insisted that the Commission must show how, in the absence of a common policy in this area, the development of direct trade between producers and consumers would have been possible.[86] In line with the general requirements in this respect for competition law and state aid, this would seem to require as a minimum an appreciable effect and therefore not potential effects.[87] However, to my knowledge there are so far no examples where this has led to a finding of illegality of a measure that would have passed muster on the three other grounds of Article 106(2) TFEU that have just been discussed. We now move on to the third paragraph of Article 106 TFEU.

Article 106(3) TFEU: enforcement powers

This provision serves two purposes. First, it establishes the Commission as the party that is responsible for the enforcement of Article 106 TFEU. In its position as guardian of the Treaties it would have had this responsibility in any event, but spelling this out presumably strengthens its position and fortifies its resolve when tackling problems in this area that tend to be fraught with

[83] Cf. for instance A. Sinnaeve, 'State financing of public services: The Court's dilemma in the *Altmark* Case', *European State Aid Law Quarterly*, 2 (2003) 351–62; E. Szyszczak and J. W. van de Gronden (eds.), *Financing services of general economic interest: Reform and modernization* (TMC Asser Press, The Hague, 2013).

[84] Case T-354/05 *Télévision française 1 SA (TF1)* v. *Commission* [2009] ECR II-471, para. 135 and the references cited there.

[85] Above, n. 4.

[86] C-157/94 *Commission* v. *Netherlands*, above n. 8; C-158/94 *Commission* v. *Italy*, above n. 8; C-159/94 *Commission* v. *France*, above n. 8; C-160/94 *Commission* v. *Spain*, above n. 8.

[87] Cf. Commission Notice – Guidelines on the effect on trade concept contained in Articles 81 and 82 of the Treaty, OJ 2004, C101/81; Commission Regulation 69/2001/EC on the application of Articles 87 and 88 of the EC Treaty to de minimis aid, OJ 2001, L10/30; Commission Regulation on de minimis aid to undertakings providing SGEI (2012), above n. 4.

political sensitivities. Second, for this purpose the Commission is provided with the power of adopting two types of legal instruments: Directives and Decisions. The power to adopt Decisions is in itself not remarkable because the Commission is generally able to enact Decisions in areas where it is competent to act. In principle this regards individual cases. However, it is unique in the Treaties that the Commission is given a power to unilaterally – that is without having to rely on the European Parliament and the Council – adopt legislation. Commission Directives are not rare outside the area of Article 106(3) TFEU but in these cases it usually concerns delegated powers on technical implementing measures with regard to Regulations that are adopted by the European Parliament and Council and where the latter tends to stay involved at least indirectly by means of Committee structures where the Member States are represented.

This said, the Article 106(3) TFEU legal basis has only rarely been used to adopt Directives. The three instances where this has occurred are the Transparency Directive regarding public undertakings (1980)[88] as well as the Directives on Telecommunications terminal equipment (1988) and Telecommunications services (1990).[89] All three have survived legal challenges and have been repeatedly amended. A weakness of the Directive as a legal instrument is that it is not normally directly applicable but must first be implemented in national law. This also implies that individuals cannot easily directly invoke Directives against Member States (although there are certain possibilities of vertical direct effect and regarding compensation for damages) nor at all against third parties (the horizontal direct effect of Directives is not recognized in EU law). Hence a certain measure of give and take between the institutions seems likely and the Commission has made the effort to at least consult the European Parliament and the Council on its subsequent amendments to Article 106(3) TFEU Directives even while maintaining that this was a matter of inter-institutional courtesy rather than a legal obligation. At the same time, concerns regarding the democratic legitimacy of the European institutions, including the executive, have only increased in recent years. Hence today it appears unlikely that the abolition of special and exclusive rights undertaken in the two telecommunications Directives just cited will ever be repeated in another sector.

The legal instrument of the Article 106(3) TFEU Decision is more likely to see further use. So far it has been of particular significance in the area of state

[88] Commission Directive 80/723/EEC of 25 June 1980 on the transparency of financial relations between Member States and public undertakings, OJ 1980, L195/35; now Commission Directive 2006/111/EC of 16 November 2006 on the transparency of financial relations between Member States and public undertakings as well as on financial transparency within certain undertakings, OJ 2006, L318/17.

[89] Commission Directive 88/301/EEC of 16 May 1988 on competition in the markets in telecommunications terminal equipment, OJ 1988, L131/73; Commission Directive 90/388/EEC of 28 June 1990 on competition in the markets for telecommunications services, OJ 1990, L192/10.

aid, where it was used in 2005 and 2012 to create a block exemption regime especially for the financial compensation of social services.[90] Here a Decision is used not to address individual cases but to provide a block (or general) exemption that applies directly to all relevant categories of undertakings if the relevant requirements are met. It is therefore difficult to distinguish from general rule-making.

Finally, as regards the legal basis for legislation concerning public services, I want to take a quick look at the relationship between Article 14 TFEU, which, as we have seen, provides for the possibility of adopting European Parliament and Council Regulations, and Article 106(3) TFEU. In my view, this relationship remains largely undetermined and I am not aware of any case law so far that sheds light on this issue. Both provisions regard SGEI (as does Article 36 CFREU). Yet Article 14 TFEU remains to be activated as a basis for framework legislation for SGEI by a reluctant Commission which has nevertheless been active in legislating on SGEI based on its exclusive competence set out in Article 106(3) TFEU. For the Commission there is a clear advantage to using Article 106(3) TFEU instead of Article 14 TFEU because in this manner it retains closer control over the risk-fraught topic that is SGEI. By using Article 14 TFEU it would risk losing the initiative (not in the formal sense of the right to propose legislation, but at the stage of legislative deliberations) to the European Parliament and Council with unpredictable results. However, in terms of both direct (involving the European Parliament) and indirect (via the Council) democratic legitimacy the Article 14 TFEU route is clearly preferable.

This means that, for the Commission, issues dealt with under Article 106(3) TFEU would preferably be regarded as less contentious, or technical. To an important degree that would mean instances where the Court has already provided some clarification. Arguably the standard of compensation under the state aid rules, where this competence was last used, meets these criteria: the Court had already set out the basic framework in the *Altmark* case but a translation to daily practice was necessary, as well as a clarification on the interaction between the different rules. This is a different approach from the above-mentioned 1988 and 1990 telecommunications Directives where the Commission imposed solutions which were only (largely) approved by the Court after the fact. Hence, the Commission seems to have become more risk averse in applying Article 106(3) Directives, without surrendering the use of this instrument entirely.

Article 345 TFEU

This provision dates back to the Rome Treaty (then Article 222 EEC, later Article 295 EC) and forms part of the original compromise on the economic

[90] SGEI compensation Decision, above n. 4.

constitution of the EU (market freedoms versus guarantees for public undertakings). It reads as follows:

> The Treaties shall in no way prejudice the rules in Member States governing the system of property ownership.

There has not been much case law on Article 345 TFEU.[91] It was invoked to little effect in *Italy* v. *Commission* (1985) relative to the legality of the suppression of fax forwarding services, the first liberalized telecommunications services at the time, by British Telecom, the incumbent UK operator that also exercised regulatory functions.[92] In *Van den Bergh* (2003), concerning mandatory access to freezer cabinets under the EU competition rules, Article 345 TFEU was linked to the freedom of private property as a principle of EU law. The General Court stated:

> [A]lthough the right to property forms part of the general principles of Community law, it is not an absolute right but must be viewed in relation to its social function. Consequently, its exercise may be restricted, provided that those restrictions in fact correspond to objectives of general interest pursued by the Community and do not constitute a disproportionate and intolerable interference, impairing the very substance of the rights guaranteed.[93]

According to the General Court, this approach includes a system to ensure that competition is not distorted and the application of Articles 101 and 102 TFEU – even though the system of undistorted competition was never formally an objective of EU law. This view is presumably still good law in spite of the fact that since the Lisbon Treaty the competition rules are now no longer mentioned independently (and certainly not as objectives, as had been proposed in the Draft Constitution) but appear in Article 3(1)b TFEU and in Protocol 27 where they are linked to the functioning of the internal market.

Consequently, proportionate restrictions of public ownership that serve legitimate EU public interest objectives are possible or, vice versa, Article 345 TFEU is not an exemption from the fundamental rules of the Treaty. Thus, in the recent *Essent* case (2013) the Court ruled that Article 345 TFEU may cover a national prohibition on privatization as well as ancillary restrictions on ownership and control links and provisions to bar cross-subsidization:[94]

[91] An exception is the 'golden share' cases of privileged public ownership rights in nominally private undertakings. Cf. Case C-483/99 *Commission* v. *France* [2002] ECR I-4781, paras. 43–4. Here the Court reaffirmed that the national system of property rights must still be consistent with principles of EU law, in this case free movement of capital. Cf. Case C-503/99 *Commission* v. *Belgium* [2002] ECR I-4809.

[92] Case 41/83 *Italy* v. *Commission* [1985] ECR 873, paras. 21–2.

[93] Case T-65/98 *Van den Bergh Foods Ltd* v. *Commission* [2003] ECR II-4653, para. 170, with reference to inter alia Case 44/79 *Liselotte Hauer* v. *Land Rheinland-Pfalz* [1979] ECR I-3727.

[94] Joined cases C-105/12 to C-107/12 *Netherlands Staat* v. *Essent NV, Essent Nederland BV, Eneco Holding NV and Delta NV*, Judgment of 22 October 2013.

> Article 345 TFEU does not mean that rules governing the system of property ownership current in the Member States are not subject to the fundamental rules of the FEU Treaty, which rules include, inter alia, the prohibition of discrimination, freedom of establishment and the free movement of capital.
>
> ... Accordingly, the prohibition of privatisation falls within the scope of Article 63 TFEU and must be examined in the light of that article.[95]

Although such restrictions are tested against the freedom of capital in Article 63 TFEU, the Member States may invoke overriding reasons of public interest to justify them.

However, since 1957 the practical significance of Article 345 TFEU has in any event decreased steadily because the popularity of using public undertakings as a vehicle for the provision of public services has declined. Another factor is that the state aid rules are increasingly also imposed on public undertakings, making them less attractive as instruments to promote job schemes, for regional development and other redistributive purposes. The demise of socialism as an alternative economic model and therefore of the popularity of social ownership of the means of production as a policy instrument has also played a role – although the banking crisis has generated a presumably temporary rash of public interventions to save banks which left a significant number of them publicly owned. In sum, it appears that Article 345 TFEU primarily sets out a position of principle which is of limited significance when it comes to deciding actual issues.

Protocol 26 on services of general interest

Together with the new legal basis for legislation on SGEI in Article 14 TFEU, Protocol 26 on SGI is the main accomplishment of those who wished to promote the use of SGEI in the Lisbon Treaty. An important role in this respect was played by the French and Dutch governments. After presiding over rejections of the Constitutional Treaty by their respective voters, they led the way in thinking up amendments to this text that might make the result more palatable, which became the Lisbon Treaty. Protocol 26 was one of their crowning achievements (along with the relegation of the competition rules to Protocol 27). It reads:

> *Protocol (No 26) on Services of General Interest*
>
> The high contracting parties, wishing to emphasise the importance of services of general interest, have agreed upon the following interpretative provisions, which shall be annexed to the Treaty on European Union and to the Treaty on the Functioning of the European Union:
>
> Article 1: The shared values of the Union in respect of services of general economic interest within the meaning of Article 14 of the Treaty on the Functioning of the European Union include in particular:

95 Ibid., paras. 36 and 38.

- the essential role and the wide discretion of national, regional and local authorities in providing, commissioning and organising services of general economic interest as closely as possible to the needs of the users;
- the diversity between various services of general economic interest and the differences in the needs and preferences of users that may result from different geographical, social or cultural situations;
- a high level of quality, safety and affordability, equal treatment and the promotion of universal access and of user rights.

> Article 2: The provisions of the Treaties do not affect in any way the competence of Member States to provide, commission and organise non-economic services of general interest.

This Protocol 26 is the first time SGI are mentioned in a legally binding text of EU law, and subsequently this has become the overarching category which I assimilate with the vernacular term public service, as set out in Chapter 1.[96] SGI are in effect only the topic of Article 2 of the Protocol which reaffirms the power of the Member States to designate and run public services that are not economic (hence not SGEI). In itself this is not new and it is an open question whether a reaffirmation in a Protocol should be read as a sign of strength or of weakness: are not SGI under pressure from angles other than EU law? This provision nevertheless raises questions because the scope of intervention based on the various dimensions of the Treaty is potentially broader than the economic aspects of the demand and supply for (or access to) public services. This regards in particular the requirements of non-discrimination and citizenship which would appear to apply to SGI as well. Is this now ruled out by this provision with its explicit assertion that the provisions of the Treaties do not affect the powers of the Member States in any way? Or, one step further, would this provision excuse violations of fundamental principles of EU law? Presumably this was not intended, but it does call into question the scope and meaning of this provision.

The first article of Protocol 26 does not relate to SGI but to its subcategory of services of general *economic* interest (SGEI). In material terms SGEI are of course the main category to which EU law rights and obligations are attached. (See also the remarks on Articles 14 and 106(2) TFEU above.) Article 1 refers back to the shared values of the EU in Article 14 TFEU and in effect it specifies these values for the first time. Its first indent highlights the role of different levels of authorities (notably including regional and local authorities), and the subsidiarity principle (also set out in Article 5(3) TEU) of allocating powers at the lowest effective level – that is also to say closest to the users. The reverse of this obligation is that if they are most effective at EU level, powers must be allocated there. The focus on diversity in the second indent, however, squares with leaving the initiative at national level. Finally, the third indent, which

[96] Cf. Communication from the Commission, A quality framework for services of general interest in Europe, COM(2011) 900.

highlights quality, safety and affordability, equal treatment, universal access and user rights, provides the substance of a catalogue of common values of the Union with respect to SGEI. Elsewhere I have argued that this further underlines the core principle of universal service at the heart of SG(E)I in the EU context. It should be noted, however, as the recent *Libert* case (2013) on public housing subsidies illustrates, that direct services to final consumers need not always be involved in order to qualify as a public service in the context of the *Altmark* test.[97]

Protocol 29 on public broadcasting

This Protocol was introduced by the Amsterdam Treaty in 1999.[98] It is mentioned here because, in my view, public broadcasting services fall within the remit of public services. The Protocol, which, like the other protocols, has equal force to the provisions of the Treaties, is intended to ensure that funding for public service broadcasting is not jeopardized by, in particular, the application of the state aid rules (although these are not mentioned explicitly). The precondition for this is that funding is proportional to the fulfilment of the public service remit. The latter is conferred, defined and organized by the Member States. It is clear that once again we are looking at a *lex specialis* that mirrors the model found in Article 106(2) TFEU on SGEI. That model is: (i) public services are defined by the Member State, (ii) but may rely on an exception in the event it impinges on the Treaty rules, (iii) which is moderated by a proportionality test. This system closely resembles the overriding reasons test in relation to the free movement rules. The difference is that it relates not to a public policy, but to a public service.

Article 36 of the Charter of Fundamental Rights of the European Union

This Charter was proclaimed by the European Parliament, the Council and the Commission in 2000. It eventually became binding with equal force to the provisions of the Treaties by reason of Article 6(1) TEU in 2009. Since then the EU Courts have treated its provisions as justiciable.[99] Article 36 CFREU, however, has not yet been the subject of legal proceedings. Its title is 'Access to services of general economic interest' and the accompanying text reads as follows:

[97] Sauter (2008), above n. 71. However, universality may be served indirectly by means of a PSO at 'wholesale' level. Cf. Joined cases C-197/11 and C-203/11 *Eric Libert et al.* v. *Gouvernement flamand and All Projects & Developments NV et al.* v. *Vlaamse Regering*, Judgment of 8 May 2013.

[98] Cf. Communication from the Commission on the application of State aid rules to public service broadcasting, OJ 2009, C257/1.

[99] Cf. Case C-93/12 *ET Agrokonsulting-04-Velko Stoyanov* v. *Izpalnitelen direktor na Darzhaven fond «Zemedelie» – Razplashtatelna agentsia*, Judgment of 27 June 2013.

> The Union recognises and respects access to services of general economic interest as provided for in national laws and practices, in accordance with the Treaty establishing the European Community, in order to promote the social and territorial cohesion of the Union.

Although universal service is not mentioned explicitly, access and universality are clearly part of the same domain. Access to SGEI is listed in Chapter IV of the Charter, on solidarity, alongside employment-based rights, the right to family life, social services, healthcare and environmental protection. Hence it does not appear in the preceding Chapter I on citizenship, which deals more with political rights, non-discrimination and rights to free movement, and diplomatic and consular representation. Perhaps this categorization does not immediately plead strongly against views favouring a citizenship role for SGEI but neither does it plead in favour. In any event, the text of Article 36 CFREU, which is largely repeated in Article 14 TFEU, has not played an independent role so far. With this rather practical qualification on the fundamental right of access to SGEI, I conclude the section on the legal basis for public services in the Treaties. We will now move on to the internal market rules.

2.3 The material rules on the internal market and competition

In this section, I will briefly cover the main rules of the internal market as comprising not only the rules on free movement but also those on competition and state aid. As Ulla Neergaard points out, the treatment of SSGI in the context of the four freedoms rules is asymmetrical vis-à-vis that under the competition rules.[100] Broadly speaking, the competition (and state aid) rules are more likely to be infringed than the free movement rules.[101] This is a logical consequence of the fact that where SGEI are concerned we are talking about undertakings, which are the basic category of entities addressed by competition and state aid law, but not free movement, which concerns the acts of Member States. This is something that will come out more clearly in Chapters 3 and 4 where the case law on free movement, respectively competition and state aid, with respect to public services will be dealt with. Consequently the discussion below will mainly be a concise overview of the relevant provisions.

The four freedoms

The four freedoms (goods, services, persons including establishment, and capital) are generally considered to form the very core of EU law. Their purpose is to abolish tariff and non-tariff barriers (measures having equivalent effect). At

[100] U. Neergaard, 'The concept of SSGI and the asymmetries between free movement and competition law', in U. Neergaard et al. (eds.), *Social services of general interest in the EU* (TMC Asser Press, The Hague, 2013), 205–44.

[101] An exception is provided by Joined cases C-147/97 and C-148/97 *Deutsche Post*, above n. 42.

the same time, proportional public interest exceptions to these rules are possible. These exceptions can be based either on specific provisions in the Treaty (such as public health) or on overriding reasons of public interest (such as planning of healthcare systems) that are freely adopted by the individual Member States as a matter of national policy.[102]

Freedom of services

The deepest roots of the EU are found in the primary industries of coal and steel production of the European Coal and Steel Community (ECSC). Subsequently, the free movement of goods has long been the dominant vector in the internal market. Today, however, services account for 70 per cent of GDP in the EU and have become increasingly important both economically and socially, as well as in the study of EU law.[103] The freedom of services includes the freedom to provide services and to receive them both on each side of the borders between the Member States (so there are four basic scenarios). This essential freedom is defined in Article 57 TFEU, which states:

> Services shall be considered to be 'services' within the meaning of the Treaties where they are normally provided for remuneration, in so far as they are not governed by the provisions relating to freedom of movement for goods, capital and persons.

In addition, Article 57 TFEU states that services shall in particular include: activities of an industrial character; of a commercial character; of craftsmen; and of the professions. This raises the question whether services in the sense of Article 49 TFEU are the same as services in the context of SGEI. Is there a different standard with respect to Article 106(2) TFEU? There are two points to be made here.

First, it should be emphasized that not all public services (SGI) are also services for remuneration. Examples abound, and can be sought for instance in the context of social services or, more controversially, education.[104] By contrast, in the healthcare setting the provision of care to patients from other Member States has consistently been regarded as a service in the sense of Article 57 TFEU, even if domestically a tax-funded National Health Service (what is in a name?) was the organizing principle for the sector.[105] In both cases, whether or not services are provided for consideration appears to be key. Second, SGEI

[102] Case C-385/99 *Müller-Fauré*, above n. 44.

[103] Cf. V. Hatzopoulos, *Regulating services in the European Union* (Oxford University Press, 2012); F. S. Benyon (ed.), *Services and the EU Citizen* (Hart Publishing, Oxford, 2013).

[104] Cf. Case 263/86 *Belgium* v. *René Humbel and Marie-Thérèse Edel* [1988] ECR 5365; Case C-76/05 *Herbert Schwarz and Marga Gootjes-Schwarz* v. *Finanzamt Bergisch Gladbach* [2007] ECR I-6849; Case C-56/09 *Emiliano Zanotti* v. *Agenzia delle Entrate – Ufficio Roma 2* [2010] ECR I-4517.

[105] Case C-158/96 *Raymond Kohll* v. *Union des caisses de maladie* [1998] ECR I-1931 and Case C-120/95 *Nicolas Decker* v. *Caisse de maladie des employés privés* [1998] ECR I-1831; Case

have an additional requirement that is not explicitly set for services in the sense of Article 57 TFEU: they must be provided by an undertaking as defined consistent with the rules on competition and state aid. This does not exclude the existence of a logically consistent EU law universe on this count, but a difference in emphasis may well lead to divergence at the level of individual cases.

The 2006 Services Directive, which aims to codify and streamline the relevant internal market case law, covers both services and establishment.[106] This is logical because both involve ways in which services can cross borders, either temporarily (services) or permanently (establishment). It does not provide an exception for SGEI as such, but certain public services (such as transport, healthcare and postal services) are excluded. The Services Directive does not concern the funding of SGEI nor does it deal with 'the liberalisation of services of general economic interest, reserved to public or private entities, nor with the privatisation of public entities providing services'.[107] This important Directive will be discussed in detail in Chapter 5 as a horizontal measure regarding public services.

Ancillary freedoms: persons and establishment

Regarding the free movement of persons today in addition to the provisions on the free movement of workers in Article 45–48 TFEU, we also have to consider the general prohibition of Article 18 TFEU on non-discrimination and Article 20(2) TFEU on the freedom to move and reside for citizens. The question is how the latter two provisions are different from the former.[108] As regards the relevance of SGEI, it appears to me that access to public services is the main issue – which seems to be primarily related to Article 18 TFEU and the citizenship provisions.

The line between the freedom of services and that of establishment in Article 49 TFEU is drawn by reference to the question whether there is a permanent presence of the provider of the service in another Member State. If so, then establishment is involved. If there is no presence or if it is intermittent, the freedom to provide services is likely to be concerned. Finally, concerning exceptions to the freedom of establishment, a new norm appears to have been developed: in particular, instead of a strict proportionality test (looking at a least restrictive means test comparing different solutions), the consistency or coherence of the policy is tested. Also there is no reading across jurisdictions to

C-372/04 *The Queen, on the application of Yvonne Watts* v. *Bedford Primary Care Trust and Secretary of State for Health* [2006] ECR I-4325.

[106] Directive 2006/123/EC of the European Parliament and of the Council of 12 December 2006 on services in the internal market, OJ 2006, L376/36. Cf. C. Barnard, 'Unravelling the Services Directive', *Common Market Law Review*, 45 (2008), 323–94.

[107] Directive 2006/123/EC, above n. 106, Article 1(2).

[108] C. Barnard, *The substantive law of the EU: The four freedoms*, 4th edn (Oxford University Press, 2013).

identify solutions that are more in conformity with market principles and less restrictive.[109]

The role of competition

Since the Lisbon Treaty came into force in 2009 the rules on competition are now deeply linked to the internal market, which, according to Article 3(3) TEU, is an objective of the Union: 'The Union shall establish an internal market.' According to its Article 3(1)b TFEU, the Union shall have exclusive competence regarding the establishing of the competition rules necessary for the functioning of the internal market. This is substantively repeated in Protocol 27 on the internal market and competition, which reads:

> The high contracting parties, considering that the internal market as set out in Article 3 of the Treaty on European Union includes a system ensuring that competition is not distorted, have agreed that: To this end, the Union shall, if necessary, take action under the provisions of the Treaties, including under Article 352 of the Treaty on the Functioning of the European Union.

These provisions are to be seen as a form of compensation for removing the reference to competition rules as such (that is, not in relation to the internal market) from the body of the EC Treaty, or indeed as an objective of European integration as had been proposed in the failed draft Constitutional Treaty. This had been one of the points renegotiated after the draft Constitutional Treaty was voted down in the French and Dutch referenda in 2005. Explicitly linking the competition rules to the internal market, the jewel in the crown of European integration, is of course the surest way of safeguarding them. It is also consistent with the original rationale of the competition rules, which was to avoid private parties resurrecting the barriers that had been levelled by the Member States.[110] But it is a disappointment to those who had advocated competition policy as an economics-driven value in its own right and the only necessary type of regulation.

The substantive rules on competition

These rules are to be found in Articles 101 and 102 TFEU on antitrust – merger control is based on secondary law in the merger control regulation.[111] In addition, the rules on state aid are found in Articles 107 and 108 TFEU. As is the case for the internal market rules, libraries have been filled with specialized works on these topics, so I will limit myself to setting out what I believe is useful

[109] Cf. Hancher and Sauter (2010), above n. 26.

[110] Cf. W. Sauter, *Competition law and industrial policy in the EU* (Oxford University Press, 1997).

[111] Council Regulation (EC) No 139/2004 of 20 January 2004 on the control of concentrations between undertakings, OJ 2004, L24/1.

for an understanding of the law on public services in the EU.[112] The antitrust provisions (and the merger rules) only apply to undertakings. They prohibit respectively anticompetitive agreement and abuse of a dominant position. In both cases market power is involved. In the first instance under Article 101 TFEU this is due to a cartel, or several undertakings acting jointly on key competitive variables such as price, volume and territory. In the second (and less frequent) instance under Article 102 TFEU this is due to dominance where one company or a close oligopoly dominates the market to the extent that it can neglect its competitors and the interest of consumers. Such behaviour is illegal and can be fined. In order to determine the existence of market power, a market definition in a geographical and product sense is necessary. Finally, exemptions exist, primarily with regard to efficiencies. Here the SGEI exception adds an important dimension because it may regard not only efficiency but equity as well. In addition, Article 21(4) of the merger control Regulation allows a derogation from the broadly dominance-based test on public policy grounds that are compatible with EU law:

> Member States may take appropriate measures to protect legitimate interests other than those taken into consideration by this Regulation and compatible with the general principles and other provisions of Community law.[113]

As we have seen in the section on special and exclusive rights, most cases concerning the competition rules and public services have been in regard to (alleged) forms of dominance abuse.[114]

A topic regarding the competition rules and public intervention with which I will not deal in this book is the doctrine of *effet utile* – or useful effect. This is a mechanism whereby Member States who encourage and abet or even impose breaches of the competition rules can be found guilty of neglecting the EU good faith requirement and the principle of sincere cooperation in Article 4(3) TEU in combination with the relative substantive provisions of the Treaty (such as Article 101 or 102 TFEU). The undertakings involved can claim a 'state action' defence unless they have restrained competition independently from the state in any remaining areas of freedom.[115] In my view this is too far removed from the topic of public services to warrant further attention (as this ground has already been well covered by others).[116]

After long neglect, state aid has more recently become an intensely studied academic topic. This coincides with the initial elaboration of secondary rules

[112] Cf. G. Monti, *EC competition law* (Cambridge University Press, 2007); Faull and Nikpay, above n. 7. M. Motta, *Competition policy, theory and practice* (Cambridge University Press, 2004).

[113] Council Regulation (EC) No 139/2004, above n. 111.

[114] Cf. for instance Joined cases C-147/97 and C-148/97 *Deutsche Post*, above n. 42.

[115] Joined cases C-359/95 P and C-379/95 P *Commission and France* v. *Ladbroke Racing Ltd* [1997] ECR I-6265.

[116] Cf. T. Prosser, *The limits of competition law: Markets and public services* (Oxford University Press, 2005); E. Szyszczak, *The regulation of the state in competitive markets in the EU* (Hart Publishing, Oxford, 2007).

and the subsequent modernization of state aid which aims at a more economic approach.[117] Again I will only set out some general features. Most forms of aid are in principle illegal unless they are found to be compatible. Aid exists if four cumulative conditions are met: where an undertaking benefits from (i) a transfer of state resources which is (ii) selective (provides an advantage), has (iii) a distorting effect on competition, and (iv) an effect on trade between the Member States. National courts are entitled to apply these criteria and make a finding that aid exists. However, the European Commission alone can apply an exemption and declare an existing aid to be compatible with the internal market. This is the capstone of a centralized mechanism of notifications to, and (first and second phase) investigations by, the Commission. Normally compatibility is decided based on Article 107(3) TFEU. In the case of SGEI, however, Article 106(2) TFEU is normally applied. Non-economic SGI or SSGI that are not economic are likely to fall outside the state aid rules because they are not carried out by entities that qualify as undertakings. As I have already mentioned, the Commission has adopted a framework for dealing with compensation for SGEI in the setting of state aid.[118] This will be examined in detail in Chapter 5 on horizontal rules regarding public services. Here I will instead follow up with a discussion on the economic orientation of the Treaties.

I will now move on to discuss constitutional dimensions of SGEI and citizenship, before concluding this chapter.

2.4 The mixed economic constitution

A mixed economic constitution

The economic orientation of the Treaty is a contentious issue. On the one hand, it is possible to defend the position that it was liberal in origin and has been diluted by successive Treaty amendments to include items such as industrial policy and social policy that qualify or even compromise the earlier strict market orientation.[119] On the other hand, it is equally possible to point to the fact that the original market orientation was largely hypothetical because in practice it applied only to a very small segment of the economy of which large swathes were outside the reach of EU law in any real sense.[120] Subsequent expansion of the scope of EU law has entailed certain trade-offs in terms of

[117] Cf. L. Hancher, T. Ottervanger and P. J. Slot (eds.), *EU state aids*, 4th edn (Sweet & Maxwell, London, 2012); F. de Cecco, *State aid and the European economic constitution* (Hart Publishing, Oxford, 2013); E. Szyszczak (ed.), *Research handbook on European state aid law* (Edward Elgar, Cheltenham, 2011).

[118] Above, n. 4.

[119] Cf. M. E. Streit and W. Mussler, 'The economic constitution of the European Community: From "Rome" to "Maastricht"', *European Law Journal*, 1 (1995), 5–30.

[120] For instance, it should be noted that although services account for 70 per cent of GDP, they have been less likely to be caught by EU law than goods. Cf. Hatzopoulos, above n. 103; Benyon, above n. 103.

relaxing its stringency, or opening up new exceptions.[121] However, many commentators warn of an opposite trend: a hollowing out of public services and of the welfare state itself due to unrestricted liberalization by means of negative integration by directly effective EU law that, given certain inherent weaknesses of the decision-making process at EU level, cannot be compensated politically by positive European policies.[122]

Christian Joerges has pointed out that, following the outset of the global financial crisis, the economic constitution of the EU appears to have an unlimited range and is no longer governed (or at least not exclusively so) by the rule of law.[123] It is clear that a general lack of boundaries and the absence of legal justification and coherence would explode most understandings of what it means to have a constitution. At the same time every constitution needs a degree of malleability. It is not clear whether what is observed in practice should be regarded as a weakening of the EU system of governance: in my view it demonstrates that the EU has now entered the realm of economic politics, which does not observe the limits Joerges mentions because it must address a different range of often unpredictable events.

I will not go into the issue whether this is inherently undesirable or unavoidable. However, it appears to me that at least where the internal market and competition rules are concerned, we can continue to speak of a mixed economic constitution, as underpinning the objective of a social market economy. Thus, in contrast to the Ordoliberal view of the economic constitution, the social market economy provides a third way between capitalism and socialism. In Joerges' view the social market economy may, however, suffer from a social deficit – this is in line with the critique by Fritz Scharpf on the imbalance between positive and negative integration. This Euroscepticism can be contrasted with the position taken by the economic historian Alan Milward: he believed the European welfare states would have been unsustainable long ago without European integration, which was motivated primarily by self-interest.[124]

This discussion is relevant to my topic because public services are one of the main examples of services that long remained inviolate by EU law, a situation which first changed with respect to the utilities, and may now be in the process of changing regarding social services. A question that I hope to answer in this book is whether this simply means a market-oriented regime or even a neo-liberal free for all. Or does the applicable legal framework leave room for the pursuit of the public interest consistent with EU law in a manner that need not be substantively inferior to what had earlier been achieved at national level

[121] Cf. Sauter and Schepel, above n. 11.

[122] For a steadfast proponent of this thesis: F. W. Scharpf, *Community and autonomy: Institutions, policies and legitimacy in multilevel Europe* (Campus, Frankfurt am Main, 2010).

[123] C. Joerges, '*Rechtsstaat* and social Europe: How a classical tension resurfaces in the European integration process', *Comparative Sociology*, 9 (2010), 65–85.

[124] Cf. A. S. Milward, *The European rescue of the nation state*, 2nd edn (Routledge, London, 1999).

outside the scope of EU legal strictures? It is too early to answer these questions now. In either case, however, it is clear that the current Treaty regime is that of a mixed economic constitution, because it does not subscribe to a pure market orientation nor to unfettered public intervention.[125] At a sectoral level this is reflected by the managed competition regimes for the utilities that we will discuss in Chapter 6. More broadly, this is newly symbolized by the commitment to the objective of establishing a highly competitive social market economy in Article 3(3) TEU, just as at an earlier stage the old Article 345 TFEU on the neutrality of the Treaty to the national regime of – public or private – ownership had been interpreted in a similar vein. What this means will be addressed below.

Article 3(3) TEU and the social market economy

The relevant segment of Article 3(3) TEU reads as follows:

> The Union shall establish an internal market. It shall work for the sustainable development of Europe based on balanced economic growth and price stability, a highly competitive social market economy, aiming at full employment and social progress, and a high level of protection and improvement of the quality of the environment.

This provision sounds the language of the third road between capitalism and socialism. That is remarkable at a time when, following the events of 1989 and the demise of the Soviet Bloc, the socialist orientation has little practical significance left anywhere and capitalism (the Washington consensus) garnered broad support at least until the 2008 global financial crisis was unleashed. However, it fits in with a broader trend. At the same time as it embraced a form of societal fairness as its guiding principle, the EU has attempted to bootstrap its economy with the ill-fated (as it was scuppered by the global financial crisis) 2000 Lisbon Programme[126] and the ensuing Europe 2020 strategy that was proposed in 2010.[127] It would deviate too far from my topic to discuss the plausibility of these initiatives, in particular because the key documents do not assign a key role to public services. In fact, the policy bibles do not refer to public services at all except for a single reference in the 2000 Council

[125] On the different dimensions of the economic constitution see M. Poiares Maduro, *We the Court: The European Court of Justice and the European economic constitution* (Hart Publishing, Oxford, 1998) on the internal market; J. Baquero Cruz, *Between competition and free movement: The economic constitutional law of the European Community* (Hart Publishing, Oxford, 2002) on the internal market and competition; Sauter, above n. 110, on competition; and de Cecco, above n. 117, on state aid.

[126] Presidency Conclusions, Lisbon European Council, 23 and 24 March 2000 – regarding employment, economic reform and social cohesion, as well as preparing the transition to a competitive, dynamic and knowledge based economy.

[127] Communication from the Commission, Europe 2020: A strategy for smart, sustainable and inclusive growth, COM(2010) 2020.

Conclusions that they should be accessible electronically. Instead, therefore, I just want to highlight that, on the one hand, at least on paper the economic constitutional framework is now more favourable to public services than ever before, but that, on the other hand, this does not mean that they are freely governed at national level without EU interference. Paradoxically, by trying to secure guarantees for public services at EU level, in EU constitutional texts, the Member States have also outlined and legitimized the application of EU law to public services, albeit within (at least marginally) clearer boundaries.

It is too early to say what the social market economy will entail: the language chosen no doubt deliberately suggests a broader application of the German (or Rhineland) economic model. Whether this is copying as the sincerest form of flattery, merely a calculated public relations exercise or something that will have a practical dimension is not yet clear. In any event, it seems that the EU is choosing as its banner a concept that worked well in a single large Member State during a relatively distinct period when it was possible to combine an internal market with national welfare states pursuing independent economic policies. This contrasts with the present when independent national economic policies are increasingly no longer a realistic prospect. Moreover, comparative advantage may not favour universal adoption of a single model across the EU, no matter how virtuous.

The social market economy is in any event a concept that is inherently not inimical to the concept of public services. Provided proportionally, in competition and/or more efficiently and/or according to new standards set at EU level, or according to the subsidiarity principle locally or regionally, public services may eventually help to give meaning to the EU social market economy. But whether this concept itself will be influential time will show.

Article 345 TFEU and the mixed economic constitution

As we have seen, by contrast with the newly minted Article 3(3) TEU, this provision on the national freedom to choose a property regime was already found in the original Rome Treaty of 1957. It is a throwback to the time when centralized planning and public ownership of the means of production were not yet discredited as ineffective at achieving their objectives of 'from each according to his abilities, to each according to his needs'. Public ownership was widely found in the Member States but unevenly dispersed between and across sectors within them. Article 345 TFEU means that in the EU legal framework neither is public ownership officially outlawed or discouraged nor is private ownership treated preferentially.

However, in practice the universal applicability of the state aid rules (and transparency requirements that facilitate their enforcement) and the introduction of competition in previously sheltered sectors can make public undertakings unattractive to use, ineffective at carrying out their tasks as originally intended, and ultimately unsustainable. Member States' efforts to rule beyond the grave through private law instruments such as golden shares in formerly public sectors have been snuffed out systematically – without offending Article 345 TFEU.[128] Article 3(3) TEU and Article 345 TFEU therefore act as the bookends of the mixed economy, in the latter case propping up a formal neutrality that is rarely met in effect. Meanwhile, different perceptions have also developed: it is no longer the status of ownership that is key but the quality and accessibility of the services that are delivered to consumers.

2.5 Citizenship (solidarity) and legitimacy

The concept of citizenship was introduced by the 1993 Maastricht Treaty. It has two main dimensions: first, political rights relating to elections and representation, and the right to diplomatic and consular assistance abroad, which are largely new; and second, the rights to freely move between and reside in the Member States in Article 20 TFEU which are largely a recast of pre-existing EU law rights. The latter dimension is that which is relevant here, and which is closely linked to Article 18 TFEU on non-discrimination which supplements the non-discrimination provisions that are scattered throughout the Treaty. (The fact that Article 18 TFEU is grouped separately also means that non-discrimination is applied more broadly than just to citizens.) Citizenship was originally conceived as a way of bolstering the legitimacy of the EU, and implicitly as part of a federative process, which was to have culminated in the Constitutional Treaty that was eventually aborted. It is not clear to what extent this purpose has so far been served effectively: few Europeans would spontaneously identify themselves as EU citizens. At the same time, citizenship has a practical legal value that is in the course of being expanded by the case law of the CJEU.

The question that interests me here is whether citizenship is also relevant to EU law on public services. This can be construed by equating universal service and consumer rights to citizenship at EU level. Several authors have gone down this road,[129] and I have tried linking the strategic compromise in telecommunications liberalization that revolved around defining USO and liberalizing the remaining bulk of services to the citizenship concept myself.[130]

[128] Above, n. 28.

[129] H.-W. Micklitz, 'Universal services: Nucleus for a social European private law', in M. Cremona (ed.), *Market integration and public services in the European Union* (Oxford University Press, 2011), 63–102; T. Prosser, 'Competition law and public services: From single market to citizenship rights', *European Public Law*, 11 (2005), 543–63; J. Davies and E. Szyszczak, 'Universal service obligations: Fulfilling new generations of services of general economic interest', in E. Szyszczak et al. (eds.), *Developments in services of general interest* (TMC Asser Press, The Hague, 2011), 155–77.

[130] W. Sauter, 'Universal service obligations and the emergence of citizens' rights in European telecommunications liberalization', in M. Freedland and S. Sciarra (eds.), *Public services and citizenship in European law: Public and labour law perspectives* (Oxford University Press, 1998), 117–43.

The issue has recently been raised again with the innovative use of hybrid concepts such as the 'market citizen' and the 'consumer citizen' by authors such as Jim Davies, H.-W. Micklitz and Tony Prosser.[131] I cannot do justice to their work here but will raise only a few points: for me the question remains whether the concepts of market rights and citizenship are truly compatible. One argument raised is that informed consumers would manifest a kind of moral authority akin to voting in their purchasing decisions.[132] Another argument is that, akin to political rights, but unlike them because they are not listed in the Treaties, there are economic rights with respect to public services of which the basic provision forms a guarantee of citizenship. Such rights would revolve around USO set at EU level. It is a difficult question: if so, why would the right to nourishment or basic healthcare not be included, while free-to-air broadcasting of key sports events or reduced fares for ferry travel to peripheral islands would be? And, as was suggested at the end of the first chapter, so would public services that are for profit and can be afforded by only part of the population. This raises the question whether a citizenship dimension that is so patchy could still be meaningful or would only be a necessary step towards its further completion.

Nevertheless, the Court has enforced access to certain public services, in particular social services such as in the *Grzelczyk* (2001) case, on citizenship grounds.[133] Also it has ruled that residence rights are subject to an individualized proportionality test in *Baumbast* (2002).[134] Cases such as *De Cuyper* (2006)[135] and *Tas-Hagen* (2006)[136] concern the coincidence of free movement and equal treatment as discussed by Michael Dougan.[137] This suggests that at least some public services must be available to citizens, but not necessarily all public services, nor possibly even to all citizens: in the *Grzelczyk* case the Belgian authorities were authorized to set certain conditions (just not the ones they had initially applied). Catherine Barnard sets up the model of attenuated citizenship, which is graduated based on the quality and the

[131] J. Davies, *The European consumer citizen in law and policy: Consumption and public life* (Palgrave Macmillan, London, 2011); Micklitz, above n. 129; Prosser, above n. 129. Cf. Monti, above n. 5.

[132] As these authors acknowledge, this would presuppose having the capabilities of doing so. See also the perspective of behavioural economics: C. R. Sunstein and R. H. Thaler, *Nudge: Improving decisions about health, wealth, and happiness* (Yale University Press, New Haven, 2008).

[133] Case C-184/99 *Rudy Grzelczyk* v. *Centre public d'aide sociale d'Ottignies-Louvain-la-Neuve* [2001] ECR I-6193.

[134] Case C-413/99 *Baumbast and R* v. *Secretary of State for the Home Department* [2002] ECR I-7091.

[135] Case C-406/04 *Gérald De Cuyper* v. *Office national de l'emploi* [2006] ECR I-6947.

[136] Case C-192/05 *K. Tas-Hagen and R.A. Tas* v. *Raadskamer WUBO van de Pensioen- en Uitkeringsraad* [2006] ECR I-10451.

[137] M. Dougan, 'Expanding the frontiers of Union citizenship by dismantling the territorial boundaries of national welfare states?' in C. Barnard and O. Odudu (eds.), *The outer limits of European Union law* (Hart Publishing, Oxford, 2009), 119–66.

duration of the link with the host society.[138] This she contrasts with absolutist approaches such as those related to patients' rights.[139]

In my view, it is premature to regard public services as citizen-based or oriented per se. Citizenship is about a combination of inclusion and exclusion. Public services are about access and provision, categories that do not map onto the previous ones flawlessly. Their legitimation is in large part directed towards the Member States that have defined SGEI, and not towards the EU. Quite to the contrary: the EU is frequently accused of undermining them. To the extent that USO and consumer rights are defined at EU level they might help to legitimize the EU, but it is not clear that consumers would perceive their rights as coming from this direction.[140] However, it is worth exploring this issue in detail by looking at the relevant legislation, which is what we will do in Chapter 6 on vertical rules on public services.

2.6 Conclusion

The first question asked above was what is the relevant primary EU law. It turns out that there is not a systematic framework for public services or in any event (if we accept that the Treaties as a whole provide a general framework for EU law) not a specific one. As we have seen, there are a number of provisions that concern public services but the few mentions of this concept (as related to transport, public administration, broadcasting), even in the form of SGI (a single sentence stating a platitude), do not constitute a coherent whole. They do make clear that the general idea is that public services are defined at national level, and that the Treaty rules do not stop them from being so. SGEI are more extensively covered by several provisions. Of these, Article 106(2) TFEU is the most important. Here a three-step system becomes evident: SGEI may be defined freely if they represent a legitimate public interest, and may involve necessary and proportional restrictions to the rule of the Treaty.

This brings us to the second question: what are the limits that EU law imposes on public services? In principle, EU law applies fully to SGEI, except where necessary to allow them to fulfil their objectives. It is their economic nature, meaning the fact that they are performed by undertakings providing services in a market at least potentially subject to competition, that brings SGEI within the scope of the Treaty rules – especially those on competition and state aid.

Third, what scope do EU law exceptions leave for national policies on public services? As we have seen, the SGEI provision in Article 106(2) TFEU allows both efficiency and equity defences, which are generally tested according to a

138 C. Barnard, 'EU citizenship and the principle of solidarity', in M. Dougan and E. Spaventa (eds.), *Social welfare and EU law: Essays in European law* (Hart Publishing, Oxford, 2005), 157–80.

139 Case C-158/96 *Kohll*; Case C-120/95 *Decker*; Case C-372/04 *Watts*, all above n. 105.

140 For an attempt in this direction see Regulation (EU) No 531/2012 on roaming, above n. 39.

manifest disproportionality standard. Only if the EU has occupied the field by means of defining SGEI – or more properly the USO that are its core content – is a stricter test likely. However, we have so far not seen any practical examples of this.

The fourth question was what the role of the concept of service of general (economic) interest, SGI and SGEI, is. Regarding SGEI this question has already been largely answered in the course of the preceding paragraph.

In addition, we have dealt with several issues in this chapter that were not explicitly raised as research questions at the beginning: at a conceptual level the mixed economic constitution appears fully compatible with the social market economy and an ideal habitat for public services. But does it provide a useful framework for discussing the issues at hand, or just a convenient container category? It appears to be the latter rather than the former. A guiding idea is yet to emerge.

As regards social services and SGI versus SGEI, we have seen that these services are relatively more difficult to classify.

- First, they are often SGI rather than SGEI. Because they are non-economic in nature they are immune from the rules on competition and state aid. However, in my view they are nevertheless still subject to the provisions on anti-discrimination and citizenship.
- Second, the anti-discrimination and citizenship case law leads to a perspective of service recipients rather than public service providers. This reversal of roles makes social services that are SGI and SGEI services that are social services or utilities difficult to compare.
- Third, several authors have launched hybrid concepts like the market citizen or the consumer citizen. It is difficult to see how useful this is: calling everything citizenship may suggest it is a concept still in development, but it may also debase the currency involved.

At the same time, it may well be that in the detailed USO provisions that have now been adopted for several sectors in combination with the right to access in Article 36 CFREU there is a nascent basis for a development towards EU citizenship rights with regard to public services. I propose examining this in Chapter 6 on sector-specific rules, and taking it up in the concluding Chapter 7.

3

Public services and the free movement and citizenship case law

3.1 Introduction

My purpose in this third chapter is to provide an overview of the relevant case law with regard to free movement and public services. As far as I am aware, so far this mainly involves welfare: the healthcare, education and social security services that I will take as examples here, including their citizenship dimension. The utilities are rarely relevant here. This is because they are normally provided by undertakings and therefore the free movement rules, which pertain to limitations imposed by public authorities, generally do not apply. Public services that are welfare services, however, are frequently provided publicly and therefore limitations imposed by public authorities tend to play a more important role.[1]

Welfare services have in common the fact that they are based on exclusion and inclusion of beneficiaries, generally as a result of the territoriality principle, depending on either residency or work (or both). As we will see, drawing the circle of beneficiaries is the subject matter of most of the cases in this area. Hence boundary issues often dominate the debate,[2] in a comparable manner to the question of what is an undertaking which precedes much of competition law with regard to public services, as we will see in the next chapter. On the substantive side, the proportionality of public restrictions is essential. This means that the benefits in terms of the public interests involved must be balanced against their costs, or at least pursued in a coherent manner.

In view of the above, my focus will be on the welfare-type services and boundary issues; the utilities will only be addressed summarily, jointly, in a separate section. Here, as throughout this book, I will only deal with cases that were decided at EU level, not only because these are most readily accessible but also because the principles of EU law are established there. The order proposed is loosely that of the ascending degree to which the relevant services are so far

[1] Cf. L. Nistor, *Public services and the European Union: Healthcare, health insurance and education services* (TMC Asser Press, The Hague, 2011).

[2] M. Dougan, 'Expanding the frontiers of Union citizenship by dismantling the territorial boundaries of national welfare states?' in C. Barnard and O. Odudu (eds.), *The outer limits of European Union law* (Hart Publishing, Oxford, 2009), 119–66.

subject to harmonization rules: first healthcare, then education and finally social security. I have chosen this approach because the degree to which the EU is involved in setting public policy goals has an impact on the degrees of freedom to pursue such objectives at national level.

A number of the research questions that were set out in Chapter 1, slightly modified, will be addressed here:

- What are the limits that the primary EU law on free movement imposes on public services?
- What scope is left for national policies regarding public services under EU law exceptions?
- What are the common elements regarding public services in the free movement case law?
- Are EU standards emerging here and what is their role?
- What is the role of EU citizenship?

I will first address these questions sector by sector (albeit not always explicitly). The emphasis will be on the primary law and the relevant case law (the secondary law will be discussed in Chapter 6). In addition, I will look at the influence of EU citizenship on the right to receive public services as a horizontal issue. I will then attempt to draw comparisons across sectors and bring out common trends in the conclusion.

3.2 Free movement, citizenship and the utilities

As I have already stated in the introduction, the utilities are generally provided by undertakings. This is all the more true in the network industries that have been subject to large-scale liberalization and EU-driven (re)reregulation, in particular as regards electronic communications, energy (gas and electricity), postal services and, to a lesser extent, transport. Where competition starts to play a role it is a constant source of friction if public authorities and private undertakings are rubbing shoulders in providing the same, similar or related services. Moreover, where competing activities must be organized at arm's length there are few advantages to maintaining public services that are provided by public authorities, public undertakings or even private undertakings with a significant share of public ownership. This is not so much true for other utilities-type sectors where, at least so far, there is both not as much competition and a lesser degree of EU-level regulation in place, such as regarding water, sanitation, waste management and public broadcasting (or primary banking services). However, the general trend is clear.

As I have likewise already mentioned, the free movement rules do not address undertakings but Member States, with respect to barriers to the internal market, hence entry barriers to market access. In other words, they concern free movement of consumers and products (goods and services) and production factors (labour and capital). Because they regard the Member States they are less relevant to undertakings other than as beneficiaries from the public policies involved; because the public services that are utilities are generally provided by undertakings, the free movement case law does not apply to them. The same, *ceteris paribus*, applies with regard to citizenship, although some authors have attempted to link the latter to universal service obligations which are imposed on undertakings providing public services in the utilities sectors.[3] For various reasons, including potentially both the effectiveness and the legitimacy of European integration (although some authors have doubts about the legitimation potential of EU citizenship, see below in section 3.6), this is an attractive idea. However, as far as I am aware, there is so far no significant case law linking citizenship as defined in the TFEU and consumer rights.

3.3 Healthcare

The Treaty provisions on healthcare

I will start with healthcare as this is the most recent welfare service to be drawn within the sphere of EU law. The Treaty contains a single provision with regard to healthcare as such, in Article 168 TFEU, alongside references elsewhere to (human) health and safety and public health as admissible public policy exceptions to the application of the rules of the Treaty and/or policy objectives of EU action.[4] Article 168(7) TFEU includes a clause that can be called a sector-specific subsidiarity provision, stating that

> Union action shall respect the responsibilities of the Member States for the definition of their health policy and for the organisation and delivery of health services and medical care. The responsibilities of the Member States shall include the management of health services and medical care and the allocation of the resources assigned to them.

It is worth noting that in spite of this sector-specific subsidiarity clause the 2012 Patients' Rights Directive was jointly based on the general harmonization provision Article 114 TFEU and on Article 158 TFEU.[5]

[3] H.-W. Micklitz, 'Universal services: Nucleus for a social European private law', in M. Cremona (ed.), *Market integration and public services in the European Union* (Oxford University Press, 2011), 63–102; T. Prosser, 'Competition law and public services: From single market to citizenship rights', *European Public Law*, 11 (2005), 543–63; J. Davies and E. Szyszczak, 'Universal service obligations: Fulfilling new generations of services of general economic interest', in E. Szyszczak et al. (eds.), *Developments in services of general interest* (TMC Asser Press, The Hague, 2011), 155–77; J. Davies, *The European consumer citizen in law and policy: Consumption and public life* (Palgrave Macmillan, London, 2011).

[4] See Articles 6, 9, 36, 45(3), 52(1), 114(8), 153(1)a, 164, 191, 202 and 207 TFEU.

[5] Directive 2011/24/EU of the European Parliament and of the Council of 9 March 2011 on the application of patients' rights in cross-border healthcare, OJ 2011, L88/45. Cf. L. Hancher and W. Sauter, *EU competition and internal market law in the healthcare sector* (Oxford University Press, 2012).

The case law on healthcare services

The national healthcare systems in the EU can be classified broadly as either tax-based NHS systems, also called Beveridge systems (after their architect in the UK), and insurance-based Bismarck systems (with a further distinction between benefits in kind and restitution in cash-based systems). Both types of system struggle to contain costs, which are driven up by ageing populations, technological change and rising expectations. Everywhere in the EU healthcare funding issues tend to be highly sensitive politically.

In its early healthcare case law (*Luisi and Carbone*, 1984) the Court established that the freedom to provide services includes the freedom for the recipients of services to go to another Member State in order to receive those services there.[6] The fact that healthcare was a service was established in the landmark Irish abortion rights case *SPUC* v. *Grogan* (1991).[7] This set the scene for subsequent cases where especially the right to receive reimbursement for treatment received abroad was at stake.

First a set of ground-breaking decisions established rights to reimbursement of medical treatment across national borders within the EU, sidestepping the secondary law regime of Regulation 883/2004 (then 1408/71) which provided rights to health benefits originally to workers and their dependants.[8] Next the new case law was codified in the above-mentioned Patients' Rights Directive. The initial landmark cases were *Kohll* (1998) and *Decker* (1998).[9] In *Kohll* the Court ruled that a prior authorization requirement for the reimbursement of medical services enjoyed in another Member State was an infringement of the freedom to purchase services.

> While the national rules at issue in the main proceedings do not deprive insured persons of the possibility of approaching a provider of services established in another Member State, they do nevertheless make reimbursement of the costs incurred in that Member State subject to prior authorisation, and deny such reimbursement to insured persons who have not obtained that authorisation. Costs incurred in the State of insurance are not, however, subject to that authorisation.
>
> Consequently, such rules deter insured persons from approaching providers of medical services established in another Member State and constitute, for them and their patients, a barrier to freedom to provide services.[10]

6 Joined cases 286/82 and 26/83 *Graziana Luisi and Giuseppe Carbone* v. *Ministero del Tesoro* [1984] ECR 377, paras. 10 and 16.

7 Case C-159/90 *Society for the Protection of Unborn Children Ireland Ltd* v. *Stephen Grogan et al.* [1991] ECR I-4685.

8 Regulation (EC) No 883/2004 of the European Parliament and of the Council of 29 April 2004 on the coordination of social security systems, OJ 2004, L166/1.

9 Case C-158/96 *Raymond Kohll* v. *Union des caisses de maladie* [1998] ECR I-1931; Case C-120/95 *Nicolas Decker* v. *Caisse de maladie des employés privés* [1998] ECR I-1831.

10 Case C-158/96 Kohll, above n. 9, paras. 34–5.

The same applied to the purchase of medical devices (a pair of spectacles, in *Decker*) as an infringement of the free movement of goods. Initially Member States with National Health Services (NHS) that are characterized by tax-funded services free of charge at the point of delivery, as well as Member States with insurance systems that were based on benefits in kind (as opposed to restitution systems where the patient pays the physician's fees but is reimbursed by the insurer), maintained that they were not affected by the scope of these cases.

However, in successive cases such as *Geraets-Smits and Peerbooms* (2001),[11] *Müller-Fauré and van Riet* (2003)[12] and *Watts* (2006)[13] the Court clarified that first, benefits in kind, and second, NHS systems, were fully subject to the free movement rules, and had to provide for reimbursement based on the level applicable in the home Member State. At one level the argument was a simple one: even if in the home system no direct payments were required, once these had been made in another Member State that required reimbursement to be made. At another level it is remarkable that the Court sidestepped an EU system of secondary legislation that was already in place (albeit based on prior authorization and reimbursement according to the rules of the host Member State). These cases were widely perceived as ominous for the possibilities of the Member States to operate their healthcare systems, and thereby for the sustainability and legitimacy of the latter.[14] The provision of healthcare became sufficiently controversial as a topic to eventually require their explicit exclusion from the Services Directive which was then under discussion.[15]

Beginning with *Geraets-Smits* and as confirmed in *Müller-Fauré* the Court accepted that a prior authorization system could be proportional to the pursuit of overriding reasons of public interest, in particular the need for planning of healthcare systems as well as their financial sustainability, which was linked to the policy objective of providing access to healthcare services. An economic objective could thus justify a restriction, which is remarkable because generally

[11] Case C-157/99 *B. S. M. Geraets-Smits* v. *Stichting Ziekenfonds VGZ and H. T. M. Peerbooms* v. *Stichting CZ Groep Zorgverzekeringen* [2001] ECR I-5473.

[12] Case C-385/99 *V. G. Müller-Fauré* v. *Onderlinge Waarborgmaatschappij OZ Zorgverzekeringen UA and E. E. M. van Riet* v. *Onderlinge Waarborgmaatschappij ZAO Zorgverzekeringen* [2003] ECR I-4509.

[13] Case C-372/04 *The Queen, on the application of Yvonne Watts* v. *Bedford Primary Care Trust and Secretary of State for Health* [2006] ECR I-4325.

[14] Cf. G. Davies, 'The effect of Mrs Watts' trip to France on the National Health Service', *King's Law Journal*, 18 (2007), 158–67; A. Dawes, '"Bonjour Herr Doctor": National healthcare systems, the internal market and cross-border medical care within the European Union', *Legal Issues of Economic Integration*, 33 (2006), 167–82; V. G. Hatzopoulos, 'Killing national health and insurance systems but healing patients? The European market for health care services after the judgments of the ECJ in *Vanbraekel* and *Peerbooms*', *Common Market Law Review*, 39 (2002), 683–729; C. Newdick, 'Citizenship, free movement and health care: Cementing individual rights by corroding social solidarity', *Common Market Law Review*, 43 (2006), 1645–68.

[15] Directive 2006/123/EC of the European Parliament and of the Council of 12 December 2006 on services in the internal market, OJ 2006, L376/36.

exceptions under free movement must be equity based, not efficiency related.[16] Thus in *Müller-Fauré* the Court held:

> It is well known that the number of hospitals, their geographical distribution, the way in which they are organised and the facilities with which they are provided, and even the nature of the medical services which they are able to offer, are all matters for which planning must be possible.
>
> As may be seen, in particular, from the system of agreements involved in the main actions, this kind of planning generally meets a variety of concerns.
>
> For one thing, it seeks to achieve the aim of ensuring that there is sufficient and permanent accessibility to a balanced range of high-quality hospital treatment in the State concerned.
>
> For another thing, it assists in meeting a desire to control costs and to prevent, as far as possible, any wastage of financial, technical and human resources. Such wastage would be all the more damaging because it is generally recognised that the hospital care sector generates considerable costs and must satisfy increasing needs, while the financial resources which may be made available for health care are not unlimited, whatever the mode of funding applied.[17]

However, to balance this exception to the rule of free movement, the Court also ruled that in any event the individual circumstances of the case must be taken into account, notably the health status of the patient and the effect on his or her employment,[18] the degree of pain and the possibilities of providing speedy and effective treatment in the home Member State. Thus in *Watts*:

> [A] refusal to grant prior authorisation cannot be based merely on the existence of waiting lists enabling the supply of hospital care to be planned and managed on the basis of predetermined general clinical priorities, without carrying out in the individual case in question an objective medical assessment of the patient's medical condition, the history and probable course of his illness, the degree of pain he is in and/or the nature of his disability at the time when the request for authorisation was made or renewed.[19]

In so ruling the Court opened the door to a 'citizenship-type' reading of the rights of patients in the context of cross-border healthcare, creating rights that had not previously been granted within national healthcare systems at national level. A direct link with citizenship has however not yet been established in the

[16] Cf. Case C-542/09 *Commission* v. *Netherlands*, Judgment of 14 June 2012, paras. 57–8 and the references cited there.

[17] Case C-385/99 *Müller-Fauré*, above n. 12, paras. 77–80.

[18] Ibid., para. 90: 'the national authorities are required to have regard to all the circumstances of each specific case and to take due account not only of the patient's medical condition at the time when authorisation is sought and, where appropriate, of the degree of pain or the nature of the patient's disability which might, for example, make it impossible or extremely difficult for him to carry out a professional activity, but also of his medical history'. Cf. Case C-157/99 *Geraets-Smits*, above n. 11, para. 104.

[19] Case C-372/04 *Watts*, above n. 13, para. 119.

case law.[20] The above-mentioned Patients' Rights Directive does not change this equation but it does create rights for patients vis-à-vis both their home Member State and their host Member State – the latter mainly with regard to transparency and non-discrimination. We will get back to this Directive in Chapter 6 on vertical (or sector-specific) secondary law.

The case law on healthcare establishment

In contrast with the other sectors dealt with below (education and social services), the healthcare sector has given rise to a relatively extensive body of case law regarding establishment. This starts with the *Sodemare* judgment in 1997, where the Court held that there was no discrimination involved between domestic or foreign providers in barring for-profit organizations from reimbursement for the provision of care for the elderly.[21] Hence it found no restriction, nor therefore a need to rely on a justification. More recently even non-discriminatory rules that bar market access are now caught by the prohibition. However, the exceptions thereto are generous, based on the four-part *Gebhard* test with regard to the conditions imposed. They must: (i) be non-discriminatory; (ii) be justified by imperative requirements in the general interest; (iii) be suitable for securing the attainment of their objective; and (iv) not go beyond what is necessary.[22] In practice this means that systems based on public provision or self-regulation are protected from market access and competitive entry.[23]

This observation is subject to an important exception, however: to be protected the applicable national regulation must be coherent, or the disputed measure may yet fail the proportionality test (necessity or appropriateness).[24] Finally, restrictions of competition between undertakings may lead to barriers to establishment, especially where corporate bodies are involved that may abuse rule-making powers that they have been granted in the public interest to this

[20] Case C-345/09 *J. A. van Delft and Others* v. *College voor zorgverzekeringen* [2010] ECR I-9879, where Article 21 TFEU was invoked in the context of health insurance coverage for migrant pensioners, perhaps comes closest.

[21] Case C-70/95 *Sodemare SA, Anni Azzurri Holding SpA and Anni Azzurri Rezzato Srl* v. *Regione Lombardia* [1997] ECR I-3395. Cf. L. Hancher and W. Sauter, 'One step beyond? From *Sodemare* to *Docmorris*: The EU's freedom of establishment case law concerning healthcare', *Common Market Law Review*, 47 (2010), 117–46.

[22] Case C-55/94 *Reinhard Gebhard* v. *Consiglio dell'Ordine degli Avvocati e Procuratori di Milano* [1995] ECR I-4165.

[23] Case C-141/07 *Commission* v. *Germany* [2008] ECR I-6935; Joined cases C-171/07 and C-172/07 *Apothekerkammer des Saarlandes and Others and Helga Neumann-Seiwert* v. *Saarland and Ministerium für Justiz, Gesundheit und Soziales* [2009] ECR I-4171; Joined cases C-570/07 and C-571/07 *José Manuel Blanco Pérez and María del Pilar Chao Gómez* v. *Consejería de Salud y Servicios Sanitarios and Principado de Asturias* [2010] ECR I-4629.

[24] Cf. Case C-500/06 *Corporación Dermoestética SA* v. *To Me Group Advertising Media* [2008] ECR I-5785; Case C-169/07 *Hartlauer Handelsgesellschaft mbH* v. *Wiener Landesregierung and Oberösterreichische Landesregierung* [2009] ECR I-1721; Case C-89/09 *Commission* v. *France* [2010] ECR I-12941.

end.[25] Such bodies are plentiful in the healthcare sector. I will deal with this topic under the competition rules and will now move on to the next welfare sector, that of education.

3.4 Education

The Treaty provisions on education

Education is one of the most important public services in terms of both its scope and (as a consequence) the numbers involved: at one stage or another it will affect the lives of all EU citizens. Similarly to what is the case for healthcare, as regards education the subsidiary role of EU action is likewise emphasized by the Treaty, in this case Title XII TFEU on education, vocational training, youth and sport. Hence Article 165(1) TFEU reads:

> The Union shall contribute to the development of quality education by encouraging cooperation between Member States and, if necessary, by supporting and supplementing their action, while fully respecting the responsibility of the Member States for the content of teaching and the organisation of education systems and their cultural and linguistic diversity.

However, Article 165(2) TFEU provides for encouraging the mobility of students and teachers, and Article 166 TFEU entrusts the Union with the power to develop a vocational training policy. As we will see below, vocational training has been the original source of much of the case law on education because this is linked more closely with the rights of workers, and therefore with the internal market.

General principles

The Commission's 2013 Communication on public services and state aid, more precisely services of general economic interest and compensation, cites the case law to show that public education that is organized and supervised by the state does not constitute an economic activity.[26] This means that the rules on state aid and competition are not applicable because no undertakings are involved. Even a requirement that fees must be paid does not change this equation in so far as they cover only a fraction of the costs of the public education system which is otherwise funded from the public purse. These observations apply to all types of education, that is to say from kindergarten to primary and secondary schools, and universities (which are subsumed

[25] Cf. Summary of Commission Decision of 8 December 2010 relating to a proceeding under Article 101 TFEU (Case COMP/39.510 – LABCO/ONP), OJ 2011, C92/11.

[26] Communication from the Commission on a European Union framework for state aid in the form of public service compensation, OJ 2012, C8/15, paras. 26ff, citing Case C-318/05 *Commission* v. *Germany* [2007] ECR I-6957, para. 68.

under the EU definition of vocational training).[27] However, commercial enterprises offering education financed entirely by students are undertakings. This means that difficulties are evidently presented by cases with mixed financing. Thus in the 2007 case *Schwarz* the CJEU stated that it

> has . . . excluded from the definition of services within the meaning of Article 50 EC [now Article 57 TFEU] courses offered by certain establishments forming part of a system of public education and financed, entirely or mainly, by public funds . . . The Court thus held that, by establishing and maintaining such a system of public education, financed as a general rule by the public budget and not by pupils or their parents, the State did not intend to involve itself in remunerated activities, but was carrying out its task in the social, cultural and educational fields towards its population.
>
> However, the Court has held that courses given by educational establishments essentially financed by private funds, notably by students and their parents, constitute services within the meaning of Article 50 EC [now Article 57 TFEU], since the aim of those establishments is to offer a service for remuneration.[28]

The Court tends to regard teaching activities as coming within the scope of the free movement rules (in particular Article 57 TFEU on the freedom of services) in so far as they are provided for remuneration, even if they are carried out as part of a public education system, irrespective of whether they are aimed at making a profit.[29] Finally, Article 18 TFEU on the general application of non-discrimination and Article 21 TFEU on the right to move and reside freely in the citizenship context can come into play. Thus in the above-mentioned *Schwarz* case the CJEU ruled as follows:

> National legislation which places at a disadvantage certain of the nationals of the Member State concerned simply because they have exercised their freedom to move and to reside in another Member State is a restriction on the freedoms conferred by Article 18(1) EC [now Article 21 TFEU] on every citizen of the Union . . .
>
> Article 18 EC [now Article 21 TFEU] precludes legislation which allows taxpayers to claim as special expenses conferring a right to a reduction in income tax the payment of school fees to certain private schools established in national territory, but generally excludes that possibility in relation to school fees paid to a private school established in another Member State.[30]

[27] Cf. Case 242/87 *Commission* v. *Council* [1989] ECR 1425, on the European Community action scheme for the mobility of university students (Erasmus), paras. 24ff and the references cited there.

[28] Case C-76/05 *Herbert Schwarz and Marga Gootjes-Schwarz* v. *Finanzamt Bergisch Gladbach* [2007] ECR I-6849, paras. 39–40, with reference to Case 263/86 *Belgium* v. *René Humbel and Marie-Thérèse Edel* [1988] ECR 5365, paras. 17–18; Case C-109/92 *Stephan Max Wirth* v. *Landeshauptstadt Hannover* [1993] ECR I-6447, paras. 15–17.

[29] Case C-281/06 *Hans-Dieter Jundt and Hedwig Jundt* v. *Finanzamt Offenburg* [2007] ECR I-12231, paras. 32 and 33, with reference to Case C-157/99 *Geraets-Smits*, above n. 11, paras. 50 and 52.

[30] Case C-76/05 *Schwarz*, above n. 28, paras. 93–8.

Moreover, the citizenship right to move and reside freely is found to apply here. Hence it is necessary that a difference in treatment is objective and proportional.[31] This means it may be allowed to prevent maintenance costs from becoming an unreasonable burden. Excluding fees paid abroad from tax allowances, and barring students from receiving grants, however, is disproportionate. I will now look in more detail at the various aspects.

First we will examine a number of cases regarding discriminatory fees – or access rights to national education for inbound students. However, many of the education cases in EU law do not concern a right of access to education per se, or characteristics such as the quality of the education provided. Instead in recent years they mainly involve the right to financial assistance and/or tax exemptions for private financial contributions in the setting of funding either public or private education in another Member State than that where the funding system or the tax facility involved originated. Generally speaking, this does not involve an EU law-based right to educational funding. Rather, it concerns the export of such rights as exist nationally in cases where education is enjoyed in another Member State by outbound students. This is the second category of cases that I will look at. Finally, rights to non-educational funding for inbound students are covered under social security.

Discriminatory fees

The early cases generally revolve around vocational training because this was set out in Article 128 EEC (now Article 166 TFEU) as an area of activity of the EU.[32] In addition, where the student or their parents lived in the Member State where access to education was sought, it was linked to Regulation 1612/68 on free movement of workers.[33] The first such case appears to be *Forcheri* (1983)[34] involving Italian nationals residing and working in Belgium. Here the Court held that access to vocational education fell within the scope of the Treaty, and that consequently requiring an enrolment fee for such training only from foreign nationals constituted discrimination by nationality that was prohibited by Article 7 EEC (now Article 18 TFEU).

31 Case C-192/05 *K. Tas-Hagen and R. A. Tas* v. *Raadskamer WUBO van de Pensioen- en Uitkeringsraad* [2006] ECR I-10451; Case C-406/04 *Gérald De Cuyper* v. *Office national de l'emploi* [2006] ECR I-6947; Case C-224/98 *Marie-Nathalie D'Hoop* v. *Office national de l'emploi* [2002] ECR I-6191.

32 Article 166(1) TFEU reads: 'The Union shall implement a vocational training policy which shall support and supplement the action of the Member States, while fully respecting the responsibility of the Member States for the content and organisation of vocational training.'

33 Regulation (EEC) No 1612/68 of the Council of 15 October 1968 on freedom of movement for workers within the Community, OJ 1968, L257/2 (English special edition: Series I Volume 1968(II) p. 475); repealed by Regulation (EU) No 492/2011 of the European Parliament and of the Council of 5 April 2011 on freedom of movement for workers within the Union, OJ 2011, L141/1.

34 Case 28/83 *Sandro Forcheri* v. *Commission* [1984] ECR 1426.

Likewise in *Gravier* (1985) the Court held that charging a fee for admission to higher arts education (as a form of vocational training) exclusively to non-Belgian nationals constituted an illegal form of discrimination on grounds of nationality with respect to citizens from other Member States.[35] The Belgian defence was that the numbers of outbound and inbound students in Belgium were not in balance, with more students entering Belgium to study there than Belgian students studying abroad, and that the relevant costs of education would otherwise be borne primarily by Belgian citizens, with the benefits accruing to nationals from the other Member States. Belgium argued that imposing a proportional contribution to the costs did not constitute discrimination in a material sense. This argument was not accepted: instead a formal definition of discrimination (on grounds of nationality) was used that compared only the position of Belgian and foreign students, not the broader financing context.[36] Hence Article 7 EEC (now Article 18 TFEU) was held to be infringed.

This can be contrasted with *Humbel* (1988) where an enrolment fee was charged for secondary (vocational) education provided to a French national residing in Belgium.[37] Here the question of education as a service was addressed as follows:

> The essential characteristic of remuneration ... lies in the fact that it constitutes consideration for the service in question, and is normally agreed upon between the provider and the recipient of the service.
>
> That characteristic is, however, absent in the case of courses provided under the national education system. First of all, the State, in establishing and maintaining such a system, is not seeking to engage in gainful activity but is fulfilling its duties towards its own population in the social, cultural and educational fields. Secondly, the system in question is, as a general rule, funded from the public purse and not by pupils or their parents.
>
> The nature of the activity is not affected by the fact that pupils or their parents must sometimes pay teaching or enrolment fees in order to make a certain contribution to the operating expenses of the system. A fortiori, the mere fact that foreign pupils alone are required to pay a minerval can have no such effect.[38]

So far this definition has stood the test of time.[39] Consequently the education services concerned were not regarded as services in the sense of Article 57 TFEU and charging a fee would therefore not be in breach of this provision. In

[35] Case 293/83 *Françoise Gravier* v. *City of Liège* [1985] ECR 593, para. 26. In this case the Court also defined vocational training as 'any form of education which prepares for a qualification for a particular profession, trade or employment or which provides the necessary training and skills for such a profession, trade or employment'. Ibid., para. 30. Cf. Case 197/86 *Steven Malcolm Brown* v. *Secretary of State for Scotland* [1988] ECR 3205, para. 10; Case 24/86 *Vincent Blaizot* v. *University of Liège et al.* [1988] ECR 379, paras. 19–20.

[36] See C. Barnard, 'EU citizenship and the principle of solidarity', in M. Dougan and E. Spaventa (eds.), *Social welfare and EU law: Essays in EU law* (Hart Publishing, Oxford, 2005), 157–80.

[37] Case 263/86 *Humbel*, above n. 28. [38] Para. 12. [39] See Case C-76/05 *Schwarz*, above n. 28.

Humbel Article 12 of Regulation 1612/68 (now Regulation 492/2011)[40] on free movement of workers was found not to apply because it referred only to the children of workers who wished to access the education system in the Member State where they and their parents resided.

The right to funding

The above-mentioned Article 12 of Regulation 1612/68 (now Regulation 492/2011) has been at the heart of several cases on access to education for children of workers from other Member States.[41] It reads:

> The children of a national of a Member State who is or has been employed in the territory of another Member State shall be admitted to that State's general educational, apprenticeship and vocational training courses under the same conditions as the nationals of that State, if such children are residing in its territory.

In *Casagrande* (1974), with regard to the claim of a German monthly educational grant by the child of an Italian worker in Germany, the Court found that equal admission to educational courses in Article 12 of Regulation 1612/68 'under the same conditions as nationals' referred to all measures intended to facilitate attendance.[42] In *Brown* (1988) the Court held that this provision only applies to a child who resides in a Member State simultaneously with at least one of his parents who is a worker.[43] In both *Brown* and *Lair* (1988) the Court confirmed that grants for university studies are to be regarded as a social advantage to which workers are entitled under Article 7 of Regulation 1612/68. In *Lair* it ruled that during a period of attending studies following a period of occupational activity that status of 'worker' was not lost: this meant that a right to an educational grant would exist if there was a link between the occupational activity and the studies involved.[44]

A similar funding case is *Wirth* (1993), which concerned the restriction of the right of a German national to claim a German educational grant only for the pursuit of higher education in Germany and not (in this case) in the Netherlands.[45] Here the Court held that in establishing and maintaining an education system, Member States are not seeking to engage in gainful activity (even though pupils or their parents might sometimes make a contribution). Hence there was no question of services being provided for remuneration and the freedom of services did not apply to the refusal of grants for studies in other Member States. Reliance on non-discrimination was therefore deemed to be foreclosed – a position that was to change in later cases.

[40] Above, n. 33. [41] Ibid.
[42] Case 9/74 *Donato Casagrande* v. *Landeshauptstadt München* [1974] ECR 773.
[43] Case 197/86 *Brown*, above n. 35.
[44] Case 39/86 *Sylvie Lair* v. *Universität Hannover* [1988] ECR 3161.
[45] Case C-109/92 *Wirth*, above n. 28.

Several cases involve tax deductions for educational expenses.[46] In *Commission* v. *Germany* (2007)[47] the Court held that privately run educational establishments provided services in the sense of EU law. Drawing an interesting but not very clear parallel with the 2006 *Watts* case, where it had held that even an NHS system must reimburse the costs of healthcare provided to UK residents abroad,[48] although domestically it provides services for free at the point of delivery, the CJEU ruled that to provide tax deductions to German nationals in order to offset the charges of private schools in Germany that were not available with regard to private schools in other Member States infringed the freedom to provide services. Germany justified its system with reference to the 2005 *Bidar* case (see the next section)[49] and the principle established there that it could limit benefits in order to avoid grants becoming an unreasonable burden. However, the categorical denial of tax relief for private school fees in other Member States failed the proportionality test that was applied to this restriction since other means, such as limiting the amount deductible for school fees, would have been available.[50]

In *Commission* v. *Germany* the Court also applied the rule that the general citizenship's rights to reside and move freely of Article 20 TFEU are not applicable if their more specific elaboration in Article 56 and Article 49 TFEU on the freedom of services and of establishment is applicable.[51] In *Schwarz* (2007) substantially the same conclusions were drawn with regard to the freedom to provide services in relation to the deductibility of private school fees and Article 56 TFEU. Here, however, the Court examined Article 20 TFEU in the alternative (if no services would be involved) and found that in this case the disputed measures would impose an unjustified disadvantage on citizens who had availed themselves of their rights to free movement. Hence benefits (tax deductions) regarding fees for private schools at home could be transposed to fees for public schools in other Member States.

[46] Case C-281/06 *Jundt*, above n. 29, concerned unjustified discriminatory tax allowances for university teaching. Interestingly here, teaching was considered to be covered by the freedom to provide services even if in the other cases cited enjoying and/or providing public education were not. A case regarding the use of academic titles where the Court ruled that Member States may not penalize their own nationals for making use of free movement was Case C-19/92 *Dieter Kraus* v. *Land Baden-Württemberg* [1993] ECR I-1663.

[47] Case C-318/05 *Commission* v. *Germany*, above n. 26.

[48] Case C-372/04 *Watts*, above n. 13.

[49] Case C-209/03 *The Queen, on the application of Dany Bidar* v. *London Borough of Ealing and Secretary of State for Education and Skills* [2005] ECR I-2119, paras. 56 and 57.

[50] Case C-318/05 *Commission* v. *Germany*, above n. 26, paras. 32–3.

[51] In Case C-147/03 *Commission* v. *Austria* [2005] ECR I-5969, a condition that in order to obtain admission to Austrian universities students from other Member States must in addition to a diploma provide proof that they would be eligible for admission to comparable studies in their home Member State was considered an unjustified form of discrimination that breached Article 18 TFEU.

This case law was confirmed in *Zanotti* (2010), where the Court held that both Article 20 TFEU and Article 56 TFEU precluded national legislation that allowed tax deductions for national university fees but barred such deductions for tuition fees at a private university in another Member State.[52] However, setting a limit on such deductions at the level of the national state university nearest to the taxpayer's residence was not precluded. This suggests that an effective and practical balance could be struck between, on the one hand, the free movement and citizenship rights of students and, on the other hand, the financial equilibrium of the educational system. Finally, in *Giersch* (2013) the Court held that a residency requirement for financial aid for higher education discriminated materially against the children of frontier workers and was not proportional to the public interest objective of raising the percentage of the population with advanced education.[53] The loan could have been made conditional upon the recipient returning to the Member State that granted it (Luxembourg) to reside and work there after their studies.[54]

Discriminatory access conditions

There are two leading cases concerning Member States imposing additional requirements for admission to university education on nationals from other Member States. In *Commission* v. *Belgium* (2004) nationals of other Member States who wished to gain access to a number of forms of higher education in Belgium (medical studies, dental and veterinary science, and agricultural engineering) were required to pass an additional aptitude test apart from having completed the requisite level of secondary education.[55] This system applied if they could not prove that they qualified for university admission in their own country of origin without further entry requirements. This was considered to be at odds with the general non-discrimination obligation of Article 18 TFEU and Belgium did not claim recourse to overriding reasons of public interest in its justification.

Likewise in *Commission* v. *Austria* (2005) students who were nationals of other Member States who wished to study medicine in Austria had to demonstrate that they would have been admitted unconditionally in their home Member State.[56] Material discrimination was held to be at stake here as well,

[52] Case C-56/09 *Emiliano Zanotti* v. *Agenzia delle Entrate – Ufficio Roma 2* [2010] ECR I-4517.

[53] Case C-20/12 *Elodie Giersch et al.* v. *Luxembourg*, Judgment of 20 June 2013. It is worth noting that, in accepting the public interest objective of raising standards of learning, the Court referred to the Commission Communication of 3 March 2010, Europe 2020: A strategy for smart, sustainable and inclusive growth, COM(2010) 2020 final, as well as other EU initiatives in this area. Ibid., paras. 54–5.

[54] A three out of six years residency requirement was likewise held to be too restrictive in Case C-542/09 *Commission* v. *Netherlands*, above n. 16.

[55] Case C-65/03 *Commission* v. *Belgium* [2004] ECR I-6427.

[56] Case C-147/03 *Commission* v. *Austria*, above n. 51.

and moreover non-discriminatory measures such as an entry exam or the requirement of a minimum grade point average could have been applied instead. Finally, Austria had failed to show specific evidence substantiating its claims that derogation was necessary because the existence and the homogeneity of the Austrian education system were at stake. Hence in this case the additional requirements were likewise struck down for infringing the non-discrimination requirement.

In both cases we see a smaller Member State struggling with the influx of students from a larger neighbour (France for Belgium, and Germany for Austria) that may put pressure on the financial sustainability or at least the organizational structure of its system. Both countries have since adopted quota systems for a number of especially sensitive studies (medicine, dentistry, physiotherapy and veterinary studies), first in 2007 and then in 2012, which were tolerated for a five-year period to assess the effects of this system. During this period the Commission suspended infringement proceedings against these Member States.[57] Hence there is a potential basis here for a balanced test similar to that arrived at in the cross-border healthcare case law (and eventually codified in the Patients' Rights Directive), albeit that here there does not appear to be a requirement of an assessment based on the personal circumstances of the individual involved. This assessment changes, however, when we look more closely at the citizenship dimension.

Education and citizenship

A number of cases are more specifically dedicated to the link between education and citizenship. In *Morgan* (2007) the Court specified that students enjoy citizenship status and may therefore rely on the relevant rights to move and reside, including against their home Member State.[58] In addition, it held that a requirement for financial assistance for studies in another Member State that they should have been preceded by at least a year of studies in the home Member State and that those same studies should be continued abroad infringed Article 20 TFEU. Citing *Bidar* (discussed further below), on the other hand, the Court also found that it was legitimate for a Member State to require the existence of a certain degree of integration in the society of that state as a precondition for making grants available to students from other Member States. Such a requirement could serve to ensure that the relevant maintenance costs do not become an unreasonable burden that could have consequences for the overall level of assistance that could be granted.

[57] Austria and Belgium were given more time to justify quotas, European Commission – IP/12/1388, 18 December 2012.

[58] Joined cases C-11/06 and C-12/06 *Rhiannon Morgan* v. *Bezirksregierung Köln and Iris Bucher* v. *Landrat des Kreises Düren* [2007] ECR I-9161.

In *Bressol* (2010)[59] the Court examined access to medical training against the background of Directive 2004/38 on the rights of citizens to move and reside freely.[60] It held there was no need to exercise an economic activity in order to be able to rely on the relevant freedoms. There is overlap with the healthcare case law cited above, albeit from a supply side perspective rather than one of demand for healthcare services, because the justification of the condition applied here – a residency requirement – was based on the objective of the protection of public health. The Court demanded that a link between this residency requirement and public health, including the existence of a risk to the latter, be established based on an objective and detailed analysis and solid and consistent data. In addition, the measure must be shown to be appropriate in terms of increasing the number of graduates available to provide future public health services and the least restrictive means available for this purpose. By setting such a stringent evidence requirement the Court (unusually enough) gave real substance to the proportionality requirement.

A different type of link is that between the student and the Member State where financial aid is requested. Recently, in the *Prinz* case (2013) with regard to the right of financial assistance for studies in another Member State, this was formulated as follows:

> [A]ccording to settled case-law, the proof required to demonstrate the genuine link must not be too exclusive in nature or unduly favour one element which is not necessarily representative of the real and effective degree of connection between the claimant and this Member State, to the exclusion of all other representative elements.[61]

Hence a flat eligibility requirement of three years' residency without allowing for other factors to be taken into account was held to be unacceptable.[62] Therefore it appears that a general condition may be imposed but that the circumstances of the individual case may have to be taken into account, as was the case for patients' rights and free movement in the healthcare setting.[63] Having noted this incipient parallel, I will now move on to the third welfare sector that I will discuss in this chapter, that of social security.

[59] Case C-73/08 *Nicolas Bressol et al. and Céline Chaverot et al.* v. *Gouvernement de la Communauté française* [2010] ECR I-2735.

[60] Directive 2004/38/EC of the European Parliament and of the Council of 29 April 2004 on the right of citizens of the Union and their family members to move and reside freely within the territory of the Member States amending Regulation (EEC) No 1612/68 and repealing Directives 64/221/EEC, 68/360/EEC, 72/194/EEC, 73/148/EEC, 75/34/EEC, 75/35/EEC, 90/364/EEC, 90/365/EEC and 93/96/EEC, OJ 2004, L158/77.

[61] Joined cases C-523/11 and C-585/11 *Laurence Prinz* v. *Region Hannover and Philipp Seeberger* v. *Studentenwerk Heidelberg*, Judgment of 18 July 2013, para. 37.

[62] In Case C-158/07 *Jacqueline Förster* v. *Hoofddirectie van de Informatie Beheer Groep* [2008] ECR I-8507, citizenship and non-discrimination was held to give a student a right to a maintenance grant, but a five-year residence requirement was held to be acceptable.

[63] Case C-372/04 *Watts*, above n. 13.

3.5 Social security

A complex regime

Social security presents us with a complex EU law regime. The judgment in *Partena* (2012) neatly sums up the division of competencies in the EU with regard to social security.

> Although EU law does not detract from the power of the Member States to organise their own social security systems and, in the absence of harmonization at Community level, it is for the legislation of the Member State concerned to determine the conditions governing the right or duty to be insured with a social security scheme, it is nonetheless necessary, when the Member State concerned exercises that power, that it comply with EU law.[64]

Such compliance is not as straightforward as it may seem. As regards social security a complex regime is in place, or in fact several parallel regimes are.[65] The EU law system is in part based on the now extensive provisions in Treaty Articles 151–61 TFEU, in part on the citizenship provisions, and partly on the secondary legislation on social security coordination in Regulation 883/2004,[66] regarding migrant workers in Regulation 492/2011[67] or regarding citizens in Regulation 2004/38/EC.[68] For instance, the rights under Regulation 883/2004 are to be read in the context of citizenship.[69] Also, the same situation can fall under different regulations,[70] with the citizenship rights in the Treaty as a catch-all in the background. In addition, free movement rights may be involved.[71] Because I will dedicate Chapter 5 to horizontal secondary legislation, I will try to focus here on the primary law, that is to say the Treaty texts themselves and their interpretation with regard to social services.

The Treaty provisions on social policy and social security

As mentioned, the provisions in the TFEU on social policy are extensive. They go back to the European Social Charter signed at Turin on 18 October 1961 and the 1989 Community Charter of the Fundamental Social Rights of Workers. During the UK opt-out period between the 1993 Treaty of Maastricht and the 1998 Treaty of Amsterdam the relevant rules were set aside as the Social Policy

[64] Case C-137/11 *Partena ASBL* v. *Les Tartes de Chaumont-Gistoux SA*, Judgment of 27 September 2012, para. 59. Cf. N. Rennuy, 'The emergence of a parallel system of social security coordination', *Common Market Law Review*, 50 (2013), 1221–66, at 1222.

[65] Cf. A. P. van der Meij, *Free movement of persons within the European Community: Cross-border access to public benefits* (Hart Publishing, Oxford, 2003); F. Pennings, *European social security law*, 5th edn (Intersentia, Antwerp, 2010).

[66] Regulation 883/2004, above n. 8. [67] Above, n. 3. [68] Above, n. 60.

[69] Case C-140/12 *Pensionsversicherungsanstalt* v. *Peter Brey*, Judgment of 19 September 2013.

[70] Case C-111/91 *Commission* v. *Luxembourg* [1993] ECR I-817. Dougan, above n. 2, at 124.

[71] Case C-287/05 *D. P. W. Hendrix* v. *Raad van Bestuur van het Uitvoeringsinstituut Werknemersverzekeringen* [2007] ECR I-6909.

Protocol. The provisions on social policy involve topics such as working conditions, health and safety at work, and the conditions for termination of employment that go well beyond the scope of what I understand as social security, which are essentially subsistence benefits of various types. Instead, therefore, Article 153(1)c TFEU on social security and social protection of workers is what I am primarily interested in.

The case law on social security

The case law on social security is extensive, in part because the rights involved are interpreted broadly. In the first place, just as we have seen with regard to education, the Member States may not penalize their own nationals for exercising their free movement rights under EU law.[72] In addition, the Court has further widened the scope of EU law on social services by ruling that even where secondary social security legislation does not confer rights on citizens even formally non-discriminatory barriers to free movement could still be caught by Article 20 TFEU. The same holds for non-discriminatory barriers outside the context of secondary legislation.

There is some overlap here between the case law on education and on social services in those cases where students claim social benefits in order to finance their continued education. The most celebrated example of this is the *Grzelczyk* case (2001).[73] Here the Court held that the request for social assistance by a student from another Member State could conceivably justify withdrawal of his residence permit but could not automatically lead to that consequence.

> Articles 6 and 8 of the Treaty [now Articles 18 and 20 TFEU] preclude entitlement to a non-contributory social benefit, such as the minimex, from being made conditional, in the case of nationals of Member States other than the host State where they are legally resident, on their falling within the scope of Regulation No 1612/68 when no such condition applies to nationals of the host Member State.[74]

The Regulation 1612/68 cited here was already mentioned above and applies to the free movement of workers.[75] In this case therefore primary EU law (on citizenship) supplements or even substitutes secondary law, which is in itself not problematic within a hierarchy of legal norms, but it may be more difficult to justify from a perspective of political legitimacy in a multi-level polity. In addition, residence rights could not be revoked automatically from the national of another Member State as a consequence of his becoming dependent on social

[72] Cf. Case C-18/95 *F. C. Terhoeve* v. *Inspecteur van de Belastingdienst Particulieren/ Ondernemingen buitenland* [1999] ECR I-345.

[73] Case C-184/99 *Rudy Grzelczyk* v. *Centre public d'aide sociale d'Ottignies-Louvain-la-Neuve* [2001] ECR I-6193. Cf. M. Dougan and E. Spaventa, 'Educating Rudy and the non-English patient: A double bill on residency rights under Article 18 EC', *European Law Review*, 28 (2003), 699–712.

[74] Case C-184/99 *Grzelczyk*, above n. 73, para. 46.

[75] Regulation 1612/68, above n. 33.

assistance in the host Member State. In this context the existence of a certain degree of financial solidarity between EU citizens – nationals and non-nationals of host and home Member States – was presupposed.

In the *Bidar* case (2005) the Court held it permissible for a Member State to limit the maintenance costs of students from other Member States in order to ensure that they did not become an unreasonable burden – which could have a negative impact on the ability of the Member State to grant assistance at all.[76] Unlike with regard to tide-over allowances in *D'Hoop* (2002)[77] or job-seeking allowances in *Collins* (2004),[78] requiring a link with the employment market could not be required in *Bidar* because the nature of higher education is generally not restricted to a particular geographical employment market. However, a requirement of proof of the existence of a degree of integration by means of having resided in the host Member State for a certain length of time was accepted. In the case in point a genuine link with the host society (as opposed to its employment market) was found to exist. In other words, the possibilities for relying on the principle of a genuine link were extended considerably – from the job market to society more generally. Yet at the same time affordability was accepted as a legitimate constraint.

It is worth noting that this argument is similar to that which was used in *Müller-Fauré* (2003)[79] and *Geraets-Smits* (2001)[80] regarding the sustainability of healthcare systems (and the objective of maintaining a balanced medical and hospital service open to all), in the light of access to healthcare. That is to say, at a minimum, indirect economic justifications that can be linked to ensuring universal availability or in any event widespread access rights are held to be acceptable even if the general rule is that public policy exceptions and overriding reasons of public interest under the free movement rules are in principle equity and not efficiency based. In addition, it appears that the Court requires attention to be paid to the merits and details of the individual case, respectively the personal situation involved.

The case law however is subtle. A case which illustrates that national rules are not always trumped is *De Cuyper* (2006), regarding the beneficiary of social security in the sense of Regulation 1408/71 (now Regulation 883/2004).[81] A requirement to reside in the Member State where the benefit was granted was found not to be precluded by the freedom of movement and residence in Article 18 EC (now Article 20 TFEU) because this restriction was justified by the need to monitor the employment and family situation of unemployed persons:

[76] Case C-209/03 *Bidar*, above n. 49, para. 63.

[77] Case C-224/98 *D'Hoop*, above n. 31, para. 38.

[78] Case C-138/02 *Brian Francis Collins* v. *Secretary of State for Work and Pensions* [2004] ECR I-2703, para. 67.

[79] Case C-385/99 *Müller-Fauré*, above n. 12.

[80] Case C-157/99 *Geraets-Smits*, above n. 11.

[81] Case C-406/04 *De Cuyper*, above n. 31.

> [L]ess restrictive measures, such as the production of documents or certificates, would mean that the monitoring would no longer be unexpected and would consequently be less effective.
>
> Accordingly, it must be found that the obligation to reside in the Member State in which the institution responsible for payment is situated, which is justified in domestic law by the need to monitor compliance with the statutory conditions governing the compensation paid to unemployed persons, satisfies the requirement of proportionality.[82]

In *Hendrix* (2007)[83] the CJEU accepted that a residency requirement was objectively justified with regard to an incapacity benefit for disabled young people. However, it held that implementation of the relevant legislation should not go beyond what is necessary and infringe the rights of the applicant who had maintained all of his social links to the Member State of origin, even while living abroad. In addition, it held that since the case fell under the free movement of workers, recourse to Article 20 TFEU on the freedom to move and reside for citizens was not necessary. In the *Petersen* case (2008), under the Social Security Regulation and the free movement of workers, however, a residency requirement for an invalidity pension which qualified as an unemployment benefit was regarded as disproportionate as the potential beneficiaries were exempt from obligations concerning the capacity, willingness and availability to work.[84] Finally, in *Bartlett* (2011) the EU legislature's choices were respected instead of trumped by primary law.[85] Here the CJEU held that a derogation from the principle of exportability of social security benefits, based on Article 48 TFEU, was permissible. In this case the grant of benefits 'closely linked with the social environment' – a disability living allowance – were made subject to a residence requirement in the host Member State.

The picture that emerges is therefore one where individual rights based on primary law trump secondary legislation, and where free movement, especially for workers, constitutes a *lex specialis* with regard to the more general citizenship-based rights.

3.6 Public services, free movement and citizenship

Discrimination and reverse discrimination

As we have seen, the general relevance of free movement and citizenship to public services concerns access and funding. However, this does not mean this case law is grounded in the special status of public services. Rather it is the reverse: because free movement and/or citizenship are involved, a right accrues

[82] Ibid., paras. 46–7. [83] Case C-287/05 *Hendrix*, above n. 71.

[84] Case C-228/07 *Jörn Petersen* v. *Landesgeschäftsstelle des Arbeitsmarktservice Niederösterreich* [2008] ECR I-6989.

[85] Case C-537/09 *Ralph James Bartlett et al.* v. *Secretary of State for Work and Pensions* [2011] ECR I-3417.

that is not much more – but also no less – than a very broad entitlement to non-discrimination.[86] Citizenship also means that the free movement rules are extended to economically inactive persons.[87] Finally, secondary EU law is rewritten by recourse to primary law.[88]

Generally, discrimination on the basis of nationality is illegal in EU law with regard to parties from other Member States. In principle this does not exclude so-called reverse discrimination by Member States against their own citizens, at least where there was no free movement dimension:[89] a purely internal situation. Thus in 2008 the Court found that it was lawful under EU law for the Flemish regional government to deny the right to affiliation with, and benefits from, a long-term care insurance scheme to Belgian nationals who lived in the Walloon region, but not in relation to nationals from other EU Member States who lived in that region.[90]

Citizens of the EU may however invoke their citizenship rights, including non-discrimination, against their Member State of origin. Thus in *D'Hoop* (2002) the Court ruled that it would be incompatible with freedom of movement if a citizen were to receive less favourable treatment in her home Member State as the result of having availed herself of the free movement rights under the Treaty.[91] More recently, the citizenship rights of Article 20 TFEU were applied to a purely internal situation in the *Zambrano* case (2011),[92] regarding the rights to residency and employment (a work permit) for the Colombian parents of two Belgian children living in that Member State.

The existence of a real link

Benefits need not be awarded to all comers. In fact, so far exclusion and inclusion are the key to any welfare regime. As far as deciding who is regarded as entitled to national benefits is concerned, the existence of a real link with the host society may be demanded, provided that the condition imposed is necessary and therefore proportionate.[93] In the *D'Hoop* case (2002) the Court found that a link could be required between, on the one hand, the applicant for a tide-over allowance for the period between completing university education and

[86] Cf. Case C-85/96 *María Martínez Sala* v. *Freistaat Bayern* [1998] ECR I-2691.

[87] Cf. Case C-413/99 *Baumbast and R* v. *Secretary of State for the Home Department* [2002] ECR I-7091.

[88] Cf. Dougan and Spaventa, above n. 73; M. Dougan, 'The constitutional dimension to the case law on Union citizenship', *European Law Review*, 31 (2006), 613–41.

[89] Where nationals of a Member State have exercised their right to move and reside in another Member State, the free movement rules do apply. Cf. Case C-192/05 *Tas-Hagen*; and Case C-406/04 *De Cuyper*, both above n. 31.

[90] Case C-212/06 *Government of Communauté française and Gouvernement wallon* v. *Gouvernement flamand* [2008] ECR I-1683.

[91] Case C-224/98 *D'Hoop*, above n. 31, para. 30.

[92] Case C-34/09 *Gerardo Ruiz Zambrano* v. *Office national de l'emploi (ONEm)* [2011] ECR I-1177.

[93] Case C-224/98 *D'Hoop*, above n. 31, para. 39.

finding work and, on the other hand, the geographic employment market concerned. However, the single condition based on where applicants had obtained their secondary education diploma was held to be too general and exclusive in nature, and therefore not proportional.[94] More fundamentally, as mentioned in *Bidar* (2005), a real or genuine link with the host society (as opposed to just the employment market) could be based inter alia on a certain term of residency.[95]

Again therefore we see a screening device being allowed to the Member States provided that it is non-discriminatory and proportional to its legitimate objective.

Citizenship: access versus content

As we will see in the following chapters, there is an argument that secondary rules regarding universal service obligations in the utilities sectors are leading to the emergence of a market citizenship or a consumer citizenship.[96] However, these rights are not based on the citizenship provisions in the Treaty and it is difficult to construe a connection between them in any meaningful legal sense. The citizenship dimension that we have seen with regard to welfare services is squarely based on the Treaty. It trumps not only national regimes but even EU secondary legislation in terms of regulating access on a strictly non-discriminatory basis. However, in terms of the content of the rights involved, such as the amounts of reimbursement, or the conditions covered, the Member States remain independent in what is ultimately an assessment that is based on national politics.

The trump status of citizenship versus legitimacy

The significance of citizenship to the topic of public services is unquestionable. In the *Grzelczyk* case (2001) the Court defined the status of citizenship as follows:

> Union citizenship is destined to be the fundamental status of nationals of the Member States, enabling those who find themselves in the same situation to enjoy the same treatment in law irrespective of their nationality, subject to such exceptions as are expressly provided for.[97]

As was mentioned above, in this line of cases the Court trumps not just national rules but even EU secondary law with the primary EU law on citizenship. This is in conformity with the functioning of a constitutional hierarchy of norms, but it does raise questions from the perspective of political legitimacy in a multi-level polity. Such a tension would already exist in any federal system; however, the

[94] Ibid., paras. 38–9. [95] Case C-209/03 *Bidar*, above n. 49. [96] Above, n. 3.
[97] Case C-184/99 *Grzelczyk*, above n. 73, para. 31.

Union today is not a federal state but a federation of nation states, albeit subject to a dynamic development that may be moving towards a federation. As in any hand of cards, the number of trumps available is limited and should be played with caution to obtain maximum effect. And effectively we do see for all three types of welfare services that were examined above the emergence of a balance between, on the one hand, regulation, be it at EU or national level, and, on the other hand, the protection by the Court of individual rights along the vectors of material non-discrimination and the proportional pursuit of legitimate means.

Citizenship tends to be associated with increased legitimacy for the EU as it now is, or for future federal aspirations. At the same time, it is questionable whether it is always the case that citizenship provides such legitimacy. In the words of Jo Shaw:

> While it is often said that citizenship of the Union, in its current Treaty form, is a vapid and impoverished version of the membership concept which has been central to liberal democratic and constitutionally based (national) polities, there does not seem to be any obvious popular legitimacy driving the argument that EU citizenship *should* be developed in more substantial ways than it is at present.[98]

Of course, popular legitimacy is not the only reason to have or develop EU citizenship. Nevertheless this is a caveat that I will keep in mind when I get back to this topic in subsequent chapters, and especially the general conclusion.

3.7 Conclusion

As we have seen above, there are significant parallels between the public services that can be classified as welfare services as regards the primary law on free movement. The utilities sectors, however, are scarcely affected, at least by the primary law. Instead, as we shall see in Chapters 5 and 6 on secondary law, they are influenced by the horizontal secondary rules and, evidently to an even greater extent, by their respective sector-specific regulatory regimes.

For healthcare, education and social security services the reverse holds: there are some important secondary horizontal rules in place relating to the rights of workers (Regulation 883/2004) and the free movement rights of citizens (Directive 2004/38/EC) that have already been touched upon here.[99] However, in relation to these welfare services direct recourse to the internal market freedoms as well as citizenship occurs frequently. In Michael Dougan's words:

> Welfare law is one of those intriguing fields where EU regulatory power is relatively weak ... yet the Member State's duty to respect the free movement

98 J. Shaw, 'Citizenship: Contrasting dynamics at the interface of integration and constitutionalism', in P. Craig and G. de Búrca, *The evolution of EU law*, 2nd edn (Oxford University Press, 2011), 575–609, at 605 (emphasis in the original).

99 Above at n. 8 and n. 57 respectively.

> obligations derived from the Treaty itself manages to exert an increasingly profound influence on the exercise of domestic competence and the character of national welfare provision.[100]

This involves both cases of nationals of a (home) Member State invoking the free movement rules when seeking benefits while residing abroad and the reverse, foreign nationals claiming benefits in the (host) Member State where they are residing. In both cases recourse to citizenship is also available, sometimes in parallel, and sometimes as a trump – by referring to a rule of a higher order. If we can draw one main lesson from the case law on such issues it is that the Court now seems to have settled on the requirement that a 'real link' must exist between the Member State and the claimant involved for rights in EU law to accrue to the latter.

It should be noted, however, that the level at which welfare services are provided (that is to say: their content) more generally is not directly affected. Also, it is questionable whether in most cases even the indirect effect is likely to be substantial. For instance, according to figures provided by the Commission in 2013, only 1 per cent of patients would travel across borders to receive medical treatment.[101] In some instances the effects may be concentrated enough locally to have a more significant impact but this pales against the needs to control costs in the light of other factors such as technological change, an ageing population and rising expectations.

There are three further aspects of this case law that are worth highlighting here:

- First, the primary reason why the Court is prepared to accept proportional restrictions on free movement and/or citizenship rights with regard to public services is that it accepts that otherwise the financial sustainability of the system and thereby the very access to the benefits involved may be at stake for consumers at large. In doing so, the Court effectively accepts an economic (or efficiency) justification in an area, free movement, where in principle public policy exceptions and overriding reasons must be equity based.
- Second, as part of its proportionality test the Court will require in each of the three areas examined that the Member State looks into the individual circumstances of the claimant in those cases where he or she fails to meet the standard test adopted to establish the real link – or in the case of healthcare, for prior approval. Here there is potential tension between individual

[100] Dougan, above n. 2, at 119. Also, the Union 'may not have the power to tax and spend and therefore no welfare system of its own; but the Union now plays a decisive role in organising welfare rights between individuals and national authorities, and creating new rights to supranational welfare support'. Ibid., at 129.

[101] Demand for cross-border healthcare represents only around 1 per cent of public spending on healthcare, which is currently around €10 billion. This estimate includes cross-border healthcare which patients had not planned in advance, such as emergency care. European Commission, MEMO, Q&A: Patients' Rights in Cross-Border Healthcare, Brussels, 22 October 2013.

rights under EU law and efficient administration at national level based on general rules, where the Court clearly chooses to promote the former over the latter.

- Third, the effect of the case law is to promote access and funding of such access in various combinations of inbound and outbound free movement. The result in my view induces a greater degree of universality with regard to welfare services at the boundaries of territoriality and nationality, although the content of the relevant rights remains determined at national level, not that of the EU. Thus there is a certain affinity with the EU rules on universal service obligations in the utilities sectors which also revolve around access but set minimum content standards as well. However, there is no direct connection.

Based on what I have discussed above, it appears obvious to me now that criticizing this case law as dismantling national systems of public services by law (negative integration) while failing to erect new structures by means of legislation (positive integration) fails to capture what is actually occurring.[102] To start with, the numbers involved in the cross-border consumption of health-care, social services and education are generally not staggering and they are only a single factor among many that may put pressure on the sustainability of national welfare systems, with debt crises and Euro criteria more recently prominent among them. Hence in practice we simply do not witness national regimes being stripped or crippled as a result of the more expansive reading of EU law (for instance on citizenship) favoured by the Court in recent years.

Instead we see that benefits continue to be defined nationally, as is the standard that determines to whom they are extended. It is only the latter dimension which is increasingly codetermined by EU law, by setting limits on what type of test is acceptable to determine access to the respective national systems, both for outbound own nationals and inbound nationals from other Member States. The immediate net effect appears to be that more, not fewer, rights to social services are created. At least in theory, a secondary effect may be that national regimes are trimmed down in response to growing demand, although to my knowledge so far it has not been demonstrated that this in fact the case. In other words, it is dubious whether EU law requirements are a direct and significant cause of welfare reform in any Member State.

Finally, I found an unexpected parallel with the utilities. There intensive EU law-based regulation has become the norm, which is not the case here. However, here too we see the EU not so much funding public services as regulating their provision, or at least the relevant access and funding (which can be seen as a type of access) rights. This means that governance, not spending power, is the EU's ticket to influence over public services (and

[102] Cf. F. W. Scharpf, *Community and autonomy: Institutions, policies and legitimacy in multilevel Europe* (Campus, Frankfurt am Main, 2010), and Chapter 1 above.

arguably much else that escapes the scope of this book). Unlike the utilities sectors where the rules are now largely identical across the Member States, the net effect is not uniformity. Then again, like utilities regulation, the overriding consequence of this process is rationalization of social, or welfare, services. Rationalization of public policy with regard to the provision of public services at large finally fits in well with the current need for austerity and cost-cutting to constrain public finances against the backdrop of the global financial crisis.

4

Public services and the rules on competition and state aid

4.1 Introduction

Within the system of the EU Treaties, the rules on competition form the counterpoint to the free movement rules that I have discussed in the preceding chapter. Whereas the free movement rules aim to constrain the Member States from discriminatory action that divides national markets within the EU by obstructing market access, the competition rules aim to prevent private actors from distorting competition in various ways: by forming cartels, by abusing dominant positions, or by mergers creating such positions.

Albeit preceded by competition rules in the ECSC Treaty on coal and steel, inclusion of such rules addressing private parties at large in what was at the outset simply an international agreement – the 1957 Rome Treaty – was noteworthy.[1] The objective in doing so was to ensure that private actors did not resurrect the barriers that the Member States would have levelled based on the free movement provisions. In this sense the two sets of rules are complementary.[2] From early on in the life of the EU, then the Community, the competition rules have played a significant role. The state aid rules, however, have come to fruition only since the late 1990s. They take an intermediate position with regard to competition and free movement: they are aimed at the Member States, prohibiting discriminatory advantages from being bestowed on private parties (or more precisely as we shall see: undertakings) who are therefore affected indirectly.

Both for the competition rules on antitrust (the prohibitions on cartels and on dominance abuse) and mergers, and as regards the state aid rules, the concept of undertaking is key: undertakings are the addressee of the competition rules and undertakings are the beneficiaries of state aid. Other types of entity are not relevant in terms of these rules. As is frequently the case in EU

[1] The 1951 Treaty on the European Coal and Steel Community (ECSC) included not only sectoral antitrust and abuse of dominance provisions but also merger control powers to ensure that concentrations of economic power in what were perceived as potential war industries were checked. The EU eventually obtained merger powers only in 1989.

[2] Cf. the Spaak report, Comité intergouvernemental creé par la Conférence de Messine, *Rapport des Chefs de délégation aux Ministres des Affaires étrangères* (Brussels, 1956), p. 16.

law, a functional definition of the concept of undertaking is used to avoid reliance on categories established in national law and the difficulties caused by possible inconsistencies between or even within the legal systems of the Member States. This brings me back to public services: the competition and state aid rules are only relevant to public services to the extent that they are being provided by undertakings. Regarding welfare services this will frequently not be the case, whereas in the case of the utilities this will almost always be so. Hence what we find here mirrors the situation found with respect to free movement, which was frequently relevant to welfare services, but seldom so for the utilities.

In this chapter I want to discuss both the system of the competition and state aid rules, and the exceptions that are relevant to public services. Hence I will give a concise description of the various instruments in order to facilitate understanding of the issues with reference to the case law on public services. In addition, there are three secondary themes that I want to address in this chapter:

- Citizenship does not play a role with regard to competition and state aid: the consumer interest, however, does – especially under the competition rules. Whether or not the concepts of the citizen as found in free movement and the consumer under the competition rules can be linked in terms of EU law or in a more general conceptual sense is one of the questions that I will try to address.
- Another concept that I will study more closely is that of market failure, which is relevant primarily (but no longer exclusively) to state aid. Is the existence of market failure a condition for reliance on the exception for services of general economic interest (SGEI)? This will be linked to the next topic.
- Both in relation to competition and in relation to state aid I will look at the application of the SGEI concept, which has been elaborated especially with regard to state aid and compensation for public service obligations. In this context universal service will be a significant issue.

The organization of this chapter is as follows. To set the scene I will briefly discuss the competition rules in the context of the concept of the mixed economic constitution that I have already introduced in Chapter 2 above. Next I will discuss the concept of undertaking, especially with regard to welfare services, because this is the most complex category. Following this I will discuss the competition rules, with a focus on antitrust. Then I will look at state aid, in particular with regard to the concept of compensation for public service obligations and the application of SGEI in this context. Finally, I will draw some conclusions from the above. This will wrap up the discussion of the primary EU law on public services. In the next two chapters I will look at the secondary rules.

4.2 Competition, public services and the economic constitution

Complementarity between competition and free movement

I have mentioned in the introduction how the framers of the Rome Treaty intended the free movement and competition rules to be complementary. Both were designed to ensure the proper functioning of the internal market. Thus in the words of the celebrated *Consten* case (1966) regarding a vertical distribution agreement on consumer electronics:

> [A]n agreement between producer and distributor which might tend to restore the national divisions in trade between Member States might be such as to frustrate the most fundamental objections of the Community. The Treaty, whose preamble and content aim at abolishing the barriers between states, and which in several provisions gives evidence of a stern attitude with regard to their reappearance, could not allow undertakings to reconstruct such barriers. Article 85(1) [now Article 101(1) TFEU] is designed to pursue this aim, even in the case of agreements between undertakings placed at different levels in the economic process.[3]

Today, vertical agreements are no longer seen as particularly harmful in EU competition law and have little bearing on public services. However, the suggestion that the competition rules serve the internal market is still relevant. It is at odds with two competing and, in some important ways, contrasting schools of thought on antitrust: Ordoliberalism and Chicago school neo-liberalism.

Ordoliberalism, neo-liberalism and the economic constitution

The first (historically) is that of Ordoliberalism, a German school of law and economics originating in Freiburg in the 1930s, which assigned a key role to competition policy as a guarantor of economic freedom.[4] In the case of Ordoliberalism, protecting the competitive process as an objective of competition policy is supplemented by protecting competitors who have a 'right' to compete in the marketplace. In addition, competition law serves to keep politics out of the marketplace. The Ordoliberals saw the original EC Treaty as an ideal economic constitution because it was limited to rules of market governance with no discernible role for the political process. Even better in their view was that, due to the EU law doctrines of supremacy and direct effect, the European economic constitution could trump the compromised (because politicized)

[3] Joined cases 56 and 58–64 *Établissements Consten S.à.R.L. and Grundig-Verkaufs-GmbH* v. *Commission* [1966] ECR English special edition 299. Cf. more recently the Commission Notice – Guidelines on vertical restraints, OJ 2010, C130/1, para. 7.

[4] Cf. D. Gerber, 'Constitutionalising the economy: German neo-liberalism, competition law and the "new" Europe', *American Journal of Comparative Law*, 42 (1994), 24–84. D. J. Gerber, *Law and competition in twentieth century Europe: Protecting Prometheus* (Oxford University Press, 1998).

national constitutional arrangements. (Interestingly this view of the role of EU law is shared by critics on the left, such as Fritz Scharpf, but valued strongly negatively.)[5]

The second school is that of neo-liberalism, also known as the Chicago school of law and economics, which originated in the 1960s.[6] This school of thought is very critical of antitrust as being prone to promoting inefficiencies and quaint ideas of competition. It pioneered new economic insights into the functioning of markets, such as the generally benevolent nature of vertical restraints and various commercial practices such as price discrimination and product differentiation, and the unlikelihood of the occurrence of anticompetitive excessive pricing, predatory pricing and bundling. To the extent that competition policy serves a purpose in Chicago school terms, it is that of promoting a single variable: consumer welfare.

Both schools have had an (arguably profound) impact on EU competition policy but neither has ultimately prevailed.

- First, the link between competition policy and the internal market has been emphasized by the 2007 Lisbon Treaty, notably the text of Article 3(1)b TFEU and that of Protocol 27, both of which affirm the importance of this relationship. Only the internal market is an objective of European integration, not competition policy per se.
- Second, the Treaty has been expanded with such a range of policies – industrial policy, social policy and economic policy coordination, to name just a few contentious examples – that it is now impossible to see it as an Ordoliberal constitution: if anything it is the constitution of a mixed economy (see further Chapter 2).

Third, whereas the Commission and the General Court have tried applying the theory that only the consumer interest determines the scope of competition policy in practice, as we will see below the CJEU has differed forcefully. I will now move on to look more closely at the view of the ultimate arbiter of EU law: the CJEU.

The Court's perspective on the objectives of EU competition law

Two quotations from the case law may serve to illustrate the Court's views. Thus in response to a preliminary reference in *T-Mobile* (2009) the CJEU stated

> Article 81 EC [now Article 101 TFEU], like the other competition rules of the Treaty, is designed to protect not only the immediate interests of individual competitors or consumers but also to protect the structure of the market and thus competition as such.

[5] F. W. Scharpf, *Community and autonomy: Institutions, policies and legitimacy in multilevel Europe* (Campus, Frankfurt am Main, 2010).

[6] R. H. Bork, *The antitrust paradox: A policy at war with itself* (Basic Books, Chicago, 1978).

> Therefore . . . in order to find that a concerted practice has an anti-competitive object, there does not need to be a direct link between that practice and consumer prices.[7]

Three months later in its 2009 *GlaxoSmithKline* case the CJEU comprehensively overruled both the Commission and the General Court, stating with regard to the application of Article 101(1) TFEU:

> First of all, there is nothing in that provision to indicate that only those agreements which deprive consumers of certain advantages may have an anti-competitive object. Secondly, it must be borne in mind that the Court has held that, like other competition rules laid down in the Treaty, Article 81 EC [now Article 101 TFEU] aims to protect not only the interests of competitors or of consumers, but also the structure of the market and, in so doing, competition as such. Consequently, for a finding that an agreement has an anti-competitive object, it is not necessary that final consumers be deprived of the advantages of effective competition in terms of supply or price.[8]

The interests of competitors, market structure and competition as such are therefore of equal importance to EU competition policy, as are the direct effects on consumers. In addition, it is possible to pursue not only efficiency objectives but also equity goals under the exceptions to competition policy, notably that on SGEI (as I will argue, although some others would claim the same for Article 101(1) and 101(3) TFEU as well, as we will see below), which would have been an anathema to both the Ordoliberal and the Chicago school.[9] Finally, since the Lisbon Treaty came into force in 2009 the purpose of the competition rules is now more than ever linked to the internal market.[10] The Court expressed this clearly in the 2011 *TeliaSonera* case on dominance abuse (price squeeze) in broadband markets:

> [I]t must be observed at the outset that Article 3(3) TEU states that the European Union is to establish an internal market, which, in accordance with Protocol No 27 on the internal market and competition, annexed to the Treaty of Lisbon . . ., is to include a system ensuring that competition is not distorted.

7 Case C-8/08 *T-Mobile Netherlands BV, KPN Mobile NV, Orange Nederland NV and Vodafone Libertel NV* v. *Raad van bestuur van de Nederlandse Mededingingsautoriteit* [2009] ECR I-4529, paras. 38–9.

8 Joined cases C-501/06 P, C-513/06 P, C-515/06 P and C-519/06 P *GlaxoSmithKline Services Unlimited* v. *Commission and Commission* v. *GlaxoSmithKline Services Unlimited and European Association of Euro Pharmaceutical Companies (EAEPC)* v. *Commission and Asociación de exportadores españoles de productos farmacéuticos (Aseprofar)* v. *Commission* [2009] ECR I-9291, para. 63; cf. Case C-8/08 *T-Mobile*, above n. 7, para. 38.

9 It also appears to have been overlooked by Fritz Scharpf. Cf. J. Baquero Cruz, 'Social services of general interest and the state aid rules', in U. Neergaard et al. (eds.), *Social services of general interest in the EU* (TMC Asser Press, The Hague, 2013), 287–313.

10 For an early example with regard to the link between effective competition and the objective of attaining the internal market, see Case 26/76 *Metro SB-Großmärkte GmbH & Co. KG* v. *Commission* [1977] ECR 1875, para. 20.

> Article 102 TFEU is one of the competition rules referred to in Article 3(1)(b) TFEU which are necessary for the functioning of that internal market.
>
> The function of those rules is precisely to prevent competition from being distorted to the detriment of the public interest, individual undertakings and consumers, thereby ensuring the well-being of the European Union.[11]

The view of the Court is therefore clear: there is a range of objectives to EU competition policy and consumer welfare is only one among others.

Competition, state aid and the mixed economic constitution

This is not to say that a constitutional perspective on competition law is impossible, provided that this takes into account the fact that the economic constitution of the EU is the constitution of a mixed economy. This raises issues on internal tension and compatibility and/or consistency that must be resolved not just in theory but also in practice on a case-by-case basis. Whether the categories that I have identified in the introduction – market failure, universality and the consumer interest – play a key role here remains to be seen. As far as the role of public services in this context is concerned, I refer to what I have said in the first two chapters on the strategic compromise whereby the 'liberal' Member States obtained the four freedoms and the competition rules, and the 'statist' Member States obtained exceptions to the above and special provisions for public enterprises, state monopolies and SGEI – although in practice all Member States rely on both types of rules. As we will see, in particular, the rules governing SGEI are relevant to public services in the context of competition and state aid law.

The organizational structure of competition and state aid policy

I will make just a few remarks here on the organizational arrangements of EU competition law and state aid policy. Although the antitrust prohibitions have always been considered to be directly effective so they could be invoked by interested parties before national courts, the Commission long had a monopoly on the application of the efficiency exception provided for in Article 101(3) TFEU. This clogged the system and frustrated direct effect, problems which were only partially addressed by means of tools like block exemptions for certain categories of agreements.[12] These drawbacks were remedied by an ambitious decentralization scheme that came into force in 2004. First, all

[11] Case C-52/09 *Konkurrensverket* v. *TeliaSonera Sverige AB* [2011] ECR I-527, paras. 19–20. Cf. U. Neergaard, 'The concept of SSGI and the asymmetries between free movement and competition law', in Neergaard et al., above n. 9, 205–44.

[12] Such as Commission Regulation 330/2010 of 20 April 2010 on the application of Article 101(3) of the Treaty on the Functioning of the European Union to categories of vertical agreements and concerted practices, OJ 2010, L102/1; Commission Regulation (EU) No 461/2010 of 27 May 2010 on the application of Article 101(3) of the Treaty on the Functioning of the

Member States were required to have created national competition authorities (NCAs) that could apply Articles 101 and 102 TFEU to cases with an appreciable effect on competition and an effect on trade between the Member States on their national territory. Second, direct application of Article 101(3) TFEU was introduced – so the parties affected could make their own assessment. Third, the Commission was given certain coordinating powers – mainly the right to claim any competition case with an EU dimension, even where it was already under investigation by an NCA.[13] Finally, a network of NCAs was created, coordinated by the European Commission. The justification behind this modernization was that the rules were now known widely enough to make direct application possible. While this argument was largely spurious (the interpretations change, and numerous issues remain to be clarified), the new system has so far worked reasonably well.

State aid enforcement lags one generation behind antitrust in this respect. Although national courts can make a finding that state aid exists, only the European Commission (with very minor exceptions) can make a finding that the aid involved is nevertheless compatible with the internal market. Moreover, compared to the competition policy of the EU, in my view its State aid policy remains under-theorized.[14] This may in large part be due to the fact that state aid law exists mainly at EU level and only in Europe: there is no Chicago school of state aid theory because there is no state aid control in the US. This does not mean that general economic theories do not apply here, but mainly that they have scarcely been developed with respect to this particular application. More recently, however, in the context of state aid control the concept of market failure is gaining traction.

4.3 Public services and the concept of undertaking

The general rule

The main variable to determine whether or not the competition and state aid rules apply is the concept of undertaking. As I have already mentioned in the introduction, this is a functional concept: hence the definitions under national law are not decisive in this regard. With regard to the production of goods,

European Union to categories of vertical agreements and concerted practices in the motor vehicle sector, OJ 2010, L129/52.

13 Council Regulation (EC) No 1/2003 of 16 December 2002 on the implementation of the rules on competition laid down in Articles 81 and 82 of the Treaty, OJ 2003, L1/1.

14 A positive change in this respect has been made by the appearance of the *European State Aid Law Quarterly* since 2002. Legal resources as such are not scarce: cf. an introduction in P. Nicolaides, M. Kekelekis and M. Kleis, *State aid and practice in the European Community: Principles and practice*, 2nd edn (Kluwer, Alphen aan den Rijn, 2008); a comprehensive overview in L. Hancher, T. Ottervanger and P. J. Slot (eds.), *EU state aids*, 4th edn (Sweet & Maxwell, London, 2012); and more selective contributions such as E. Szyszczak (ed.), *Research handbook on European state aid law* (Edward Elgar, Cheltenham, 2011). An exception to the relative scarcity of theory is F. de Cecco, *State aid and the European economic constitution* (Hart Publishing, Oxford, 2013).

defining undertakings has rarely been an issue, but regarding services – which is evidently more central to our topic of public services – this question has been more complex. The leading cases remain *Höfner* (1991) on job placement services – then considered a public service in Germany – and *Glöckner* (2001) which concerned ambulance services, for which likewise the existence of an SGEI had been claimed. In *Höfner* the Court stated:

> It must be observed, in the context of competition law, first that the concept of an undertaking encompasses every entity engaged in an economic activity, regardless of the legal status of the entity and the way in which it is financed and, secondly, that employment procurement is an economic activity.

Significantly the Court added the following:

> The fact that employment procurement activities are normally entrusted to public agencies cannot affect the economic nature of such activities. Employment procurement has not always been, and is not necessarily, carried out by public entities.[15]

In the *Glöckner* case (ten years after *Höfner*) the definition of undertaking was spelled out as follows:

> [T]he concept of an undertaking, in the context of competition law, covers any entity engaged in an economic activity, regardless of the legal status of the entity or the way in which it is financed.

Moreover the Court added:

> Any activity consisting in offering goods and services on a given market is an economic activity.[16]

This meant that entities providing ambulance services, where the provision of services in a market was already a given, constituted undertakings. Effectively the test could be read as expressing a general rule that where services are actually or potentially provided in competition the entities involved are undertakings, and the competition rules are therefore applicable. However, at the same time the assessment can differ over time and between different Member States.

[15] Case C-41/90 *Klaus Höfner and Fritz Elser* v. *Macrotron GmbH* [1991] ECR I-1979, paras. 21–2. The authorities were held to have infringed Article 106(1) TFEU if they had granted an SGEI to an undertaking that was manifestly unable to meet demand, as appeared to be the case.

[16] Case C-475/99 *Firma Ambulanz Glöckner* v. *Landkreis Südwestpfalz* [2001] ECR I-8089, para. 35, with reference to Joined Cases C-180/98 to C-184/98 *Pavel Pavlov et al.* v. *Stichting Pensioenfonds Medische Specialisten* [2000] ECR I-6451, paras. 74–5 (with regard to an occupational pension fund). Case C-218/00 *Cisal di Battistello Venanzio & C. Sas* v. *Istituto nazionale per l'assicurazione contro gli infortuni sul lavoro (INAIL)* [2002] ECR I-691, para. 23 (concerning insurance against accidents at work), and Joined cases T-231/06 and T-237/06 *The Netherlands and Nederlandse Omroep Stichting (NOS)* v. *Commission* [2010] ECR II-5993, paras. 92–5 (with regard to public service broadcasting).

The broad sweep of this approach to defining an undertaking can be contrasted with the Commission's more recent (2012) approach in its Communication on compensation under the state aid rules to the question whether assigning an SGEI – that is to say, after determining the status of an entity as an undertaking – is justifiable. Here it does consider whether an activity is already provided or could be provided satisfactorily and under conditions including price, quality, continuity and access to services – consistent with the public interest – by undertakings operating under normal market conditions.[17] However, the test applied is a weak one based on manifest disproportionality. (The example given in the Communication is the broadband sector, which we will take up in the section on state aid at the end of this chapter.)

Read in conjunction with the above-mentioned assessment of the existence of an SGEI in the context of market provision, this would mean that the rule on whether an undertaking is involved is strict and favours application of EU law, whereas the exception for SGEI which lets undertakings back off the hook is wide and tolerates national peculiarities to a greater degree (within the relatively mild constraints of a manifest disproportionality test).

Providing versus purchasing services

The Commission in its above-mentioned 2012 Communication added that the for-profit or not-for-profit status is not decisive. Non-profit organizations that are active in a market are undertakings too:

> [T]he application of the State aid rules as such does not depend on whether the entity is set up to generate profits. Based on the case-law of the Court of Justice and the General Court, non-profit entities can offer goods and services on a market too.[18]

This line can be contrasted with two healthcare cases: the *AOK* case (2004) on German sickness funds,[19] and the *FENIN* case (2006) on the purchasing activities of Spanish national health service providers.[20] Both types of entity

[17] Communication from the Commission on the application of the European Union state aid rules to compensation granted for the provision of services of general economic interest, OJ 2012, C8/4, para. 48, with reference to Case C-205/99 *Asociación Profesional de Empresas Navieras de Líneas Regulares (Analir) et al.* v. *Administración General del Estado* [2001] ECR I-1271, para. 71 (with regard to public service obligations and maritime cabotage). Cf. Draft Commission Notice on the notion of state aid pursaunt to Article 107(1) TFEU (March 2014).

[18] SGEI compensation Communication, above n. 17, para. 9. Cf. Case C-49/07 *Motosykletistiki Omospondia Ellados NPID (MOTOE)* v. *Elliniko Dimosio* [2008] ECR I-4863.

[19] Joined cases C-264/01, C-306/01, C-354/01 and C-355/01 *AOK Bundesverband et al.* v. *Ichthyol-Gesellschaft Cordes, Hermani & Co., Mundipharma GmbH, Gödecke GmbH and Intersan, Institut für pharmazeutische und klinische Forschung GmbH* [2004] ECR I-2493.

[20] Case C-205/03 P *Federación Española de Empresas de Tecnología Sanitaria (FENIN)* v. *Commission* [2006] ECR I-6295.

were active in markets but were nevertheless not held to be undertakings for purposes of the competition rules. An (in my view) all too subtle difference in offering goods and services in a market (unambiguously defined as an economic activity) and purchasing goods and services (possibly not or not necessarily an economic activity) appears to be responsible for this approach. It also results in a divergence from the way economic activity is defined in the context of the free movement rules, which is remuneration based and does not revolve around offering or receiving a service.[21]

A possible defence of the more restrictive view under the competition rules that I have not yet come across could be that buying power is inherently less anticompetitive than selling power, in particular where the resulting benefits are passed on to consumers.[22] Also buying power may play a role as countervailing market power to neutralize the effects of selling power.[23] Both of these aspects may plead in favour of a lenient approach to buying power, but in my view not necessarily for leaving it outside the scope of the competition rules because additionally the likelihood of passing on benefits and/or compensating for selling power must be examined. This I believe would require a competition analysis and therefore purchasing should be seen as an economic activity even if these aspects are taken into account.

In the document already cited, the Commission suggests that the classification of an entity as an undertaking is always relative to a specific activity, meaning that an entity carrying out economic and non-economic activities will be treated as an undertaking only with regard to the former and not to the latter.[24] It seems that in the two above-mentioned cases, *AOK* and *FENIN*, this approach (separating economic and non-economic activities) might have provided a solution more conformative with the general approach to competition

21 Joined cases 286/82 and 26/83 *Graziana Luisi and Giuseppe Carbone* v. *Ministero del Tesoro* [1984] ECR 377. Cf. a detailed comparison between the relevant aspects of the free movement and competition law regimes in O. Odudu, 'Economic activity as a limit to Community law', in C. Barnard and O. Odudu (eds.), *The outer limits of European Union law* (Hart Publishing, Oxford, 2009), 225–43. The Commission acknowledges the discrepancy in its Communication (2012), above, n. 17, para. 15: 'In the absence of a definition of economic activity in the Treaties, the case-law appears to offer different criteria for the application of internal market rules and for the application of competition law.'

22 A. Ezrachi and K. de Jong, 'Buyer power, private labels and the welfare consequences of quality erosion', *European Competition Law Review* 33 (2012), 45–50.

23 Cf. Communication from the Commission – Guidance on the Commission's enforcement priorities in applying Article 82 of the EC Treaty to abusive exclusionary conduct by dominant undertakings, OJ 2009, C45/7, para. 18; Guidelines on the assessment of horizontal mergers under the Council Regulation on the control of concentrations between undertakings, OJ 2004, C31/5, paras. 64–7. Cf. the promotion of an effects-based and consumer-interest-oriented approach by the academic economist advising the Commission: Report by the EAGCP (antitrust subgroup), *An economic approach to Article 82*, July 2005.

24 SGEI compensation Communication, above n. 17, para. 9. Examples are Case T-155/04 *SELEX Sistemi Integrati SpA* v. *Commission* [2006] ECR II-4797; and Case C-81/01 P *Aéroports de Paris* v. *Commission* [2002] ECR I-9297. Cf. V. Hatzopoulos, *Regulating services in the European Union* (Oxford University Press, 2012).

law. In line with the 2012 Communication on compensation and state aid, below I will go into more detail on a limited number of welfare sectors: social security, education and healthcare.[25]

Social security and solidarity

For social security, the definition of an undertaking is based on the question whether it is the solidarity principle or instead an economic motive that is decisive for the purposes of a particular scheme. Solidarity is a possible (equity-based) explanation for regulation that is an alternative to an (efficiency-based) economic motivation. Both types can be subsumed under the concept of market failure (discussed in Chapter 1.5), depending on whether a wide (efficiency and equity) or a narrow (just efficiency) definition of market failure is used.[26] It is important to note that while equity arguments are not generally a valid motivation for claiming an exception to the competition rules (with the notable exception of SGEI), they can form a valid reason why the competition rules are not applicable at all. The principle of solidarity is somewhat elusive in that the risks that are insured against, such as old age, disability and ill health, are frequently exactly the same as those of economic schemes. It is thus not the risk involved that is decisive but the way the provision of the service involved is funded and structured.

We have seen the Commission's position, quoted at the beginning of the previous section, regarding the neutrality with regard to the for-profit or non-profit status of an entity. However, in the social security context, the for-profit or non-profit status is an important factor alongside the social function of a scheme and the question whether affiliation is compulsory or not. In the pension insurance case *Poucet* (1993) the Court ruled:

> The principle of solidarity is, in the sickness and maternity scheme, embodied in the fact that the scheme is financed by contributions proportional to the income from the occupation and to the retirement pensions of the persons making them . . . Solidarity entails the redistribution of income between those who are better off and those who, in view of their resources and state of health, would be deprived of the necessary social cover.
>
> In the old-age insurance scheme, solidarity is embodied in the fact that the contributions paid by active workers serve to finance the pensions of retired workers. It is also reflected by the grant of pension rights where no contributions have been made and of pension rights that are not proportional to the contributions paid.

[25] The Draft Notice on the notion of State aid (above n. 17) covers the same ground but also includes infrastructure. Cf. Chapter 2 of the present volume.

[26] Cf. N. Boeger, 'Solidarity and EC competition law', *European Law Review*, 32 (2007), 319–40; more broadly, T. Prosser, 'Regulation and social solidarity', *Journal of Law and Society*, 33 (2006) 364–87. Earlier A. Winterstein, 'Nailing the jellyfish: Social security and competition law', (1999) *European Competition Law Review*, 19 (1999), 324–33.

And

> It follows that the social security schemes, as described, are based on a system of compulsory contribution, which is indispensable for application of the principle of solidarity and the financial equilibrium of those schemes.[27]

Apart from the non-profit status, therefore, compulsory affiliation and an exclusively social function are relevant, as well as whether benefits are independent from, and not proportionate to, the individual contributions of the participants,[28] and whether the scheme is supervised by the state. Whether solidarity is involved depends especially on whether the risk profile or personal characteristics of the person insured are taken into account.[29] Thus in *Albany* (1999) the Court held:

> [O]peration of the sectoral pension fund is based on the principle of solidarity. Such solidarity is reflected by the obligation to accept all workers without a prior medical examination, the continuing accrual of pension rights despite exemption from contributions in the event of incapacity for work, the discharge by the fund of arrears of contributions due from an employer in the event of the latter's insolvency and by the indexing of the amount of the pensions in order to maintain their value. The principle of solidarity is also apparent from the absence of any equivalence, for individuals, between the contribution paid, which is an average contribution not linked to risks, and pension rights, which are determined by reference to an average salary. Such solidarity makes compulsory affiliation to the supplementary pension scheme essential. Otherwise, if 'good' risks left the scheme, the ensuing downward spiral would jeopardise its financial equilibrium.[30]

Nevertheless, in this case the Court ultimately held that the supplementary pension funds involved were undertakings because it turned out that they were at least in some respects in competition with private insurance companies. In my view therefore it is ultimately this question, whether the services compete or not ('are provided in competition') that decides the score. The Court, however, has not always taken this view, as is illustrated in two cases that will be discussed in more detail below. In *AOK* (2004), already mentioned above, the existence of a 'degree of competition' as regards prices – but not benefits – that did lead to actual switching behaviour of customers was not held to be decisive and the

[27] Joined cases C-159/91 and C-160/91 *Christian Poucet* v. *Assurances Générales de France and Caisse Mutuelle Régionale du Languedoc-Roussillon* [1993] ECR I-637, paras. 10, 11 and 13.

[28] Cf. with regard to compulsory affiliation to supplementary sectoral pension funds: Case C-67/96 *Albany International BV* v. *Stichting Bedrijfspensioenfonds Textielindustrie* [1999] ECR I-5751; Joined cases C-115/97, C-116/97 and C-117/97 *Brentjens' Handelsonderneming BV* v. *Stichting Bedrijfspensioenfonds voor de Handel in Bouwmaterialen* [1999] ECR I-6025; and Case C-219/97 *Maatschappij Drijvende Bokken BV* v. *Stichting Pensioenfonds voor de Vervoer- en Havenbedrijven* [1999] ECR I-6121.

[29] Cf. Case C-437/09 *AG2R Prévoyance* v. *Beaudout Père et Fils SARL* [2011] ECR I-973 (supplementary health insurance), paras. 47–52.

[30] Case C-67/96 *Albany*, above n. 28, para. 75.

health insurance funds were deemed not to be undertakings.[31] In *FENIN* (2006) the providers of medical devices were in competition, so the goods concerned were bought in a market, but the purchasers themselves were not active in a market regarding their primary activity as providers of national health services.[32] Whether this case law reflects a subtle use of meaningful criteria (such as price competition not competition on benefits; purchasing not providing services) or merely a convenient basis for distinguishing difficult individual cases, remains an open question.

Economic schemes, by contrast, are deemed to be likely to be for-profit, have optional membership, and are based on a link between entitlements and contributions.[33] In a particular case the balance of the factors listed above is used to determine whether or not an economic activity and therefore an undertaking is involved. However, in those cases where the Court does not find there is sufficient solidarity to exclude application of the concept of undertaking it may still accept that there is sufficient solidarity involved to successfully invoke the applicability of the SGEI exception in Article 106(2) TFEU.[34] A strict application of its functional criterion of undertaking and therefore of the limits of EU law (the 'rule') is therefore combined with a liberal interpretation of the exceptions: this is a theme that is present throughout EU law but has been remarked upon especially with regard to the competition rules.[35] By applying exceptions instead of ruling activities out of bounds, the authorities involved evidently gain leverage over the undertakings/entities involved. The drawback involved is that, as a result of this approach, rules tend not to be self-executing and enforcement issues (related to bottlenecks and effectiveness) arise.

Healthcare

With regard to the definition of the concept of undertaking, for healthcare the *FENIN* (2006) exception that I have already mentioned is made. Concerning national health services that are tax financed and based on the principle of solidarity, the Commission holds the view that 'the relevant organisations do not act as undertakings'.[36] This position does not provide much clarity as to who the relevant organizations are – would healthcare providers competing

31 Joined cases C-264/01, C-306/01, C-354/01 and C-355/01 *AOK*, above n. 19.

32 Case C-205/03 *FENIN*, above n. 20.

33 Cf. SGEI compensation Communication, above n. 17, paras. 17–20.

34 Cf. the cases discussed above and J. W. van de Gronden and W. Sauter, 'Taking the temperature: EU competition law and health care', *Legal Issues of Economic Integration*, 38 (2011), 213–41.

35 Cf. O. Odudu, above n. 21; O. Odudu, *The boundaries of EC competition law: The scope of Article 81* (Oxford University Press, 2006); more generally cf. T. Prosser, *The limits of competition law: Markets and public services* (Oxford University Press, 2005). W. Sauter and H. Schepel, *State and market in European Union law: The public and private spheres of the internal market before the EU Courts* (Cambridge University Press, 2009).

36 SGEI compensation Communication, above n. 17, para. 22.

with each other and/or with private operators count as being excluded?[37] Moreover:

> Where that structure exists [a national health service], even activities that in themselves could be of an economic nature, but are carried out merely for the purpose of providing another non-economic service, are not of an economic nature. An organisation that purchases goods – even in large quantities – for the purpose of offering a non-economic service does not act as an undertaking simply because it is a purchaser in a given market.[38]

Surely, purchasing goods in a market is an economic activity with an impact on competition, even if the buyer involved is a monopsonist. As regards sickness funds, in *AOK* (2004) the decisive factor was that their benefits were defined by law and not the subject of competition, although they did compete on other parameters:

> The latitude available to the sickness funds when setting the contribution rate and their freedom to engage in some competition with one another in order to attract members does not call this analysis into question. As is apparent from the observations submitted to the Court, the legislature introduced an element of competition with regard to contributions in order to encourage the sickness funds to operate in accordance with principles of sound management, that is to say in the most effective and least costly manner possible, in the interests of the proper functioning of the German social security system. Pursuit of that objective does not in any way change the nature of the sickness funds' activity.[39]

Hence some competition as a form of cost-control was non-competition from a perspective of competition law. On the purchasing side the Court's position on the definition of undertaking therefore looks contestable. On the other hand, where healthcare services are provided in competition, their public non-profit status does not protect them from being seen as undertakings. Private doctors, even individually, are regarded as undertakings.[40] Hence it appears that healthcare providers are categorized between two extremes depending on the nature of their system as tax (and solidarity) or insurance (and competition) based even while in practice most national systems are in fact to some degree a mixture of the two.

Education

Here the Court has ruled that public education financed mainly by public funds is not an economic activity as it is not provided for remuneration but the

[37] Cf. O. Odudu, 'Are state-owned health-care providers undertakings subject to competition law?' *European Competition Law Review*, 32 (2011), 231–41.
[38] SGEI compensation Communication, above n. 17, para. 23.
[39] Joined cases C-264/01, C-306/01, C-354/01 and C-355/01 *AOK*, above n. 19, para. 56.
[40] Joined Cases C-180/98 to C-184/98 *Pavlov*, above n. 16.

fulfilment of a social, cultural and educational public task.[41] Where education is classified as not constituting an economic activity this automatically means no undertakings are involved and the competition rules do not apply. However, the definition of economic activities has so far not come up specifically with regard to the applicability of the competition rules to education. Instead this classification issue has frequently come up in the financing disputes already discussed in Chapter 3 where it primarily regards the question whether remuneration is involved and the freedom to provide or purchase services is affected.

> The Court has thus excluded from the definition of services within the meaning of Article 50 EC [now Article 57 TFEU] EC courses offered by certain establishments forming part of a system of public education financed, entirely or mainly, by public funds. The Court has made clear that, by establishing and maintaining such a system of public education, funded as a general rule from the public purse and not by pupils or their parents, the State was not seeking to engage in gainful activity, but was fulfilling its duties towards its own population in the social, cultural and educational fields.
>
> However, the Court has held that courses offered by educational establishments essentially financed by private funds, in particular by students and their parents, constitute services within the meaning of Article 50 EC [now Article 57 TFEU], since the aim of those establishments is to offer a service for remuneration.[42]

Even if pupils or parents pay tuition or enrolment fees that contribute to operating costs these are likely to cover only a fraction of the costs of the service. Hence they are not considered to be remuneration in the sense of the Treaties. Commercial provision of higher education does involve an economic activity that is provided in competition if it is financed entirely by students and if competing private organizations exist. This appears to be a necessary specification because if public education was said to be in competition with private schools the question of whether the former was not after all provided by undertakings would raise its head.

Competition in education and the application (or applicability) of the competition rules in this sector is a topic that is heating up academically, and in which national competition authorities have started taking an interest.[43] However, at the time of writing there are no significant EU-level cases to report or discuss. I will therefore now move on from the limits of competition law based on the concept of undertaking, to the substantive rules and their

[41] Case C-318/05 *Commission* v. *Germany* [2007] ECR I-6957; SGEI compensation Communication, above n. 17, paras. 26–8.

[42] Case C-56/09 *Emiliano Zanotti* v. *Agenzia delle Entrate – Ufficio Roma 2* [2010] ECR I-4517, paras. 31–2. Cf. Case 263/86 *Belgium* v. *René Humbel and Marie-Thérèse Edel* [1988] ECR 5365, paras. 18–19.

[43] Cf. A. Gideon, 'Higher education institutions and EU competition law', *Competition Law Review*, 8 (2012), 169–84; J. P. Myklebust and B. O'Malley, 'Netherlands: Dawn raids over "illegal" tuition fees', *University World News* issue 188, 7 September 2011.

application with regard to public services. Following that, I will turn to look at the same themes with regard to state aid.

4.4 The competition rules applied to public services

Three sets of rules

As before, I will continue to make a distinction between the competition rules and the rules on state aid. The rules on competition themselves can be divided into three parts that regard respectively: anticompetitive practices (formerly usually called anticompetitive agreements); abuse of a dominant position; and mergers.[44] Whereas both anticompetitive practices that have an appreciable effect on trade and competition and dominance abuse are prohibited as such, mergers above a quantitative threshold establishing their EU dimension are only vetted to see whether they will result in a dominant position. If that risk is established, such mergers are either blocked or, more frequently, modified to address the concerns raised. Mergers below the threshold may be vetted at national level or not at all. In all three cases a form of market power at the expense of other market participants – suppliers, competitors or consumers – is involved. As was discussed above, this system was originally administered mainly by the European Commission, but (with the exception of merger control) has now largely been decentralized to national competition authorities and private enforcement in national courts.

Below I shall limit myself to discussing some of the main applications of competition law to public services, so I will not give a full account of the functioning of the system of competition law with its complex interplay of rules and exceptions.[45] The relevance of the EU competition rules evidently increases to the extent that there is competition and/or scope for competition. However, as we have seen above, welfare services are often excluded because they are not deemed to be provided by undertakings. At the same time, the utilities, which generally are provided by what are indisputably undertakings, are often subject to sectoral competition rules (which are the result of harmonization legislation and are discussed in Chapter 6) that are more stringent – but especially more predictable – than the general competition rules which are the subject of the present chapter. This means that despite the political commotion about the application of competition law to public services, in actual practice this occurs relatively rarely, and generally with a limited impact outside the sector at hand.

I will first discuss the public interest and the consumer interest in competition law. Next I will look at a number of competition cases involving public services.

44 Cf. G. Monti, *EC competition law* (Cambridge University Press, 2007); J. Faull and A. Nikpay, *The EC law of competition*, 3rd edn (Oxford University Press, 2014).

45 Cf. for a sectoral example van de Gronden and Sauter, above n. 34, 213; W. Sauter, 'The impact of EU competition law on national healthcare systems', *European Law Review*, 38 (2013), 456–78.

The public interest and EU competition law

Competition law was not originally designed with the public interest as a ground for exceptions. Effectively it is not included in the text of the relevant provisions of EU law (aside from the exception for SGEI in Article 106(2) TFEU discussed below). The admissible exceptions to the competition rules themselves are in principle efficiency – not equity – based. An important example is the 'efficiency defence' that has now been extended to include dominance abuse as well as anticompetitive practices and mergers.[46] This system, which has been transplanted from Article 101(3) TFEU, checks whether the economic benefits claimed: (i) exist; (ii) are shared fairly with consumers; (iii) are specific to the restriction involved (necessary); and (iv) do not eliminate competition entirely (although potential competition may suffice). The benefits that are claimed at the level of undertakings and consumers are efficiency based.

Legitimate public interests that are not efficiency but equity based can be a reason to keep the anticompetitive practices concerned outside the scope of the competition rules altogether, even where undertakings are concerned. The most well-known example is the *Wouters* case (2006), where the Court decided that the rules of the national bar association in the Netherlands that banned partnerships including both lawyers and accountants were permissible, although restrictive, because they were necessary in the pursuit of a legitimate public interest:

> [N]ot every agreement between undertakings or every decision of an association of undertakings which restricts the freedom of action of the parties or of one of them necessarily falls within the prohibition laid down in Article 85(1) of the Treaty [now Article 101(1) TFEU]. For the purposes of application of that provision to a particular case, account must first of all be taken of the overall context in which the decision of the association of undertakings was taken or produces its effects ... More particularly, account must be taken of its objectives ... It has then to be considered whether the consequential effects restrictive of competition are inherent in the pursuit of those objectives.[47]

[46] 'The Commission considers that a dominant undertaking may also justify conduct leading to foreclosure of competitors on the ground of efficiencies that are sufficient to guarantee that no net harm to consumers is likely to arise.' Guidance on exclusionary conduct, above n. 23, para. 30. Cf. Case C-209/10 *Post Danmark A/S* v. *Konkurrencerådet*, Judgment of 27 March 2012, para. 41, with reference to Case C-95/03 P *British Airways* v. *Commission* [2007] ECR I-2331, para. 86; Case C-52/09 *TeliaSonera*, above n. 11, para. 76.

[47] Case C-309/99 *J. C. J. Wouters, J. W. Savelbergh and Price Waterhouse Belastingadviseurs BV* v. *Algemene Raad van de Nederlandse Orde van Advocaten* [2002] ECR I-1577, para. 97. Cf. Case C-519/04 P *David Meca-Medina and Igor Majcen* v. *Commission* [2006] ECR I-6991; Case C-136/12 *Consiglio nazionale dei geologi* v. *Autorità garante della concorrenza e del mercato and Autorità garante della concorrenza e del mercato* v. *Consiglio nazionale dei geologi*, Judgment of 18 July 2013. The *Wouters* standard was clearly not met in regard to permanent education rules of the Portuguese bar association in Case C-1/12 *Ordem dos Técnicos Oficiais de Contas* v. *Autoridade da Concorrência*, Judgment of 28 February 2013. Cf. E. Loozen, 'Professional ethics and restrictions of competition', *European Law Review*, 31 (2006), 29–48; R. O'Loughlin, 'EC competition rules and free movement rules: An examination of the parallels

Following this approach, the promotion of legitimate public interests may cause anticompetitive practices ('inherent restrictions') to fall outside the scope of the prohibition set out in Article 101(1) TFEU under a rule of reason, instead of being based on a balancing test under Article 101(3) TFEU as had long been standard practice for normal exceptions.[48] There is an increasing debate on the question whether public interest cartels should be exempted under Article 101(3) TFEU instead, or as well.[49] From a competition policy perspective, such an approach might have been feasible while the exemption power remained concentrated in the hands of the Commission. Yet, following modernization, undertakings must make their own assessment (guidance is not usually provided in advance) and so must national competition authorities and courts. It is difficult to see how the very undertakings that stand to gain from restrictive practices could be expected to successfully weigh variable public interests, as well as their own, against the benefits to the internal market of free competition. Likewise competition authorities are not well placed to rule on non-economic matters: they lack both the expertise and the democratic legitimacy to do so.

These drawbacks are all the more important because there are two perfectly good alternatives to privatizing public interest regulation.

The alternatives to private definition of public interest exceptions

The first alternative approach is Member State regulation in the public interest which, if it is made binding on the undertakings involved, even if it entails restrictions on competition variables such as volume, price, quality and so forth, provides them with immunity from the competition rules. In EU competition law this is known as the 'state action defence'.[50] State action arrangements that are proportional and respect procedural safeguards, such as setting clear standards, involving balanced interest representation and reserving the right of

and their furtherance by the ECJ *Wouters* Decision', *European Competition Law Review*, 23 (2003), 62–9.

48 However, see Case T-238/03 *O2 (Germany) GmbH & Co. OHG* v. *Commission* [2006] ECR II-1231.

49 Cf. S. A. C. M. Lavrijssen, 'The protection of non-competition interests: What role for competition authorities after Lisbon?' *European Law Review*, 35 (2010), 634–59; G. Monti, 'Article 81 and public policy', *Common Market Law Review*, 39 (2002), 1057–99; Odudu (2006), above n. 35; C. Townley, *Article 81 EC and public policy* (Hart Publishing, Oxford 2009); H. Vedder, 'Of jurisdiction and justification: Why competition is good for "non-economic" goals, but may need to be restricted', *Competition Law Review*, 6 (2009), 51–75.

50 Joined Cases C-359/95 P and C-379/95 P *Commission and France* v. *Ladbroke Racing Ltd* [1997] ECR I-6265; Case C-198/01 *Consorzio Industrie Fiammiferi (CIF)* v. *Autorità Garante della Concorrenza e del Mercato* [2003] ECR I-8055. Cf. D. Gerard, 'EU competition policy after Lisbon: Time to review the "state action doctrine"?' *Journal of European Competition Law and Practice*, 1 (2010), 202–10; J. Baquero Cruz, 'The state action doctrine', in G. Amato, C.-D. Ehlermann and A. Komninos (eds.), *EC competition law: A critical assessment* (Hart Publishing, Oxford, 2007), 551–90. P. J. Slot, 'Public distortions of competition: The importance of Article 106 TFEU and the state action doctrine', in Neergaard et al., above n. 9, 245–62.

public authorities to take final decisions, are not touched by EU competition law.[51] Arguably the existence of a market failure must also be demonstrated.[52]

However, the state intervention involved may itself infringe the good faith clause of Article 4(3) TFEU (the principle of sincere cooperation) in combination with Article 101 TFEU if it is primarily designed to benefit, create or impose a cartel instead of promoting a bona fide public interest. Thus in *Van Eycke* (1988), the Court specified this rule as follows:

> It must be pointed out . . . that Articles 85 and 86 of the Treaty [now Articles 101 and 102 TFEU] per se are concerned only with the conduct of undertakings and not with national legislation. The Court has consistently held, however, that Articles 85 and 86 of the Treaty, in conjunction with Article 5 [now Article 4(3) TEU], require the Member States not to introduce or maintain in force measures, even of a legislative nature, which may render ineffective the competition rules applicable to undertakings. Such would be the case, the Court has held, if a Member State were to require or favour the adoption of agreements, decisions or concerted practices contrary to Article 85 or to reinforce their effects, or to deprive its own legislation of its official character by delegating to private traders responsibility for taking decisions affecting the economic sphere.[53]

This is known as an infringement of the *effet utile* of the relevant Treaty provisions.[54] From a systemic perspective, therefore, the state action defence is disciplined by that of the *effet utile*. This method relies on the democratically legitimized Member States taking their responsibility for formulating the public interest within the constraints of their responsibility as parties to the Treaties – instead of making undertakings that are inherently conflicted if acting on their own accord responsible for doing so. In my view, that is vastly preferable to the *Wouters* rule of reason approach as a solution to dealing with the public interest in competition law.

The second and, in my view, main alternative to the above-mentioned approaches that has emerged in recent years is evidently the exception for SGEI in Article 106(2) TFEU. This provides a by-now finely tuned framework for assessments on the scope of the public interest invoked and the

51 Cf. Case C-35/99 *Criminal proceedings against Manuele Arduino, third parties: Diego Dessi, Giovanni Bertolotto and Compagnia Assicuratrice RAS SpA* [2002] ECR I-1529; Joined cases C-94/04 and C-202/04 *Federico Cipolla* v. *Rosaria Fazari, née Portolese and Stefano Macrino and Claudia Capoparte* v. *Roberto Meloni* [2006] ECR I-11421; Case T-513/93 *Consiglio Nazionale degli Spedizionieri Doganali* v. *Commission* [2000] ECR II-1807. Cf. H. Schepel, 'Delegation of regulatory powers to private parties under EC competition law: Towards a procedural public interest test', *Common Market Law Review*, 39 (2002), 31–51.

52 Lavrijssen, above n. 49, at 658.

53 Case 267/86 *Pascal Van Eycke* v. *ASPA NV* [1988] ECR 4769, para. 16. Cf. Case C-446/05 *Criminal proceedings against Ioannis Doulamis* [2008] ECR I-1377.

54 Cf. Baquero Cruz, above n. 50; J. Baquero Cruz, *Between competition and free movement: The economic constitutional law of the European Community* (Hart Publishing, Oxford, 2002); E. Szyszczak, *The regulation of the state in competitive markets in the EU* (Hart Publishing, Oxford, 2007).

proportionate restrictions of competition that are allowed in pursuit of public interest objectives. We will discuss this exemption at length under the heading of state aid, but it applies to the competition rules as well. In view of these two tried alternatives, I see no useful or indeed legitimate purpose to the *Wouters* exception and the ideas about its follow-up. They entail grave risks of corporatist gold-plating masquerading as privately developed public interest guarantees as well as the erection of private barriers to market entry. These problems can easily be avoided by taking the public route while achieving a more sound end result, including in terms of democratic legitimacy. As we will see with regard to public services, the SGEI avenue is increasingly the preferred option both for the Commission and for the authorities of the Member States.

The consumer interest in EU competition law

While the consumer interest is not co-extensive with the concept of public services, there is surely some overlap in terms of the objectives pursued. At the same time, the consumer interest – or in more technical economic terms, consumer welfare – plays a role in competition law. Whether or not the consumer interest is central to EU competition law or even its key driver has been the subject of debate.[55] Above I have already cited the *GlaxoSmithKline* case (2009), where the CJEU made clear that consumer welfare is not the exclusive standard, but that instead the interests of competitors, the competitive process itself and market structure are variables that also play a role as objectives of EU competition law.[56] Although this perspective may not be compatible with the strictures of Chicago School economics,[57] it appears to be fully consistent with the focus on the internal market that characterizes the EU's competition policy, as has been highlighted by Article 3(1)b TFEU and Protocol 27 and the *TeliaSonera* case cited above.[58]

Consistent with this broader approach, the EU does not focus on exploitative abuses, such as excessive pricing or bundling, that directly concern consumers.[59] Rather it is the opposite: the enforcement of the rules on dominance abuse

[55] Cf. E. Buttigieg, *Competition law: Safeguarding the consumer interest. A comparative analysis of US antitrust law and EC competition law* (Kluwer Law, Alphen aan den Rijn, 2009); K. Cseres, 'The controversies of the consumer welfare standard', *Competition Law Review*, 3 (2007), 121–73; K. J. Cseres, *Competition policy and consumer protection* (Kluwer Law, Alphen aan den Rijn, 2005).

[56] Joined cases C-501/06 P, C-513/06 P, C-515/06 P and C-519/06 P *GlaxoSmithKline*, above n. 8.

[57] Cf. Bork, above n. 6; H. Hovenkamp, *The antitrust enterprise: Principle and execution* (Harvard University Press, Cambridge, Mass. 2005).

[58] Cf. Case C-52/09 *Konkurrensverket*, above n. 11.

[59] Sometimes legislation is used instead: Regulation (EU) No 531/2012 of the European Parliament and of the Council of 13 June 2012 on roaming on public mobile communications networks within the Union, OJ 2012, L172/10. Its legality was confirmed in Case C-58/08 *The Queen, on the application of Vodafone Ltd and Others* v. *Secretary of State for Business, Enterprise and Regulatory Reform* [2010] ECR I-4999. Current proposals aim to abolish some roaming charges for the use of mobile phones abroad altogether.

concentrates on (an economic approach to) exclusionary abuses. The underlying logic is that addressing exclusion will solve exploitation by imposing competitive pressure on the undertaking with market power. A supplementary practical consideration is that exploitative abuses are generally difficult (if not impossible) to prove.[60] This approach is consistent with that found in sectoral regulation in the network industries – the utilities. There regulators tend to impose wholesale level intervention that is aimed at facilitating efficient market entry with the objective of generating the discipline of competitive pressure. This is preferred over the open-ended regulation of consumer products and prices, where feasible.

This does not mean that the consumer interest does not play an important role in EU competition law: ever since the original 1957 Rome Treaty the consumer interest is found explicitly in Article 101(3) TFEU. There it is stated that a restrictive practice that 'contributes to improving the production or distribution of goods or to promoting technical or economic progress, while *allowing consumers a fair share of the resulting benefit*' (emphasis added) is allowed, provided the other two conditions (necessity, and no elimination of competition) are met. A related example is the standard that the Commission must take into account in its appraisal of mergers under the Merger Control Regulation 139/2004, which test includes:

> the interests of the intermediate and ultimate consumers, and the development of technical and economic progress provided that it is to consumers' advantage and does not form an obstacle to competition.[61]

A related procedural aspect in merger proceedings is the right of consumer organizations (where the proposed concentration concerns products or services used by final consumers) to be heard. Even if the effects on consumers are secondary in nature, this does not deprive them of their right to be heard.[62] Finally, based on Article 21(4) of the Merger Control Regulation, Member States are allowed to take other interests than competition into account in merger procedures (apart from a limited set of predefined reasons), subject to Commission approval.[63]

[60] Guidance on exclusionary conduct, above n. 23. An exception is Case T-201/04 *Microsoft Corp.* v. *Commission* [2007] ECR II-3601, which involved tying of a media player to PC operating systems as one of a range of abuses – however this was oriented more towards the effects on competitors.

[61] Article 2(1)b, Council Regulation (EC) No 139/2004 of 20 January 2004 on the control of concentrations between undertakings, OJ 2004, L24/1.

[62] Commission Regulation (EC) No 802/2004 of 7 April 2004 implementing Council Regulation (EC) No 139/2004 on the control of concentrations between undertakings, OJ 2004, L133/1. Cf. Case T-224/10 *Association belge des consommateurs test-achats ASBL* v. *Commission* [2011] ECR II-7177, concerning the (indirect) consumer interest in an energy merger.

[63] This provision reads: 'Member States may take appropriate measures to protect legitimate interests other than those taken into consideration by this Regulation and compatible with the general principles and other provisions of Community law. Public security, plurality of the media and prudential rules shall be regarded as legitimate interests within the meaning of the first subparagraph. Any other public interest must be communicated to the Commission by

In sum, therefore, the manner in which the consumer interest is dealt with in EU competition law is multi-faceted, but there is a discrepancy between consumer-oriented rhetoric and the actual practice which targets the intermediate or wholesale economic level or the interests of competitors. Nevertheless, this practice seems both to represent sound economics and to be in line with pursuit of the internal market objective. Giving consumer organizations access to competition procedures may help to bridge the gap observed to some extent.

Following these reflections on the more theoretical themes of the way in which the public interest may be pursued with respect to the competition rules and the role of the consumer interest, I will now move on to discuss some individual competition cases involving the providers of public services, notably utilities.

Reflections on the competition case law

So far, competition cases with regard to public services that touch on their relationship to the public in the shape of a public service obligation are rare. The cases that do exist concerning public services tend to concern behaviour vis-à-vis competitors instead. This usually regards dominance abuse, and not anti-competitive practices. The reason for this is simple: the majority of cases relate to former statutory monopolists in the utilities sectors ('incumbents') that try to frustrate or snuff out the competition that is fostered by liberalization. Although in some of these cases sector-specific regulatory frameworks already existed, the competition rules have continued to play a role in the background as regulation of last resort. This can be explained not least by the fact that whereas the European Commission can act directly under the competition rules, it must rely on national authorities to enforce the sectoral rules.

A relatively early (1985) case, which presaged by thirteen years the full EU-wide telecommunications liberalization that took place in 1998, regarded behaviour by British Telecom that had been penalized by the European Commission as dominance abuse. In spite of the fact that it concerned a British undertaking, this case was brought against the Commission by Italy as a matter of principle: it felt that British Telecom should be regarded as a public authority and hence as immune from the competition rules. The Court, however, found that the Commission was within its rights to find an infringement of Article 102 TFEU where British Telecom (then still an integrated monopolist cum regulator) had abused its rule-making powers to frustrate the emergence of fax forwarding services (then considered innovative).[64] Because they were

the Member State concerned and shall be recognised by the Commission after an assessment of its compatibility with the general principles and other provisions of Community law before the measures referred to above may be taken. The Commission shall inform the Member State concerned of its decision within 25 working days of that communication.' Cf. D. Gerard, 'Protectionist threats against cross-border mergers: Unexplored avenues to strengthen the effectiveness of Article 21 ECMR', *Common Market Law Review*, 45 (2008), 987–1025.

64 Case 41/83 *Italy* v. *Commission* [1985] ECR 873.

freely exercised by British Telecom (at least without detailed official guidance), these rule-making powers were seen as an integral part of its business activities.

Similar examples existed in other sectors, as was illustrated in the 1997 *GT-Link* case where the Court found that the public undertaking which owned and operated a commercial port in Denmark occupied a dominant position that was abused if it levied charges on competitors from which its own ferry services were exempt.[65] In addition, it held that dock work (loading, unloading and storage of goods) cannot be regarded as a service of general economic interest. From a present-day perspective, I would concur as there is no link to key SGEI variables such as market failure, universality or the consumer perspective.

In recent years a number of cases have been decided regarding pricing abuses in the utilities sectors, notably electronic communications, such as predatory pricing in the *France Télécom* case (2009).[66] In the *Deutsche Telekom* case (2010) and *Telefónica* case (2012) retail prices for end-users were also involved. However, this was mainly in relation to price squeezes (the difference between retail and wholesale price levels being too small to allow efficient market entry) that were imposed on competitors and not as a matter of protecting the consumer interest directly.[67] In principle this problem could have been solved by means of applying the sector-specific rules whereby the national regulator could set both the relevant wholesale and retail rates. Because the objective was promoting competition, it could have set these rates at levels encouraging efficient entry. However, if we look at the *Deutsche Telekom* case we see that it is precisely the regulation by the national regulatory authority (NRA), RegTP, that helped cause the squeeze. Presumably RegTP at the time was reluctant to rebalance or raise consumer prices (never a popular policy) and lower wholesale rates for political reasons. Hence the Commission overruled the NRA based on its general competition powers and the CJEU pointed to the independent responsibility of a dominant undertaking to abide by the competition rules:

> According to the case-law of the Court, dominant undertakings have a special responsibility not to allow their conduct to impair genuine undistorted competition on the common market.
>
> It follows from this that the mere fact that the appellant was encouraged by the intervention of a national regulatory authority such as RegTP to maintain the pricing practices which led to the margin squeeze of competitors who are at least as efficient as the appellant cannot, as such, in any way absolve the appellant from responsibility under Article 82 EC [now Article 102 TFEU].

[65] Case C-242/95 *GT-Link A/S* v. *De Danske Statsbaner* (DSB) [1997] ECR I-4449. Cf. earlier 94/119/EC: Commission Decision of 21 December 1993 concerning a refusal to grant access to the facilities of the port of Rødby (Denmark), OJ 1994, L55/52.

[66] Case C-202/07 P *France Télécom SA* v. *Commission* [2009] ECR I-2369.

[67] Case C-280/08 P *Deutsche Telekom AG* v. *Commission* [2010] ECR I-9555; Case T-336/07 *Telefónica SA and Telefónica de España SA* v. *Commission*, Judgment of 29 March 2012. Cf. Case C-52/09 *TeliaSonera*, above n. 11.

> Since, notwithstanding such interventions, the appellant had scope to adjust its retail prices for end-user access services, the General Court was entitled to find, on that ground alone, that the margin squeeze at issue was attributable to the appellant.[68]

Similarly, abuse cases in the postal sector regard, for instance, selectively low pricing to target the customers of third-party operators.[69] In sum, the competition cases involved concern not so much universal service as the effects of dominant behaviour that is deleterious to third-party providers: these cases reflect a desire by the European Commission to promote competition in the market and thereby address consumer benefits only indirectly (but arguably ultimately more effectively). This is in line with the focus on exclusionary abuses that has been adopted by the European Commission,[70] and with promoting competition as an alternative to policing retail practices. These cases stiffen the backbone of the NRAs when they apply their harmonized sectoral liberalization regimes that we will discuss in Chapter 6. For now I will only remark that there too wholesale intervention is preferred over retail regulation.

Sectoral competition regimes: guidance

To complicate matters, not only are there (i) general competition rules and (ii) sector-specific harmonized liberalization regimes that aim to promote competition, but there is also (iii) an intermediate category of rules that are based on the general competition rules and that aim to promote competition in specific sectors. This includes competition regimes for public services, in the cases of postal services,[71] electronic communications networks and services,[72] as well as transport by rail, road and inland waterway.[73] (There are also separate rules for air transport[74] and maritime transport,[75] but I do not consider these to be public services here.) These sectoral competition rules are partly a form of soft-law guidance offered by the Commission that is based upon an elaboration of the general competition rules for the specific context – as in the case of the Notice on postal services and the Guidelines and Notice on electronic communications.

[68] Case C-280/08 P *Deutsche Telekom*, above n. 67, paras. 83–5.

[69] Case C-209/10 *Post Danmark*, above n. 46.

[70] Guidance on exclusionary conduct, above n. 23.

[71] Notice from the Commission on the application of the competition rules to the postal sector and on the assessment of certain state measures relating to postal services, OJ 1998, C39/2.

[72] Commission Directive 2002/77/EC of 16 September 2002 on competition in the markets for electronic communications networks and services, OJ 2002, L249/21.

[73] Council Regulation (EC) No 169/2009 of 26 February 2009 applying rules of competition to transport by rail, road and inland waterway, OJ 2009, L61/1.

[74] Council Regulation (EC) No 487/2009 of 25 May 2009 on the application of Article 81(3) of the Treaty to certain categories of agreements and concerted practices in the air transport sector, OJ 2009, L148/1.

[75] Guidelines on the application of Article 81 of the EC Treaty to maritime transport services, OJ 2008, C245/2.

However, there are also two examples where the sectoral competition regimes for public services take the binding form of legislation – the Commission Directives on electronic communications and the Council Regulation on transport by rail, road and inland waterway. Because they are primarily elaborations on the Treaty provisions on competition, in my view these rules are different from the internal-market-oriented sectoral regimes that are based on harmonization legislation by the European Parliament and the Council and will be discussed in Chapter 6. Because they are sectoral in nature, these rules are also different from the horizontal rules of general application that I will review in Chapter 5. This pleads in favour of discussing them here. However, because in the interest of the overall balance of the book it would go too far to describe each of these regimes in detail, I will only provide a short summary.

Postal services

The postal services sector has traditionally been one of the most intractable public services as far as liberalization is concerned. On the one hand, these services are (at least in theory) highly valued by the public and highly unionized, with postal workers having enjoyed a protected status as public officials in a number of Member States. On the other hand, there is a steady decline in the actual use of traditional postal services. Much of postal services is now concerned with direct mail (business communications) and courier services, and letter mail is increasingly being replaced by e-mail and electronic access to official bodies and services (such as taxation and local government). Managing this decline and reorientation at EU level has involved a very slow liberalization process. In this context the Commission adopted a Notice with guidance on the competition and state aid rules in postal services in 1998, which I will discuss briefly below.[76] This was accompanied by a harmonization Directive which was adopted in 1997 (amended in 2002 and 2008) that also deals extensively with universal service in this sector and that will be discussed in Chapter 6 below.[77]

The objectives of EU regulation for the postal services at large are to safeguard the postal service as a universal service in the long term; to limit the extent of the reserved areas which the Member States may grant their providers of universal service; and to facilitate a process of gradual market

[76] Postal Guidelines, above n. 71.

[77] Directive 97/67/EC of the European Parliament and of the Council of 15 December 1997 on common rules for the development of the internal market of Community postal services and the improvement of quality of service, OJ 1998, L15/14; Directive 2002/39/EC of the European Parliament and of the Council of 10 June 2002 amending Directive 97/67/EC with regard to the further opening to competition of Community postal services, OJ 2002, L176/21; Directive 2008/6/EC of the European Parliament and of the Council of 20 February 2008 amending Directive 97/67/EC with regard to the full accomplishment of the internal market of Community postal services, OJ 2008, L52/3.

opening to competition. In the Guidelines the concept of universal service is generally described as

> the provision of a high-quality service to all [at] prices anyone can afford. Universal service is defined in terms of principles: equality, universality, continuity and adaptability; and in terms of sound practices: openness in management, price-setting and funding and scrutiny by bodies independent of those operating the services.[78]

As this definition illustrates, the Commission is linking universal service with transparency (on state aid relevant variables) as well as with independent regulatory supervision, neither of which is generally or strictly speaking a competition law concern. They are all the more relevant in a broader context of liberalizing a public service while guaranteeing services and creating a regulatory framework that replaces state ownership and public provision.

The Guidelines warn that conferring exclusive rights when an operator is unable to meet demand for particular services infringes the competition rules. Likewise it spells out that cross-subsidization by allocating costs to reserved services in order to subsidize competitive services may infringe the prohibition on dominance abuse. With regard to state aid,[79] and SGEI, the Guidelines provide the following more detailed outline of universal service:

> Without prejudice to the rights of the Member States to define particular requirements of services of general interest, that task consists primarily in the provision and the maintenance of a universal public postal service, guaranteeing at affordable, cost-effective and transparent tariffs nationwide access to the public postal network within a reasonable distance and during adequate opening hours, including the clearance of postal items from accessible postal boxes or collection points throughout the territory and the timely delivery of such items to the address indicated, as well as associated services entrusted by measures of a regulatory nature to those operators for universal delivery at a specified quality. The universal service is to evolve in response to the social, economical and technical environment and to the demands of users.[80]

Special and exclusive rights outside the areas which can remain reserved under the terms of the Postal Directive are to be withdrawn, and the monitoring of the performance of public service tasks is to be entrusted to an independent body: regulatory powers may no longer be conferred on dominant operators but must be organized at arm's length from such entities. There is thus an interplay between the competition-law-based liberalization measures and the internal-market-based harmonization measures that is also found in the telecommunications context. This may reflect a common history: for reasons that are less

[78] Postal Guidelines, above n. 71, at 3.

[79] With reference to Case T-106/95 *Fédération française des sociétés d'assurances (FFSA) et al.* v. *Commission* [1997] ECR II-229 on tax advantages to a postal operator that were held to be covered by Article 106(2) TFEU.

[80] Postal Guidelines, above n. 71, at para. 8.1.

obvious with hindsight, postal and telecommunications services were in the past frequently organized and provided by the same public body, a post, telephony and telegraphy operator or PTT.

Electronic communications

This sector is subject to an extensive harmonization regime that has been updated several times.[81] The harmonization rules cover not only third-party access rules and other extensive regulatory powers but also universal service provisions. They will be dealt with in greater detail in Chapter 6 on vertical secondary rules. Under the competition rules, which we are looking at here, guidance has been provided by the Commission in 1991 (the Telecommunications Guidelines)[82] and 1998 (the Access Notice).[83] Much like the Postal Services Notice discussed above, which especially the Telecommunications Guidelines resemble, these two documents are by now mainly of historical significance. The Telecommunications Guidelines, written eight years before telecommunications networks and services were liberalized, set out the basic features of the competition rules for a telecommunications audience. They also deal with cross-subsidization and set out how this can be justified in the context of funding and providing a universal service.[84]

The Access Guidelines are more specific and deal primarily with third-party access – that is to say, in practical terms, access for competitors entering the market to the vertically integrated network of the dominant incumbent operator (the former legal monopolist). They deal with issues like refusal to deal, tying and price squeezes and were intended to provide soft-law backing for private enforcement of the competition rules on such issues. The Guidelines

[81] Most recently Directive 2009/140/EC of the European Parliament and of the Council of 25 November 2009 amending Directives 2002/21/EC on a common regulatory framework for electronic communications networks and services, 2002/19/EC on access to, and interconnection of, electronic communications networks and associated facilities, and 2002/20/EC on the authorisation of electronic communications networks and services, OJ 2009, L337/37; Directive 2009/136/EC of the European Parliament and of the Council of 25 November 2009 amending Directive 2002/22/EC on universal service and users' rights relating to electronic communications networks and services; Directive 2002/58/EC concerning the processing of personal data and the protection of privacy in the electronic communications sector and Regulation (EC) No 2006/2004 on cooperation between national authorities responsible for the enforcement of consumer protection laws, OJ 2009, L337/11.

[82] Guidelines on the application of EEC competition rules in the telecommunications sector, OJ 1991, C233/2.

[83] Notice on the application of the competition rules to access agreements in the telecommunications sector – framework, relevant markets and principles, OJ 1998, C/265/2.

[84] 'The Commission has recognized in the Green Paper the central role of the TOs, which justifies the maintenance of certain monopolies to enable them to perform their public task. This public task consists in the provision and exploitation of a universal network or, where appropriate, universal service, i.e. one having general coverage and available to all users (including service providers and the TOs themselves) upon request on reasonable and non-discriminatory conditions.' Telecommunications Guidelines, above n. 82, para. 84.

also emphasize the parallel application of the general competition rules and the harmonized liberalization legislation. At the time it was still widely thought that the harmonization framework would quickly converge with, or be superseded by, the general competition rules. We now know this has not happened and is unlikely to occur in the foreseeable future: not only does liberalization require reregulation instead of deregulation, but also the rules involved have a tendency to become permanent even if they were meant to be temporary and transitional at the outset.

In addition, in 1999 a Commission Directive was adopted on competition in the markets for telecommunications services that has been updated and amended several times, most recently in 2002.[85] This Directive is what may be not only the latest but also the last Article 106(3) TFEU Directive, because of the democratic objections against this unilateral type of legislation by the Commission with only a 'voluntary' submission of the proposed text for comments to the European Parliament and the Council. Originally used to eliminate special and exclusive rights in electronic communications, it repeats this prohibition and states that instead general authorization procedures are to be used, and licences issued only when necessary. Spectrum rights for mobile communications are to be awarded based on objective, transparent and non-discriminatory criteria.[86] Finally, Member States should ensure that vertically integrated public telecommunications operators which enjoy a dominant position do not discriminate against their competitors. Set against the background of the comprehensive harmonization framework that was meanwhile adopted and the paradigm shift towards full competition that has taken place, the added value of the 2002 Article 106(3) Directive largely appears to have been limited to requiring special and exclusive rights to be abolished in new Member States in so far as they had not already been.

Rail, road and inland waterway transport

The 2008 Council Regulation updates the earlier (repeatedly amended) 1968 regime[87] by providing a block exemption for particular forms of cooperation by undertakings active in the transport sector. Public service obligations and/or universal service do not play a role here. Instead the Regulation exempts standardization, exchange and pooling arrangements, successive,

[85] Commission Directive 90/388/EEC of 28 June 1990 on competition in the markets for telecommunications services, OJ 1990, L192/10, 'recast' by Commission Directive 2002/77/EC, above n. 72.

[86] Cf. D. Gabathuler and W. Sauter, 'The allocation of scarce resources and spectrum assignment in mobile communications: The case of UMTS', in P. A. Buigues and P. Rey (eds.), *The economics of antitrust and regulation in telecommunications: Perspectives for the new European regulatory framework* (Edward Elgar, Cheltenham, 2004), 213–38.

[87] Regulation (EEC) No 1017/68 of the Council of 19 July 1968 applying rules of competition to transport by rail, road and inland waterway, OJ 1968, L175/1. Cf. T. M. Rusche and S. Schmidt, 'Transport', in E. Szyszczak and J. W. van de Gronden (eds.), *Financing services of general economic interest: Reform and modernization* (TMC Asser Press, The Hague, 2013), 217–48.

complementary or combined transport operations and related rate fixing, the establishment of uniform rules for the structure of rates as well as a number of other more technical forms of cooperation as falling outside the scope of the cartel prohibition in Article 101(1) TFEU. There is an additional exemption for small and medium-sized enterprises (SMEs). In both respects – the absence of USO considerations and the wholesale exemption of various types of cooperation instead of focusing on the applicability of the competition rules – there is a stark contrast with the regimes above on postal services and electronic communications, although evidently it should be no surprise that a block exemption exempts particular practices that might normally be thought objectionable. Moreover, there are no supplementary harmonization rules here.

In sum, it appears that the transport sector is trailing well behind the other two sectors just mentioned in terms of a public services sensitive application of the competition rules. However, as we will see, universal service type arrangements do come up with regard to ferry services in the context of the *Altmark* framework that I will discuss in the next section on state aid.[88]

4.5 The application of the state aid rules to public services

The rules on state aid

The state aid rules in Articles 107 and 108 TFEU serve to ensure that Member States do not confer discriminatory advantages upon undertakings that distort competition in the internal market. The addressees are therefore the Member States although the beneficiaries of the aid are (or must be in order to fit the definitions) undertakings. Conceptually therefore the state aid rules occupy a sort of middle ground between the competition and the free movement rules. For a state aid to exist four conditions (sometimes stretched by commentators into five or even six conditions) must be met. A measure must: (i) be provided at a cost to the public purse; (ii) confer a selective advantage on only some undertakings; that (iii) distorts competition; and (iv) has an effect on trade. This can involve all types of advantages as long as they can be expressed in monetary value, such as interest free loans, loan guarantees, tax deferrals,

[88] Cf. Commission Decision of 20 December 2011 on the application of Article 106(2) of the Treaty on the Functioning of the European Union to state aid in the form of public service compensation granted to certain undertakings entrusted with the operation of services of general economic interest, OJ 2012, L7/3. In its Article 2(1) this provides an exemption for: '(d) compensation for the provision of services of general economic interest as regards air or maritime links to islands on which the average annual traffic during the 2 financial years preceding that in which the service of general economic interest was assigned does not exceed 300,000 passengers; (e) compensation for the provision of services of general economic interest as regards airports and ports for which the average annual traffic during the 2 financial years preceding that in which the service of general economic interest was assigned does not exceed 200,000 passengers, in the case of airports, and 300,000 passengers, in the case of ports.'

preferential awards of land as well as more straightforward cash injections and periodic subsidies.

Since 2005 the Commission has taken a more refined economic approach to state aid based more on an analysis of market failures, with the objective of obtaining less and better targeted state aid.[89] In its state aid action plan it formulated this as follows:

> State aid measures can sometimes be effective tools for achieving objectives of common interest. They can correct market failures, thereby improving the functioning of markets and enhancing European competitiveness. They can also help promote e.g. social and regional cohesion, sustainable development and cultural diversity, irrespective of the correction of market failures.
>
> However, state aid should only be used when it is an appropriate instrument for meeting a well defined objective, when it creates the right incentives, is proportionate and when it distorts competition to the least possible extent. For that reason, appreciating the compatibility of state aid is fundamentally about balancing the negative effects of aid on competition with its positive effects in terms of common interest.[90]

The focus of this change in approach is the so-called balancing test in Article 107(3) TFEU which is used to decide whether state measures are compatible with the internal market. As sketched out in the quotation above, this test asks: (i) whether there is a well-defined common interest objective (defined in efficiency or equity terms), such as market failure; (ii) whether the aid effectively addresses this objective, provides the right incentives and is itself both necessary and proportionate; and (iii) whether the resulting restrictions on competition and on trade are limited so on balance the measure has a positive effect.[91]

As I have briefly mentioned above, in contrast to the competition rules which since 2004 have been characterized by decentralized enforcement, the Commission retains the monopoly on declaring aid compatible with the internal market under Article 107(3) TFEU. This frustrates the application of the state aid rules by national courts who can declare that (in principle illegal) state aid exists but cannot exclude that compatibility might be declared to exempt the aid. The solution adopted by the Commission is reliance on block exemptions (just as had been the case in antitrust prior to 2004), the applicability of which

[89] Communication from the Commission, State aid action plan: Less and better targeted state aid: A roadmap for state aid reform 2005–2009 (Consultation document) COM(2005) 107, 7 June 2005. Cf. N. Fiedziuk, 'Towards a more refined economic approach to services of general economic interest', *European Public Law*, 16 (2010), 271–88; D. Neven and V. Verouden, 'Towards a more refined economic approach in state aid control', in W. Mederer, N. Pesaresi and M. Van Hoof (eds.), *EU competition law – Volume IV: State aid* (Claeys and Casteels Publishing, Deventer, 2008).

[90] State aid action plan, above n. 89, paras. 10–11.

[91] Cf. Common principles for an economic assessment of the compatibility of state aid under article 87.3, Commission non-paper, para. 9; Fiedziuk, above n. 89; Neven and Verouden, above n. 89, para. 1.3.

national courts are able to decide on.[92] The Commission also provides non-binding (or soft-law) guidance. Below, we will examine these various approaches in more detail with relation to their application to public services.

The *Altmark* case

The importance of the state aid rule with regard to public services has increased exponentially since the adoption of the Court's decision in the *Altmark* case in 2003.[93] *Altmark* concerned compensation for public transport services (regional bus services) in Germany. In this case the Court resolved a theoretical dispute among state aid specialists concerning the way compensation for public services should be dealt with under the state aid rules. One view (the 'state aid approach') was that compensation should be considered to constitute aid, but should be subsequently declared compatible with the internal market.[94] This was the view advocated in two separate Opinions by Advocate General Léger and broadly in line with a general trend in EU law where behaviour is easily caught by a prohibition only to be released again based on a (sometimes conditional) exception. The competing view ('the compensation approach'), which carried the day in *Altmark*, was that provided certain criteria were met, compensation formed remuneration for the performance of a service so there was no question of an advantage, and hence state aid did not exist.[95] This looks more like a rule of reason approach.

[92] Commission Regulation (EC) No 800/2008 of 6 August 2008 declaring certain categories of aid compatible with the common market in application of Articles 87 and 88 of the Treaty (General block exemption Regulation), OJ 2008, L214/3.

[93] Case C-280/00 *Altmark Trans GmbH and Regierungspräsidium Magdeburg* v. *Nahverkehrsgesellschaft Altmark GmbH, and Oberbundesanwalt beim Bundesverwaltungsgericht* [2003] ECR I-7747. Cf. F. Louis and A. Vallery, '*Ferring* revisited: The *Altmark* case and state financing of public service obligations', *World Competition*, 27 (2004), 53; A. Sinnaeve, 'State financing of public services: The Court's dilemma in the *Altmark* Case', *European State Aid Law Quarterly*, 2 (2003), 351–62; M. Ronellenfitsch, 'Das Altmark-Urteil des Europäischen Gerichtshofs', *Verwaltungsarchiv*, 95 (2004), 425–42; S. Bracq, 'Droit communautaire matériel et qualification juridique: Le financement des obligations de service public au coeur de la tourmente', (2004) *Revue trimestrielle de droit européen*, 40 (2004), 33–70.

[94] A state aid approach was found in Case T-106/95 *FFSA*, above n. 79; Case T-46/97 *SIC – Sociedade Independente de Comunicação SA* v. *Commission* [2000] ECR II-2125; Case C-332/98 *France* v. *Commission (aid for the Coopérative d'Exportation du Livre Français)* [2000] ECR I-4833.

[95] On the compensation approach the Court referred especially to Case 240/83 *Procureur de la République* v. *Association de défense des brûleurs d'huiles usagées (ADBHU)* [1985] ECR 531 and Case C-53/00 *Ferring SA* v. *Agence centrale des organismes de sécurité sociale (ACOSS)* [2001] ECR I-9067. A third, 'quid pro quo' approach is identified in C. H. Bovis, 'The conceptual links between state aid and public procurement in the financing of services of general economic interest', in M. Krajewski, U. Neergaard and J. van de Gronden (eds.), *The changing legal framework for services of general interest in Europe, between competition and solidarity* (TMC Asser Press, The Hague, 2009), 149–70.

Given their importance it is worth again citing the four conditions set by the Court:

> First, the recipient undertaking must actually have public service obligations to discharge, and the obligations must be clearly defined . . .
>
> Second, the parameters on the basis of which the compensation is calculated must be established in advance in an objective and transparent manner, to avoid it conferring an economic advantage which may favour the recipient undertaking over competing undertakings . . .
>
> Third, the compensation cannot exceed what is necessary to cover all or part of the costs incurred in the discharge of public service obligations, taking into account the relevant receipts and a reasonable profit for discharging those obligations . . .
>
> Fourth, where the undertaking which is to discharge public service obligations, in a specific case, is not chosen pursuant to a public procurement procedure which would allow for the selection of the tenderer capable of providing those services at the least cost to the community, the level of compensation needed must be determined on the basis of an analysis of the costs which a typical undertaking, well run and adequately provided with means of transport so as to be able to meet the necessary public service requirements, would have incurred in discharging those obligations, taking into account the relevant receipts and a reasonable profit for discharging the obligations.[96]

These conditions have provided the template for all future decisions on compensation for the provision of public services and, because the judgment was not limited in time, even for evaluating decisions that had been taken prior to this ruling. In addition, the Commission has adopted two legislative packages, the first published in 2005 and the second in 2012,[97] which are designed to implement the *Altmark* judgment by providing a framework for decisions based on the first three above-mentioned criteria. They are tailored to situations where the parties concerned cannot meet the relatively strict fourth, or efficiency, condition – which requires either reliance on a public tender procedure or setting costs at the level of an efficient undertaking, where it is often difficult to find a comparator if monopoly services are involved. As regards public tender procedures, public procurement is subject to separate 'horizontal' legislation which will be covered in the next chapter.

To maintain chronology, below I will first discuss the 2008 *BUPA* case,[98] which is both an important example of the application of the *Altmark* criteria

[96] Case C-280/00 *Altmark*, above n. 93, paras. 90–3.

[97] SGEI compensation Decision, above n. 88; Communication from the Commission on a European Union framework for state aid in the form of public service compensation, OJ 2012, C8/15; SGEI compensation Communication, above n. 17; Commission Regulation on the application of Articles 107 and 108 of the Treaty on the Functioning of the European Union to de minimis aid granted to undertakings providing services of general economic interest, OJ 2012, L114/8.

[98] Case T-289/03 *British United Provident Association Ltd (BUPA), BUPA Insurance Ltd and BUPA Ireland Ltd* v. *Commission of the European Communities* [2008] ECR II-81.

and comprises some significant amendments to the *Altmark* approach, or suggests a considerable degree of flexibility. (To some extent this has already come up in Chapter 1.) Next I will discuss the *Altmark* package, in particular the 2012 version which is still in force. Finally, I will briefly discuss two sectoral regulatory regimes that are based on the state aid rules: the guidelines on broadband networks and on public broadcasting.

The *BUPA* case

BUPA is a case that concerned the issue whether the prospective Irish risk equalization scheme between competing providers of private health insurance was allowed under the state aid rules. The economic logic behind this scheme is that because minimum benefits were defined publicly and as the insurers were required to accept all customers and could not price discriminate between them based on their health status, risk selection must be avoided. Risk selection reflects a market failure because insurers prefer to insure healthy persons who in turn do not need or want insurance, leaving the part of the population that does require insurance out of the market. Hence the idea is that in addition to the public law guarantees already mentioned insurers would compensate each other for above-average risk profiles in their population (for example, a disproportionate percentage of older people). In theory this would lead to competition on the merits. In practice this meant that the new entrant in the market, BUPA, with younger customers, would have to compensate the incumbent, VHI, which catered to a more elderly population.

On an appeal against a state aid clearance (no aid was found on the ground that compensation was at the minimum level necessary to compensate for an SGEI) by the Commission that predated the *Altmark* judgment, the General Court in *BUPA* applied both the four-part *Altmark* test and that of Article 106(2) TFEU (checking for a public service obligation, and no more than necessary as well as proportionate restraints). It gave the Commission Decision a clean bill of health on both counts, but in the process significantly reinterpreted the *Altmark* conditions.

The first issue was whether there was a legitimate public service obligation in place. As regards universality, the General Court was prepared to accept that this condition could even be satisfied if, as in the case at hand, only the healthier and wealthier part of the population (albeit some 50 per cent of the total) availed themselves of the service. Nor was it deemed relevant that the service was for profit, included priced discrimination (there were luxury and basic packages) and formed voluntary (supplementary) insurance. The only requirement was whether the provider of the public service obligation must do business with any interested customer, and on identical terms:

> [I]t is sufficient, in order to conclude that a service is compulsory, that the operator entrusted with a particular mission is under an obligation to provide that service to any user requesting it. In other words, the compulsory nature of the service and, accordingly, the existence of an SGEI mission are established if the service-provider is obliged to contract, on consistent conditions, without being able to reject the other contracting party. That element makes it possible to distinguish a service forming part of an SGEI mission from any other service provided on the market and, accordingly, from any other activity carried out in complete freedom.[99]

Second, the issue was whether costs could be contained and verified where they were not known in advance. Here the Court held that the parameters were complex but set out ex ante, specific, clearly identifiable and capable of being controlled. This is notwithstanding that actual compensation occurred ex post, which was favoured for reasons of certainty, but led to the compensation of cost instead of risk, and therefore gave the wrong incentives. There was no direct relationship between the provision of an SGEI and the amount of compensation (which was dependent on risk and performance of the healthcare insurer). However, because a 'link' existed between the cost of SGEI and compensation the Court accepted that cost played a role, and was satisfied.

It is perhaps self-evident that the *Altmark* criteria may be easier to apply in the more predictable world of subsidies for public transport than in the more complex world of risk equalization schemes. However, the conclusion seems warranted that the General Court is prepared to take a flexible view of public interest schemes that are perceived as bona fide even where the costs involved cannot be controlled quite to the standard set in *Altmark*. A similar line was taken by the CJEU itself in the *Chronopost* v. *UFEX* case (2008). Although *Altmark* was not applied here, just as in *BUPA* there was no efficiency test (or for that manner any specific test) required in relation to the compensation scheme involving the French postal operator La Poste. The Court was nevertheless satisfied with the Commission's finding that no aid had been involved.[100] Whether this case law should be seen as encouraging or as quite worrying depends on one's perspective on the need for exceptions to the state aid rules to be tightly controlled.

In contrast to the EU Courts, however, the Commission's practice shows that it is more likely to find that the fourth *Altmark* condition (on efficiency) is not met and that it will instead apply its *Altmark* framework, to which I will now turn.

[99] Ibid., para. 190.

[100] Cf. Joined cases C-341/06 P and C-342/06 P *Chronopost SA and La Poste* v. *Union française de l'express (UFEX) et al.* [2008] ECR I-4777; discussed in H. Vedder and M. Holwerda, 'The European Court's jurisprudence after *Altmark*', in Szyszczak and van de Gronden, above n. 87, 53–67. Cf. de Cecco, above n. 14, at 144ff.

The *Altmark* package

Towards a more economic approach to SGEI

In 2005 the Commission adopted its first *Altmark* package for cases where the four conditions set in the *Altmark* case cannot be met.[101] Like its successor in 2012, the 2005 package was centred on a block exemption and a framework for individual decisions regarding compensation for public services.[102] In addition, the 2012 package provides an explanatory Communication and a Regulation setting out a new de minimis threshold at €500,000 over three fiscal years.[103] The Commission also provides extensive public guidance.[104] The justification for both packages was by and large the same: the fourth *Altmark* condition could not be met in many cases, for which the Commission intended to provide legal certainty under the state aid rules by using Article 106(3) TFEU to exempt them (either under the above-mentioned block exemption or in individual decisions). In effect this meant reintroducing the very 'state aid approach' that had been sidestepped by *Altmark*.

The *Altmark* package was enthusiastically received by academic economists, notably by the Economic Advisory Group to the Commission's Competition and State Aid Directorate General.[105] In its view, market failure should be at the heart of all state aid policy, as is enabling competition on the market or competition for the market (as in a tender procedure) wherever possible, and using a cost versus benefits assessment to determine whether intervention is warranted (or from a legal perspective: proportional). In the view of the Advisory Group, SGEI services should be defined by universal coverage and universal pricing requirements under conditions that would by definition lead to their provision at a loss – otherwise there would be no need to define an SGEI. I am not an economist but it seems to me that any public service obligation that would lead to a disadvantage given more profitable alternative uses of an economic operator's assets – opportunity costs – would equally qualify.

[101] Cf. Joined cases T-231/06 and T-237/06, *The Netherlands*, above n. 16, paras. 153–5.

[102] Cf. W. Sauter, 'The *Altmark* package mark II: New rules for state aid and the compensation of services of general economic interest', *European Competition Law Review*, 33 (2012), 307–13; E. Szyszczak, 'Modernising state aid and the financing of SGEI', *Journal of European Competition Law and Practice*, 3 (2012), 332–43. Cf. Szyszczak and van de Gronden, above n. 87.

[103] This is significantly higher than the general threshold for state aid in Commission Regulation (EC) No 1998/2006 of 15 December 2006 on the application of Articles 87 and 88 of the Treaty to de minimis aid, OJ 2006, L379/5, which sets a ceiling of €200,000 over three fiscal years.

[104] Commission staff working document, Guide to the application of the European Union rules on state aid, public procurement and the internal market to services of general economic interest, and in particular to social services of general interest, SWD(2013) 53.

[105] EAGCP (state aid subgroup), *Services of general economic interest*, June 2006. An internal precursor was the DG Competition 'Non-paper on services of general economic interest and state aid', of 12 November 2002.

The Advisory Group applauded the criteria set out in *Altmark* and substantively repeated in the *Altmark* package, with exception of the fourth, or efficiency, condition. This may come as a surprise coming from economic commentators. However, the fourth criterion is also in their view the most difficult to implement, for instance because no appropriate comparator may exist. In my own view, it should be noted that the fourth condition makes no sense either if services are being provided in competition: arguably this is even better for efficiency than a public tender would have been. However, in this case there is perhaps no scope for SGEI. Nevertheless the *Altmark* package does provide for efficiency incentives, as we will see further below after looking at the different elements of the *Altmark* package.

The block exemption for welfare services

The 2012 Decision provides a block exemption for transport services and, more importantly, an unlimited block exemption (no quantitative threshold applies) for social services of general interest – or welfare services, to stick with my usage so far – that are subject to an SGEI:

> the provision of services of general economic interest by hospitals providing medical care, including, where applicable, emergency services; ... services of general economic interest meeting social needs as regards health and long term care, childcare, access to and reintegration into the labour market, social housing and the care and social inclusion of vulnerable groups.

This exemption applies provided certain requirements are met, which are essentially that there must be an act of entrustment which sets out an SGEI,[106] the terms of compensation must be clear and set out in advance, and there must be control for overcompensation as well as a recovery mechanism. In other words, the amount of aid must be justified in relation to the SGEI provided, and in relation to cost parameters set out in advance, but not in relation to an extraneous competition standard. It should be noted that even these relatively relaxed requirements are often not met in practice, where there is no act of entrustment, and the existence of an SGEI must be derived from the context.[107] This approach has many drawbacks, an important one of which is that if the objectives are not crystal clear it becomes difficult or impossible to apply an effective proportionality test, which after all requires testing the restraints involved against these objectives.

[106] This must contain: '(a) the content and duration of the public service obligations; (b) the undertaking and, where applicable, the territory concerned; (c) the nature of any exclusive or special rights assigned to the undertaking by the granting authority; (d) a description of the compensation mechanism and the parameters for calculating, controlling and reviewing the compensation; (e) the arrangements for avoiding and recovering any overcompensation; and (f) a reference to this Decision'.

[107] Case T-289/03 *BUPA*, above n. 98; Case T-137/10 *Coordination bruxelloise d'institutions sociales et de santé (CBI)* v. *Commission*, Judgment of 7 November 2012.

The individual exemptions regime for the utilities

The framework that forms the other main element of the *Altmark* package sets out the conditions under which individual exemptions will be provided. Although the conditions are substantially identical to those in the block exemption, such aid will have to be notified and cannot be disbursed prior to a Commission decision on the individual case. Given the filter for welfare services in the general interest set out in the block exemption, this means that effectively the individual exemptions regime is targeted at the utilities. First of all, this is in line with the objective of focusing more on the economically most significant cases (and where there are prospects for cross-border provision and/ or investment), which has also been one of the motives of the earlier (2004) competition policy modernization and decentralization.[108] Second, a more economic approach is chosen.[109]

The economic objectives are: (i) avoiding overcompensation; and (ii) avoiding cross-subsidies that distort compensation. Because more detailed economic analysis will be required to determine the costs, the rules on cost parameters here are more specific with respect to the net avoidable cost methodology to be used and the concept of a reasonable profit (requiring a benchmark rate of return). The test does not require meeting the standard of an efficient provider (the fourth *Altmark* condition) but the inclusion of an efficiency incentive:

> In devising the method of compensation, Member States must introduce incentives for the efficient provision of SGEI of a high standard, unless they can duly justify that it is not feasible or appropriate to do so.[110]

Whether SGEI are an appropriate instrument at all and whether competitive provision could not have sufficed is covered in the general Communication that accompanies the package:

> The Commission thus considers that it would not be appropriate to attach specific public service obligations to an activity which is already provided or can be provided satisfactorily and under conditions, such as price, objective quality characteristics, continuity and access to the service, consistent with the public interest, as defined by the State, by undertakings operating under normal market conditions. As for the question of whether a service can be provided by the market, the Commission's assessment is limited to checking whether the Member State has made a manifest error.[111]

Because I have already discussed this condition in Chapters 1 and 3 above, I will be brief here. The Commission combines the principle of an ambitious and

[108] Cf. L. Hancher and P. Larouche, 'The coming of age of EU regulation of network industries and services of general economic interest', in P. Craig and G. de Búrca (eds.), *The evolution of EU law*, 2nd edn (Oxford University Press, 2011), 743–81.

[109] Cf. J. Kavanagh, 'Financing services of general economic interest: The European Commission's economic tests', in Szyszczak and van de Gronden, above n. 87, 149–59.

[110] SGEI compensation framework, above n. 97, para. 39.

[111] SGEI compensation Communication, above n. 17, para. 48.

intrusive standard (consistent with the existence of potential competition) for excluding services from SGEI with a weak instrument to control and enforce that standard in practice. Most likely comparisons across Member States will not survive this test, so the situation in each Member State will be examined on its own terms. It is also striking that the concept of market failure seems to have been spelled out here in substance but is not mentioned explicitly. Possibly this standard is intended as a stub for future elaboration.

Methodology of the *Altmark* package

The methodology of the *Altmark* package for public service compensation is summarized well in the flowchart shown below (see Figure 4.1) that formed part of the Commission's comment and information that accompanied the package. The process consists of two instruments (the block exemption Decision and the Framework for individual decisions) and three stages.

The first question is whether there is aid (if not there is no issue). If so, the second question is whether the aid fulfils the criteria of the Decision, in which

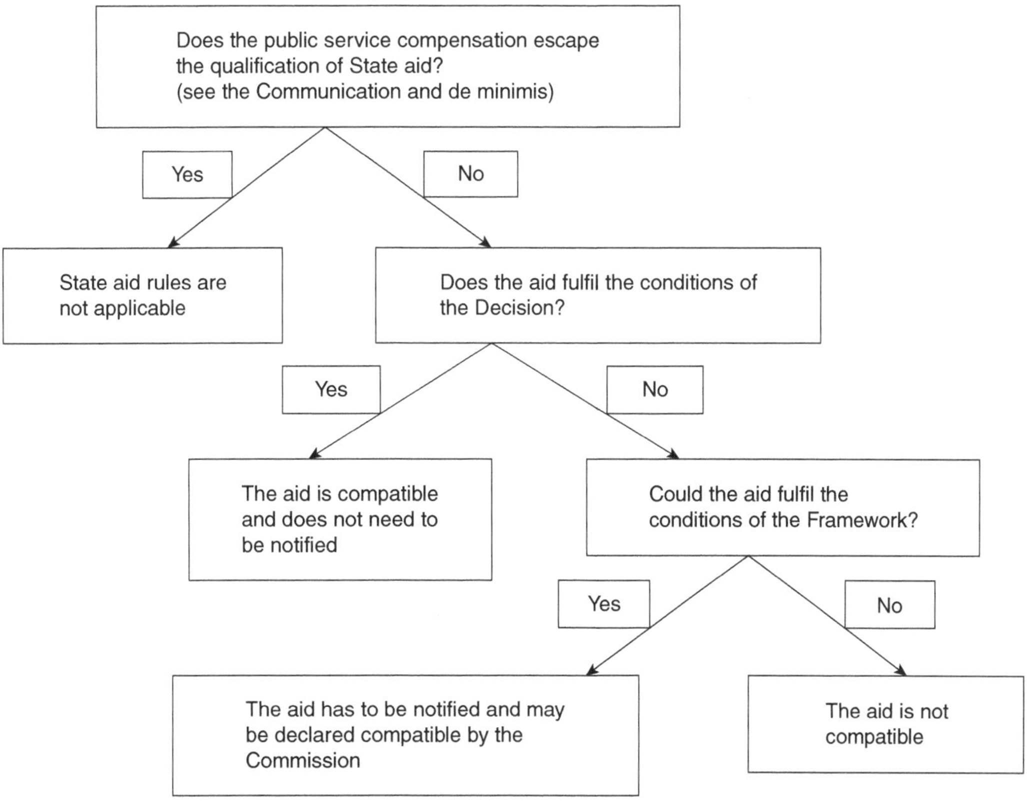

Figure 4.1 Analysis tree (source: N. Pesaresi et al., 'The new state aid rules for services of general economic interest (SGEI): The Commission Decision and Framework of 20 December 2011', *Competition Policy Newsletter* (2012) 1

case it is compatible aid. As we have seen, this step is tailored to be met by the welfare services (and certain transport services). If the public service compensation does not fulfil the criteria it could still be declared compatible based on an individual notification if it passes muster under the Framework (which is the third question). If not, the aid is not compatible.

Efficiency

As we have seen, there is no requirement to use public procurement or the standard of a well-run (efficient) undertaking as there is under the *Altmark* test set out by the CJEU. However, all three elements of the *Altmark* package include reference to efficiency incentives that may be introduced by the Member States to determine what constitutes a reasonable profit.[112] There is a marked difference on this point between the various instruments that constitute the package.

The Communication states that the Member States 'may' introduce efficiency incentives when determining what constitutes a reasonable profit. According to the Decision,

> In determining what constitutes a reasonable profit, Member States may introduce incentive criteria relating, in particular, to the quality of service provided and gains in productive efficiency. Efficiency gains shall not reduce the quality of the service provided. Any rewards linked to productive efficiency gains shall be set at a level such as to allow balanced sharing of those gains between the undertaking and the Member State and/or the users.[113]

It is therefore up to the Member States themselves whether they wish to introduce efficiency incentives for the public services that are covered by the block exemption contained in the Decision. The Framework Communication, however, states imposing efficiency incentives as a conditional obligation:

> In devising the method of compensation, Member States must introduce incentives for the efficient provision of SGEI of a high standard, unless they can duly justify that it is not feasible or appropriate to do so . . .
>
> Rewards linked to productive efficiency gains are to be set at a level such as to allow balanced sharing of those gains between the undertaking and the Member State and/or the users.
>
> Any such mechanism for incentivising efficiency improvements must be based on objective and measurable criteria set out in the entrustment act and subject to transparent ex post assessment carried out by an entity independent from the SGEI provider.[114]

[112] Cf. SGEI compensation Communication, above n. 17, para. 61. SGEI compensation Decision, above n. 88, Article 5(6); SGEI compensation framework, above n. 97, paras. 39–43.

[113] SGEI compensation Decision, above n. 88, Article 5(6).

[114] SGEI compensation framework, above n. 97, paras. 39, 41–2.

Consequently, efficiency incentives are effectively required in order to obtain a finding of compatibility with the internal market in individual cases notified to the Commission under the framework. It should be noted that the gains are to be shared between the undertaking and the Member State or the users, and therefore need not accrue to the Union, as would normally be expected where efficiency benefits in the context of Article 107(3) TFEU are concerned. This can be explained by the fact that here we are dealing with the context of SGEI and Article 106(3) TFEU. The flexibility of the SGEI provision in this respect can be seen as an additional advantage to using this test.

I will not go into further detail on the *Altmark* package.[115] Instead I will now briefly present two sectoral regimes that can also be regarded as case studies with regard to state aid: first, public broadcasting; and second, broadband.

The Public Broadcasting Guidelines

For obvious reasons related to the role of media in the shaping of popular culture and politics, public service broadcasting has long been a politically sensitive sector in the EU. This is reflected in Protocol 29 on the system of public broadcasting in the Member States that was added to the Amsterdam Treaty in 1998. This Protocol cites the 'democratic, social and cultural needs of each society and . . . the need to preserve media pluralism' as public objectives of the Member States, and states that the Treaty rules do not affect the funding of public broadcasting in so far as this does not infringe competition and the EU common interest.

Monopolies have long been abolished in the broadcasting sector and consequently public broadcasting has come under economic pressure from commercial broadcasters who generate (more) funding from advertising and offer more popular formats. Technological change has added to the complexity as the range of audiovisual services offered has multiplied while audiences have fragmented: more recently the internet-based new (social) media have become both an opportunity and a threat. They broaden media pluralism while undermining traditional media. In this context state aid to public broadcasters has become an especially sensitive issue. Both single funding (public funding) and dual funding (mixing commercial income with public funding) are in principle acceptable, in line with the strictures of Protocol 29.

In 2009 the Commission adopted the current regime of soft-law guidance for public service broadcasting.[116] This 2009 Communication superseded earlier guidance that had been issued in 2001,[117] and accompanied the 2010 Directive

[115] Cf. J. L. Buendia Sierra and J. M. Panero Rivas, 'The *Almunia* package: State aid and services of general economic interest', in Szyszczak and van de Gronden, above n. 87, 125–48.

[116] Communication from the Commission on the application of state aid rules to public service broadcasting OJ 2009, C257/1.

[117] Communication from the Commission on the application of state aid rules to public service broadcasting OJ 2001, C320/5.

on audiovisual media services that will be discussed in more detail in Chapter 6 on vertical secondary legislation.[118] At the time of writing, some thirty-six Commission Decisions have been adopted based on the Broadcasting Guidelines. Although the principle of public or mixed funding is accepted, the Commission will verify whether the broadcaster concerned has been entrusted with the provision of a clearly defined service of general economic interest and will check the proportionality of the funding concerned. The proportionality test is mainly one for overcompensation. The delicate balance set out in the Broadcasting Guidelines is therefore a sector-specific variation on the SGEI test.

The reasons for exempting state aid for public broadcasting are, as is set out in Protocol 29 and cited above, unreservedly equitable in nature, not efficiency based. Unsurprisingly therefore, the Guidelines consider a qualitative definition of obligations to provide a wide range of (balanced and varied) programming to be legitimate in meeting the SGEI standard.[119] The Commission's test is limited to checking for manifest error, which would be the case if advertising, e-shopping, the use of premium rate numbers in prize games, sponsoring and merchandising are involved, or when state aid is used to finance activities with no added value in terms of serving social, democratic or cultural needs.[120] At the same time, payment for new services 'does not necessarily mean that these services are manifestly not part of the public service remit'. The Commission suggests that in deciding on this remit (apart from social, democratic and cultural needs) the universality of the service provided will play a role, which may be affected when services must be remunerated directly by viewers.[121]

In the relevant case law it is generally the proportionality of the aid involved and the scope of market activities by public service broadcasters that is primarily contested by third parties.[122] Given the fluid nature of the services provided – and of the benefits for users which are difficult to pinpoint other than in terms of aspirations – this involves difficult decisions. I will now move on to broadband where a more structured test appears to be involved.

[118] Directive 2010/13/EU of the European Parliament and of the Council of 10 March 2010 on the coordination of certain provisions laid down by law, regulation or administrative action in Member States concerning the provision of audiovisual media services (Audiovisual Media Services Directive) OJ 2010, L95/1.

[119] Broadcasting Guidelines, above n. 116, para. 47, with reference to Joined cases T-309/04, T-317/04, T-329/04 and T-336/04 *TV. 2/Danmark A/S and Others* v. *Commission* [2008] ECR II-2935 and Case T-442/03 *SIC – Sociedade Independente de Comunicação SA* v. *Commission* [2008] ECR II-1161.

[120] Broadcasting Guidelines, above n. 116, para. 48.

[121] Ibid., para. 83. The nature of the funding (public or private) does not determine the SGEI status of a service. Instead an SGEI is defined in relation to the general interest that it is intended to satisfy. Joined cases T-309/04, T-317/04, T-329/04 and T-336/04 *TV. 2*, above n. 119, paras. 107–9.

[122] Case T-275/11 *Télévision française 1 (TF1)* v. *Commission*, Judgment of 16 October 2013; Case T-520/09 *Télévision française 1 (TF1), Métropole télévision (M6) et Canal +* v. *Commission*, Judgment of 10 July 2012.

The Broadband Guidelines

In 2013 the Commission adopted soft-law guidance similar to that in public service broadcasting for state aid in the broadband sector.[123] These 2013 Guidelines replaced largely similar earlier Commission guidance adopted in 2009.[124] Broadband is shorthand for a variety of technologies that offer 'next generation' electronic communications networks for information technology, media and communications that are often largely fibre optic based (however, mobile and satellite networks are also possible). Promoting broadband roll-out is part of the Europe 2020 Strategy objectives of the EU[125] and its Digital Agenda:[126] by 2020 all of Europe must have access to higher internet speeds at above 30 Mbps and 50 per cent or more of European households must have speeds at above 100 Mbps. These industrial policy objectives are in fact quoted in the 2013 Guidelines.

At the time of writing, there were 132 Commission state aid decisions listed in this area – of which there was only one where there had been a finding of incompatible aid, all the other cases having been flagged through based on *Altmark*, or the SGEI test, or because the market economy investor principle (MEIP) had been applied.

The principle of the guidelines is that broadband markets are divided into three types: black, grey and white areas. Black areas are already served by two or more commercial providers on their own account and it is not normally permissible to give state aid there (although public authorities may still invest in accordance with the MEIP cited above). In grey areas there is at least one commercial provider which is active. Here public investment in a competing network is only permitted provided that the subsidized network offers third-party access to competitors and universal service is offered on this basis. In white areas where no commercial operations are active and there would be no investment other than public investment, there are no objections against the latter.

The 2013 Guidelines in my view undermine their own principles by stating that in exceptional circumstances, to promote the highest of high-speed networks, occasionally public investment in black areas that does not qualify as

[123] Communication from the Commission on EU Guidelines for the application of state aid rules in relation to the rapid deployment of broadband networks, OJ 2013, C25/1. Cf. A. Kliemann and O. Stehmann, 'EU state aid control in the broadband sector – The 2013 broadband guidelines and recent case practice', *European State Aid Law Quarterly*, 12 (2013), 493.

[124] Communication from the Commission, Community Guidelines for the application of State aid rules in relation to rapid deployment of broadband networks, OJ 2009, C235/7.

[125] Communication from the Commission, Europe 2020: A strategy for smart, sustainable and inclusive growth, COM(2010) 2020; Council conclusions on Europe 2020, 16 March 2010. Cf. W. Sauter, 'Squaring EU competition law and industrial policy: The case of broadband', TILEC Discussion Paper 2013/21.

[126] Communication from the Commission, A digital agenda for Europe, COM(2010) 245; Communication from the Commission, The digital agenda for Europe – Driving European growth digitally, COM(2012) 784.

MEIP is allowed. Not surprisingly, this serves to meet the overly ambitious industrial policy goals set out in the Digital Agenda and copied into the Guidelines. Other drawbacks aside, this distracts public investment from areas where more basic coverage may still be needed and displaces private investment. The contribution of the Guidelines on the topics of market failure and universal service is more encouraging. On market failure, the Guidelines state:

> A 'market failure' exists if markets, left to their own devices, without intervention fail to deliver an efficient outcome for society. This may arise, for instance, when certain investments are not being undertaken even though the economic benefit for society exceeds the cost. In such cases, the granting of State aid may produce positive effects and overall efficiency can be improved by adjusting the economic incentives for firms. In the broadband sector, one form of market failure is related to positive externalities. Such externalities arise where market players do not internalise the whole benefit of their actions ... The market outcome would therefore generate insufficient private investment in broadband networks.[127]

Apart from this efficiency-based ground for intervention, the Guidelines also mention equity reasons: investment is likely to focus on more densely populated and wealthier areas. Public intervention may also serve to remedy social and regional inequalities. Finally, on universal service the Guidelines state clearly that this is not to be provided directly by subsidized networks, but indirectly by service providers, which can obtain access to the publicly funded network (which is to serve as passive, neutral and open infrastructure) and use this as a platform.[128]

> [T]he SGEI mission should only cover the deployment of a broadband network providing universal connectivity and the provision of the related wholesale access services, without including retail communication services. Where the provider of the SGEI mission is also a vertically integrated broadband operator, adequate safeguards should be put in place to avoid any conflict of interest, undue discrimination and any other hidden indirect advantages.[129]

The recent decision by the General Court in *Colt* (2013)[130] appears to affirm that such wholesale services should actually then be regarded as SGEI when they are subject to public service obligations as the result of having to provide

[127] 2013 Broadband Guidelines, above n. 123, para. 37.

[128] Cf. 'a publicly funded network set up within the context of an SGEI should be available to all interested operators. Accordingly, the recognition of an SGEI mission for broadband deployment should be based on the provision of a passive, neutral and open infrastructure. Such a network should provide access seekers with all possible forms of network access and allow effective competition at the retail level, ensuring the provision of competitive and affordable services to end-users.' Ibid., para. 23.

[129] Ibid., para. 24.

[130] Case T-79/10 *Colt Télécommunications France* v. *Commission*, Judgment of 16 September 2013. This case refers to the earlier version of the Guidelines (2009 Broadband Guidelines); however, on this point they are identical with the 2013 Broadband Guidelines.

access to service providers on a non-discriminatory basis. They would then provide 'universal connectivity' even although they do not directly provide universal services to end-users themselves.

Market failure and state aid: the *Colt* case

Market failure is a key criterion for the justification of state aid. This efficiency-based standard is not the only criterion because equity-based defences can likewise be accepted. The same holds true for SGEI: both efficiency and equity interest may be invoked. There is a difference between the two however, because generally speaking an EU interest must be served to warrant a state aid exemption, whereas in the case of SGEI an interest of a Member State is balanced against an EU interest. In the above-mentioned *Colt* case (2013) on broadband services in France, the General Court specified that the market failure concept plays a role not only in the test whether a state aid measure is compatible with the internal market,[131] but also with regard to the preliminary question whether a state aid is involved at all and/or whether an SGEI is involved. In fact, sidestepping equity, the General Court states that the existence of a market failure is a precondition for finding an SGEI and thereby to establish the absence of a state aid:

> l'appréciation de l'existence d'une défaillance du marché constitue une préalable à la qualification d'une activité de SEIG et ainsi à la constatation de l'absence d'aide d'État.[132]

In other words, the General Court appears to suggest that a genuine SGEI (based on addressing a real market failure which can be established as a matter of fact) would not constitute state aid. This would be at least a different emphasis and possibly a serious divergence from the *Altmark* package approach which assumes that, with respect to SGEI, there can be aid but that it is (or will be declared) compatible based on Article 106(2) TFEU. The *Colt* case suggests a type of rule of reason instead. Moreover, the *Altmark* approach focuses on conditions with regard to the precise level of costs and reimbursement in order to avoid overcompensation that do not involve questioning the legitimacy of the public interest justification that is invoked as such. On the financial dimension, the ruling in the *Colt* case reaches back to the early postal case *Corbeau* (1993) to justify cross-subsidies.[133] It seems to me that at a minimum a genuine SGEI should satisfy both the legitimate objective and the no-overcompensation requirements. Finally, so far legitimate objectives in state

[131] Case T-79/10 *Colt*, above n. 130, para. 150, with reference to two broadcasting cases of 6 October 2009: T-8/06 *FAB* v. *Commission* [2009] ECR II-196; and T-21/06 *Germany* v. *Commission*, and para. 154.

[132] Case T-79/10 *Colt*, above n. 130, para. 154.

[133] Ibid., para. 185, with reference to Case C-320/91 *Criminal proceedings against Paul Corbeau* [1993] ECR I-2533. The General Court also refers to Case T-289/03 *BUPA*, above n. 98.

aid SGEI cases may include equity motives as much as reasons of efficiency. No doubt further procedures will cast new light on the questions raised by the *Colt* case.

4.6 Conclusion

The EU state aid and competition rules are both concerned with undertakings. The competition rules are addressed to undertakings and undertakings are the beneficiaries of state aid. This means that welfare services are often excluded as they are provided by public authorities and/or in accordance with conditions of solidarity, which means that they are not provided as a service in a market as an economic activity, and/or (potentially) under competitive conditions. Following liberalization, there has been no comparable discussion to the effect that the entities providing utilities are not undertakings: as a rule they are. The definitions used are functional in nature, but diverge between free movement (remuneration based) and competition (based on provision of goods or services in markets). The purchasing of services, which would be pertinent under free movement, is sometimes not regarded as relevant to the competition rules, in spite of the fact that this appears to make little economic sense.

In principle the EU competition rules allow only exceptions for practices that are efficiency based and share benefits with consumers, as is the case under Article 101(3) TFEU. However, a rule of reason that excludes restrictions in the public interest (under Article 101(1) TFEU) is sometimes applied, and some observers have claimed that public interest defences should also be allowed under Article 101(3) TFEU as well. I have serious doubt about both approaches: public policy should be set publicly and be subject to democratic scrutiny. It can be imposed on undertakings which will then enjoy antitrust immunity. Moreover, there is another alternative which is growing in significance: SGEI.

The exception for SGEI has become a common feature of the EU competition and state aid regimes. The application of the concept of SGEI in this context means that proportional restrictions that are necessary in relation to a legitimate public interest objective can be justified. In this case both equity and efficiency justifications are acceptable, and the interest is defined at the level of the Member State (although it must be balanced against the effect on the internal market). Especially in the field of state aid, it is no longer the Article 107(3) TFEU decision on the compatibility with the internal market (which could accommodate both equity and efficiency defences, but only based on the EU interest), but that based on SGEI in Article 106(2) TFEU that has come to dominate legal practice with regard to public services.

Because the choice of objectives itself is in this context only subject to a manifest disproportionality test, the risk of overcompensation has become the primary EU law concern instead. With the adoption of the 'compensation' approach (compensation for public service obligations is seen as remuneration, not as a state aid, provided certain conditions are met), the *Altmark* case (2003) and the subsequent *Altmark* packages (2005 and 2012) have determined the criteria that will henceforth be used. These are based on entrustment with a public service obligation; known and verifiable cost standards; preventing and retrieving overcompensation; as well as in the case of the *Altmark* test, an efficiency requirement. The 2012 package now also requires efficiency incentives.

My findings on the three secondary themes identified in the introduction can be summed up in just a few remarks. The consumer interest for the competition rules is one among several objectives. In many instances the competition process, not competition policy, and intervention at wholesale, not retail level, is deemed to be most beneficial for consumers. As regards market failure, this category is relevant primarily under the state aid rules, where it is gaining traction. So far, however, equity reasons can also be invoked to obtain an exception under the state aid rules (and could be covered by a broad understanding of market failure). The most important exception which covers both aspects is that for SGEI. Here universality is both a key precondition and a category that is in the process of being modified and stretched.

As we have seen, wholesale infrastructure services that do not directly reach final consumers and insurance-based services that are not mandatory and are consumed only by part of the population have been accepted as SGEI. The full extent of the flexibility of this model has not yet been tested, but at the same time its application has to remain consistent. This consistency requirement will come up again, especially in relation to the sector-specific regimes in Chapter 6. First, however, I will take up the horizontal rules of secondary law in Chapter 5. There I will look in greater detail at the public procurement rules and the link with the fourth *Altmark* criterion.

5

Horizontal secondary rules – services, procurement and transparency

5.1 Introduction

In this chapter I will look into those rules of secondary law that are relevant to public services and that are horizontal in nature. In other words: in principle these rules apply to all public services alike and they are not sector-specific. Nevertheless certain exceptions to these secondary horizontal rules may be sector specific or they may sometimes contain some sector-specific provisions. That is all the more relevant because public services, with their mixture of public and market aspects, appear to be prone to being subject to all manner of exceptions and to have obtained a special status. However, the broad gist is clear: these are rules that are meant to be of general application.

After winnowing down the set of rules to those that are truly secondary and horizontal and relevant to public services, I have ended up with a rather limited set of only three: the Services Directive,[1] the Public Procurement Directives (recently reviewed and subject to replacement in 2016)[2] and the Transparency Directive.[3]

At first sight, there does not appear to be much that these three sets of rules have in common: the first deals with all manner of services in the internal market; the second only with public purchasing with an internal market dimension and competition for the market (instead of on the market, as is generally the concern

[1] Directive 2006/123/EC of the European Parliament and of the Council of 12 December 2006 on services in the internal market, OJ 2006, L376/36. Cf. C. Barnard, 'Unravelling the Services Directive', *Common Market Law Review*, 45 (2008), 323–94; U. Neergaard, R. Nielsen and L. M. Roseberry (eds.), *The Services Directive: Consequences for the welfare state and the European social model* (Djøf Publishing, Copenhagen, 2008); V. Hatzopoulos, *Regulating services in the European Union* (Oxford University Press, 2012) at 257–65.

[2] Directive 2004/17/EC of the European Parliament and of the Council of 31 March 2004 coordinating the procurement procedures of entities operating in the water, energy, transport and postal services sectors, OJ 2004, L134/1; Directive 2004/18/EC of the European Parliament and of the Council of 31 March 2004 on the coordination of procedures for the award of public works contracts, public supply contracts and public service contracts, OJ 2004, L134/114. Cf. C. H. Bovis, *European public procurement law*, 2nd edn (Edward Elgar, Cheltenham, 2012); A. Sánchez Graells, *Public procurement and the EU competition rules* (Hart Publishing, Oxford, 2011).

[3] Commission Directive 2006/111/EC of 16 November 2006 on the transparency of financial relations between Member States and public undertakings as well as on financial transparency within certain undertakings, OJ 2006, L318/17.

for competition rules); and the third with accounting practices of public undertakings and undertakings enjoying special and exclusive rights. Apart from the fact that both the Services Directive and the Public Procurement Directives deal with opening up the internal market and the Transparency Directive primarily deals with enabling state aid enforcement, the common denominator seems to be establishing a level playing field for the provision of services. Taking the Public Procurement and Transparency Directives together instead, the role of public authorities as participants in the market rather than as regulators of the market also plays a role. This said, the interaction between the three sets of rules appears to be minimal. The common thread in my discussion will therefore be the relevance to public services. This also means that the rules concerned will not be dealt with in detail in their own right.

I have chosen to deal with the three topics of this chapter in the order in which they are presented in the title above because this seems to involve moving from the general (all services) down to the particular – via all services subject to public procurement – to only those provided by public undertakings. For the sake of comprehensiveness, I will in addition touch briefly on two topics that belong in this chapter systematically – as horizontal secondary law with a bearing on public service – but not in terms of their content. These are the Commission Decision on public service compensation and state aid, and the Framework Regulation of the European Parliament and Council on SGEI that remains to be adopted under Article 14 TFEU – but for which the Commission has so far not submitted a proposal. They fit in with the general sequence of the chapter sketched out above because they are each yet more specifically concerned with public services and services of general (economic) interest: SG(E)I.

The three questions that I want to examine here are the following:

- What is the horizontal secondary EU law and what limits does it impose on the provision of public services?
- What scope is left for national policies regarding public services under EU law exceptions to horizontal secondary law?
- What is the role of the concept of service of general (economic) interest in this context?

I will summarize and discuss the answers to these questions in the conclusion. In contrast to the horizontal rules that are the focus of the present chapter, in the next chapter I will then move on to the separate sector-specific rules for individual types of public services, that is to say the (harmonized) vertical secondary rules.

5.2 The Services Directive

A troubled background

Because in the EU services account for 70 per cent of GDP it should come as no surprise that more efficient provision of services carries considerable economic potential. The Services Directive was proposed to unlock this potential. This Directive has a heroic history, having emerged from the most contentious legislative process of any piece of secondary EU legislation in living memory, at least any piece of legislation that was ultimately adopted, albeit in severely amended form. The Services Directive was originally proposed by Internal Market Commissioner Frits Bolkestein in 2004 as a classic home country control (or country of origin principle) based Directive, with the purpose of providing a service provider who met the requirements in at least one Member State with a passport for operating in all Member States. Effectively the proposal was to apply to services the mutual recognition principle that had been established in the1979 *Cassis de Dijon* case for goods.[4]

This idea, personified by the mythical Polish plumbers who would allegedly wash over the borders to undermine working and social standards throughout the (wealthier) old Member States, alongside provisions on healthcare and on social standards (rules on the applicability of posted workers),[5] became the target of political protest and even street demonstrations. The Services Directive (or 'Frankenstein Directive' as it was dubbed by its detractors) eventually became shorthand for everything associated with rampant free-market Anglo-Saxon capitalism and social dumping.

The eventual Services Directive

Under Bolkestein's successor as Internal Market Commissioner, Charlie McCreevey, the home country control principle, the healthcare and social provisions were dropped from the proposal in order to assuage its many critics. Instead the conditions that host Member States could impose were curtailed.

- First, this concerns freedom of establishment. Here imposing an authorization requirement means that conditions must be non-discriminatory, justified by overriding reasons of public interest and proportional. In addition, the conditions for granting an authorization must meet those same requirements (that is: they must be non-discriminatory, justified by overriding reasons and proportional) as well as being clear and non-ambiguous, objective, made public in advance and transparent.
- Second, the freedom to provide services itself can only be curtailed by measures that respect the principles of non-discrimination, necessity and

[4] Case 120/78 *Rewe-Zentral AG* v. *Bundesmonopolverwaltung für Branntwein* [1979] ECR 649 (*Cassis de Dijon*). Cf. Regulation (EC) No 764/2008 of the European Parliament and of the Council of 9 July 2008 laying down procedures relating to the application of certain national technical rules to products lawfully marketed in another Member State and repealing Decision No 3052/95/ECOJ 2008, L218/21.

[5] Which gave primacy to Directive 96/71/EC of the European Parliament and of the Council of 16 December 1996 concerning the posting of workers in the framework of the provision of services, OJ 1997, L18/1. Cf. F. Hendrickx, 'The Services Directive and social dumping: National labour law under strain?' in Neergaard, Nielsen and Roseberry, above n. 1, 243–58.

proportionality, and a list of non-admissible restrictions was provided (such as an obligation to have an establishment in the territory).

- Third, the Services Directive includes rights of the recipients of services, which includes a list of prohibited restrictions, as well as a non-discrimination requirement with relation to nationality and place of residence and rights to information, assistance and dispute resolution (in what appears to be a generic version of what was subsequently spelled out for healthcare services in the Patients' Rights Directive).[6]

With these changes and this new focus the Services Directive was finally adopted in December 2006. I will now look more closely at the relationship between the Services Directive and public services. As has been discussed in the first chapter, in EU law terms this means looking at services of general interest (SGI), which includes both economic and non-economic services of general interest, and its more significant subcategory of services of general economic interest (SGEI). The latter, SGEI, is more significant because it covers economic services – that is to say, services provided for remuneration, in markets and potentially in competition. Therefore this category is relevant to the free movement and competition rules as well as the rules on state aid and the secondary legislation in those fields, in this case the Services Directive.

Services of general (economic) interest in the Services Directive

The Services Directive grapples with SGI and SGEI extensively. Its Article 1, paragraphs 2, 3 and 4 concern SGI and SGEI, stating that the Directive does not deal with liberalization of SGEI nor with privatization of public services, does not deal with the abolition of services monopolies nor with the application of the rules on state aid[7] and does not affect the freedom of the Member States to define SGEI. Contrary to what might be expected after this somewhat defensive opening gambit (a Directive focusing on what it does not concern), the Services Directive does not provide a blanket exception for SGI and SGEI but takes a staggered approach.[8] The recitals already make this clear:

[6] Directive 2011/24/EU of the European Parliament and of the Council of 9 March 2011 on the application of patients' rights in cross-border healthcare, OJ 2011, L88/45. This is discussed in Chapter 6.

[7] 'This Directive does not deal with the abolition of monopolies providing services nor with aids granted by Member States which are covered by Community rules on competition. This Directive does not affect the freedom of Member States to define, in conformity with Community law, what they consider to be services of general economic interest, how those services should be organised and financed, in compliance with the State aid rules, and what specific obligations they should be subject to.' Directive 2006/123/EC, above n. 1, Article 1(3).

[8] Cf. J. van de Gronden, 'The Services Directive and services of general (economic) interest', in M. Krajewski, U. Neergaard and J. van de Gronden (eds.), *The changing legal framework for services of general interest in Europe: Between competition and solidarity* (TMC Asser Press, The Hague, 2009), 233–54; U. Neergaard, 'Services of general (economic) interest and the Services

> This Directive covers only services which are performed for an economic consideration. Services of general interest are not covered by the definition in Article 50 of the Treaty and therefore do not fall within the scope of this Directive. Services of general economic interest are services that are performed for an economic consideration and therefore do fall within the scope of this Directive. However, certain services of general economic interest, such as those that may exist in the field of transport, are excluded from the scope of this Directive and certain other services of general economic interest, for example, those that may exist in the area of postal services, are the subject of a derogation from the provision on the freedom to provide services set out in this Directive.[9]

Mirroring this approach, I will deal successively with: (i) the general rule; (ii) exceptions; and (iii) derogations with regard to SGI and SGEI.

Non-economic SGI are not covered

Some confusion may have been sown here by the first phrase of the above quotation, which states that SGI are not performed for consideration and hence not covered, while SGEI are. However, as we have seen in Chapter 1 and as mentioned in the introduction above, SGI is the overarching category for two subcategories: economic (or SGEI) and non-economic SGI. Therefore it makes no sense to claim that the broader category is not covered but the narrow category contained within it is. In the body of the Services Directive, however, there is no misunderstanding on this basic point. As becomes clear from Article 2(1)a on the scope of the Services Directive, it does not apply to 'non-economic services of general interest', which is consistent with the current general understanding of the relationship between SGI and SGEI: this means that SGI that are also SGEI are covered (unless specifically excluded) but those SGI that are not economic in nature are not. Because Article 4(1) of the Services Directive, by defining 'service' as any self-employed economic activity normally provided for remuneration (as in the sense of Article 57 TFEU), implicitly already excludes non-economic SGEI, the explicit provision in Article 2(1)a of the Services Directive can be seen as emphasizing this point and making it unequivocal.

The sectoral exceptions for SGEI

Apart from the non-economic services of general interest already mentioned, the Services Directive excepts a number of public services explicitly in its Article 2: electronic communications services and networks, in so far as covered by the sector-specific rules on this topic; transport services (including port facilities); all healthcare services (irrespective of their organization, financing and public or private provision); audiovisual services; and social services relating to social

Directive – What is left out, why and where to go?' in Neergaard, Nielsen and Roseberry, above n. 1, 65–120.

9 Directive 2006/123/EC, above n. 1, recital 17.

housing, childcare and support of families and persons permanently or temporarily in need (as provided by the state, by providers mandated by the state or charities recognized by the state). This amounts to a significant number of sectoral exceptions for SGEI, although in some cases (transport, public broadcasting, healthcare and electronic communications) meanwhile a (vertical) sectoral framework has been created. In combination with the general exception for non-economic SGI which are likely to cover a large part of welfare services like education and social services, a broad swathe of public services is left outside the scope of the Services Directive. However, the exact scope of what is left outside is not known because the Member States are free to define new SGEI.

The definition of a service as an SGI or SGEI can thus have a significant bearing on the relevance of the Services Directive. However, because specific types of public services are identified and exempted, the strategic use of the former two categories is in large part superfluous.

The derogations from the freedom to provide services

Article 16 of the Services Directive spells out the freedom to provide services, including that any requirements imposed must be non-discriminatory, necessary and proportional (as well as a list of conditions that may not be imposed). Article 17 of the Services Directive provides additional derogations from the freedom to provide services in relation to the exceptions in Article 2 that I have just discussed. This essentially regards the remaining utilities: postal services, services in the electricity and gas sectors, water distribution and treatment of waste. With regard to these services therefore, the establishment rules of the Services Directive, but not its provisions purely relating to the provision of services, apply. Equally important, the rights of service recipients in Articles 19 to 21 of the Services Directive still apply (see further below). Moreover, the derogation in Article 16 does not mean that discriminatory rules are henceforward justified but, first, that it is the Treaty freedom to provide services which applies, and second, where they exist, the relevant secondary (vertical) sector-specific rules apply. This approach could therefore be explained as an application of the *lex specialis* rule: where specific rules already exist the general rule does not apply.

A complex balance with a bias favouring sectoral rules

In addition, the recitals of the Services Directive specify that it does not deal with state aid and public financing issues with regard to SGEI. In this respect therefore, the Services Directive and the specific rules on the application of SGEI to public service compensation in the context of state aid (discussed in Chapter 4 above) are complementary. Meanwhile the first case law on the application of the Services Directive to SGEI has emerged, which predictably concerns the limits of the definitions (in this case of the healthcare exception).[10] In sum, what we see therefore is a complex picture: (i) non-application of the most important piece of horizontal liberalization legislation to date to non-economic SGI based on the familiar categories of remuneration and economic activity; (ii) the principled application of the Services Directive to SGEI; (iii) which is, however, largely gutted by exceptions and derogations; (iv) that can, however, largely be explained by the existence of more specific sectoral rules; (v) and reference to the complementary state aid rules on public service compensation. Overall this appears to be a complex balance with a bias favouring sectoral rules.

I now move on to the next set of secondary legislation that concerns access to the market, albeit a special case where markets are only accessible periodically: the public procurement rules.

5.3 The Public Procurement Directives

What is public procurement?

Like state aid, public procurement is a hybrid between the internal market and the competition rules. Again like state aid, it aims to combat unjust preferment of some undertakings over others. Like state aid, it has only recently attracted more widespread scholarly attention. Unlike state aid, however, it does not have a direct basis in the Treaties but is based almost completely (with the exception of certain generally applicable Treaty principles, including in particular transparency and non-discrimination) on secondary law that is of horizontal application.

Public procurement is economically significant because in the EU it accounts for some 18 per cent of GDP.[11] Systematically, the public procurement rules supplement the state aid and competition rules in those cases where continual competition on the market is not feasible, and where instead competition for the market is organized on a periodic basis.[12] The public procurement rules are

[10] Case C-57/12 *Fédération des maisons de repos privées de Belgique (Femarbel) ASBL* v. *Commission communautaire commune de Bruxelles-Capitale*, Judgment of 11 July 2013.

[11] *A new strategy for the internal market: At the service of Europe's economy and society.* Report to the President of the European Commission, José Manuel Barroso, by Mario Monti, 9 May 2010, at 76.

[12] C. H. Bovis, 'The conceptual links between state aid and public procurement in the financing of services of general economic interest', in Krajewski, Neergaard and van de Gronden (eds.), above n. 8, 149–70; I. Clarke, 'The role of procurement and SGEI after *Altmark*', in E. Szyszczak and J. W. van de Gronden (eds.), *Financing services of general economic interest: Reform and modernization* (TMC Asser Press, The Hague, 2013), 69–84; N. Fiedziuk, 'Putting services of general economic interest up for tender: Reflections on applicable EU rules', *Common Market Law Review*, 50 (2013), 87–114; E. Manunza and W. J. Berends, 'Social services of general interest and the EU public procurement rules', in U. Neergaard et al. (eds.), *Social services of general interest in the EU* (TMC Asser Press, The Hague, 2013), 347–84; A. Sánchez Graells, 'The Commission's modernisation agenda for procurement and SGEI', in Szyszczak and van de Gronden, above (this note), 161–81.

aimed at the contracting authorities, not at the providers of the service, and determine the selection conditions and procedures that may be applied. The objective is that competition for the market should be organized on a strictly non-discriminatory basis. The public procurement rules refer to public service contracts (as listed in Annex IIA and IIB of Directive 2004/18) but they do not refer to public service obligations or SGEI.

The rules on public procurement may nevertheless be relevant to public services for at least one of the following three reasons:

- First, because the provider of public services may (have to) be selected according to a public tender;
- Second, as public authorities may use public tenders to organize public services – even where they are not obliged to do so because self-provision by public authorities falls outside the scope of the public procurement rules;
- Third, the *Altmark* package gives preferential treatment to services selected by public tender, because they are presumed to meet the fourth (efficiency) condition.[13] This means no aid is involved and notification to the Commission is not necessary.

It is especially this third aspect that makes public procurement topical in the context of public services. At the same time, there is a basic tension between the freedom of Member States to identify public services and designate undertakings as responsible for carrying out public service obligations and requirements that in doing so they must respect the public procurement rules or similar regimes that we will come to discuss below.[14]

As we have also seen with regard to the state aid and competition rules (and to a lesser degree the freedom of services), a large part of the discussion focuses again on applicability and the boundaries of EU law, that is to say on the question whether the public procurement rules are applicable or not. Here the main question is whether the entity involved is a contracting authority or not. This revolves around the issue whether the contracting authority is an emanation of the state and is determined based on three criteria that are discussed below.

At present the EU's public procurement regime consists of two Directives, of which one is aimed at public works, supply and services contracts, and the other targets utilities (water, energy, transport and postal services). These Directives will be repealed and replaced in 2016 (see further below).[15] Meanwhile a third Directive on concessions has recently been adopted, that will likewise enter into

[13] Cf. Communication from the Commission on the application of the European Union state aid rules to compensation granted for the provision of services of general economic interest, OJ 2012, C8/4.

[14] Fiedziuk, above n. 12.

[15] Directive 2014/24/EU of the European Parliament and of the Council of 26 February 2014 on public procurement and repealing Directive 2004/18/EC, OJ 2014, L94/65; Directive 2014/25/EU of the European Parliament and of the Council of 26 February 2014 on procurement by entities

effect in 2016.[16] The latter is discussed at the end of this section. Otherwise I will discuss the law as it stands.

For several important types of public services (such as for healthcare) a relatively mild regime is applicable, which mainly boils down to a transparency and non-discrimination requirement. However, apart from the Procurement Directives there are requirements which relate to transparency in the internal market. Finally, for dominant operators similar conditions apply regardless of their contracting authority status: their special responsibilities entail a non-discrimination obligation.[17] The procurement, general transparency and dominant undertaking regimes are thus similar and apply in parallel – although as regards dominance the addressee is evidently an undertaking and not a public authority.

The criteria for the application of the Public Procurement Directives

The three conditions for the applicability of the EU public procurement rules are that: (i) the purchasing party qualifies as a contracting authority; (ii) the value of the contract exceeds the threshold values set in the Procurement Directives; and (iii) none of the exceptions applies. The main question is whether the contracting authority is a body governed by public law. According to Article 1(9) of Directive 2004/18/EC (with an analogous provision in Article 2(1) of Directive 2004/17/EC):

> 'Contracting authorities' means the State, regional or local authorities, bodies governed by public law, associations formed by one or several of such authorities or one or several of such bodies governed by public law.

And

> A 'body governed by public law' means any body: (a) established for the specific purpose of meeting needs in the general interest, not having an industrial or commercial character; (b) having legal personality; and (c) financed, for the most part, by the State, regional or local authorities, or other bodies governed by public law; or subject to management supervision by those bodies; or having an administrative, managerial or supervisory board, more than half of whose members are appointed by the State, regional or local authorities, or by other bodies governed by public law.

Public services (contracts) are defined by ways of reference to the lists attached to Directive 2004/18/EC summing up the relevant services.

operating in the water, energy, transport and postal services sectors and repealing Directive 2004/17/EC, OJ 2014, L94/243.

16 Directive 2014/23/EU of the European Parliament and of the Council of 26 February 2014 on the award of concession contracts, OJ 2014, L94/1.

17 On the special responsibility of dominant operators cf. Case C-202/07 P *France Télécom SA* v. *Commission* [2009] ECR I-2369; Case C-52/09 *Konkurrensverket* v. *TeliaSonera Sverige AB* [2011] ECR I-527.

> 'Public service contracts' are public contracts other than public works or supply contracts having as their object the provision of services referred to in Annex II.[18]

This list in Annexes IIA and IIB includes services like transport, telecommunications and financial services, as well as health, social services and education. This looks like a familiar set, but the list also includes apparently random services like personnel placement, legal services and hotel and restaurant services. It is not possible to identify a single objective criterion that justifies inclusion on this list, and there is no reason to assume that there is a tight logical fit between what we have generally understood as public services so far, or with what constitutes SGEI in terms of EU law, and what is listed in the Public Procurement Directives. Admittedly none of these three groups is based on strict criteria; other than that for SGEI, they are defined by the Member State concerned in a proportional manner and in relation to a legitimate public interest, subject only to a manifestly disproportionate test.

The thresholds

After meeting the definitions, the next step is formed by applying the thresholds. Under the public services Procurement Directive 2004/18/EC with regard to services contracts listed in Annex IIB, the threshold is €207,000; for Annex IIA this is €134,000 (although the Treaty principles apply in any event – see below).[19] For the utilities Procurement Directive 2004/17/EC the thresholds are €5,186,000 with regard to public works and €414,000 with regard to services.

The obligations under the Public Procurement Directives

The Public Procurement Directives spell out the rules for the various phases of the tendering procedure that contracting authorities must respect. These include the invitations to tender, rules on advertising and transparency, and the setting of time limits. Competitions can be open or restricted. In some cases a competitive dialogue procedure (for complex contracts) or a negotiated procedure with or without publication of a contract notice can be used (such as when prior overall pricing is not possible). However, as we will see for welfare services (and to some extent electronic communications), a milder regime applies. The criteria for selection are to be published in advance and the results at the end of the procedure. The selection criteria can be either price only, or the

[18] In the new procurement Directive 2014/24/EU, above n. 15, this system is changed: there public service contracts are defined as having as their object the provision of services other than those covered by public works contracts, inter alia as covered by Annex II to the Directive.

[19] For public works the threshold is €5,186,000. The thresholds have been modified most recently by Commission Regulation (EU) No 1336/2013 of 13 December 2013 amending Directives 2004/17/EC, 2004/18/EC and 2009/81/EC of the European Parliament and of the Council in respect of the application thresholds for the procedures for the awards of contract, OJ 2013, L335/17. (Directive 2009/81/EC deals with defence and security contracting.)

most economically advantageous tender (MEAT) where price and non-price variables can be taken into account.

Exceptions

Public authorities remain free to determine whether they wish to outsource the public service concerned or to provide it directly (including though an in-house service provider). In addition, when outsourcing the service public authorities can grant (in an open, transparent and non-discriminatory process) licences and authorizations to all service providers prepared to meet conditions for the provision of the services concerned that are set out beforehand. In none of these cases does the public authority pay an external party for the service, and in none of these cases do the public procurement rules apply. They do apply where a public authority outsources the provision of a service to a (for-profit or non-profit) provider that it pays for delivering the service.[20]

In the public services Procurement Directive there are exceptions for service concessions as well as for services that are based on the reward of an exclusive right: in the latter case therefore the Member States are only constrained by Article 106(1) TFEU and the possibility that granting such a right leads to a per se infringement and is therefore illegal. Telecommunications services are excluded from both Public Procurement Directives, given the situation of effective competition that prevails following liberalization of the sector.

Even within the terms of the Procurement Directives there is a light regime based on Article 21 of Directive 2004/18/EC in combination with non-priority Annex IIB services, which include social services, education and healthcare services, as well as rail and water transport (only the obligations in Articles 23 and 35(4) of the Directive apply). For such services, the requirements are purely transparency based: the technical specifications must be spelled out at the start of the award procedure and a notice of the results must be provided (and/or published) at the end of the procedure. This regime comes very close to that which is generally applicable based directly on the TFEU, and may even amount to a less demanding regime because it does not specify the requirement of a non-discriminatory selection procedure.

The Treaty principles

The CJEU has determined that even where the public procurement principles are not themselves applicable, public authorities must nevertheless apply the Treaty principles of transparency, equal treatment, non-discrimination, mutual

[20] Commission staff working document, Social investment package: Third biennial report on social services of general interest, SWD(2013) 40, at 19.

recognition and proportionality.[21] In its interpretative notice on this matter, the Commission cites the Court as follows:

> [A]lthough certain contracts are excluded from the scope of the Community directives in the field of public procurement, the contracting authorities which conclude them are nevertheless bound to comply with the fundamental rules of the Treaty.[22]

In effect this requires first, advertising tenders, and second, treating interested parties in a non-discriminatory manner.[23] As the Court held in *Parking Brixen* (2005):

> The principles of equal treatment and non-discrimination on grounds of nationality imply, in particular, a duty of transparency which enables the concession-granting public authority to ensure that those principles are complied with. That obligation of transparency which is imposed on the public authority consists in ensuring, for the benefit of any potential tenderer, a degree of advertising sufficient to enable the service concession to be opened up to competition and the impartiality of procurement procedures to be reviewed.[24]

So far this case law has been relevant especially to public service concessions, which are not covered by the Public Procurement Directives as they are currently in force. Concessions are not based (exclusively) on remuneration under a contract, but instead are based on the right to exploit and therefore collect payment (wholly or partially) from the consumers of a service.[25] For service concessions, the transparency regime based on the Treaty principles at present constitutes the default regime. However, in December 2011 the Commission proposed new public procurement legislation which, alongside other changes directly pertinent to public services, would explicitly address concessions. In February 2014 the Concessions Directive was adopted, and following transposition into national legislation it will become effective in 2016 (respectively 2018 for e-procurement).[26] This new regime is discussed below,

[21] Case C-324/98 *Telaustria Verlags GmbH and Telefonadress GmbH* v. *Telekom Austria AG* [2000] ECR I-10745; Case C-458/03 *Parking Brixen GmbH* v. *Gemeinde Brixen and Stadtwerke Brixen AG* [2005] ECR I-8585; Case C-231/03 *Consorzio Aziende Metano (Coname)* v. *Comune di Cingia de' Botti* [2005] ECR I-7287. Cf. B. J. Drijber and H. Stergiou, 'Public procurement law and internal market law', *Common Market Law Review*, 46 (2009), 805–46.

[22] Commission interpretative Communication on the Community law applicable to contract awards not or not fully subject to the provisions of the Public Procurement Directives, OJ 2006, C179/2, at 1.2, citing Case C-59/00 *Bent Mousten Vestergaard* v. *Spøttrup Boligselskab* [2001] ECR I-9505, para. 20.

[23] Commission staff working document (2013), above n. 20, at 20.

[24] Case C-458/03 *Parking Brixen*, above n. 21, para. 49.

[25] '"Service concession" is a contract of the same type as a public service contract except for the fact that the consideration for the provision of services consists either solely in the right to exploit the service or in this right together with payment.' Article 1(4) of Directive 2004/18/EC, above n. 2.

[26] Directive 2014/23/EU, above n. 16. On defining concessions and the test whether the concession holder assumes the risk of operating the service as the deciding principle under the (pre-)existing

but first I will look at the link between the state aid regime for public services compensation and the public procurement rules.

The link with *Altmark*

As we have already seen in Chapter 4, the *Altmark* case (2003) sets out the four conditions under which public service compensation is not regarded as state aid.[27] The fourth *Altmark* condition selects public procurement as the preferred modus operandi to ensure that by definition the compensation paid does not constitute a state aid. This condition reads as follows:

> Fourth, where the undertaking which is to discharge public service obligations, in a specific case, is not chosen pursuant to a public procurement procedure which would allow for the selection of the tenderer capable of providing those services at the least cost to the community, the level of compensation needed must be determined on the basis of an analysis of the costs which a typical undertaking, well run and adequately provided with means of transport so as to be able to meet the necessary public service requirements, would have incurred in discharging those obligations, taking into account the relevant receipts and a reasonable profit for discharging the obligations.[28]

The default to a more complex process of demonstrating efficiency based on a comparison with an efficient competitor – a comparator which may not always exist[29] – is therefore public procurement. Although some authors (including the economic advisers to the Competition Directorate General of the European Commission)[30] doubt whether this is always a realistic assumption, it has the benefit of clarity, simplicity and tying together the different EU law frameworks into a coherent whole. Another option is to forgo the *Altmark* test on the fourth condition and instead opt for the standard of actual costs plus a reasonable return that is applied by the Commission under its *Altmark* package test, which is not subject to a strict efficiency condition (however, see the next section on

rules, cf. Fiedziuk, above n. 12, citing Case C-206/08 *Wasser- und Abwasserzweckverband Gotha und Landkreisgemeinden (WAZV Gotha)* v. *Eurawasser Aufbereitungs- und Entsorgungsgesellschaft mbH* [2009] ECR I-8377; and Case C-274/09 *Privater Rettungsdienst und Krankentransport Stadler* v. *Zweckverband für Rettungsdienst und Feuerwehralarmierung Passau* [2011] ECR I-1335. This could also be an interesting additional variable in defining whether something is an economic activity.

27 Case C-280/00 *Altmark Trans GmbH and Regierungspräsidium Magdeburg* v. *Nahverkehrsgesellschaft Altmark GmbH, and Oberbundesanwalt beim Bundesverwaltungsgericht* [2003] ECR I-7747.

28 Ibid., para. 93.

29 Cf. Case T-137/10 *Coordination bruxelloise d'institutions sociales et de santé (CBI)* v. *Commission*, Judgment of 7 November 2012. L. Hancher and W. Sauter, 'This won't hurt a bit: The Commission's approach to services of general economic interest and state aid to hospitals', in Szyszczak and van de Gronden, above n. 12, 249–72.

30 Cf. *Services of general economic interest*, Opinion prepared by the State Aid Group of EAGCP, 29 June 2006.

efficiency incentives). The SGEI compensation Communication spells out in detail how this is to be assessed.[31]

An important feature is that the fourth *Altmark* condition states that services must be provided 'at the least cost to the community'. It is open to debate whether this allows for a selection on criteria other than price, such as the economically most effective tender, which can include quality criteria.[32]

Efficiency

As we have seen in the *Altmark* package, there is no requirement to use public procurement or the standard of a well-run (efficient) undertaking as there is under the *Altmark* test set out by the CJEU. However, all three of the *Altmark* criteria that are elaborated in the *Altmark* package include reference to efficiency incentives that may be introduced by the Member States to determine what constitutes a reasonable profit.[33] There is a marked difference on this point between the different instruments that constitute the package.

The Communication states that the Member States 'may' introduce efficiency incentives when determining what constitutes a reasonable profit. According to the Decision,

> In determining what constitutes a reasonable profit, Member States may introduce incentive criteria relating, in particular, to the quality of service provided and gains in productive efficiency. Efficiency gains shall not reduce the quality of the service provided. Any rewards linked to productive efficiency gains shall be set at a level such as to allow balanced sharing of those gains between the undertaking and the Member State and/or the users.[34]

It is therefore up to the Member States themselves whether they wish to introduce efficiency incentives for the public services that are covered by the block exemption contained in the Decision. As I have already cited above in Chapter 4, the Framework Communication, however, states imposing efficiency incentives as a conditional obligation:

> In devising the method of compensation, Member States must introduce incentives for the efficient provision of SGEI of a high standard, unless they can duly justify that it is not feasible or appropriate to do so . . .

[31] SGEI compensation Communication, above n. 13, paras. 63–77.

[32] Cf. Sánchez Graells, above n. 2.

[33] Cf. SGEI compensation Communication, above n. 13, para. 61. Commission Decision 2012/21/EU of 20 December 2011 on the application of Article 106(2) of the Treaty on the Functioning of the European Union to state aid in the form of public service compensation granted to certain undertakings entrusted with the operation of services of general economic interest, OJ 2012, L7/3, Article 5(6); Communication from the Commission on a European Union framework for state aid in the form of public service compensation, OJ 2012, C8/15, paras. 39–43.

[34] SGEI compensation Decision, above n. 33, Article 5(6).

> Rewards linked to productive efficiency gains are to be set at a level such as to allow balanced sharing of those gains between the undertaking and the Member State and/or the users.
>
> Any such mechanism for incentivising efficiency improvements must be based on objective and measurable criteria set out in the entrustment act and subject to transparent ex post assessment carried out by an entity independent from the SGEI provider.[35]

Consequently, efficiency incentives are effectively required in order to obtain a finding of compatibility with the internal market in individual cases notified to the Commission under the framework. It should be noted that the gains are to be shared between the undertaking and the Member State or the users, and therefore need not accrue to the Union, as would normally be expected where efficiency benefits in the context of Article 107(3) TFEU are concerned. This can be explained by the fact that here we are dealing with the context of SGEI and Article 106(3) TFEU. The flexibility of the SGEI provision in this respect can be seen as an additional advantage of using this test.

Future directions

As I have mentioned, so far service concessions have been excluded from the scope of the Public Procurement Directives. However, in December 2011 the Commission proposed a new regime for concessions alongside revisions of the existing Directives that was adopted in February 2014. The proposals were announced in parallel with the *Altmark* package I have just discussed. Also the 2010 Monti report had referred to the need to revise public procurement,[36] and it had been announced as one of the levers for growth by the Commission in its document on the Single Market Act.[37] The reform has seen the introduction of a revamped utilities Procurement Directive (2014/25/EU replacing Directive 2004/17/EC) and a revamped Directive on public procurement (2014/24/EU replacing Directive 2004/18/EC),[38] as well as a third wholly new Directive 2014/23/EU on the award of concession contracts.[39]

In particular these changes will involve a more relaxed regime for welfare services, or 'services to the person, such as certain social, health and educational services'.[40] A higher threshold of €5,186,000 will apply, and Member States will be free to choose procedures as long as these respect the Treaty principles of

35 SGEI compensation framework, above n. 33, paras. 39, 41–2. 36 Above, n. 11.

37 Communication from the Commission, Single Market Act. Twelve levers to boost growth and strengthen confidence 'Working together to create new growth', COM(2011) 206.

38 Above, n. 15. 39 Above, n. 16.

40 Directive 2014/24/EU, above n. 15, recital 114. Its Title III, Chapter I, provides a special regime for social and other specific services. Annex XIV lists health and social services; administrative, educational, healthcare and cultural services; compulsory social security services; benefit services; other community, social and personal services (as well as services furnished by trade unions and religious organizations).

transparency (publishing a contract notice and a contract award notice) and non-discrimination. This is no great change: as we have seen, the Court had already created a parallel transparency regime that would apply in any event. However, the Member States are now encouraged to define criteria that are sensitive to quality, continuity and accessibility of public services. In addition, Member States will also be allowed to decide that social services will always be awarded only based on criteria combining quality and price (the 'most economically advantageous tender', or MEAT, instead of only on price). There is thus an ongoing push by the Commission to ensure that the EU law requirement of public tendering for welfare services is no longer perceived as an alien intervention based on a cold economic calculus that neglects the nature of the services involved. Instead it is to combine efficiency and equity incentives for the benefit of the persons concerned.

In addition, the Concessions Directive highlights the remaining freedom of the Member States to determine the mode of provision of welfare services:

> Member States and/or public authorities remain free to provide these services themselves or to organise social services in a way that does not entail the conclusion of concessions, for example through the mere financing of such services or by granting licences or authorisations to all economic operators meeting the conditions established beforehand by the contracting authority or contracting entity, without any limits or quotas, provided such systems ensure sufficient advertising and compl[y] with the principles of transparency and non-discrimination.[41]

Having referred so often to the need for transparency as a fundamental Treaty principle in the procurement context, this provides a convenient link to my next topic: that of transparency not in relation to private operators jostling for contracts in a public tender, but rather transparency with regard to parties that are preferred almost by definition – public undertakings.[42]

5.4 The Transparency Directive

Background

If the significance and popularity of the principle of transparency in EU law may be gauged by numbers, the fact that there are no fewer than three fundamentally different Directives that go under the name 'Transparency Directive' bodes well. These Directives are respectively concerned with

[41] Directive 2014/23/EU, above n. 16, recital 54.

[42] For a recent argument in favour of public provision see M. Finger and D. Finon, 'From the "public service" model to the "universal service" obligation', in M. Finger and R. Künneke (eds.), *International handbook of network industries: The liberalisation of infrastructure* (Edward Elgar, Cheltenham, 2011), 54–69.

securities trading;[43] with the pricing of pharmaceuticals;[44] and with financial relations between Member States and public undertakings.[45] It is the latter Transparency Directive on the relations with public undertakings that concerns us here.

The text of the Transparency Directive that is in force today dates back to 2006. The original instrument was adopted in 1980, during the doldrums years of the European Union, in the days of stagnation before the 1985 Single European Act and the 1992 programme that reinvigorated European integration.[46] This makes the Transparency Directive all the more daring both in content and in form.

- As far as the content was concerned, the terms 'public authorities' and 'public undertakings' were defined, as were the types of financial operations that must be reported, and operations (excepting cases where there was no effect on trade or that were de minimis) and sectors (energy, transport, credit institutions, telecommunications and posts) that were exempt. Periodic reporting requirements to the European Commission were imposed.
- As regards its form, the Transparency Directive was the first binding legal instrument that has been based directly on Article 106(3) TFEU, in other words on the independent legislative powers of the Commission with regard to public undertakings, special and exclusive rights, and SGEI. This is therefore the main instance where the 'public undertakings' reference in Article 103(1) TFEU takes centre stage.

Below, we will look at the case law on the first Transparency Directive before moving on to discuss the contents of the current text of the Directive in greater detail.

Early case law on the Transparency Directive

As mentioned above, the Transparency Directive was adopted by the Commission based on Article 106(3) TFEU. The Commission's power to legislate in this form (as Directive) and on this basis were contested as a matter of principle by a number of Member States. However, it was upheld by the Court in 1982.[47] The Court refused to accept that only (the European

[43] Directive 2004/109/EC of the European Parliament and of the Council of 15 December 2004 on the harmonisation of transparency requirements in relation to information about issuers whose securities are admitted to trading on a regulated market and amending Directive 2001/34/EC, OJ 2004, L390/38.

[44] Council Directive 89/105/EEC of 21 December 1988 relating to the transparency of measures regulating the prices of medicinal products for human use and their inclusion in the scope of national health insurance systems, OJ 1989, L40/8.

[45] Commission Directive 2006/111/EC, above n. 3.

[46] Commission Directive 80/723/EEC of 25 June 1980 on the transparency of financial relations between Member States and public undertakings, OJ 1980, L195/35.

[47] Joined cases 188 to 190/80 *France, Italy and United Kingdom* v. *Commission* [1982] ECR 2545.

Parliament and) the Council could enact legislation of general application. The argument that the Court rejected was based on a literal reading of the text: it had been argued that Article 106(3) TFEU Directives were somehow of narrower application than regular Directives, and were to be addressed to individual Member States. Nor did it accept that the powers of the Council to legislate in the field of state aid were exclusive. The Court focused on the fact that a specific provision in the Treaty enabled the Commission to legislate:

> [I]n comparison with the Council's power under Article 94 [now Article 109 TFEU], that which is conferred upon the Commission by Article 90(3) [now Article 106(3) TFEU] thus operates in a specific field of application and under conditions defined by reference to the particular objective of that article. It follows that the Commission's power to issue the contested directive depends on the needs inherent in its duty of surveillance provided for in Article 90 and that the possibility that rules might be laid down by the Council, by virtue of its general power under Article 94, containing provisions impinging upon the specific sphere of aids granted to public undertakings does not preclude the exercise of that power by the Commission.[48]

The definitions (and thereby the scope of the Transparency Directive) were likewise upheld. As an aside, this ruling laid the foundations not only for the subsequent amendments and extensions of the Transparency Directive itself, but also for the 1988 Terminal Equipment and 1990 Services Directives regarding telecommunications, which were adopted on the same legal basis and survived legal challenges by the Member States.[49] Subsequently, however, Article 106(3) TFEU has fallen into disuse, at least as far as the adoption of Directives is concerned. This is due to concerns about the lack of democratic validation of Article 106(3) TFEU Directives because the democratically legitimate legislature (European Parliament, directly elected, and Council, indirectly representative) is circumvented, apart from playing a non-binding advisory role. A Commission Decision on state aid and public service compensation based on Article 106(3) TFEU was however adopted relatively recently, in 2011 (published in 2012).[50] Because it is a block exemption it effectively also legislates for a range of particular cases (and of an undetermined number).

Some years after the 1980 *Transparency Directive* case the application of the definitions that had been drafted in a functional manner – which is to say not in accordance with the definitions under national law but according to the purpose or the function of the entities concerned – was upheld in *Italy*

[48] Ibid., para. 14.

[49] Commission Directive 88/301/EEC of 16 May 1988 on competition in the markets in telecommunications terminal equipment, OJ 1988, L131/73; Commission Directive 90/388/EEC of 28 June 1990 on competition in the markets for telecommunications services, OJ 1990, L192/10; upheld in Case C-202/88 *France* v. *Commission* [1991] ECR I-1223; and (except in relation to abolishing special rights) in Joined cases C-271/90, C-281/90 and C-289/90 *Spain, Belgium and Italy* v. *Commission* [1992] ECR I-5833.

[50] SGEI compensation Decision, above n. 33.

v. *Commission* (1987). Here Italy had argued that the so-called independent state monopolies administration (Amministrazione Autonoma dei Monopoli di Stato) was not covered since it did not have a separate legal personality. This case provides a clear presentation of the reasons for applying a functional definition in EU law:

> [T]he purpose of Directive 80/723 . . . would be called into question if its application depended on whether or not state bodies had legal personality distinct from that of the state. The result would be that, according to the legal form chosen by the Member States, the economic activities of an industrial or commercial nature carried on by certain state bodies would be covered by the Directive whereas those carried on by other bodies would not. Furthermore, the application of the Directive in regard to the same activity would differ from one Member State to another according to the legal form which each Member State gives to the public undertakings carrying on that activity.[51]

In addition,

> [T]he fact that a body carrying out economic activities of an industrial or commercial nature is integrated into the state administration and does not have legal personality separate therefrom does not prevent the existence of financial relations between the state and that body.[52]

So far the Commission has thus been very fortunate in the outcome of the legal challenges to its legislation based on Article 106(3) TFEU, more in particular with regard to the Transparency Directive. It is likely that the changed public climate with regard to the EU would have made similar outcomes with regard to this type of legislation which lacks democratic credentials doubtful in more recent years. This is less of an issue with regard to Decisions – although in effect the Commission's recent Decision on compensation for state aid forms a block exemption, and not a decision in an individual case. I will now look at the text of the current (2006) version of the Transparency Directive.

Scope and definitions

The purpose of the Transparency Directive, first, is to ensure clarity regarding the public funds that public authorities make available to public undertakings either directly or indirectly through intermediacy of public undertakings or financial institutions, and the use to which these funds are put. Second, in addition, the financial and organizational structure of the undertakings concerned must be made transparent so the allocation of costs and revenues and the method to assign or allocate them can be verified. This is deemed necessary to ensure a fair and effective application of the rules on state aid. The main definitions are as follows:

[51] Case 118/85 *Commission* v. *Italy* [1987] ECR 2599, para. 10. [52] Ibid., para. 13.

> 'public authorities' means all public authorities, including the State and regional, local and all other territorial authorities;
>
> 'public undertakings' means any undertaking over which the public authorities may exercise directly or indirectly a dominant influence by virtue of their ownership of it, their financial participation therein, or the rules which govern it.[53]

This shows clearly that the concept of undertaking is once again key – which should come as no surprise since the rationale behind the text is to check for state aid relevance.

There is no notion of public services connected to these terms, nor is the provision of services dealt with separately, although there are special reporting rules dealing with the manufacturing sector,[54] which suggests that services are in the mainstream. The Transparency Directive also contains definitions of special and exclusive rights, as we have seen in Chapter 2.2. Finally, SGEI moreover are not defined by, but referred to in, the Transparency Directive, and accordingly have to be accounted for separately.

Transparency requirements and exemptions

As mentioned in the previous section, the substance of the Transparency Directive consists of two conditions that regard: (i) the flow and use of funds; and (ii) accounting separation. For the flow and use of funds transparency requirement (the first condition) there is a de minimis threshold of €40 million (€800 million for credit institutions), an appreciability threshold, and an exception for central banks and public credit institutions operating on commercial terms. For the structural and accounting separation transparency requirement (the second condition) there are comparable exemptions, and in addition SGEI are exempted if their compensation was fixed for an appropriate period, following an open, transparent and non-discriminating procedure.

SGEI do have to provide transparency under the first condition on the way operating losses are offset, the provision of capital, non-refundable grants or privileged loans, financial advantages granted by forgoing profits of the recovery of sums due, the forgoing of normal profits on public funds used and compensation for financial burdens imposed by the authorities. That is to say that for SGEI financial transfers must be notified but not the allocation of funds and the internal organization of the undertakings concerned. However, as we have seen in Chapter 4 above, the undertakings receiving public service compensation already have to provide detailed information on their costs in the context of the state aid rules.[55] This regime for public service compensation could arguably be regarded as a *lex specialis* with regard to the general regime of

[53] Commission Directive 2006/111/EC, above n. 3, Article 2(a) and 2(b).

[54] Covering the provision of share capital, non-refundable grants, loans, loan guarantees, dividends and profits and any other form of state intervention.

[55] Cf. SGEI compensation Decision, above n. 33; SGEI compensation framework, above n. 33.

the Transparency Directive. The Commission, however, stresses in its information on the *Altmark* package that the provisions of the Transparency Directive remain applicable. The reason may be that the Commission deems this useful in order to obtain more general information than that related only to the cost of providing the public service obligations concerned.

To stay with the *Altmark* package for now: the block exemption that forms the core of this framework is covered next.

5.5 The Commission Decision on public services compensation and SGEI

This Decision, which was adopted in 2011 and published in 2012, has already been discussed in more detail in Chapter 4, because it is closely related to the non-binding (soft-law) explanatory texts with regard to public services compensation in the state aid context that together with this Decision form the *Altmark* package (of 2005 and 2012).[56] Like the Transparency Directive that I have just discussed, the Decision on public services compensation is based on Article 106(3) TFEU. It sets out how the Commission applies its powers with regard to SGEI that concern compensation for public services in the context of its state aid control. Effectively, provided certain conditions are met, the Decision constitutes an unlimited block exemption for welfare services: 'medical care, health and long term care, childcare, access to and reintegration into the labour market, social housing and the care and social inclusion of vulnerable groups'. In addition, it covers certain types of transport (maritime and air transport) up to specific passenger numbers. In itself it is therefore not fully horizontal in the sense implied in this chapter, which is to say with regard to all public services.

Although they are based on the Commission's reading of Article 106(2) TFEU, the conditions applied effectively cover the same ground as the first three conditions that are set out in the *Altmark* case (2003): the fourth or efficiency condition, which sets public procurement procedures as a benchmark, is left out. If not, the *Altmark* judgment could have been applied directly and there would have been no aid, nor any need to revert to the Commission. The conditions regard, first, the contents of the act of entrustment (including the cost data and a mechanism for recovering overcompensation) and second, the rules with regard to admissible costs (essentially net costs for providing the SGEI plus a reasonable profit).

A companion Framework Communication sets out the rules for what are de facto the utilities sectors, which are subjected to a notification requirement and individual Commission Decisions, because they are deemed to be economically more significant as well as perhaps politically less sensitive.[57] Jointly with the block exemption Decision just discussed, the framework forms a horizontal set

[56] SGEI compensation Decision, above n. 33. [57] SGEI compensation framework, above n. 33.

of rules applicable to all public services. In practical terms, they are also the most significant such rules to date, because they deal with state aid and compensation. This is an issue affecting almost all public services: after all, they are provided by economic actors but generally not under purely market-based conditions. A market failure is therefore usually at issue, or an equity reason to provide more services than the market alone could bear. Jointly they also form the most complete horizontal framework targeting specifically SGEI, although in theory at least in this sense they could be replaced by the framework legislation that is covered in the section immediately below.

5.6 The European Parliament and Council Framework Regulation on SGEI

Somewhat metaphysically, this section deals with an as-of-yet non-existing Regulation which may however well become a game-changer if it is ever enacted.[58] It would also be the most targeted piece of horizontal secondary legislation regarding SGEI: this is why, although it does not exist, I am dealing with it here as the final topic of this chapter. The 2007 Lisbon Treaty has introduced the basis for legislating a framework for SGEI, a proposal which would have to be prepared by the Commission and adopted by the European Parliament and Council in the ordinary (that is to say, standard) legislative procedure. Somewhat disingenuously, however, the Commission in its 2007 Communication on the internal market in the twenty-first century has claimed that Protocol 26 on SGI and SGEI had already clarified all the issues and itself formed a coherent framework for EU action, boldly implying that therefore legislation based on Article 14 TFEU was no longer necessary:

> *The Protocol: A Coherent Framework for EU Action*
>
> The Protocol annexed to the Treaty of Lisbon provides a coherent framework that will guide EU action and serves as a reference for all levels of governance. By clarifying the principles and setting out the common values underpinning EU policies, it gives visibility, transparency and clarity to the EU approach applicable to services of general interest.[59]

This interpretation by the Commission is scarcely credible because the legislative competence of SGEI was introduced at the same time as Protocol 26 so there was no clear intention among the parties to the Treaties to simply fill in one with the help of the other. Instead it is likely these instruments should be

[58] Cf. S. Rodrigues, 'Towards a general EC framework instrument related to SGEI? Political considerations and legal constraints', in Krajewski, Neergaard and van de Gronden, above n. 8, 255–66.

[59] Communication from the Commission to the European Parliament, the Council, the European Economic and Social Committee and the Committee of the Regions accompanying the Communication on 'A single market for 21st century Europe' – Services of general interest, including social services of general interest: A new European commitment, COM(2007) 725, section 3.

seen as no more than complementary. At the same time, the Commission has prepared a new *Altmark* package (published in 2012), which for the first time included an explanatory Communication.[60] This use of a Communication does not suggest that all is clear in the world of SGI and SGEI, at least as regards their relationship with state aid – arguably the most important topic in this context.

It appears to me that instead of observing actual clarity in Protocol 26 where there is little to be found, the Commission is simply stalling on proposing SGEI framework legislation because there is a risk that this may be hijacked by the representatives of unpredictable interventionist sentiments both in the Member States and in the European Parliament, with the risk of gutting the internal market. This may well be a realistic assessment, even if it is hidden by dissimulation behind the SGI/SGEI Protocol. At the same time, this defensive approach means missing out on the opportunity to draft a coherent framework bringing together the welfare services and the utilities, as well as arguments concerning market failure, universal service and consumer rights, and clarifying their relationship with EU citizenship. If these factors are accepted as potential sources of legitimacy, then not linking them also means missing out on strengthening support for the EU.[61]

The 2007 Communication that I have already cited highlights a number of themes that appear in the Protocol, which notably include equal treatment, universal access and users' rights. In my view, and in Fritz Scharpf's terminology (but not according to his interpretation of events),[62] there are two complementary dimensions here which can be linked to positive (new EU rules) and negative (scrapping national rules) integration. Alongside the usefulness of SGEI as a source of relatively closely controlled efficiency and equity exceptions to negative integration for legitimate public policy objectives, there is a further untapped potential in this concept on the side of positive integration. I will get back to these issues in the concluding Chapter 7.

I will now conclude this chapter before moving on to Chapter 6 on the vertical, harmonized, sector-specific legislation which, perhaps unsurprisingly, is a good deal more extensive than the general horizontal rules that we have charted here.

5.7 Conclusion

Going back to the three questions set out in the introduction to the chapter, we can conclude that there are indeed horizontal secondary rules that are relevant to public services with regard to the freedom of services, public procurement

60 SGEI compensation Communication, above n. 13.

61 For a contrasting view on the legitimacy of EU citizenship cf. J. Shaw, 'Citizenship: Contrasting dynamics at the interface of integration and constitutionalism', in P. Craig and G. de Búrca, *The evolution of EU law*, 2nd edn (Oxford University Press, 2011), 575–609.

62 F. W. Scharpf, *Community and autonomy: Institutions, policies and legitimacy in multilevel Europe* (Campus, Frankfurt am Main, 2010).

and transparency. However, in the first place, these rules tend to exclude non-economic SGI, and therefore many welfare services. Second, they are riddled with exceptions, either for SGEI in general, or for particular types of public services. The SGEI concept therefore only partly determines the outcome. Third, there may be a minimalist regime for public services as in the case of 'Annex IIB services' under public procurement, which is arguably even less demanding than the general requirements of the Treaty with regard to transparency and non-discrimination would have been. Even exclusive rights are accommodated under public procurement. The result appears to be somewhat patchy, but not hostile or even particularly demanding with regard to public services.

Most demanding with regard to public services is arguably the *Altmark* package on the public service compensation which has been covered here only in part because it is only partly horizontal secondary legislation and mostly soft-law guidance on the application of the state aid rules.

To a dispassionate observer, it would appear that if the EU wants to give direction to public services short of adopting a harmonized regime to do so, applying the state aid rules – which involve looking at the act of entrustment and examining the proportionality of the measures concerned against the legitimacy of the public policy objective invoked – is indeed the most effective method. The Commission appears to have grasped this point fully. In effect this means leveraging its central position in state aid control by using the legal basis of Article 106(3) TFEU for maximum effect. Two of the Commission's trump cards thus reinforce each other here, so it controls the outcome.

The opposite is true for the adoption of a European Parliament and Council Regulation based on the SGEI provision in Article 14 TFEU: at least in theory this horizontal instrument might appear to be an attractive vehicle for organizing the various objectives and instruments relating to public services in a neat and comprehensive way. In practice, however, there is a risk it could degenerate into an open invitation to wild-eyed believers in state interventionism who favour public provision of everything, and more cynical supporters of cosy corporatist arrangements, to drive a battering ram into the delicately balanced edifice of the internal market, backfiring badly. However, if it is not derailed in this way, the Regulation could also link negative and positive integration in a manner that might add support to the legitimacy of the EU. The Commission may yet try if it feels it has to.

6

Vertical secondary rules – the harmonized sectoral legislation for public services

6.1 Introduction

This penultimate chapter provides a catalogue of individual regimes for each of the public services for which such a regime (to my knowledge) exists in EU law. There are several things that I intend to accomplish by this. In the first place, I want to provide a reasonably accurate overview of the law as it stands on public services. But this book is not intended as a reference source for the black letter law on public services – if any black letter account would adopt that category as an organizing principle. Instead the law as it stands is intended as a dataset on which to base a discussion of the law in context, which is my objective here. Apart from providing an overview, the obvious objective is therefore to chart some of the main similarities and differences in the regimes concerned in order to be able to perform a secondary analysis looking at trends and future developments.

For various reasons, I will be discriminating in my descriptions, more so in their scope than in their number. That is to say, I will concern myself primarily with the rules that are pertinent to public service and universal service obligations, their formulation and their financing, and any ancillary restraints that are deemed necessary to guarantee their performance. Third-party access and other conditions for promoting competition in the various sectors will not be discussed, except perhaps in passing: I am primarily interested in competition only as a variable concerning the manner in which public services are provided – such as under a concession, by competing providers, based on a cross-subsidy, under an exclusive right or through a universal service fund sponsored by competitors. (Although from an economic perspective direct subsidies for consumers raised by way of general taxation would be preferable, I will not enter this discussion.)[1]

This is because, in my view, which I hope to test against and illustrate with the material presented here, the public service obligations form the core of public services, their *raison d'être*, and in fact what ultimately defines them as

[1] Cf. M. Harker, A. Kreutzmann and C. Waddams, *Public service obligations and competition*, Final Report, February 2013, CERRE Centre for regulation in Europe, at 80.

public services. This aspect should therefore be at the heart of this investigation. At the same time, it is my impression that, since I first reported on these matters,[2] over the past fifteen-odd years public service obligations have been subject to development, and are in the course of becoming increasingly sophisticated. To account for this, I will organize the discussion of the respective frameworks roughly in chronological order, which is intended to illustrate this development. In addition, I hope to catch up with the latest advances.

For these purposes, I will use a somewhat modified set of questions compared to that presented in the introductory chapter. The general assumption is that public service obligations exist – this is how the regimes were selected – and are generally related in some form to universal service and to protecting consumers (although some are imposed at wholesale level). The latter in turn raises the question of what is the relationship between public service obligations and general consumer protection (which I will deal with in a separate section). A question which reflects subsidiarity is at what level of government public service obligations are defined and what margins of freedom there are. Apart from the dimension of universality, the concepts of market failure and the consumer interest are likely to play a role. Finally, the role of SGEI is examined. This can be summarized as follows:

- What are the sector-specific regimes for public services and what do they have in common?
- What role do they assign to public service obligations and how are these guaranteed?
- What dimensions do public service obligations have: are they universal service based?
- Are public service obligations organized at EU or at national level?
- What is the role for the consumer interest, for market failure?
- What is the link to consumer protection more broadly?
- What is the role, if any, for SGEI?

In selecting the sectors discussed, I have based myself on the availability of a relevant sector-specific framework more than on a preconceived list of public services: where previous chapters have been more discriminating, I have chosen to be less selective here. This also means that I will not be able to go into comparable levels of granularity for each sector, as there are differences in the degree of detail and the relevance of the respective sectoral regimes.

The ten sectors that I will review in this chapter are listed below. It is worth noting that five are utilities, two are welfare services (healthcare and social

[2] W. Sauter, 'Universal service obligations and the emergence of citizens' rights in European telecommunications liberalization', in M. Freedland and S. Sciarra (eds.), *Public services and citizenship in European law: Public and labour law perspectives* (Oxford University Press, 1998), 117–43.

security) and three are indeterminate in nature in the sense of not clearly belonging to either category (broadcasting, air transport and banking).

- Electronic communications (2002)[3]
- Postal services (2008)[4]
- Electricity (2009)[5]
- Gas (2009)[6]
- Broadcasting (2010)[7]
- Rail and road transport (2007)[8]
- Maritime and air transport (2008)[9]
- Social security (2004)[10]
- Healthcare (2011)[11]
- Payment services (2011)[12]

Following this review, I will look briefly at the relationship between public service guarantees and general measures of consumer protection. Next I will

[3] Directive 2002/22/EC of the European Parliament and of the Council of 7 March 2002 on universal service and users' rights relating to electronic communications networks and services, OJ 2002, L108/51; as amended by Directive 2009/136/EC of the European Parliament and of the Council of 25 November 2009 amending Directive 2002/22/EC on universal service and users' rights relating to electronic communications networks and services, Directive 2002/58/EC concerning the processing of personal data and the protection of privacy in the electronic communications sector and Regulation (EC) No 2006/2004 on cooperation between national authorities responsible for the enforcement of consumer protection laws, OJ 2009, L337/ 11.

[4] Directive 2008/6/EC of the European Parliament and of the Council of 20 February 2008 amending Directive 97/67/EC with regard to the full accomplishment of the internal market of Community postal services, OJ 2008, L52/3.

[5] Directive 2009/72/EC of the European Parliament and of the Council of 13 July 2009 concerning common rules for the internal market in electricity and repealing Directive 2003/54/EC, OJ 2009, L211/55.

[6] Directive 2009/73/EC of the European Parliament and of the Council of 13 July 2009 concerning common rules for the internal market in natural gas and repealing Directive 2003/55/EC, OJ 2009, L211/94.

[7] Directive 2010/13/EU of the European Parliament and of the Council of 10 March 2010 on the coordination of certain provisions laid down by law, regulation or administrative action in Member States concerning the provision of audiovisual media services, OJ 2010, L95/1.

[8] Regulation (EC) No 1370/2007 of the European Parliament and of the Council of 23 October 2007 on public passenger transport services by rail and by road and repealing Council Regulations (EEC) Nos 1191/69 and 1107/70, OJ 2007, L315/1.

[9] Council Regulation (EEC) No 3577/92 of 7 December 1992 applying the principle of freedom to provide services to maritime transport within Member States (maritime cabotage), OJ 1992, L364/7; Regulation (EC) No 1008/2008 of the European Parliament and of the Council of 24 September 2008 on common rules for the operation of air services in the Community (Recast), OJ 2008, L293/3.

[10] Regulation (EC) No 883/2004 of the European Parliament and of the Council of 29 April 2004 on the coordination of social security systems, OJ 2004, L166/1.

[11] Directive 2011/24/EU of the European Parliament and of the Council of 9 March 2011 on the application of patients' rights in cross-border healthcare, OJ 2011, L88/45.

[12] Commission Recommendation 2011/442/EU of 18 July 2011 on access to a basic payment account, OJ 2011, L190/87.

conclude with reference to the questions set out above and try to draw some general lessons.

6.2 Electronic communications

The liberalization background

With the exception of transport, which will be discussed further below, in my view telecommunications was the first public service that was addressed as such at EU level. More in particular it is the sector where the concept of universal service was coined in EU law. The definition of universal service at EU level formed an integral part of the trade-off between the competition-minded Commission and the initially reluctant Member States and European Parliament, which allowed liberalization to occur.[13]

In broad outline this took place as follows. Historically, public monopolies dominated and foreclosed each national market. Public service obligations and users' rights that were frequently not legally enforceable were used as arguments to block market-based provision and the introduction of competition. Nevertheless, the right to provide new services and networks (such as mobile and satellite) and eventually existing services and networks were lopped off from the incumbent monopoly in a piecemeal fashion until a grand compromise emerged: the merger between the French and German incumbent operators was cleared by the European Commission on the condition that these two key Member States enable market entry. This turned them from opponents of liberalization into proponents and the merged entity into a potential market entrant elsewhere (although as many merged entities do, the new entity eventually failed).

Meanwhile the Commission had already issued Article 106(3) Directives to abolish the special and exclusive rights that underpinned the monopolies of the national operators,[14] actions that had been upheld by the Court of Justice.[15] In combination with the about-face of France and Germany, this meant that from 1 January 1998 full competition became possible, albeit within the context of a system of sector-specific legislation adopted at EU level, initially called open network provision (ONP). The original idea was that this sectoral legislation,

[13] Cf. Sauter, above n. 2; P. Nihoul and P. Rodford, *EU electronic communications law: Competition and regulation in the European telecommunications market*, 2nd edn (Oxford University Press, 2011); P. Larouche, *Competition law and regulation in European telecommunications* (Hart Publishing, Oxford, 2000).

[14] Commission Directive 88/301/EEC of 16 May 1988 on competition in the markets in telecommunications terminal equipment, OJ 1988, L131/73; Commission Directive 90/388/EEC of 28 June 1990 on competition in the markets for telecommunications services, OJ 1990, L192/10, both successively amended.

[15] Case C-202/88 *France* v. *Commission* [1991] ECR I-1223; and (except in relation to abolishing special rights) in Joined cases C-271/90, C-281/90 and C-289/90 *Spain, Belgium and Italy* v. *Commission* [1992] ECR I-5833.

which contained rules on universal service, but not least on third-party access and the regulation of wholesale and retail rates as well, would be temporary. It was the intention that eventually this system would be replaced by general competition law. Hence competition policy concepts like market definition and significant market power, based on dominance, were introduced in the ONP regime that was administered by a network of national regulatory authorities (NRAs). This regulatory framework has been instrumental in market opening but it has not led to a single regulatory space, let alone a single market for electronic communications: national markets persist.[16] Politically and socially this new regime was made acceptable in large part because the public service objections had been channelled and provided for in a new universal service regime.

At the same time, this meant that significant universal service obligations were formulated for the first time, not just at EU level, but as far as most Member States were concerned, at any level. This provides a strong argument why liberalization and the provision of public services, or the performance of public service obligations, are not only not necessarily at odds with one another, but can even be mutually reinforcing. Admittedly the electronic communications example is characterized by a number of peculiarities, such as network effects (each new user adds value not just for themselves but also for the other users), very rapid technological change and falling costs of technology. The latter are in no small part due to large-scale adoption, which in turn favours change and declining costs. Perhaps the main difference with other utilities is the degree to which services are targeted at individuals and to which choice is possible, whereas the main difference with welfare services is the degree to which electronic communication is technology driven and has spill-over effects on other services as well as on the economy as a whole.

The original ONP regime for universal service

The groundwork for the universal service regime in the ONP framework was prepared in two Commission Communications of 1993 and 1996,[17] and a Council Resolution of 1994.[18] From the outset the general objective was to ensure social cohesion by avoiding the development of a two-tier society – also called the digital divide – in the context of electronic communications services.

[16] L. Hancher and P. Larouche, 'The coming of age of EU regulation of network industries and services of general economic interest', in P. Craig and G. de Búrca (eds.), *The evolution of EU law*, 2nd edn (Oxford University Press, 2011), 743–81, at 745.

[17] Communication from the Commission, Universal service for telecommunications in the perspective of a fully liberalized environment: An essential element of the information society, COM(96) 73; and Communication from the Commission, Developing universal service for telecommunications in a competitive environment: Proposal for a Council Resolution on universal service principles in the telecommunications sector, COM(93) 43.

[18] Council Resolution of 7 February 1994 on universal service principles in the telecommunications sector, OJ 1994, C48/1.

In addition, it was emphasized that universal service was a dynamic concept. The three objectives identified were universality (universal access, including an affordable price), equality (geographical access) and continuity (at guaranteed quality). The three regulatory dimensions were the scope of the service, its affordability and the financing of the universal service. All of these aspects had a direct bearing on the scope for competition: a broadly defined scope for universal service would automatically limit the scope for competitive provision and it might hamper the emergence of new services if they had to be universally and uniformly available from scratch; affordability could hollow out profit margins; while generous funding regimes for operators of last resort might come at the expense of would-be competitors required to feed universal service funds.

The first ONP Directive on voice telephony, which preceded full liberalization, did not cover explicit obligations with regard to universal service.[19] Two of the second-generation ONP Directives that were applied in parallel, however, contained extensive provisions on universal service: the ONP Voice Telephony Directive (intended to deal with retail-level services) and the ONP Interconnection Directive (intended to deal primarily with wholesale-level services and third-party access).[20] These were the Directives that set out the rules for the new and fully liberalized regulatory regime that entered into force on 1 January 1998. Hence universal service obligations and full competition were introduced and intended to work in tandem.

The Voice Telephony Directive

The 1998 Voice Telephony Directive set the standard for universal service in electronic communications that has by and large endured (with a few elaborations and modifications discussed below). As regards availability, the Voice Telephony Directive set Member States the task of ensuring the relevant services were made available to all users in their territory, regardless of the location, and at a price that was affordable in the light of national conditions. The services concerned were a connection to the fixed public telephone network at a fixed location and access to fixed public telephone services. This connection should enable the user to make and receive national and international calls, and should support speech, fax and/or data communications. In addition, the universal service obligations covered free directory services, the provision of

[19] European Parliament and Council Directive 95/62/EC of 13 December 1995 on the application of open network provision (ONP) to voice telephony, OJ 1995 L321/6. Its recitals and Articles 11 and 12 did mention universal service but only as possible objectives of the Member States.

[20] Directive 98/10/EC of the European Parliament and of the Council of 26 February 1998 on the application of open network provision (ONP) to voice telephony and on universal service for telecommunications in a competitive environment, OJ 1998, L101/24; Directive 97/33/EC of the European Parliament and of the Council of 30 June 1997 on interconnection in telecommunications with regard to ensuring universal service and interoperability through application of the principles of open network provision (ONP), OJ 1997, L199/32.

public payphones, and the obligation to ensure equal and affordable access for disabled users and users with special needs. Financing schemes for universal service were covered by the Interconnection Directive.

The Interconnection Directive

The Interconnection Directive (at least in so far as universal service was concerned) dealt mainly with universal service contributions and the method used for calculating them. This is logical because this Directive concerns the relationships between operators, which is to say at wholesale level. Member States were to assess whether a universal service obligation represented an unfair burden on a telecommunications operator, in which case the costs could be shared with other telecommunications operators by means of a universal service fund. This method of financing could only apply (but need not apply) to a set of services that was predefined in the Directive (essentially the fixed public telephone network and the fixed telephone network service): this suggests that universal service funding could be used for a set of services that exceeded the minimum requirement for universal service set out in the Voice Telephony Directive at the discretion of the Member State, but that there was nevertheless an outer limit set by EU law to the range of services that could be involved.[21] The cost for universal service was to be based on calculating the difference between the net cost of operating with and without the universal service obligation, taking revenues into account as well as geographic averaging of prices.

Universal service for electronic communications today

Since the two ONP Directives just discussed, there has been periodic review by the Commission of the scope of universal service in electronic communications networks and services,[22] as well as legislative change: the adoption of a new generation of ONP Directives, notably Directive 2002/22/EC on universal service and users rights (the Universal Service Directive).[23] Under the Universal Service Directive economic criteria are being applied to the question whether imposing universal service obligations is necessary. Article 3(2) of this Directive now reads:

> Member States shall determine the most efficient and appropriate approach for ensuring the implementation of universal service, whilst respecting the principles of objectivity, transparency, non-discrimination and proportionality. They shall seek to minimise market distortions, in particular the provision of services at

[21] Directive 97/33/EC, above n. 20, Article 5(1), with reference to Part 1 of Annex I.

[22] Cf. most recently Communication from the Commission, Universal service in e-communications: Report on the outcome of the public consultation and the third periodic review of the scope in accordance with Article 15 of Directive 2002/22/EC, COM(2011) 795.

[23] Directive 2002/22/EC, as amended by Directive 2009/136/EC, above n. 3.

> prices or subject to other terms and conditions which depart from normal commercial conditions, whilst safeguarding the public interest.

In other words, although this is not stated explicitly anywhere in the Directive, where the services concerned are, or can be, provided under market conditions it would not be appropriate (or necessary) to impose universal service obligations.[24] It is thus the provision of the services as such, not the provision of services by a designated operator, which must be guaranteed.

At the same time, so far the scope of universal service has remained remarkably constant.[25] Thus it remains limited to fixed connections. Member States must ensure all end-users have access at a fixed location to voice communications and functional internet access. They must minimize market distortions that can result from imposing universal service obligations, and the technology by which the services can be provided may be freely chosen by the operator. The possibility of using a universal service fund remains.

The main innovation is the increased role for data communications and the internet:

> The connection provided shall be capable of supporting voice, facsimile and data communications at data rates that are sufficient to permit functional Internet access, taking into account prevailing technologies used by the majority of subscribers and technological feasibility.[26]

In addition, the Universal Service Directive now sets the terms for the designation of undertakings to guarantee the provision of universal service; deals with the monitoring of the affordability of tariffs covered by universal service (and with providing tariff options for low-income users); and with tying of additional services (under the heading 'control of expenditure'). Apart from defining the scope of universal service and setting out the calculation and the recovery of net costs, the Universal Service Directive establishes a process for reviewing the scope of universal service. The need to do so is set out in its Article 15, the methodology in Annex V. This requires technological and social developments to be taken into account. In addition:

[24] Cf. this same argument more generally for the application of SGI in the Communication from the Commission on the application of the European Union state aid rules to compensation granted for the provision of services of general economic interest, OJ 2012, C8/4, para. 48. Here the example of broadband is used. Cf. Community Guidelines for the application of state aid rules in relation to the rapid deployment of broadband networks, OJ 2009, C235/7; replaced by EU Guidelines for the application of state aid rules in relation to the rapid deployment of broadband networks, OJ 2013, C25/01.

[25] Cf. A. Nijenhuis, 'Electronic communications and the EU consumer', in F. S. Benyon (ed.), *Services and the EU citizen* (Hart Publishing, Oxford, 2013), 47–74.

[26] Directive 2002/22/EC, above n. 3, Article 4(2).

> In considering whether the scope of universal service obligations be changed or redefined, the Commission is to take into consideration the following elements:
>
> - are specific services available to and used by a majority of consumers and does the lack of availability or non-use by a minority of consumers result in social exclusion, and
> - does the availability and use of specific services convey a general net benefit to all consumers such that public intervention is warranted in circumstances where the specific services are not provided to the public under normal commercial circumstances?

The application of this two-pronged test can be checked against the arguments for including mobile and broadband services. There are three-yearly reviews, where these issues are addressed, with so far minimal results in terms of motivating change.[27] For mobile services the conclusion was that competitive provision of these services has led to their availability at levels of widespread affordable access that leave no real risk of social exclusion. For broadband access the prospects are differentiated between various areas within the EU and within Member States. In addition, the threshold of broadband usage has not yet reached a substantial majority of consumers in the EU overall. Whereas the standard for internet access was originally narrowband, in the view of the Commission individual Member States are now 'allowed' to set specific broadband rates as a universal service requirement.[28] This is based on the following text:

> The data rate that can be supported by a connection to the public communications network depends on the capabilities of the subscriber's terminal equipment as well as the connection. For this reason, it is not appropriate to mandate a specific data or bit rate at Community level. Flexibility is required to allow Member States to take measures, where necessary, to ensure that a data connection is capable of supporting satisfactory data rates which are sufficient to permit functional Internet access, as defined by the Member States, taking due account of specific circumstances in national markets, for instance the prevailing bandwidth used by the majority of subscribers in that Member State, and technological feasibility, provided that these measures seek to minimise market distortion.[29]

Because this is only a recital of the 2009 Directive 2009/136/EC that amended the Universal Service Directive it looks more a soft-law nudge than a real obligation or a conferral of freedom of action in divergence from an obligation. It does, however, raise a fundamental question: do the EU rules set the outer limits of universal service, or just a minimum level?

[27] Most recently, Communication from the Commission, Universal service in e-communications, above n. 22.

[28] Ibid., para. 1. [29] Recital 5 of Directive 2009/136/EC, above n. 3.

Is universal service fully harmonized?

The question whether the EU rules set the outer limits of universal service or just a minimum level has a significance that goes beyond users' rights. Universal service has an obvious appeal as a demonstration of how users' rights and market provision of services are compatible in practice. However, at the same time the Commission has always been keen to ensure that universal service did not become a convenient instrument for throttling competition. National extensions of universal service obligations are after all a potential threat to free markets. It seems reasonable to expect that such an obviously relevant point would have been settled early on in the Directives or the case law. The Directives that make up the regulatory framework for electronic communications however do not mention this issue.

As we have seen above, the Universal Service Directive implicitly suggests that where the market already provides the services concerned at an adequate level, imposing universal service obligations would not be appropriate. In fact not all Member States have designated providers of universal services and some therefore rely on market provision, which is consistent with freedom in the direction of imposing fewer obligations, or at least not imposing them when they are not deemed to be necessary. (It also shows that comparisons are not made across borders.) Thus the third periodic review of the scope of universal service in 2011 reports as follows:

> Several Member States have exercised their discretion not to designate any USO provider, or have relaxed obligations concerning service elements that are already catered for by the market (e.g. public payphones and directories).[30]

At the other extreme, as we have seen in the previous section, the Commission appears to suggest that it can rule by reference to the recitals to the Directives – allowing some Member States to impose more extensive obligations with regard to broadband. In addition, the second periodic review of the scope of universal service in 2008 stated:

> Member States are free to mandate additional services extending beyond the minimum set of services set by the Directive, but any further financing associated with them must be borne by them (for example through general taxation) and not by specific market players.[31]

Hence in this Communication the Commission interpreted universal service in the Universal Service Directive as a minimum set that Member States could go beyond. However, these Member States could not finance this extension via a universal service fund (levied from other operators), but it would have to be

[30] Above, n. 21, at 3.

[31] Communication from the Commission on the second periodic review of the scope of universal service in electronic communications networks and services in accordance with Article 15 of Directive 2002/22/EC, COM(2008) 562, at 3.

tax-financed – a method which would appear to be superior on economic grounds (to maximize effective targeting and minimize market extortion).[32] This interpretation appears to be undermined by the third periodic review of the scope of universal service which, as mentioned above, claims that the Member States have regained the freedom to set broadband rates under the Universal Service Directive because this Directive itself does not specify a bit-rate – whereas their freedom to do so is established by the fifth recital of the amending Directive 2009/136/EC. In my view, this contradicts rather than strengthens the earlier reasoning, which suggests that Member States are in any event free to go beyond the minimum set, but are limited with regard to the funding of such services.

However, the recent case law appears to be more conclusive. In *Telekomunikacja Polska* (2010) the Court ruled that consumer protection measures imposed on operators could go beyond those of the Universal Service Directive (notably on tying), which did not constitute full harmonization on this point.[33] Likewise in the *Deutsche Telekom* case (2011) the CJEU ruled that the Universal Service Directive did not provide for full harmonization of all aspects of consumer protection, in this case with regard to data to be made available to undertakings providing publicly available directory enquiry services and directories.[34] Admittedly these cases left the question whether this argument applies to universal service more broadly unaddressed.

However, in *The Number* (2011) the Court ruled that the discretion conferred on the Member States by Article 3(2) of the Universal Service Directive to determine how they wish to ensure universal service does not allow them to impose on individual undertakings obligations inter alia in excess of universal service obligations.[35] This is because Article 3(2) of the Authorization Directive determines that the operators of electronic communications may only be subject to a general authorization.[36] Exceptions to this rule, such as the obligations with relation to universal service and the designation in Article 8(1) of the Universal Service Directive, are to be interpreted strictly.

> It . . . follows from the wording of that provision, taken as a whole, that a Member State can impose on a designated undertaking only the obligations specifically laid down by the provisions of the Universal Service Directive relating to the provision by that undertaking itself to end-users of one of the specific elements of universal service identified in Articles 4 to 7 and 9(2) of the Directive.[37]

[32] CERRE report, above n. 1.

[33] Case C-522/08 *Telekomunikacja Polska SA w Warszawie* v. *Prezes Urzędu Komunikacji Elektronicznej* [2010] ECR I-2079.

[34] Case C-543/09 *Deutsche Telekom AG* v. *Germany* [2011] ECR I-3441.

[35] Case C-16/10 *The Number Ltd and Conduit Enterprises Ltd* v. *Office of Communications and British Telecommunications plc* [2011] ECR I-691.

[36] Directive 2002/20/EC of the European Parliament and of the Council of 7 March 2002 on the authorization of electronic communications networks and services, OJ 2002, L108/21.

[37] Case C-16/10 *The Number*, above n. 35, para. 32.

In spite of the observations in 2008 by the Commission that I have cited above, and although the reasoning in the case cited above is not always clear to me, this does appear to mean that only the universal service obligations formulated in the Directive can be imposed. Hence as far as electronic communications is concerned, universal service, unless otherwise construed in the Directive, such as freedom on determining bandwidth or bit-rates, is a fully harmonized service. This point is underscored by Article 32 of the Universal Service Directive, which provides that additional services may be made mandatory by the Member States, but that these may not be subject to a financing mechanism involving specific undertakings.

Before moving on to the next sector, I will look briefly at financing universal service, must-carry obligations and the special case of the Roaming Regulation – where the EU intervenes directly in the provision of national electronic communications.

Financing universal service

As is set out in Articles 12 and 13 of the Universal Service Directive, financing of universal service obligations is based on their net cost, and justified only if meeting these costs would amount to an unfair burden on the undertaking charged with the obligation. For these costs a compensation mechanism can be created based on public funding (that is to say, tax-based), or they can be shared between providers of electronic networks and services (such as via a universal service fund). Several cases have arisen on this topic. In the *Arcor* case (2008) the Court held that it is illegal to levy an additional charge which can be classified neither as an interconnection charge nor as a universal service charge but which was intended to compensate the incumbent operator for a deficit that occurred because the charges for operating the local loop (the access network for subscribers) had not been rebalanced. That is to say, the Court imposed a requirement to make services meet their actual costs instead of relying on cross-subsidies.[38]

The issue of what concerns an unfair burden came up in the *Base* case (2010) and the *Commission* v. *Belgium* case (2010), which were decided on the same day.[39] In both cases the Court found that the definition of what constituted an unfair burden had not been provided by the Universal Service Directive. Hence the Belgian State was free to formulate a definition itself. However, the Court did not accept that Belgium, in designating all operators as suffering from an unfair burden, had applied an appropriate approach and in effect the CJEU itself provided the following definition:

[38] Joined cases C-152/07 to C-154/07 *Arcor AG & Co. KG, Communication Services TELE2 GmbH and Firma 01051 Telekom GmbH* v. *Germany* [2008] ECR I-5959.

[39] Case C-389/08 *Base NV et al.* v. *Ministerraad* [2010] ECR I-9073; Case C-222/08 *Commission* v. *Belgium* [2010] ECR I-9017.

> [T]he unfair burden which must be found to exist by the national regulatory authority before any compensation is paid is a burden which, for each undertaking concerned, is excessive in view of the undertaking's ability to bear it, account being taken of all the undertaking's own characteristics, in particular the quality of its equipment, its economic and financial situation and its market share.[40]

This standard had not been met. Moreover, the Court held that intangible benefits of providing the universal service must be taken into account in the calculation of the net costs of universal service provision.[41]

Must-carry obligations

It is sometimes forgotten that the Directives on electronic communications concern all infrastructure, including that which is used for broadcasting – in any event, a distinction that due to internet-based convergence is increasingly difficult to make. Broadcasting content is subject to separate regulation at EU level which is discussed in section 6.5 below. The Universal Service Directive, however, in its Article 31, contains a provision on must-carry obligations. This is a type of public service obligation with universal access aims intended for the benefit of consumers that make it closely akin to a universal service obligation – although there is no individualized right to such access in this case. It does not allow public authorities other than NRAs (such as municipalities) to set rates for a minimum set of radio and television programmes.[42] According to Article 31 of the Universal Service Directive, a must-carry obligation can only be imposed on operators on which a significant number of end-users are dependent as their principal source of media broadcasts. In substance such obligations can only be imposed in pursuit of clearly defined public interest objectives and they must be proportionate and transparent.

These conditions have been confirmed in the case law both based on the Universal Service Directive, *Commission* v. *Belgium* (2011),[43] and in an earlier case based on Article 56 TFEU on the freedom to provide services: *UPC* v. *Belgium* (2007).[44] In these cases the Court required the conditions for the objective of pluralism to be specified: it cannot automatically cover all channels transmitted by a private broadcaster but must be strictly limited to those channels that have a content which would enable the relevant general interest objective to be attained. It has also required that, in addition, the criteria for awarding must-carry status must be non-discriminatory. I now move on to the regulation of services that emerged wholly in competition and with a clear EU dimension, with regard to mobile roaming.

[40] Case C-389/08, above n. 39, para. 42 and Case C-222/08, above n. 39, para. 49.

[41] Case C-222/08, above n. 39, paras. 84 and 86.

[42] Case C-518/11 *UPC Nederland BV* v. *Gemeente Hilversum*, Judgment of 7 November 2013.

[43] Case C-134/10 *Commission* v. *Belgium* [2011] ECR I-1053.

[44] Case C-250/06 *United Pan-Europe Communications Belgium SA et al.* v. *Belgium* [2007] ECR I-11135.

The Roaming Regulations

A discussion of universal service and electronic communications is not complete without looking at the 2007 and 2012 Roaming Regulations.[45] Roaming services are characterized by a unique combination of market failure and regulatory failure.

- The market failure is due to asymmetrical information and to a lack of choice: users are generally unaware of the elevated charges involved and cannot avoid them because they are imposed by foreign (host) operators, not the domestic (home) operator with whom they have contracted. Hence consumers cannot vote with their feet. Also the domestic tariffs, rather than roaming tariffs with which they are bundled, tend to drive competition between the mobile operators in each Member State.
- Similarly the regulatory failure occurs because the high charges for visiting a mobile communications network abroad are imposed on visitors, whereas any benefits to regulating those charges at national level likewise accrue abroad and may even lead to higher rates nationally as local mobile operators seek to compensate their losses.

There are therefore few incentives and even some disincentives for NRAs to help foreign customers, while at the same time the NRAs in the other Member States have equally few incentives to act. This puzzle has proved too complex for the NRAs to solve. At the same time, high roaming rates hit EU consumers and businesses precisely when they are availing themselves of the possibility to move freely within the internal market. This is of course a direct affront to the effectiveness of European integration.

These elements may explain why in the case of roaming the EU legislator exceptionally decided to intervene directly in the relevant rates rather than attempt to do so indirectly by invoking the NRAs, or by imposing obligations upon them to act either individually or in concert. As far as I am aware, this is so far the only public service where rates (effectively a price cap) are set directly at EU level, by the EU legislature. It may not be coincidental that European Members of Parliament are almost by definition heavy users of roaming services themselves, and have therefore long been subject to the operators' price-gouging practices.

The original 2007 Roaming Regulation set maximum average wholesale rates (applied between operators) and an obligation to offer all roaming

[45] Regulation (EU) No 531/2012 of the European Parliament and of the Council of 13 June 2012 on roaming on public mobile communications networks within the Union, OJ 2012, L172/10. Preceded by Regulation (EC) No 717/2007 of the European Parliament and of the Council of 27 June 2007 on roaming on public mobile telephone networks within the Community and amending Directive 2002/21/EC, OJ 2007, L171/32, upheld in Case C-58/08 *The Queen, on the application of Vodafone Ltd and Others* v. *Secretary of State for Business, Enterprise and Regulatory Reform* [2010] ECR I-4999.

customers a choice for a price-capped retail tariff ('Eurotariff'), with the default option that consumers who did not make an active choice would be moved to the Eurotariff scheme.[46] In addition, tariffs were made transparent by a text message (SMS) to alert roaming customers to the charges they were facing. The 2012 Roaming Regulation went one step further by unbundling roaming services and enacting wholesale access for providers who wished to supply cheaper roaming access to the customers of other networks. This mechanism is intended to trigger competition that will drive roaming rates down. Wholesale rates were halved and retail rates reduced in steps by up to 80 per cent. In addition, a Eurotariff scheme for data roaming was set up and SMS roaming was price capped.

Does the Roaming Regulation concern universal service? As far as its content is concerned, the roaming services regulation imposed by the EU satisfies at least the ubiquity requirement – even if not that of a standardized quality. As we have seen above, so far it has been decided to keep mobile services outside the scope of the Universal Service Directive, yet here we have a full-fledged EU Regulation. In any event, although there is no explicit universal service element involved, this is a rare example of direct pan-European intervention in pricing levels and structures by the European legislature in the interest of European consumers and in a highly invasive but effective manner.

What is clear is that this concerns services that are key to the internal market but escape the grasp of national regulators. At the same time, these interventions are carried out in a sector (mobile communications services) that has from the outset developed in a competitive market environment. Hence, clearly competition alone is not a sufficient guarantee of the consumer interest, not even when fortified by the competition rules. Meanwhile the Commission has recently proposed a new generation of legislation aiming to create a single market for electronic communications and to wholly abolish roaming charges – and which inter alia establishes a requirement of network neutrality vis-à-vis the services carried by operators, and a new EU regulator.[47]

We will now move back from the cutting edge of information-age EU regulation to a sector that has long been more evocative of the stagecoach age – postal services.

[46] This is a clear case of 'nudging' consumers in line with behavioural economics. Cf. C. R. Sunstein and R. H. Thaler, *Nudge: Improving decisions about health, wealth and happiness* (Yale University Press, New Haven, 2008).

[47] Proposal for a Regulation of the European Parliament and of the Council laying down measures concerning the European single market for electronic communications and to achieve a Connected Continent, and amending Directives 2002/20/EC, 2002/21/EC and 2002/22/EC and Regulations (EC) No 1211/2009 and (EU) No 531/2012, COM(2013) 627 final.

6.3 Postal services

Background

There may be no other sector where universal service is as engrained in the character of the services concerned as such as in postal services.[48] The postal services sector does not rely on a physical infrastructural network as much as the other utilities do, but it does involve the use of a network and especially of a dedicated workforce (that is both very large and traditionally highly unionized) for postal delivery. The EU has been involved in attempts to liberalize these services with mixed success, with the first significant legislation adopted in the late 1990s – as part of a broader liberalization trend that also included the regulatory framework for full competition in telecommunications and the first-generation legislative package for gas and electricity.[49] At the same time, the competitive edge of postal markets was being contested by entrants resorting to various arbitrage schemes such as re-mailing domestic items via international mail when terminal dues were lower than standard national rates.[50]

The early days: universal service and postal liberalization

The very opening provisions of the 1997 Postal Services Directive on the development of the internal market for postal services were concerned with universal postal service. Thus Article 1(1) provided that the Directive established common rules concerning the provision of a universal postal service within the Community, and 'the criteria defining the services which may be reserved for universal service providers and the conditions governing the provision of non-reserved services' as well as tariff principles. Effectively the strategy of Member States who were reluctant to liberalize had evolved since the reform of telecommunications discussed in the previous section where we have seen the pivotal role of universal service in promoting liberalization: once it had been guaranteed the remainder of the services could be liberalized.

In postal services the Member States instead fully equated the existing services with universal service, and with its financing through cross-subsidies, leaving very limited scope for competition. Hence they embraced universal service, with a deleterious effect on competition and on the emergence of an internal market for postal services. The 1997 Directive defined universal service as follows:

[48] Cf. the case study on the postal sector in M. P. Smith, *States of liberalisation: Redefining the public sector in integrated Europe* (SUNY Press, Albany, 2005).

[49] Directive 97/67/EC of the European Parliament and of the Council of 15 December 1997 on common rules for the development of the internal market of Community postal services and the improvement of quality of service, OJ 1998, L15/14.

[50] Cf. Joined cases C-147/97 and C-148/97 *Deutsche Post AG* v. *Gesellschaft für Zahlungssysteme mbH (GZS) and Citicorp Kartenservice GmbH* [2000] ECR I-825.

> Member States shall ensure that users enjoy the right to a universal service involving the permanent provision of a postal service of specified quality at all points in their territory at affordable prices for all users.[51]

This was to involve at least one clearance (collection) and one delivery a day every working day and not less than five days a week. In addition, the service was to be non-discriminatory. The weight limit of the postal items concerned was up to 2 kilograms and for packages up to 10 kilograms, and services for registered items and insured items were to be provided. The Member States could raise the weight limit for packages under the universal service obligation to 20 kilograms. Member States could establish a universal service fund that would be financed by operators authorized to supply non-reserved services (see below), as was confirmed by the CJEU in an analysis based on Articles 102 and 106 TFEU (then Articles 86 and 90 EC).[52]

Separately, categories of mail that could be reserved for universal service operators (that is to say, protecting them from market entry rather than just ensuring universal service) were distinguished. They covered essentially domestic correspondence charged at less than five times the relevant standard public rate and weighing less than 350 grams. The CJEU has ruled that EU law did not preclude reserving additional postal services to the operator of the universal service without recourse to public procurement procedures, at least to the extent necessary to ensure the maintenance of the universal service.[53] This could even include cross-border mail, to the same extent.[54] However, the Court also ruled that it was not allowed to severely restrict the conditions for offering services such as self-provision that could not be reserved to universal service providers under the Directive.[55]

The logic behind this is that tariffs had generally not been rebalanced, so they relied on a system of cross-subsidies.[56] Allowing competitive courier services to cherry-pick the more profitable business customers would undermine the ability of the universal service operator to continue providing non-remunerative services to peripheral private users. If universal service obligations represented an unfair burden upon the universal service provider, a compensation fund could be installed, fed with contributions from competing operators of the non-reserved services.

[51] Above, n. 49, Article 3(1).

[52] Case C-340/99 *TNT Traco SpA* v. *Poste Italiane SpA et al.* [2001] ECR I-4109.

[53] Case C-220/06 *Asociación Profesional de Empresas de Reparto y Manipulado de Correspondencia* v. *Administración General del Estado* [2007] ECR I-12175.

[54] Case C-162/06 *International Mail Spain SL* v. *Administración del Estado and Correos* [2007] ECR I-9911.

[55] Case C-240/01 *Asociación Profesional de Empresas de Reparto y Manipulado de Correspondencia (Asempre) and Asociación Nacional de Empresas de Externalización y Gestión de Envíos y Pequeña Paquetería* v. *Entidad Pública Empresarial Correos y Telégrafos and Administración General del Estado* [2004] ECR I-2461.

[56] Case C-320/91 *Criminal proceedings against Paul Corbeau* [1993] ECR I-2533.

Tariff principles of affordability and cost-orientation, transparency and non-discrimination were imposed for services that formed part of the provision of universal service. Most importantly, Member States were allowed to impose a uniform tariff throughout the national territory – which by definition entails cross-subsidization and a departure from the cost-orientation which was also required. A complaints procedure was provided for the users of universal services (which could be extended to providers of postal services outside the scope of universal service).[57]

Finally, the 1997 Postal Services Directive set out quality standards regarding in particular routing times, regularity and reliability. This quality offensive was a political necessity because, in at least some Member States, the only reliable aspect of the postal services was the dismal nature of their quality. This had to be improved significantly not just for the sake of their unfortunate users (who were to be held hostage because liberalization was stalled) but also in order to salvage the respectability of the universal service defence claimed under EU law by the other dominant postal operators.

The 2008 Postal Services Directive

In the 2002 amendments to the 1997 Postal Directive the weight limits for the reserved area were reduced, thereby gradually increasing the scope for competition.[58] The amendments made by the 2008 Postal Services Directive maintain the scope for universal service that had been established eleven years earlier in the 1997 Directive with minimal changes (such as five working days a week instead of every working day and not less than five days a week). The main changes regard the financing of universal service: special and exclusive rights in postal services were abolished and thereby effectively so is the reserved area.[59] Instead Member States must now use public procurement, compensation based on public funds or a universal service fund fed by competitive providers and/or user fees (possibly based on conditions imposed as part of the authorization regime) and subject to principles of transparency, non-discrimination and proportionality.

Tariffs should promote affordable access, be cost-oriented and must include efficiency incentives – a principle that has also surfaced in the 2012 *Altmark* package, where it is not obligatory for the block exemption, but does apply for

[57] Case C-148/10 *DHL International NV, formerly Express Line NV* v. *Belgisch Instituut voor Postdiensten en Telecommunicatie* [2011] ECR I-9543.

[58] Directive 2002/39/EC of the European Parliament and of the Council of 10 June 2002 amending Directive 97/67/EC with regard to the further opening to competition of Community postal services, OJ 2002, L176/21.

[59] Under the 2008 Directive sixteen Member States had opened their markets by 31 December 2010. The remaining eleven did so by the end of 2012.

individual exemptions.[60] Separate accounts are to be kept for services that are part of the universal service and those that are not, in order to enable state aid scrutiny.

Consequently postal services markets have now been opened up to competition without compromising the level of universal service, which has remained constant over the past fifteen years. By contrast with electronic communications, the harmonization involved appears to be full harmonization. The role played by universal service in legitimizing a step-by-step approach whereby liberalization is phased in appears to be broadly similar between postal services and electronic communications. In the resulting liberalized sphere, general competition law can then be used to address abuses by incumbent operators.[61] However, whereas electronic communications regulation as a whole is fairly successful in its attempts to be technology neutral, postal services regulation appears to be largely locked into the past, while consumers have largely deserted its services for electronic equivalents. Messages are hardly distributed by post any longer, with the declining exception of business to consumer mail, and packages are provided in competition. As a public service therefore, postal services appear to have largely been outlived by their regulatory framework. In the next sector I will look at energy and examine whether the same holds true there.

6.4 Energy: gas and electricity

The internal market in energy

Like electronic communications and posts, the energy markets in gas and electricity in the EU are subject to liberalization: the attempt to create an internal market in energy.[62] Meanwhile the third-generation regulatory regime for these services is in place. As is the case for electronic communications, energy services are delivered via a physical network, but even more so than in the case of electronic communications bottlenecks play a role, not only as far as the distribution network is concerned, but also regarding high-capacity backbone networks and due to limited capabilities for storage vis-à-vis the need to

[60] Cf. SGEI compensation Communication, above n. 24, para. 61. Commission Decision of 20 December 2011 on the application of Article 106(2) of the Treaty on the Functioning of the European Union to state aid in the form of public service compensation granted to certain undertakings entrusted with the operation of services of general economic interest, OJ 2012, L7/3, Article 5(6); Communication from the Commission, European Union framework for state aid in the form of public service compensation, OJ 2012, C8/03, paras. 39–43.

[61] Cf. Case C-209/10 *Post Danmark A/S* v. *Konkurrencerådet*, Judgment of 27 March 2012; Case T-60/05 *Union française de l'express (UFEX) et al.* v. *Commission* [2007] ECR II-3397. An earlier state aid case in Joined Cases C-83/01 P, C-93/01 P and C-94/01 P *Chronopost SA, La Poste and French Republic* v. *Union française de l'express (Ufex), DHL International, Federal express international (France) SNC and CRIE SA* [2003] ECR I-6993.

[62] For a contextual commentary see K. Talus, *EU energy law and policy: A critical account* (Oxford University Press, 2013).

meet peaks in demand. Again, like in the realm of electronic communications - and perhaps even more so due to an even lower degree of efficient replicability of networks and a lesser degree of technological innovation – third-party access is an issue.[63]

Public service obligation, universal service and consumer protection

Below, however, I will concentrate on public service obligations, notably universal service. I will deal with both sectors together: although electricity liberalization started earlier (in 1996) than gas (in 1998), since then the rules for the two sectors have developed jointly and are in many ways highly similar in their approach to public service obligations, universal service and consumer protection measures.

First, regarding public service obligations the current Electricity Directive (2009) states the following:

> Having full regard to the relevant provisions of the Treaty, in particular Article 86 thereof [now Article 106 TFEU], Member States may impose on undertakings operating in the electricity sector, in the general economic interest, public service obligations which may relate to security, including security of supply, regularity, quality and price of supplies and environmental protection, including energy efficiency, energy from renewable sources and climate protection. Such obligations shall be clearly defined, transparent, non-discriminatory, verifiable and shall guarantee equality of access for electricity undertakings of the Community to national consumers.[64]

This is significant because the public service obligations involved are wide-ranging (from security of supply to environmental protection) and are not all focused on universal service. Unlike what is suggested for example in the 2008 *BUPA* case,[65] universality of service provision to individuals is not the key to these PSOs. The 2009 Gas Directive contains a virtually identical provision. Clearly there is a wide range of legitimate public interest objectives accompanied by a high tolerance for public service obligations in the energy sector, opening the door to a wide range of SGEI. However, these wholesale-level public service obligations do not (yet) relate to universal service.

Second, in the 2009 Electricity Directive (but not in the 2009 Gas Directive) universal service is covered in a separate provision:

> Member States shall ensure that all household customers, and, where Member States deem it appropriate, small enterprises (namely enterprises with fewer than

[63] Cf. Hancher and Larouche, above n. 16.

[64] Directive 2009/73/EC, above n. 6, Article 3(2); cf. Directive 2009/72/EC, above n. 5, Article 3(2). Cf. Case C-393/92 *Municipality of Almelo and Others* v. *NV Energiebedrijf Ijsselmij* [1994] ECR I-1477.

[65] Case T-289/03 *British United Provident Association Ltd (BUPA), BUPA Insurance Ltd and BUPA Ireland Ltd* v. *Commission of the European Communities* [2008] ECR II-81.

50 occupied persons and an annual turnover or balance sheet not exceeding EUR 10 million), enjoy universal service, that is the right to be supplied with electricity of a specified quality within their territory at reasonable, easily and clearly comparable, transparent and non-discriminatory prices. To ensure the provision of universal service, Member States may appoint a supplier of last resort.[66]

What we see here is a universal service obligation (in short: the right to be supplied with energy of a specific quality at reasonable prices) that can be imposed on a supplier of last resort. There is no mention of a funding mechanism. In addition, there is an obligation to provide a connection to the service on defined terms. These terms are not, however, defined in the Directive, but left to the Member States to define. Remarkably, the universal service is not limited to natural persons but may also involve small enterprises, effectively creating a special regime of price controls for their benefit.

The 2009 Gas Directive, however, omits comparable provisions on universal service and instead appears to rely on broader consumer protection measures discussed immediately below, and on the formulation of national energy action plans that provide social security benefits to ensure necessary gas supplies to vulnerable customers and to address energy poverty, 'including in the broader context of poverty'.[67] Thus the general social security system instead of a specific universal service obligation with provision of services on controlled terms is preferred here. Again the terms involved are not set in the Directive but are left to the Member States to define. To the extent the funding involved is tax based it may be preferable to universal service funds sponsored by providers from an economic point of view. In addition, in the 2010 *Federutility* case the Court accepted Italian price regulation measures based on the definition of reference prices as balancing the objective of liberalization and protection of final consumers under the earlier 2003 Gas Directive.[68] The general economic interest pursued by this policy was that of maintaining the price of gas for consumers at a reasonable level.

Third, both the 2009 Electricity and Gas regimes have special consumer protection provisions:

> Member States shall take appropriate measures to protect final customers, and shall, in particular, ensure that there are adequate safeguards to protect vulnerable customers. In this context, each Member State shall define the concept of vulnerable customers which may refer to energy poverty and, inter alia, to the prohibition of disconnection of electricity to such customers in critical times. Member States shall ensure that rights and obligations linked to vulnerable customers are applied. In particular, they shall take measures to protect final customers in remote areas. They shall ensure high levels of consumer protection, particularly with respect to transparency regarding contractual terms and

[66] Directive 2009/73/EC, above n. 6, Article 3(3).
[67] Directive 2009/72/EC, above n. 5, Article 3(4).
[68] Case C-265/08 *Federutility et al.* v. *Autorità per lénergia elettrica e il gas* [2010] ECR I-3377.

conditions, general information and dispute settlement mechanisms. Member States shall ensure that the eligible customer is in fact able easily to switch to a new supplier. As regards at least household customers, those measures shall include those set out in Annex I.[69]

This introduces the concept of vulnerable customers and energy poverty, which is more elaborate than the similar concept of socially disadvantaged or handicapped users in the case of electronic communications. At the same time, it appears that the level of detail of consumer protection here may reflect a lesser degree of effective competition: the latter would itself protect consumers – at least to the extent that they are able to switch providers within a reasonable timeframe. However, mobile telephony contracts in a market frequently deemed almost a model of competitiveness (and innovation) are frequently concluded for two years whereas, as we will see below, consumers must be able to switch their energy contracts within three weeks. The Annex I mentioned in the reference above contains two pages in small print of consumer protection measures that apply without prejudice to the EU rules on consumer protection.[70] This may seem odd for a *lex specialis* as is provided for energy here, but presumably means that the regime which is the most favourable to the consumer applies.

Fourth and finally, as I have already mentioned, in addition electricity and gas consumers are to be enabled to change suppliers within three weeks and are entitled to receive all the relevant consumption data. In the case of electricity, in addition, references to environmental impact data must be supplied, such as CO_2 emissions and the radioactive waste generated.

Background

The provisions on public service obligations and universal service respectively regarding vulnerable customers and energy poverty are by no means at the core of the EU energy regime: at present the concern is with unbundling of transmission systems, third-party access and effective regulatory supervision at national level. Nevertheless, the consumer-oriented rules that I have discussed above are essential to ensure that liberalization of energy markets delivers

[69] Directive 2009/73/EC, above n. 6, Article 3(7); cf. Directive 2009/72/EC, above n. 5, Article 3(3).

[70] Directive 2011/83/EU of the European Parliament and of the Council of 25 October 2011 on consumer rights, amending Council Directive 93/13/EEC and Directive 1999/44/EC of the European Parliament and of the Council and repealing Council Directive 85/577/EEC and Directive 97/7/EC of the European Parliament and of the Council, OJ 2011, L304/64; Council Directive 93/13/EEC of 5 April 1993 on unfair terms in consumer contracts, OJ 1993, L95/29; Directive 1999/44/EC of the European Parliament and of the Council of 25 May 1999 on certain aspects of the sale of consumer goods and associated guarantees, OJ 1999, L171/12. Cf. Note of DG Energy and Transport on Directives 2003/54/EC and 2003/55/EC on the internal market in electricity and natural gas, Public service obligations, 16 January 2004; Case C-92/11 *RWE Vertrieb AG* v. *Verbraucherzentrale Nordrhein-Westfalen e.V.*, Judgment of 21 March 2013.

results to end-users. This is reflected in the way that public service obligations and consumer rights have been extended with each generation of the regulatory regime for energy.[71] Thus the first generation of 1996/1998 Directives focused exclusively on public service obligations and SGEI, and did not mention universal service, vulnerable customers and energy poverty, or consumer protection. In this context, the degree of detail that has meanwhile developed (in particular regarding consumer protection) itself suggests that competition itself cannot be trusted to protect consumers via choice.

This raises the question whether the problems addressed by EU energy regulation are inherent market failures (such as information asymmetries) or whether they are related to market power and therefore potentially of a transient nature until competition becomes effective. An additional final observation is that the range of public service, universal service and consumer protection measures that are allowed under the 2009 Gas and Electricity Directives is very wide. As a result, it may itself be counterproductive by hampering competition at the same time as it is trying to substitute for the effects of competition.

6.5 Broadcasting

In earlier chapters we have looked at Protocol 29 on public service broadcasting and at the state aid Communication on public broadcasting,[72] both of which seek to carve out a space for the funding of public service broadcasting within EU law. The 2010 Audiovisual Media Services Directive, however, formulates a regime that for the most part does not reflect a public service character, or at least not one related to universal service obligations.[73] Hence it can be said that the impact of EU law on public service broadcasting has largely been indirect. While the Directive on Audiovisual Media Services does not mention public service broadcasting, it does provide a framework within which commercial providers can operate effectively.[74] Accordingly, the model adopted looks like one of opening markets to commercial operators while allowing public service

[71] The first generation: Directive 96/92/EC of the European Parliament and of the Council of 19 December 1996 concerning common rules for the internal market in electricity, OJ 1997, L27/20; Directive 98/30/EC of the European Parliament and of the Council of 22 June 1998 concerning common rules for the internal market in natural gas, OJ 1998, L204/1. The second generation: Directive 2003/54/EC of the European Parliament and of the Council of 26 June 2003 concerning common rules for the internal market in electricity and repealing Directive 96/92/EC, OJ 2003, L176/37; Directive 2003/55/EC of the European Parliament and of the Council of 26 June 2003 concerning common rules for the internal market in natural gas and repealing Directive 98/30/EC, OJ 2003, L176/57.

[72] Communication from the Commission on the application of state aid rules to public service broadcasting, OJ 2009, C257/1.

[73] Directive 2010/13/EU, above n. 7.

[74] R. Mastroianni, 'Public service media and market integration: A differential application of free movement and state aid rule?' in M. Cremona (ed.), *Market integration and public services in the European Union* (Oxford University Press, 2011), 149–77.

operators to keep their privileged access to the public purse. This is not dissimilar to the general approach to liberalization in its early stages as adopted in other sectors.

An exception is found in Chapter V of the Audiovisual Media Services Directive on exclusive rights and short news reports in television broadcasting.[75] Regarding exclusive rights the principle is established that Member States may establish a rule that broadcasters should not be allowed to broadcast on an exclusive basis those events of major importance to society:

> Each Member State may take measures in accordance with Union law to ensure that broadcasters under its jurisdiction do not broadcast on an exclusive basis events which are regarded by that Member State as being of major importance for society in such a way as to deprive a substantial proportion of the public in that Member State of the possibility of following such events by live coverage or deferred coverage on free television. If it does so, the Member State concerned shall draw up a list of designated events.[76]

This attempt to guarantee access to key public events via the broadcasting media in order to avoid social exclusion can be seen as akin to universal service: it also echoes the criterion of social inclusion that we have seen forms part of the test for applying universal service in the electronic communications context. The measures taken are to be notified to the Commission. Cross-border denial of access to such events is likewise to be avoided by way of legislation. Similarly, in regard to access to news reports, the Directive provides:

> Member States shall ensure that for the purpose of short news reports, any broadcaster established in the Union has access on a fair, reasonable and non-discriminatory basis to events of high interest to the public which are transmitted on an exclusive basis by a broadcaster under their jurisdiction.[77]

In addition, the Directive encourages the use of European content (at least half of net broadcasting time after subtracting advertising, news, teleshopping and so forth), and requires the protection of minors and the right of reply in television broadcasting to be ensured. The main gist of the Directive is, however, enabling broadcasting across national borders.

The Audiovisual Media Directive covers on-demand audiovisual media services or 'non-linear' audiovisual media services as well, thereby covering broadcasting across a wide range of devices (handheld, mobile). Hence, like the Roaming Regulation discussed above, the Audiovisual Media Directive appears to be information-age proof. However, it is not clear whether the same is true

[75] Cf. Case C-283/11 *Sky Österreich GmbH* v. *Österreichischer Rundfunk*, Judgment of 22 January 2013.

[76] Directive 2010/13/EU, above n. 7, Article 14(1). Cf. Case T-68/08 *Fédération internationale de football association (FIFA)* v. *Commission* [2011] ECR II-349. Cf. F. Benyon, 'Broadcasting and the EU consumer', in Benyon, above n. 25, 75–85.

[77] Directive 2010/13/EU, above n. 7, Article 15(1).

for the public services concerned, which are neither regulated nor really protected by the current regulatory framework. Nor, needless to say, is there an EU public service (standard) in sight.

6.6 Rail and road transport

The indeterminacy of the broadcasting regime just discussed can be contrasted with the focus found in the field of rail and road transport. Of course the 2003 *Altmark* case that triggered a revolution in public service compensation in relation to state aid was a transport case.[78] In its wake a 2007 Regulation on public passenger transport services (Public Transport Regulation) was adopted explicitly to deal with the application of Articles 14 and 106(2) TFEU on SGEI to the sector as well as Article 93 TFEU which forms a *lex specialis* to the later provision with regard to transport.[79] Accordingly, the 2007 Public Transport Regulation also forms a *lex specialis* with regard to the general framework for state aid and public service compensation set out in the 2005 and 2012 *Altmark* package.[80] Both the block exemption Decision and the Framework Communication explicitly exclude land transport.[81]

There is no question of an EU standard for public service here, or of universal service norms. Unlike in the other utilities already covered, in this sector exclusive rights are still considered to be an acceptable form of compensation, although they have to be awarded in the framework of a public service contract (but it is not obligatory to use exclusive rights). Likewise public service obligations which aim to establish maximum passenger tariffs are to be subject to general rules, which may be integrated with the public service contracts on exclusive rights. Public service contracts must clearly define the public service obligations imposed and the geographical areas concerned. The parameters of compensation and the nature and extent of the exclusive rights granted must be established in advance and are set out in detail in the Annex to the Regulation. This Annex sets compensation essentially at the level of cost plus a reasonable profit. A reasonable profit is one that is a return on capital normal for the sector in the Member State concerned, taking into account the risk profile of the public

78 Case C-280/00 *Altmark Trans GmbH and Regierungspräsidium Magdeburg* v. *Nahverkehrsgesellschaft Altmark GmbH, and Oberbundesanwalt beim Bundesverwaltungsgericht* [2003] ECR I-7747.

79 Article 93 TFEU reads: 'Aids shall be compatible with the Treaties if they meet the needs of coordination of transport or if they represent reimbursement for the discharge of certain obligations inherent in the concept of a public service.' Article 100 TFEU provides: 'The provisions of this Title shall apply to transport by rail, road and inland waterway.'

80 Cf. T. M. Rusche and S. Schmidt, 'Transport', in E. Szyszczak and J. W. van de Gronden (eds.), *Financing services of general economic interest: Reform and modernization* (TMC Asser Press, The Hague, 2013), 217–48.

81 SGEI compensation Decision, above n. 60, Article 5; SGEI compensation framework, above n. 60, para. 8.

service operator in question. Also, accounting separation is imposed in order to increase transparency and avoid cross-subsidies.

The 2007 Public Transport Regulation itself sets time limits on the duration of public service contracts (of ten years for coach and bus services and fifteen years for rail, with defined exceptions).[82] Staff may be transferred to new operators of a public service if they are associated with the provision of services.[83] As far as the award of contracts is concerned, this is to be in accordance with the rules set out in the 2007 Public Transport Regulation, except in those cases where (with regard to bus or tram services – apart from concessions for such services) the Public Procurement Directives apply.[84] Where the Public Procurement Directives are not applicable, competitive tendering is only required under the 2007 Public Transport Regulation where the competent authority concerned has decided not to provide public passenger transport services itself or through an entity over which it exercises control.

6.7 Maritime and air transport

As we have seen in Chapter 4, the block exemption of the *Altmark* package covers maritime and air transport up to specific passenger numbers provided the public service obligations concerned are consistent with the relevant sectoral legislation,[85] which is what I will discuss here.

Maritime cabotage

Maritime cabotage is a term of art that means providing shipping services between ports within the same Member State. The 1992 Maritime Cabotage Regulation contains a single article on public service obligations, which allows Member States to impose public service obligations as a precondition for the provision of cabotage services. The Maritime Cabotage Regulation states:

82 Above, n. 8. Cf. with reference to the earlier Regulation 1191/69, Case C-504/07*Associação Nacional de Transportadores Rodoviários de Pesados de Passageiros (Antrop) and Others* v. *Conselho de Ministros, Companhia Carris de Ferro de Lisboa SA (Carris) and Sociedade de Transportes Colectivos do Porto SA (STCP)* [2009] ECR I-3867.

83 By analogy to the rules in Council Directive 2001/23/EC of 12 March 2001 on the approximation of the laws of the Member States relating to the safeguarding of employees' rights in the event of transfers of undertakings, businesses or parts of undertakings or businesses, OJ 2001, L82/16.

84 Directive 2004/17/EC of the European Parliament and of the Council of 31 March 2004 coordinating the procurement procedures of entities operating in the water, energy, transport and postal services sectors, OJ 2004, L134/1; Directive 2004/18/EC of the European Parliament and of the Council of 31 March 2004 on the coordination of procedures for the award of public works contracts, public supply contracts and public service contracts, OJ 2004, L134/114.

85 SGEI compensation Decision, above n. 60, Article 2(4): 'In the field of air and maritime transport, this Decision only applies to State aid in the form of public service compensation, granted to undertakings entrusted with the operation of services of general economic interest as referred to in Article 106(2) of the Treaty, which complies with Regulation (EC) No 1008/2008 and, respectively, Regulation (EEC) No 3577/92 where applicable.' Maximum passenger numbers are found in Article 2(1)d and 2(1)e. The block exemption Decision does not apply to land transport.

> In imposing public service obligations, Member States shall be limited to requirements concerning ports to be served, regularity, continuity, frequency, capacity to provide the service, rates to be charged and manning of the vessel.[86]

Such public service obligations must be imposed, respectively contracts must be awarded on a non-discriminatory basis, and any compensation must be available for all EU shipowners. Unlike the framework for air transport that we will discuss next, this is clearly a relatively ancient and very basic regime that does not reflect the developments since *Altmark*. However, this gap is filled by the 2012 block exemption Decision on public service compensation itself up to the passenger number thresholds cited there. The designation of SGEI is subject to a manifest disproportionate standard in this sector, as elsewhere.[87] Above the block exemption Decision thresholds the 2012 Framework Communication applies, unless there is more strict sectoral regulation in place, which is not the case for maritime cabotage but in some respects exists for air transport.

Air transport

The rules on air transport were recast in 2010: that is to say, the relevant pre-existing rules were reviewed and tidied up. The 2010 Air Transport Regulation has two extensive articles dealing respectively with general principles of public service obligations and with public tendering of public service obligations. Public service obligations may be imposed for any route 'being considered vital for the economic and social development of the region which the airport serves'.[88] However, just as we have seen in relation to the other modes of public transport, there is no broader notion of universal service or of individual rights to air transport throughout the national territory or to cities of a certain size or located at a particular distance.

When identifying such routes, alternative modes of transport and the proportionality between the envisaged obligation and the need for development of the region concerned must be taken into account. Once a Member State intends to impose a public service obligation on a particular route, this must be notified to the Commission as well as to the airports on the route and the air carriers operating the route in question (and published in the Official Journal). EU air carriers who are able to meet all the conditions of the public service obligation may offer the service.

However, tendering is obligatory if there is no willing provider that can meet the public service obligation in a sustainable manner on its own accord. In this case the Member States concerned may limit the route to only one carrier for a period of up to four years, subject to review. Naturally the tendering rules set out in the 2010 Air Transport Regulation focus on transparency, and they

[86] Regulation 3577/92, above n. 9, Article 4(2).
[87] Case T-565/08 *Corsica Ferries France SAS* v. *Commission*, Judgment of 11 September 2012.
[88] Regulation 1008/2008, above n. 9, Article 16(1).

reflect a most economically attractive selection procedure. In addition, compensation may not exceed the net costs of the public service provision and a reasonable profit. The result is mixed: according to the Framework Communication, the sectoral regime applies as follows:

> The principles set out in this Communication apply to public service compensation in the field of air and maritime transport, without prejudice to stricter specific provisions contained in sectoral Union legislation.[89]

I believe that, with regard to the public tendering procedure, the 2010 Air Transport Regulation is stricter than the Framework Communication. However, as regards the justification of costs, the determination of a reasonable rate of return and the need for a claw-back mechanism for overcompensation, the Framework Communication is stricter. Presumably therefore parts of both regimes apply in parallel.

With this we round up the world of the utilities to make the transition to the – less numerous – vertical rules on welfare services: social security and healthcare.

6.8 Social security

The specificity of welfare services

The sectoral regimes for welfare services are different from those for the utilities that we have discussed above. They are less intrusive on national systems, they are much more geared towards (and limited to) cross-border situations, and the notion of universal service is virtually absent. Above I have chosen to pay limited attention to the organizational and enforcement aspects, but whereas the utilities have seen the emergence of independent national regulators coordinated (at least to some extent) by the European Commission, these are so far absent in the welfare domain, where we are more likely to observe 'contact points' instead. Likewise absent at EU level are third-party access regimes to promote competition and even liberalization as such – although at national level in various Member States the first steps in this direction are about to be taken for domestic reasons.

Social security coordination: the Regulation

Social Security Regulation 883/2004 is of central importance to determine the right to various benefits in situations in which workers and their dependants cross borders in the EU or have done so in the past.[90] The Regulation does not itself establish rights to social security benefits nor does it determine the nature

[89] SGEI compensation framework, above n. 60, para. 8.

[90] N. Rennuy, 'The emergence of a parallel system of social security coordination' *Common Market Law Review*, 50 (2013), 1221–66; F. Pennings, 'Inclusion and exclusion of persons and benefits in

or the level of such benefits: this remains the sole responsibility of the individual Member States. In this sense, there is no question of universal service set at EU level, or for that matter of universal service at all – what does exist in this regard at national level takes place across the horizon from the Regulation. What the Social Security Regulation does do is provide a coordination mechanism which is essential for workers to be able to avail themselves of their rights. Thus it plays a role in bridging the simultaneous exclusion and inclusion of rights and beneficiaries that characterizes welfare regimes, for persons who move between Member States:

> Regulation No 883/2004 does not set up a common scheme of social security, but allows different national social security schemes to exist and its sole objective is to ensure the coordination of those schemes. It thus allows different schemes to continue to exist, creating different claims on different institutions against which the claimant possesses direct rights by virtue either of national law alone or of national law supplemented, where necessary, by EU law.[91]

In particular, it guarantees the rights to social security benefits of those workers who have availed themselves of their free movement rights:

> Regulation No 883/2004 seeks to achieve the objective set out in Article 48 TFEU by preventing the possible negative effects that the exercise of the freedom of movement for workers could have on the enjoyment, by workers and their families, of social security benefits.[92]

In principle, the Regulation is therefore applicable only to that part of the EU population who have taken part in the free movement of workers, although it has meanwhile been extended: the persons covered are, roughly, nationals of Member States and their dependants.[93]

The rights to social security benefits for citizens who are not economically active can be restricted, for instance by imposing residency requirements.[94] In this context, appeals to citizenship rights linked with the 2004 Residency Rights Directive as well as the Social Security Regulation are sometimes made in tandem, leading to a complex line of case law that goes beyond the scope of

the new coordination Regulation', in M. Dougan and E. Spaventa (eds.), *Social welfare and EU law* (Hart Publishing, Oxford, 2005), 241–60; F. Pennings, *European social security law* (Intersentia, Antwerp, 2010); M. Ferrara, *The boundaries of welfare: European integration and the new spatial politics of social protection* (Oxford University Press, 2005).

91 Case C-140/12 *Pensionsversicherungsanstalt* v. *Peter Brey*, Judgment of 19 September 2013, para. 43, with reference to Case C-331/06 *K. D. Chuck* v. *Raad van Bestuur van de Sociale Verzekeringsbank* [2008] ECR I-1957, para. 27.

92 Case C-140/12 *Brey*, above n. 91, para. 51; citing Case C-331/06 *Chuck*, above n. 91, para. 32.

93 Regulation 883/2004, above n. 10, Article 2(1): 'This Regulation shall apply to nationals of a Member State, stateless persons and refugees residing in a Member State who are or have been subject to the legislation of one or more Member States, as well as to the members of their families and to their survivors.'

94 Cf. Case C-85/96 *María Martínez Sala* v. *Freistaat Bayern* [1998] ECR I-2691; Case C-158/07 *Jacqueline Förster* v. *Hoofddirectie van de Informatie Beheer Groep* [2008] ECR I-8507.

the present discussion.[95] I will just refer to the fact that an economic consideration – whether or not a resident would become an unreasonable burden – is enshrined in the Residency Rights Directive itself. This is remarkable because (i) normally only equity reasons apply; (ii) we see a similar development with regard to cross-border healthcare; and (iii) likewise, in healthcare just as with regard to social assistance, the personal circumstances of the person concerned must be taken into account. The relevant part of the recitals of the Residency Rights Directive reads as follows

> As long as the beneficiaries of the right of residence do not become an unreasonable burden on the social assistance system of the host Member State they should not be expelled. Therefore, an expulsion measure should not be the automatic consequence of recourse to the social assistance system. The host Member State should examine whether it is a case of temporary difficulties and take into account the duration of residence, the personal circumstances and the amount of aid granted in order to consider whether the beneficiary has become an unreasonable burden on its social assistance system and to proceed to his expulsion.[96]

It is worth noting, however, that in practice the Social Security Regulation – for instance, the rights with regard to healthcare benefits – sometimes also applies to persons who travel abroad precisely to avail themselves of these benefits.[97]

The services covered by the coordination regime

The social services covered are sickness, maternity and equivalent paternity benefits, benefits in respect of accidents at work and occupational diseases, death grants, invalidity benefits, old-age and survivors' pensions, unemployment benefits, pre-retirement benefits, family benefits and special non-contributory cash benefits. The basic principle applied is that time periods accumulated in other Member States serve towards the time period required for the accumulation of rights in the Member States where these are claimed, and are thus aggregated. For each type of service listed above, the coordination rules are spelled out in so far as necessary to elaborate on the general principle. With regard to sickness, there is a prior authorization system (except for emergencies) based on a right to benefits at the level of the Member State of treatment (the host Member State), which applies in parallel with the system of

[95] Directive 2004/38/EC of the European Parliament and of the Council of 29 April 2004 on the right of citizens of the Union and their family members to move and reside freely within the territory of the Member States amending Regulation (EEC) No 1612/68 and repealing Directives 64/221/EEC, 68/360/EEC, 72/194/EEC, 73/148/EEC, 75/34/EEC, 75/35/EEC, 90/364/EEC, 90/365/EEC and 93/96/EEC, OJ 2004, L158/77.

[96] Ibid., recital 16. Cf. Case C-184/99 *Rudy Grzelczyk* v. *Centre public d'aide sociale d'Ottignies-Louvain-la-Neuve* [2001] ECR I-6193; Case C-158/07 *Förster*, above n. 94.

[97] Case C-368/98 *Abdon Vanbraekel et al.* v. *Alliance nationale des mutualités chrétiennes* (ANMC) [2001] ECR I-5363; Case C-173/09 *Georgi Ivanov Elchinov* v. *Natsionalna zdravnoosiguritelna kasa* [2010] ECR I-8889.

reimbursement based on the level of the Member State of affiliation (the home Member State) of the Patients' Rights Directive that will be discussed in the next section.

6.9 Healthcare

A codification of the case law

In 2011 the EU adopted a Directive on Patients' Rights, with regard to the cross-border provision of healthcare.[98] On the one hand, this was remarkable because the Member States had long and strongly resisted EU interference in their national healthcare markets. A clear illustration of this is Article 168(7) TFEU, which enshrines a sector-specific subsidiarity clause with regard to the organization of healthcare systems and the delivery of healthcare services.[99] Also, the inclusion of healthcare in the original Services Directive (the 2004 Bolkestein proposal) on its own had already been enough to nearly scupper that initiative, and healthcare services were duly exempted from the text (the 2006 McCreevey version) which was ultimately enacted. From this perspective, the relatively recent adoption of an EU Directive on healthcare seems improbable.[100]

On the other hand, since 1998 the CJEU had been especially active in the area of cross-border healthcare. This regarded in particular the right of patients to reimbursement of healthcare expenses incurred (and paid directly by the patients) in other EU Member States. As we have seen, Regulation 883/2004 already provides a system for cross-border healthcare services based on prior approval obtained in the (home) Member State of affiliation (emergencies excepted) and reimbursement at the level applicable in the host Member State, the Member State of treatment. Because the early cases of *Kohll* and *Decker* (both 1998) regarded restitution-based insurance systems,[101] initially the Member States had resisted the idea that a right to reimbursement also existed in benefits-in-kind systems and for national health services.

Step by step, however, the case law expanded to cover all healthcare systems in the EU: the right to reimbursement at the level of the home Member State became the rule (although it existed in parallel with the system of Regulation

[98] Directive 2011/24/EU, above n. 11. Cf. L. Hancher and W. Sauter, *EU competition and internal market law in healthcare sector* (Oxford University Press, 2012); W. Sauter, 'Harmonization in health care: The EU Patients' Rights Directive', in B. Cantillon, H. Verschueren and P. Ploscar (eds.), *Social inclusion and social protection in the EU: Interactions between law and policy* (Intersentia, Antwerp, 2012), 105–29.

[99] 'Union action shall respect the responsibilities of the Member States for the definition of their health policy and for the organisation and delivery of health services and medical care. The responsibilities of the Member States shall include the management of health services and medical care and the allocation of the resources assigned to them.'

[100] Directive 2006/123/EC of the European Parliament and of the Council of 12 December 2006 on services in the internal market, OJ 2006, L376/36.

[101] Case C-158/96 *Raymond Kohll* v. *Union des caisses de maladie* [1998] ECR I-1931; Case C-120/95 *Nicolas Decker* v. *Caisse de maladie des employés privés* [1998] ECR I-1831.

883/2004).[102] At the same time, the Court accepted as an overriding reason of general interest that the planning needs of healthcare systems could justify prior authorization requirements in some cases. This is remarkable because it accepts an economic justification, whereas exceptions to free movement must normally be strictly equity based. It is not unique because we have already seen a similar development as regards the right to social assistance and the criterion of 'an unreasonable burden'. However, in order for such planning requirements to be proportional, the individual needs of the patients (the degree of pain, effects on their employment status) would always have to be considered.

The Patients' Rights Directive emerged to codify this case law and to provide a harmonized framework for cross-border healthcare services.

The Patients' Rights Directive

Just like the Social Security Regulation, the Patients' Rights Directive does not establish specific levels or modes of treatment of healthcare, nor a universal service requirement with a specific minimum standard of coverage (or for that matter any standard of coverage). Once again the objective is limited to facilitating cross-border interaction, in this case the provision of services, and the protection of persons who avail themselves of their free movement rights.

Nevertheless, when dealing with the responsibilities of the Member States of treatment, the Patients' Rights Directive refers to 'the principles of universality, access to good quality care, equity and solidarity'. In themselves they form a summary of what would constitute a universal service. Yet it is not yet clear how these principles, which suggest some form of common standards, can be translated into practice. Information that can help patients make an informed choice must be made available and non-discrimination (also as regards pricing) is to be applied to patients from other Member States. However, the latter is qualified by a provision that enables proportionate and transparent planning requirements.

The Member States of affiliation must ensure that the cost of cross-border healthcare is reimbursed. This obligation is a general one that is not specified by type of national healthcare organization, be it insurance based, benefits-in-kind based or a national health service: all must be made compliant. Prior authorization requirements are limited primarily to healthcare that is subject to planning requirements, especially hospital care requiring an overnight stay, or care that relies on highly specialized, cost-intensive infrastructure or

[102] Case C-157/99 *B. S. M. Geraets-Smits* v. *Stichting Ziekenfonds VGZ and H. T. M. Peerbooms* v. *Stichting CZ Groep Zorgverzekeringen* [2001] ECR I-5473; Case C-385/99 *V. G. Müller-Fauré* v. *Onderlinge Waarborgmaatschappij OZ Zorgverzekeringen UA and E. E. M. van Riet* v. *Onderlinge Waarborgmaatschappij ZAO Zorgverzekeringen* [2003] ECR I-4509; Case C-372/04 *The Queen, on the application of Yvonne Watts* v. *Bedford Primary Care Trust and Secretary of State for Health* [2006] ECR I-4325.

equipment. Such prior permission may only be refused primarily if there is a risk to the patient or to public health, or if

> this healthcare can be provided on its territory within a time limit which is medically justifiable, taking into account the current state of health and the probable course of the illness of each patient concerned.[103]

With this the case law of the Court has been codified. At the same time, a platform is provided for further developments – and no doubt further litigation – which may give meaning to the universality, access, equity and solidarity mentioned in the Directive but not yet connected to specific rights or duties. Article 168(7) TFEU forms a barrier here, but it has already been crossed once. Any progress in this direction is likely to require a balancing act between national prerogatives, the rights of EU citizens and consumers, and EU attempts to harness the resulting dynamics.

6.10 Payment services

Payment services can be considered as the latest branch on the family tree of public services. In fact it is perfectly possible to debate whether payment services are a public service at all. However, because a form of universal service has been introduced with regard to these services, I have decided to 'know the tree by its fruits'.[104]

The 2011 Basic Payment Account Recommendation is a non-binding measure of soft law. However, the Commission will monitor whether the Recommendation is being observed or not, and if not, whether binding legislative measures are necessary.[105] The assumption behind the Basic Payment Account Recommendation is that there are market failures in payment services which limit the right of freedom of movement and at the same time raise equity concerns:

> It is therefore necessary to establish principles on access to basic payment accounts which is a key element for promoting social inclusion and cohesion, in order to allow consumers to benefit as a minimum from a common set of essential payment services.[106]

The term 'market failure' is however not used. At the same time, the consumer interest is clear, while social inclusion and cohesion can perhaps be read as

[103] Directive 2011/24/EU, above n. 11, Article 8(6)d.

[104] Cf. N. Pesaresi and O. Pilley, 'Retail banking, social inclusion and public service', *Competition Policy Newsletter*, 10 (2003), 1: 14–20; P. de Bijl et al. *Universal service in banking*. TILEC report, 14 March 2006.

[105] The general framework is formed by Directive 2007/64/EC of the European Parliament and of the Council of 13 November 2007 on payment services in the internal market amending Directives 97/7/EC, 2002/65/EC, 2005/60/EC and 2006/48/EC and repealing Directive 97/5/EC, OJ 2007, L319/1.

[106] Basic Payment Account Recommendation, above n. 12, recital 2.

implicit references to citizenship (similarly to social exclusion with regard to universal service in electronic communications and deprivation of a substantial proportion of the population in audiovisual media).

The Basic Payment Account Recommendation requires that the Member States ensure that any legal resident has access – the right to open and use – to a basic payment account with a payment service operator in their territory. They must ensure there is at least one such operator in their territory which is charged with providing such access, while avoiding distortions of competition between payment service providers. The services concerned are the opening, operating and closing of the account, allowing money to be placed in and withdrawn from the account. In addition, there is a requirement that the service is provided either free of charge or at a reasonable charge. Regional charges are based on national income levels, average charges in the Member State concerned, costs and national consumer prices (which I take as a reference to inflation). Furthermore, awareness campaigns and out-of-court settlement procedures for dispute resolution are called for. Meanwhile, in 2013, the Commission has proposed formal EU legislation – a new Directive – that tackles the topic of payment services more broadly. Alongside access to basic payment accounts, it will serve to promote the transparency and thereby the comparability of fees, as well as the ease of switching between payment accounts from different providers.[107] Its motivation mixes universal service and internal market arguments, as well as effectiveness – because it would be formally binding.

With the Recommendation that is already in place likely to be backed up by a binding legal measure in future, we therefore see the Commission inflicting a universal service obligation on a sector that would not have guessed it was providing public services in the traditional sense. At the same time, alongside a functional internet connection, having access to a payment account forms part of the basic tool set of the modern EU citizen (not to mention internet access to a payment account). Based on the previous overview of the various sectors, I will now move on to discuss some areas of EU law that touch on universal service from different angles. These are competition; general consumer protection; and citizenship.

6.11 Universal service obligations and related EU law values

Universal service and competition

The link between these two values is threefold. First, as we have seen in some of the sectors discussed above, the adoption of universal service obligations has helped to clear the deck for liberalization and the introduction of competition. Second, these universal service obligations frequently occur alongside

[107] Proposal for a Directive of the European Parliament and of the Council on the comparability of fees related to payment accounts, payment account switching and access to payment accounts with basic features, COM(2013) 266 – 2013/0139 (COD).

third-party access requirements that are intended to promote market entry and effective competition. Here, depending on how universal service is designed – that is to say, whether it is provided by one operator or by all operators in the market – this may mean an interaction between symmetrical (universal service) and asymmetrical (access) regulations that can be at odds with one another. Universal service operators may either be placed at an advantage compared with other operators, or at a disadvantage. Third, universal service compensation can itself lead directly to overcompensation and cross-subsidies that handicap entrants. It is clear that these relationships do not all pull in the same direction, but rather introduce a variable that must be taken into consideration. Much therefore depends on the regulatory design in question.

Finally, as we have seen in the context of electronic communications, the original idea was to phase out sector-specific legislation, implicitly including the rules on universal service, and to revert to exclusive reliance on the general competition rules. In this context the question arises how universal service obligations would fare in the framework of the general competition rules, or whether they would disappear. At the same time, again in the context of electronic communications, we find that some Member States are already relying on the market to perform universal service, and are not designating operators that must do so. On the other side of the spectrum, it appears likely that once Member States are no longer obliged to impose the regime of the Universal Service Directive they might still pursue universal service policies of their own within the scope of SGEI that can accommodate both efficiency and equity concerns.

This would be so unless the Commission would no longer accept SGEI in this sector, based on the ground that it had been shown that commercial provision would suffice. However, in mobile roaming and payment account services we see intervention in a private competitive environment, where in principle the general competition rules apply. Apparently, market failures may require public interest intervention in these cases, expanding the scope of public services. There may therefore be a next generation of universal service on the horizon that does not have its roots in traditional services and a past of monopolistic provision.

Universal service and general consumer protection

Consumer protection in EU law is of course a scholarly topic in its own right that I have no intention of doing further injustice to by providing my own summary of it.[108] Nevertheless, a few remarks are in order here because it touches on

[108] Cf. S. Weatherill, *EU consumer law and policy*, 2nd edn (Edward Elgar, Cheltenham, 2013); H.-W. Micklitz, N. Reich and P. Rott, *Understanding EU consumer law* (Intersentia, Antwerp, 2009); T. Wilhelmsson, 'Services of general interest and European private law', in C. E. F. Rickett and T. G. W. Telfer (eds.), *International perspectives on consumers' access to justice* (Cambridge University Press, 2003), 149–66.

universal service in some respects. It appears that general consumer protection is in the ascendance. This involves aspects such as consumer rights, privacy and, at least sometimes, intervention to ensure 'fair pricing'. In the context of electronic communications, for instance, the Commission on its web-page professes that even effective competition itself cannot guarantee consumer needs and rights, and that therefore safeguards are necessary.[109] However, it also sketches there how a panoply of general legislation with specific consumer protection rules is already in place: the Roaming Regulation,[110] the Misleading Advertising Directive,[111] the Distance Selling Directive,[112] the Unfair Commercial Practices Directive[113] and the Regulation on cooperation in consumer protection.[114] To the unseasoned observer, this looks like a proliferation of consumer protection rules and standards. Excessive consumer protection is costly and can be anticompetitive and at odds with consumer welfare: consumers who would accept lower quality due to preference or limited availability of funds are priced out of the market, as are providers of such services.

As a rule of thumb, it would be preferable to rely as much as possible on general consumer protection rules, and as little as possible on sector-specific protection. This could also mean phasing out specific regulation over time. That in turn would mean relying on general consumer protection on the one hand, and the general competition rules on the other. Although these two dimensions, consumer protection and competition, are not necessarily directly related themselves, and reverting to one would not necessarily mean reverting to the other, entirely abolishing the sector-specific rules that cover both dimensions would in practice have the effect of doing so simultaneously. Because regulation tends to be self-perpetuating, however, it is doubtful that such sectoral regimes will be scrapped any time soon.

Universal service and citizenship

In the literature it has been suggested that market rights and EU citizenship are related concepts. In some cases the term 'market citizenship' has been

109 See http://ec.europa.eu/digital-agenda/en/users-rights.

110 Regulation (EC) No 717/2007, above n. 45.

111 Council Directive 84/450/EEC of 10 September 1984 relating to the approximation of the laws, regulations and administrative provisions of the Member States concerning misleading advertising, OJ 1984, L250/17.

112 Directive 97/7/EC of the European Parliament and of the Council of 20 May 1997 on the protection of consumers in respect of distance contracts, OJ 1997, L144/19.

113 Directive 2005/29/EC of the European Parliament and of the Council of 11 May 2005 concerning unfair business-to-consumer commercial practices in the internal market and amending Council Directive 84/450/EEC, Directives 97/7/EC, 98/27/EC and 2002/65/EC of the European Parliament and of the Council and Regulation (EC) No 2006/2004 of the European Parliament and of the Council, OJ 2005, L149/22.

114 Regulation (EC) No 2006/2004 of the European Parliament and of the Council of 27 October 2004 on cooperation between national authorities responsible for the enforcement of consumer protection laws, OJ 2004, L364/1.

used.[115] This link between two fairly disparate sets of rights is by no means self-evident, with access to (universal) services, on the one hand, meaning positive rights, and freedom from discrimination, on the other hand, being more a negative right. The two strands may meet, however, where non-discrimination means a right to access social services. A European Parliament and Council Regulation on SG(E)I based on Article 14 TFEU could form a linking pin in this process, but the Commission does not appear to regard the advantages of such an instrument as outweighing the perceived risk to the internal market. That is to say, it sees this as opening a Pandora's box.

As regards the link between, on the one hand, consumer rights and universal service and, on the other hand, universal service and citizenship, there seems to be a clear difference in that the former is concerned with procedural guarantees in relation to the purchasing and the quality of a product and the latter with more fundamental rights in relation to a service by comparison to the standard that applies nationally. Universal service itself is in an intermediate position as it concerns access rights to key services, in which case it comes close to citizenship, but also an objective quality standard, which resembles consumer rights more.

6.12 Universal service funding

Before concluding, there is one more contextual topic that I want to address with regard to universal service, which is an economic one. One of the significant dimensions of universal service is the way in which it is financed. This is important not only because it is essential for provision of the service that it should be financed in some form, but also because the mechanism used can entail greater or smaller risks for distortions of competition. Generally, the choice of the mechanism concerned is left to the Member States, which can choose between having no funding mechanism at all (usually this means imposing the burden on the incumbent operator)[116] or funding via a universal service fund. In some cases special and exclusive rights are also explicitly accepted in EU law – as in transport, but not in electronic communications or postal services. Finally, universal service can be tax-funded, in which case it is neutral in competitive terms if, instead of producers, consumers are funded directly on the basis of need.[117] From the perspective of limiting distortions of competition, the latter mechanism is preferable.[118] It is also not caught by the

[115] Cf. H.-W. Micklitz, 'Universal services: Nucleus for a social European private law', in Cremona, above n. 74, 63–102; J. Davies, *The European consumer citizen in law and policy: Consumption and public life* (Palgrave Macmillan, London, 2011).

[116] This means that it cannot be shown that this amounts to an 'unfair burden' in the sense of Articles 12 and 13 of Directive 2002/22/EC, above n. 3. Cf. Case C-389/08 *Base*, above n. 39.

[117] Cf. Harker, Kreutzmann and Waddams, above n. 1.

[118] Some authors claim that different methods of financing may be preferable depending on geography and the way the population is distributed. Cf. A. Gautier and D. Paolini, 'Universal

state aid rules, as the other mechanisms are (and as tax-based funding of producers would be), or at least must pass muster under the *Altmark* criteria or under those of the *Altmark* package.

As regards the applicability of the state aid rules to universal service funds, in my view the case law is not clear. The main relevant question is whether state resources are involved, which is one of the four requirements for a finding of state aid. Early on in *Steinike* (1977), the Court suggested that contributions imposed by the state and distributed by a fund established by the state count as aid.[119] More than twenty years later in *PreussenElektra* (2001), the Court found that there is no aid if costs are imposed on certain undertakings and the related benefits are conferred on others, even if this is done by law.[120] Finally, according to the *Pearle* case (2004), there is no aid if funding is disbursed by a private fund with privately established objectives.[121]

More recently in *Essent* (2008), the Court held that charges levied on some undertakings (purchasers of energy) in order to redistribute them to another (the joint subsidiary of domestic energy producers that had assumed their large stranded costs), imposed by law, could constitute state aid:[122]

> Article 87 EC [now Article 107 TFEU] must be construed as meaning that the amounts paid to the designated company ... constitute 'State aid' for the purposes of that provision of the Treaty to the extent that they represent an economic advantage and not compensation for the services provided by the designated company in order to discharge public service obligations.[123]

This ruling suggests that the concepts of state resources, advantage and compensation are closely linked in manner, which appears to be compatible with the emphasis on compensation in the framework of public service obligations. However, at the same time, this ruling cannot be conclusive as it was decided not in a universal service fund setting but the reverse: a situation where consumers were required to pay in order to support producers.

In sum, contrary to the generally teleological or functional approach of the CJEU, the way in which a universal service fund is structured may help determine if the state aid rules regarding compensation are applicable – and

service financing in competitive postal markets: One size does not fit all', *Review of Network Economics*, 10 (2011), 1–30; Harker, Kreutzmann and Waddams, above n. 1.

119 Case 78/76 *Steinike & Weinlig* v. *Germany* [1977] ECR 595.

120 Case C-379/98 *PreussenElektra AG* v. *Schleswag AG, in the presence of Windpark Reußenköge III GmbH and Land Schleswig-Holstein* [2001] ECR I-2099.

121 Case C-345/02 *Pearle BV, Hans Prijs Optiek Franchise BV and Rinck Opticiëns BV* v. *Hoofdbedrijfschap Ambachten* [2004] ECR I-7139.

122 Case C-206/06 *Essent Netwerk Noord BV supported by Nederlands Elektriciteit Administratiekantoor BV* v. *Aluminium Delfzijl BV, and in the indemnification proceedings Aluminium Delfzijl BV* v. *Staat der Nederlanden and in the indemnification proceedings Essent Netwerk Noord BV* v. *Nederlands Elektriciteit Administratiekantoor BV and Saranne BV* [2008] ECR I-5497. Talus, above n. 62, at 143.

123 Case C-206/06 *Essent*, above n. 122, para. 96. Nor would Article 106 TFEU cover such transfers, 'where the revenue from the charge levied on the electricity transmitted is used only in part to pay non-market-compatible costs'. Ibid., para. 57.

thereby whether the scheme must be tested against *Altmark* conditions, respectively those of the *Altmark* package, or whether it escapes because no state resources are involved.

6.13 Conclusion

Public services are a persistent irritant for economic liberals because they muddy the waters of the internal market.[124] However, because at the same time they provide tangible benefits for consumers – even rights to access services universally and at a guaranteed quality – it is hard to find fault with them. Solving the problem of the role of public services in the internal market is thus much like having one's cake and eating it. The solution appears to be distilling the active ingredients, or universal service, and ensuring their provision in a manner that is as consistent as possible with the functioning of free markets. As in any distilling process, the latter process may require repetition in successive stages or a step-by-step approach. In practice, defining a universal service may mean (at least initially) assigning additional funds (or a lifeline) to incumbent operators and cranking up the quality of their performance while opening the door to competitors, with a degree of national freedom on how to draw the balance that is gradually reduced over time. In this context, SGEI play a potentially significant role by offering a template for the provision of public service obligations that is EU law compatible. This is especially the case following the adoption of the 2005 and 2012 *Altmark* packages, which provided clarity on the Commission's approach to state aid for SGEI. Here we observe a development away from SGEI based on special and exclusive rights towards public tenders.

In spite of these commonalities, public services come in different types. In the present chapter I have discussed three varieties of public services:

- first, those primarily concerned with coordination of welfare services, where, at least in the case of healthcare, we have seen the germ of universal services;
- second, those that have been liberalized or are in the process of liberalization, broadly speaking the utilities, where universal service set at EU level is the norm (albeit with some degrees of freedom);
- third, those services that have been provided in competition from the outset, mobile roaming and payment account services, where universal services are imposed for reasons of market failure more than in response to historic claims to universality.

Another way of looking at these different categories is considering the free movement dimension that comes into play in all cases. This means either:

[124] M. Monti, *A new strategy for the single market: At the service of Europe's economy and society.* Report to the President of the European Commission, José Manuel Barroso, 9 May 2010, at 73.

- providing access to a national standard (universal service – but also non-discrimination and citizenship, not discussed in this chapter); or
- providing access to a standard combining elements from different jurisdictions (social security coordination); or
- exporting a national standard (healthcare).

Meanwhile, the right to move freely is being extended to services that had not traditionally been seen as public services: air traffic, mobile roaming and payment accounts. Although in some cases it is quite traditional (such as in maritime transport or postal services), it appears that the sector-specific legislation on public services in the EU is largely up to date and not backward looking. This is perhaps not just due to bureaucratic foresight but at least in part because the system is permeable to pressure from consumers. For instance, the healthcare reform was ultimately litigation driven: here there is an interaction between individual consumers, Treaty principles and the functional approach adopted by the CJEU. The same permeability is found – albeit based on consumer moaning rather than litigation – for mobile roaming.

It is my impression, based on the review of sectoral secondary legislation set out above, that the economic reasoning involved is not generally made explicit. Instead the benefits of the internal market are generally referred to – which can be seen as an indirect way of identifying economic benefits, albeit by now legally sanctified as an EU objective in its own right. This means that the market failures involved are not cited as such, although (as for instance in the case of payment accounts) they do play an important role. In the case of social security, coordinating between national authorities is the main point, which could be seen as a way of addressing government failure rather than market failure. Regarding roaming, finally we see a form of government failure combined with market failure where coordination has proven unable to address the root of the problem concerned. Hence the EU itself has finally grabbed the helm and legislated its way out of the conundrum, with a combination of price intervention and promotion of competition (wholesale access).

Unsurprisingly therefore, different approaches are discernible to different types of problem. Yet all are broadly consistent with a growing role for consumer interests and an increasingly direct link between the EU level and the standards of service provided to the individual. Whether this can be linked to EU citizenship will be discussed in the next (and final) chapter.

7

Conclusions and new directions

7.1 Organization

Above I have discussed various aspects of the way in which public services are classified and treated in EU law. This is relevant because it affects the way in which these services function and can continue to be provided to EU citizens and on which terms, including variables such as universality, or other aspects of equity, and efficiency. Because this conclusion aims to be concise, it focuses on the highlights and main themes of the text above. It is divided into three parts:

- First, it comprises an overview of the preceding discussion. I will attempt to summarize and present the answers that I have found to the research questions concerning the role of public services in EU law that I set out to examine. I will do this by discussing the main findings chapter by chapter and then by going down the list of questions that I have raised in the general introduction.
- Second, this conclusion provides an elaboration: I will try to build somewhat further on the answers found in the preceding chapters. This includes addressing the overall theme set out in the introduction, based on the terminology of the 2010 Monti report, the question whether public services were building blocks for the internal market or a persistent irritant.[1]
- Third, in this context I will highlight some current trends. Finally, and in line with academic custom, I will indicate some possible avenues for future research based both on issues that were raised by my findings, and on questions left open due to the limitations of my approach in this book.

7.2 An overview of the findings chapter by chapter

Questions, concepts and context

The first chapter discussed the role of the concepts of USO and SGEI and the question of what constitutes the EU law on public services. I proposed a model

[1] M. Monti, *A new strategy for the single market: At the service of Europe's economy and society.* Report to the President of the European Commission, José Manuel Barroso, 9 May 2010.

that shows the different subcategories of services of general interest (SGI), the overriding category, which I equated with the concept of public services. An SGI always includes a public service obligation (PSO, which can be at retail level or at wholesale level) and may include a universal service obligation (USO), which is sometimes (but need not be) defined at EU level. The most important concept is that of services of general economic interest (SGEI). In this context the notion 'economic' refers to the fact that these services are market based and are carried out by undertakings. In turn, an entity is an undertaking if it carries out an economic activity (at least potentially) in competition, and in this case the state aid and competition rules apply.

The concept of undertaking is thus key to the status of public services in EU law and is increasingly important now that the Commission is becoming more active with regard to SGEI in the context of state aid. Indeed, a short history of public services in the EU shows that, after an activist era promoting the adoption of sector-specific rules focusing on utilities liberalization, the Commission is now more interested in SGEI with regard to horizontal issues such as state aid and public procurement.

In the context of SGEI the relevance of the concept of market failure is increasing, but it is not always clear if this includes only efficiency (market failure narrowly defined) considerations or also equity (market failure broadly defined) considerations.[2] In accordance with its capabilities, the role of the EU in relation to market failure is one of regulation, not of spending. At the same time, even at national level there is a more general trend away from the centralized welfare state, which is limited by bounds of solidarity that do not appear to reach to the EU level. Social scientists discuss this development in terms of EU promotion of negative integration (removing market barriers) and positive integration (creating new EU-level regimes) where they see a deficit regarding the latter. As regards public services defined in EU law terms, there appear to be new trends that include competitive provision of USO, imposing PSO at wholesale level (even if the ultimate objective is to promote universal retail access for consumers), and selective provision of USO.[3]

The Treaty framework and the mixed economic constitution

Chapter 2 sketches the Treaty provisions that are specifically relevant to public services, as well as Protocol 26 on SG(E)I and the SGEI article in the Charter of Fundamental Rights of the EU. Together these can be defined as the primary EU law on public services. Here we find that Article 106 TFEU, which was present at the creation of the 1957 Rome Treaty, remains the main relevant

[2] Case T-79/10 *Colt Télécommunications France* v. *Commission*, Judgment of 16 September 2013.

[3] Cf. Case T-289/03 *British United Provident Association Ltd (BUPA), BUPA Insurance Ltd and BUPA Ireland Ltd* v. *Commission* [2008] ECR II-81.

provision. This Article and the provision on commercial monopolies in Article 37 TFEU reflect a balance that was struck between the more free-trade-oriented Northern and more statist Southern Member States. In effect this compromise, fleshed out in the case law of the CJEU, has lasted until today because the new additions to the Treaties have not yet made an impact. This concerns notably Article 14 TFEU which, since the 2007 Lisbon Treaty came into effect, enables framework legislation on SGEI but has never been used. Another provision that dates back to the Rome Treaty, Article 345 TFEU, formally guarantees the freedom of the system of property ownership chosen at Member State level. In practice, however, liberalization has swept across the utilities sector, making any effective degree of state ownership difficult to maintain. Short of state ownership, however, there is intensive EU-level regulation in the utilities sectors. For welfare services there are no comparable EU regimes in place (or even on the horizon) and national rules are dominant.

The result of these developments is that the EU has neither a free market nor a state-oriented system but one that (without claiming originality) I have called a mixed economic constitution. As is elaborated further in Chapter 4, this means that neither the economic model provided by the German Ordoliberals nor that offered by the Chicago school neo-liberals applies – but nor do state-centred models. Although on balance the mixed economic constitution favours free markets, it provides a range of possible exceptions that allow Member States to pursue efficiency but also equity goals in a proportionate manner. Article 106(2) TFEU on SGEI is one of the main sources of such exceptions with regard to public services. This appears to fit with the new EU objective of becoming a highly competitive social market economy and the newly defined role of competition policy in promoting the internal market (instead of as an objective in its own right or instrument of free competition in open markets).

With regard to citizenship, I have found that this is sometimes invoked to enforce access to public services (welfare). I have noted that some authors use the concepts of market citizens and consumer citizens, and in a context of consumer protection this may be justified. However, these concepts are at present difficult to square with, on the one hand, the very limited material content of the citizenship provisions in the Treaty, which are largely limited to non-discrimination, and, on the other hand, the differentiated experience regarding public services. (See further below.)

The free movement and citizenship case law

The utilities are almost uniformly provided by undertakings that are not concerned with the free movement rules which target public authorities. Hence, the third chapter, which studies free movement, is based on the EU case law with regard to three exemplary welfare services: healthcare, education and social security services (including their citizenship dimension). In contrast to the utilities sectors with their sector-specific frameworks and sometimes specific regulators, for these three types of welfare services the case law forms the main EU legal framework. Although the CJEU uses the concept of citizenship as a trump against national measures limiting access to welfare (at least where there is a real link between the claimant and the Member State involved), the level at which welfare services are provided and to what standard remains the prerogative of the Member States.

Under the exceptions provided in the Treaty and such overriding reasons of general interest as are established in practice, the Court is likely to accept restrictions that meet a (generally restrained, 'manifest disproportionality') proportionality test. In principle only equity reasons can be invoked with regard to free movement, but in practice efficiency reasons are accepted too, such as the planning of welfare systems and their financial balance. An observation that returns in other chapters is the trend in EU law to frame prohibitions widely while allowing for generous exceptions. As regards free movement (and citizenship), however, the Court also insists that the Member States who deny access must take into account the personal circumstances of the individuals involved. This means something resembling private or individual rights can be invoked against the Member States even where, from a general perspective, the measure would have been justified. In addition to the broadly familiar picture in EU law of rules and their exceptions, there can therefore be exceptions to the exception in order to protect individual rights.

In my view the net effect of the application of EU law promotes both access to public services and the provision of funding of such access, but the actual numbers of EU citizens who benefit directly from this are so low that they cannot realistically be seen as a serious threat to national welfare systems. Benefits continue to be defined nationally and access conditions do too to a significant extent, although some secondary EU law is in place, as has been seen in Chapter 6. The fact that, with regard to welfare services, the EU has its main impact on access forms a parallel with the utilities where, as we have seen, in spite of the existence of extensive regulatory regimes adopted at EU level, direct control over the providers of networks and services does not lie with the EU institutions. In both instances governance, not spending power, is the EU's handle on public services.

Competition and state aid

Chapter 4 forms a counterpoint to the preceding chapter: because both the competition and state aid (at least regarding its beneficiaries) rules are concerned with undertakings, this chapter primarily concerns the utilities – although, especially in the state aid field, welfare services are becoming increasingly relevant. The criteria to determine whether the concept of undertaking applies are also differentiated for the exercise of public authority and various types of public services (healthcare, social services and education), which are examined here.

In this chapter I have also discussed the scope for exceptions to these rules. For state aid there is now an extensive framework in place for SGEI that grants a block exemption to welfare services, while for the utilities a system of individual exemptions (albeit largely based on the same criteria) has been created. The content of the criteria that are applied here is largely determined by the *Altmark* case and revolves around the question whether a quid pro quo (compensation) for a genuine public service obligation has been granted that is proportional to this task.[4] If so, there is no aid, because the requirement that an advantage should be granted is not met. Where there is aid and the exception of Article 106(2) TFEU on SGEI is used, both an efficiency and an equity defence are available. The same is true for a state aid exemption based on Article 107(3) TFEU, but in the case of SGEI the interest invoked is that of the Member State, whereas in the case of a finding of compatibility with the internal market based on Article 107(3) TFEU the interest that must benefit is that of the EU.

This is in contrast to the competition rules where so far only efficiency rules in the interest of undertakings and consumers can be invoked (as well as the SGEI exception). Current voices pleading in favour of an equity defence in competition law are in my view mistaken: the SGEI defence already allows Member States to defend equity concerns under the competition rules in a structured way, and the state action defence allows them to legislate and impose conditions on market parties without aiding and abetting corporatist conspiracies among the latter. Moreover, national competition authorities are ill-suited to evaluating equity claims made by private parties even if (or perhaps especially if) these are made under the shadow of public encouragement. In my view: if public policy objectives are concerned, public authorities should face their responsibility and where necessary formulate clear obligations on private parties that can be tested according to clear EU law criteria.

Two further secondary themes addressed in this chapter were, first, the role of the consumer interest, which was found to be an important but not the predominant objective of competition law,[5] and second, the relevance of market failure. The latter, as I have already mentioned, is on the increase, especially in the state aid context.

Horizontal secondary rules: services, public procurement and transparency

Chapter 5 dealt with the relatively limited number of horizontal secondary rules, that is, legislation based on primary law that is not sector-specific but of

[4] Case C-280/00 *Altmark Trans GmbH and Regierungspräsidium Magdeburg* v. *Nahverkehrsgesellschaft Altmark GmbH, and Oberbundesanwalt beim Bundesverwaltungsgericht* [2003] ECR I-7747.

[5] Cf. Joined cases C-501/06 P, C-513/06 P, C-515/06 P and C-519/06 P *GlaxoSmithKline Services Unlimited* v. *Commission and Commission* v. *GlaxoSmithKline Services Unlimited and European Association of Euro Pharmaceutical Companies (EAEPC)* v. *Commission and Asociación de exportadores españoles de productos farmacéuticos (Aseprofar)* v. *Commission* [2009] ECR I-9291.

general application. The Services Directive and the rules on public procurement and on financial transparency for public undertakings were discussed, and finally an abbreviated coverage of the block exemption Decision on public service compensation was provided. Each of these measures serves a very different purpose. At a meta-level they may of course all be construed as serving the internal market and in particular market access. As regards public services, at least the first two have in common that they are riddled with exceptions and special regimes for public services that are intended either to leave them outside the scope of the rules concerned or to limit the effective impact of these rules on them. At the same time, the primary Treaty rules provide a background regime that, at least for public services, in some cases appears to be even stricter than the secondary law. (An example is the general EU law transparency and non-discrimination requirements compared to the mild public procurement regime for welfare services under the applicable Directives.)

An exception is provided by the (above-mentioned) Commission package that sets the rules for public service compensation with regard to SGEI and state aid. By combining its state aid (monopoly) powers and the Article 106(2) TFEU framework, the Commission mutually reinforces the impact of two of its institutional trumps to considerable effect. However, the result is not clearly a horizontal regime: different procedures apply to welfare services (the block exemption) and the utilities (with individual exemption decisions), although the substantive standards are very similar.

Finally, I have discussed and discounted the scope for a horizontal Regulation on SGEI based on Article 14 TFEU, because in the foreseeable future there is no identifiable incentive for the Commission to submit a proposal to go down this route. The risk of opening a Pandora's box of state interventionism is considerable and the advantages, such as achieving more consistency and tackling corporatism, are so far too hypothetical to change this calculus. However, the Member States and the other Community institutions which may be less sensitive to this risk (or may even welcome it) could put pressure on the European Commission to take this route.

Vertical secondary rules: harmonized framework legislation for public services

In the sixth chapter I have tried to discuss the available sectoral regimes for public services, that is to say, vertical rules of secondary EU law. This discussion does not cover the respective regulatory regimes as such, or third-party access and other competition issues, or the networks of national regulators that have emerged. Instead it focuses on public service obligations and especially universal service. It turns out that although there are similarities (for instance, the role of universal service in promoting liberalization) there are also many differences in the degree to which rules exist and are detailed, and also regarding their scope. In some cases, such as energy, there appears to be convergence and/or overlap with consumer protection, possibly to a degree that overshoots the target. In other cases intervention is more isolated within a sector that is overwhelmingly market oriented (as in access to basic banking services).

At the same time, it appears evident that sectoral regimes are here to stay: this is illustrated well by the regulation of mobile roaming services, which emerged under conditions of full competition in the electronic communications sector, but have nevertheless been price-capped at EU level. Similarly, air traffic and payment accounts suggest an ongoing forward-looking development in the EU law on public services with regard to universal service rather than a rearguard action, or merely mopping up behind utilities liberalization. At the same time, the prospect for full reliance on general competition law with regard to the utilities sectors appears remote: instead it seems that the sector-specific regimes are likely to persist for the foreseeable future. Even where competition is widely present in a sector, SGEI can be invoked to protect PSO and USO – in so far as necessary and proportional. The SGEI category is open-ended. This also means that public service obligations and universal service are likely to persist.

7.3 The answers to the research questions summarized

Following this chapter-by-chapter rendition of my findings, I will now address in turn each of the research questions that were set out in the introduction (and which I have recapitulated in each chapter as relevant). This has been organized in three sets.

The first set of issues sought to identify the rules of EU law on public services, based on the legal basis, the applicable legal rules and the exceptions to these rules.

- *What is the relevant primary and secondary EU law?* The relevant provisions have been set out in detail in the successive chapters. There are some specific provisions (Articles 14 and 106 TFEU) at the level of primary law, and in addition the free movement and competition and state aid rules are relevant: the former primarily for welfare services and the latter mainly for the utilities. In addition, general rules of secondary law and sector-specific regimes are in place, especially for the utilities. For welfare services, coordination regimes exist.
- *What are the limits that EU law imposes on public services?* Public services must conform to EU law. That is to say, that where their provision clashes with the rules on free movement or on competition, or their funding with the state aid rules, this has to be brought in line, or a successful appeal must be made for an exception. This is no different from any other appeal to the public interest in EU law that must be justified as necessary and proportionate. There is, however, a difference in that, apart from the general Treaty exceptions and overriding reasons of general interest, Article 106(2) TFEU provides a specific exception both on equity and on efficiency grounds with regard to both the competition and free movement rules.

- *What scope is left for national policies regarding public services under EU law exceptions?* Apart from the answer to the previous question, there is the fact that, especially for the utilities, there are sector-specific frameworks of secondary legislation. Generally these also aim to promote effective competition. Where such a framework is in place, national policies must be consistent with it. As regards welfare services, the situation is slightly different: there competition is generally optional, and the harmonized rules mainly concern coordination of access rights to national systems for individuals. The extent of the rights themselves remains determined at national level.

The second set of questions concerned the dynamics in the case law and the legislative process, and involved looking at the balance between positive (rule-making) and negative (market-making) integration.

- *What are the common elements regarding public services in the case law?* The Court tends to construe prohibitions widely but also gives broad scope to exceptions. A factor that is often decisive in determining how much leeway is available is the degree to which EU harmonization legislation is in place: a greater degree of harmonization reduces the scope for national policies with regard to public services that are discriminatory in some form. Also, the Court is developing its case law on citizenship (such as regarding access to social benefits) and analogies such as patients' rights. The effect is that, apart from the interests of the EU (integration based) and the Member States (various public policy objectives), now also the interests of individuals have started playing a role. Finally and most recently, the concept of market failure has begun to play a role as an explicit justification for public policy with regard to public services.
- *Are EU standards emerging and what is their role?* On the one hand, EU standards are clearly emerging in the relevant harmonization legislation. In some cases – notably the mobile roaming Regulation – there is even direct intervention in price setting and access conditions at EU level. On the other hand, this does not mean there are common EU-level standards across sectors, although in my view universality, the consumer interest and market failure are factors that in most sectors tend to play a significant role. In sum, the standards set so far have their effect primarily or even exclusively at sectoral level.
- *How does this affect legislation?* The effects on national legislation have not been examined, albeit that this will frequently consist of the need to adopt implementing measures with regard to EU Directives. In some cases there appears to be a remaining degree of freedom with regard to universal service obligations that can be topped up at national level; in other cases universal service appears to constitute maximum harmonization with a limited remaining measure of freedom (or none at all). As we have seen above, some horizontal legislation with regard to SGEI exists in the context of compensation for public services and state aid. However, in the absence of

a Regulation on SGEI based on Article 14 TFEU a genuine horizontal measure is lacking.

As regards the balance between positive and negative integration, there is no evidence of the integration process leading to fewer rules with regard to public services: if anything liberalization (where this results from negative integration) requires more rules in order to enable the new markets to function. This is relevant especially for the utilities. On the side of welfare services there is in my view no real evidence of negative integration to begin with. What does appear to be in store are experiments with market-based provision of welfare services, but this is not so far taking place in an EU law context or framework. However, if as a result of such experiments or policy shifts they are provided by undertakings (that is to say: at least potentially in competition), such welfare services will be subject to the rules on competition and on state aid.

The concluding questions concern the role and development of the main EU-level concepts.

- *What is the role of the concept of service of general (economic) interest?* The SGEI concept is the key to the role of public services in EU law: it enables their definition and provision according to national preferences but in accordance with the demands of EU law. Proportionality is a key concept here. In principle the Member States are free to define SGEI, but regarding the compensation for such services in the context of the application of the state aid rules, criteria have been set by the CJEU and the Commission. Also, where services are already adequately provided in competition, formulating an SGEI may not be acceptable, although the test applied is the mild one of manifest disproportionality. However, there is no overall framework yet, such as could be adopted under Article 14 TFEU. The role of non-economic SGI is still in its infancy. Finally, for the foreseeable future their relevance appears to be likely to be limited to non-discrimination obligations related to citizenship.
- *What is the role of universal service in this context?* Universal service is a particular type of public service obligation, which guarantees access to public services (of a defined nature and quality) at retail level, that is to say, directly to consumers. Public services can also exist at wholesale level (as they do, for instance, in the energy and broadband sectors) and affect consumers only indirectly, even though ensuring ubiquitous access (indirectly) may nevertheless be an objective here as well. Universal service, in other words, forms the underlying ratio and objective behind having public services in the first place. In my view, it is doubtful whether in the absence of any link to universal service (even indirectly) a particular service could justifiably claim to constitute a public service.
- *Is there an EU citizenship dimension?* The dimension of EU citizenship in relation to public services is difficult to define but not absent. For instance, in

the Charter of Fundamental Rights of the European Union SGEI come under the heading of solidarity and not under that of citizenship. Nevertheless, even SGI, which are not otherwise touched by EU law, must comply with the basic guarantee of non-discrimination that is based on the citizenship provisions of the TFEU. The question is whether a holistic whole that is greater than the sum of its parts can be created by linking the EU provisions on citizenship, consumer protection and universal service, under the umbrella of citizenship. For the time being this relationship remains fragmented – a positive view of this would be that these are simply different dimensions of the same basic identity. This perspective, although already adopted by some authors, has not yet been elaborated definitively.[6] I believe the reason to be the limited scope of the citizenship provisions in the TFEU. However, an alternative structure could be based on Article 14 TFEU that might complement citizenship without forming a part of it.

7.4 Broader conclusions on contextual issues

In this section I will try to take on some of the more contextual issues that were raised above. These are: (i) the relationship between positive and negative integration; (ii) the question whether public services are building blocks or irritants in the internal market context; and (iii) the impact of the EU law regime for public services on the regulation or reregulation of such services.

Positive versus negative integration

First, I will discuss what the relevance is of public services in the context of the balance between positive and negative integration where Fritz Scharpf and other political scientists presumed the deck to be stacked in favour of the latter and economic liberalism, and against the former and solidarity-based solutions.[7]

There are several points to be made here. First, in EU law solidarity is accepted as the basis for excepting entities from the application of competition law, notably in the area of welfare services. These services are thus largely ruled out of bounds when solidarity is found to be dominant. This is so because the entities concerned are then not regarded as undertakings. Second, the internal market rules have always allowed for equity-based exceptions and, at least in the area of public services, increasingly admit efficiency-based exceptions as well (such as the financial balance and planning of the social security system, respectively the healthcare system). Third, SGEI are themselves an exception

[6] Cf. J. Davies, *The European consumer citizen in law and policy: Consumption and public life* (Palgrave Macmillan, London, 2011).

[7] F. W. Scharpf, *Community and autonomy: Institutions, policies and legitimacy in multilevel Europe* (Campus, Frankfurt am Main, 2010). Earlier: F. W. Scharpf, *Governing in Europe: Effective and democratic?* (Oxford University Press, 1999).

to EU law – internal market and competition – that allows for both equity- and efficiency-based reasons. This means there are ample opportunities for invoking an exception to benefit national policies that are solidarity based.

Scharpf's underlying point may be that it is all well and good that national measures receive some protection under EU law exceptions. However, once they are exposed to the rigour of the market by economic liberalization at EU level there will be no EU measures forthcoming to remedy this exposure, and national measures alone will not suffice. Hence leaving the formal competence at national level untouched would be just another way of killing it softly. This argument appears to be more difficult to counter, but at the same time it seems that the Member States are simply not willing to cede the relevant powers to the EU level, and in line with the subsidiarity principle, are of the view that they remain best placed to exercise these powers. From the point of view of input legitimacy (justified by the democratic process if not of output legitimacy as effective results) this appears to be a plausible outcome.

In addition, I subscribe to the view on the relation between the EU and the welfare state that was developed and propagated by Alan Milward. Having a common market and more recently an internal one is what the EU at its heart is all about: it is the engine room of the economy and its continued success also allows and enables Member States to maintain their national welfare systems in the first place (or to have their cake and eat it). This is something to keep in mind when criticizing the chilling effects that EU-spurred competition and market access may have on welfare.[8]

Building block or persistent irritant?

Second, I wish to address the question whether public services are building blocks or persistent irritants that I raised in relation to the Monti report on the internal market in the introductory chapter.[9] There are essentially two prongs here: one regards public services, utilities and welfare services, and thereby the subject of this book, the other SGEI more generally.

My general view is that public services once they have been disciplined by EU law – as in the case of electronic communications and increasingly energy and posts – can play a positive role in European integration that goes beyond allowing exceptions for temporary subsidies to allow former monopolists to adjust to the market (although that aspect has certainly played a role as well). Although the initial rationale was enabling liberalization by encapsulating the public interest in a well-defined universal service bubble, there are broader public benefits associated with the utilities services and these have by and large been set out in regulatory regimes that are by now more or less permanent. Here we can see building blocks.

[8] Cf. A. S. Milward, *The European rescue of the nation state*, 2nd edn (Routledge, London, 1999).

[9] Monti, above n. 1.

For welfare services we can say that the EU has not yet decided and may never decide to install bespoke regulatory regimes and is content to regulate cross-border transactions, respectively the coordination of rights accumulated in the different Member States. By contrast, where undertakings are involved, the SGEI regime is relevant, for instance regarding public service compensation in the state aid context. Here EU norms determine the criteria that must be met by an SGEI in order to satisfy EU law scrutiny. If a public service takes this shape it is difficult to see why it should be an irritant: it is tailored to meet the procedural and economic requirements set, but in substance remains free to be defined by the Member States.

As regards SGEI more generally, as we have seen this is an open-ended category because Member States are free to define SGEI, including in new sectors, subject only to the caveat that the services concerned should not already be provided by the market in a satisfactory manner. Perhaps a public service defined as an SGEI can meet this test and still be sufficiently irritating and widespread to cause trouble in spite of the existence of a state aid regime for compensation (which should address cross-subsidization and market-spoiling events) and in spite of the applicability of the competition rules (aside from proportional exceptions in pursuit of a legitimate purpose). In this case it stands to reason that the EU should attempt to legislate. Where it cannot, the irritant will be a reminder of outstanding issues that remain to be resolved.

Regulation versus reregulation

As the sectoral regimes for, in particular, the utilities illustrate, liberalization breeds regulation and not deregulation: this is logical because markets must function within a system of transparent and predictable legal rules, whereas for a state monopolist an informal patronage system is likely to suffice or may actually be preferred. At the same time, and perhaps more surprisingly, we see that sectoral rules are not phased out to make way for regulation based on the generally applicable competition rules. There appear to be several reasons for this: once regulatory regimes are established and engrained they are difficult to displace; sectoral regimes create their own justifications; the sectors concerned are economically and politically significant, so they have systemic characteristics that make a more hands-on approach to regulation preferable; and finally, their social relevance, which is also expressed through universal service, requires closer control.

In addition, as regards the role of the EU, because it has no spending power comparable to that of the Member States, regulation is its preferred mode of intervention. This also explains that, while providing tax-based subsidies may be preferable to other types of universal service funding, from an economic perspective this model (tax and spend) is only feasible at the level of the

Member States (if they so wish) and not at EU level.[10] Regarding regulation the impact of the EU is multiplied by the European Commission's coordination of national sectoral and competition regulators. It does this in order to sort out coordination problems (obviously) as well as for broader reasons of consistency with EU law and regulatory best practice. At the same time, however, this allows EU policies to be pursued in these areas even where the Commission cannot intervene directly.

Finally, it should be noted that EU intervention is not limited to setting sectoral framework regimes by means of Directives that leave some discretion to national implementation measures and soft-law coordination by the Commission: the Roaming Regulation shows that where certain conditions are met – a pan-EU problem affecting consumers moving across borders, and a regulatory failure as well as a market failure – the EU legislature is prepared to engage in direct intervention on prices and access obligations applicable throughout the Union.[11] This set of conditions may be relatively rare, but this event nevertheless demonstrates a willingness to act on a public service issue with aspects of consumer protection, citizenship and universal service. Because mobile services emerged in a competitive environment, this also shows that public service regulation will survive the incumbent operators.

7.5 New directions in public services

In this section I want to set out some of the recent and current trends that I believe are significant to the way in which the treatment of public services in EU law is likely to develop. The first of these is the development of PSO and USO with respect in particular to consumer protection versus access obligations. The second is the competitive provision of PSO and USO. The third is the provision of PSO at wholesale instead of retail level, and the issue whether this meets the universality requirement. The fourth issue is related to partial provision of SGEI, which likewise appears at odds with the universal access requirement. The fifth and final section is on the distinction between economic and non-economic activities of the same entity.

Access rights versus consumer protection

The scope of PSO and USO is a difficult issue. In principle it is left to the Member States to decide, but any restrictions under EU law must be proportional in nature. In that context the state of development of EU law – the existence of any harmonization legislation, for instance – is an issue. In my

[10] Cf. M. Harker, A. Kreutzmann and C. Waddams, *Public service obligations and competition*, Final Report, February 2013, CERRE Centre for regulation in Europe, at 80.

[11] Regulation (EU) No 531/2012 of the European Parliament and of the Council of 13 June 2012 on roaming on public mobile communications networks within the Union, OJ 2012, L172/10.

view, USO are limited to access rights. That means to say that broader consumer protection measures may be qualified as PSO, but not as concerned with universal service. A contrary view is found in Davies and Szyszczak (2010) with reference to the plethora of new consumer rights found in the most recent electronic communications and energy legislation.[12] These developments may be linked to the perpetuation of sector-specific regulation in these sectors, which had originally been intended to revert to the framework of general competition law within a few years. To this account the 2012 Patients' Rights Directive might be added, which likewise supplements access rights for treatment across borders (or at least for reimbursement of such treatment) with notions of transparency and quality of the service provided.

At the same time, access at zero quality has nil value, strengthening the argument that the two dimensions are linked. Nevertheless, for the sake of clarity, I would advocate the approach already stated above of distinguishing between access as USO and broader PSO rights for consumers that blend into general consumer protection and cannot easily be used to justify for instance the existence of special and exclusive rights. This is also because in an infrastructural setting it is the costs for the last mile or physical connection to the consumer that are are potentially prohibitive, not those for having a toll-free information desk and the possibility to end automatically renewable contracts at a month's notice.

Competitive provision of PSO/USO?

At EU level increasingly a preference for competitive provision of USO can be discerned: this goes one step beyond the competitive provision of public services (such as electronic communications) towards competitive provision of the universal service (that is, not by a single undertaking charged with providing it – as a provider of last resort – but its provision by multiple undertakings in competition). In the liberalization context as set out in the 2002 Universal Service Directive regarding electronic communications the implementation of USO is structured both by EU law principles and by economic efficiency. It assigns priority to competitive conditions where feasible:

> Member States shall determine the most efficient and appropriate approach for ensuring the implementation of universal service, whilst respecting the principles of objectivity, transparency, non-discrimination and proportionality. They shall seek to minimise market distortions, in particular the provision of services at prices or subject to other terms and conditions

[12] J. Davies and E. Szyszczak, 'Universal service obligations: Fulfilling new generations of services of general economic interest', in E. Szyszczak et al. (eds.), *Developments in services of general interest* (TMC Asser Press, The Hague, 2011), 155–77.

> which depart from normal commercial conditions, whilst safeguarding the public interest.[13]

Similarly, in the state aid context, in its revised *Altmark* package concerning the application of Article 106(2) TFEU, the Commission clarified in 2012 that where the services concerned are already being provided at a satisfactory level by market forces:

> [I]t would not be appropriate to attach specific public service obligations to an activity which is already provided or can be provided satisfactorily and under conditions, such as price, objective quality characteristics, continuity and access to the service, consistent with the public interest, as defined by the State, by undertakings operating under normal market conditions.[14]

Hence imposing a PSO is in principle only acceptable as proportionate in the event that market provision is an insufficient guarantee. It is likely that in this setting increasingly economic criteria will play a role, in particular the concept of market failure that has been discussed above.[15]

PSO at wholesale instead of retail level

The 2013 Broadband Guidelines go one step further in the direction of competitive provision. To benefit from an exemption to the state aid rules here, undertakings charged with SGEI are required to provide third-party access to their broadband network in order to enable (but not themselves to offer) competitive retail provision. These SGEI operators are providing a public service precisely while being excluded from offering their own services directly to the public:

> Given the degree of competition that has been achieved since the liberalisation of the electronic communications sector in the Union, and in particular the competition that exists today on the retail broadband market, a publicly funded network set up within the context of an SGEI should be available to all interested operators. Accordingly, the recognition of an SGEI mission for broadband deployment should be based on the provision of a passive, neutral and open infrastructure. Such a network should provide access seekers with all possible forms of network access and allow effective competition at the retail level, ensuring the provision of competitive and affordable services to end-users.

[13] Directive 2002/22/EC of the European Parliament and of the Council of 7 March 2002 on universal service and users' rights relating to electronic communications networks and services (Universal Service Directive), OJ 2002, L108/51, Article 3(2).

[14] Communication from the Commission on the application of the European Union state aid rules to compensation granted for the provision of services of general economic interest, OJ 2012, C8/4, para. 48. Demonstrating the absence of adequate provision by the market, subject to a manifestly disproportionate test, can be the first step in defining an SGEI. My claim would be that to do so is in fact also necessary as part of the proportionality test.

[15] For instance, in the context of state aid, cf. N. Fiedziuk, 'Towards a more refined economic approach to services of general economic interest', *European Public Law*, 16 (2010), 271–88.

> Therefore, the SGEI mission should only cover the deployment of a broadband network providing universal connectivity and the provision of the related wholesale access services, without including retail communication services.[16]

In other words, under the state aid rules on broadband the EU objective of universal access to broadband services[17] is used to motivate the mandatory imposition (by the Member States concerned) of an access obligation. However, the universal service to the public is not actually provided directly by (or imposed on) the parties supplying the SGEI and receiving state aid, but by competitors who are using the network of the SGEI parties in order to provide retail services to consumers (so making them universally available). Here we see how managed competition, industrial policy (promoting broadband roll-out) and universal service are intertwined (leaving the possibly disturbing consequences regarding the incentives for private investment aside for now). Another example of a PSO at wholesale level is provided by subsidies for undertakings constructing social housing in the 2013 *Libert* case:

> [O]n account in particular of the wide discretion enjoyed by the Member States, it is not inconceivable that the social obligation may be regarded as a 'public service'. In that context, the fact, alluded to by the referring court, that the social obligation does not directly benefit individuals – the applicants for social housing – but rather the social housing companies, is irrelevant with regard to the classification of the service in question.[18]

It is clear that here we see a potentially significant direction for expansion of the PSO category which also meets the universality requirement – the subject of the next section.

Universality and partial provision

The meaning of universality is another variable that is subject to development. In order to illustrate what is in store, I will provide two examples. The first example is the General Court's ruling in the 2008 *BUPA* case that I have already cited above. Here services provided by competing health insurers in Ireland were considered SGEI in spite of providing supplementary services for payment on a voluntary basis (and therefore covering the wealthier part of the

[16] Communication from the Commission on EU Guidelines for the application of state aid rules in relation to the rapid deployment of broadband networks, OJ 2013, C25/1, paras. 23–4.

[17] Communication from the Commission, Europe 2020: A strategy for smart, sustainable and inclusive growth, COM(2010) 2020: 'The aim is to deliver sustainable economic and social benefits from a Digital Single Market based on fast and ultra fast internet and interoperable applications, with broadband access for all by 2013, access for all to much higher internet speeds (30 Mbps or above) by 2020, and 50% or more European households subscribing to internet connections above 100 Mbps.' Ibid., p 14.

[18] Joined cases C-197/11 and C-203/11 *Eric Libert et al.* v. *Gouvernement flamand and All Projects & Developments NV et al.* v. *Vlaamse Regering*, Judgment of 8 May 2013, para. 88.

population), existing alongside and on top of a more general mandatory universal service provided free of charge:

> As regards the universal nature of the PMI [private medical insurance] services, it must be noted at the outset that . . . it does not follow from Community law that, in order to be capable of being characterised as an SGEI, the service in question must constitute a universal service in the strict sense, such as the public social security scheme. In effect, the concept of universal service, within the meaning of Community law, does not mean that the service in question must respond to a need common to the whole population or be supplied throughout a territory.

Furthermore, the universality criterion does not require that the service in question be free of charge or that it be offered without consideration of economic profitability. The fact that certain potential users do not have the necessary financial resources to take advantage of all the PMI cover available on the market, in particular 'luxury' cover, does not undermine its universal nature provided that the service in question is offered at uniform and non-discriminatory rates and on similar quality conditions for all customers.[19] Hence here SGEI were held to be involved and the compensation paid was not regarded as constituting state aid (but a quid pro quo).

The second example, which mirrors the first because it refers to the least well-to-do half of the population instead of the wealthier half as in *BUPA*, is offered by the 2009 Commission Decision on aid to Dutch housing corporations.[20] Here the Dutch authorities were required to identify a clearly delimited target group amongst their population as the intended beneficiaries of social housing. This was based on an income criterion that resulted in a target group comprising 43 per cent of the population. The renting out of subsidized housing to the more affluent segment of the population was limited to 10 per cent of the housing stock involved and justified as being in the interest of social mixing and cohesion. Here therefore not universal access but access based on social criteria (household income) was decisive in determining the existence of an SGEI.

Distinguishing economic and non-economic activities of the same entity

Finally, there is a significant trend with an impact both on the rationalization of national policies and the scope of EU law with regard to public services which is reflected in the Commission's 2014 Draft Notice on the notion of state aid. This concerns the important concept of severability of the public authority tasks and the economic activities of an entity, derived from the emerging case law on this issue.[21] In the 2011 *Flughafen Leipzig-Halle* case the

[19] Case T-289/03 *BUPA*, above n. 3, paras. 186 and 203.

[20] Commission Decision, State aid No E 2/2005 and N 642/2009 – The Netherlands: Existing and special project aid to housing corporations, 15 December 2009.

[21] Communication from the Commission, Draft Commission Notice on the notion of state aid pursuant to Article 107(1) TFEU.

General Court ruled that if the operation of an activity could not be dissociated from building the underlying infrastructure, both were covered by the state aid rules.[22] It also stated that

> The classification as an activity falling within the exercise of public powers or as an economic activity must be carried out separately for each activity engaged in by a given entity.[23]

This is important because it suggests that activities ruled by competition and state aid principles can be separated effectively from non-economic tasks that are not. As is also set out in the Draft Notice, this view is reinforced by the 2012 *Compass* case, where the Court held the following:

> In so far as a public entity exercises an economic activity which can be separated from the exercise of its public powers, that entity, in relation to that activity, acts as an undertaking, while, if that economic activity cannot be separated from the exercise of its public powers, the activities exercised by that entity as a whole remain activities connected with the exercise of those public powers.[24]

Thus economic activities can be judged separately from public authority functions. Although the case law on this topic is still relatively scarce, this looks like a promising new direction.[25] This is because it will allow a rationalization of the application of the competition and state aid rules to entities with mixed tasks and will hopefully in future help to avoid anomalies such as *FENIN* where competitive activities in one market are subsumed by public tasks in another.[26] It also logically supplements the functional approach, allowing a greater degree of granularity in the analysis as well as consistency.

It is clear that the five developments signalled above show both the flexibility and the potential for further expansion of the SGEI and USO concepts. The common trend appears to be a preference for market-based provision, but with scope for proportional exceptions. It also indicates some of the more challenging ways in which competition and SGEI are intertwined in the provision of public services. It seems appropriate to follow up these trends with the prospects for future research.

[22] Joined Cases T-443/08 and T-455/08 *Freistaat Sachsen and Land Sachsen-Anhalt and Mitteldeutsche Flughafen AG and Flughafen Leipzig-Halle GmbH* v. *Commission* [2011] ECR II-1319, paras. 99–100.

[23] Ibid., para. 98.

[24] Case C-138/11 *Compass-Datenbank GmbH* v. *Republik Österreich*, Judgment of 12 July 2012, para. 38, with reference to Case C-113/07 P *SELEX Sistemi Integrati* v. *Commission* [2009] ECR I-2207, paras. 72ff.

[25] Case 107/84 *Commission* v. *Germany* [1985] ECR 2655, paras. 14–15.

[26] Case C-205/03 P *Federación Española de Empresas de Tecnología Sanitaria (FENIN)* v. *Commission* [2006] ECR I-6295.

7.6 Avenues for future research

Finally, I will just mark a number of the themes that I have mentioned above to which I have not been able to do justice in this book but that do seem to merit further attention in future research.

Welfare services versus utilities

Above I have tried to provide an approach that consistently dealt with welfare services and the utilities. The justification for doing so is that they are both (halves of the concept of) public services. In most cases, however, it appeared that these two sets of public services are mirror images of each other: in particular, one is more affected by the internal market rules (and citizenship), the other by competition and state aid.

However, I believe that in the area of state aid compensation (provided undertakings are involved) the link between the two is closest. For now this has been solved by absolving the welfare services under a block exemption; however, the conditions that they have to meet are broadly the same as would apply for an individual exemption. Also, in future, it appears likely that welfare services will increasingly be provided by undertakings, making it more likely that the (state aid and) competition rules will apply. As this happens, I believe it is likely there will be more material to examine than has been available so far, which will make it possible to extend or revise my analysis.

Efficiency versus equity

Throughout this book I have tried to mark when economic efficiency exceptions and when social equity exceptions applied. The concept of market failure is of limited help in this context because, as I understand it, this can be interpreted broadly – and cover both categories – as well as narrowly, and cover just efficiency. In addition, there is the axis of the level at which the benefits must accrue: in competition law this is the market including the consumers (efficiency based), in internal market law it is the Member State (equity based), for SGEI it is the Member State (both efficiency and equity based), but for state aid it is that of the EU (likewise both efficiency and equity based). This is summarized in Table 7.1.

This differentiation complicates the discussion, but it also shows that the SGEI instrument is relatively attractive because, as it overlaps with all of these categories, it is universally applicable. Finally, it is noteworthy that there is a discussion on whether equity arguments should be allowed in competition law (with which I disagree) and at the same time increasingly the rule on the internal market is bent to allow efficiency arguments there. For better or for worse, this suggests convergence of a kind, which means that the relevance of the proportionality requirement is likely to increase

Table 7.1 Types of exceptions and beneficiaries

I Type of EU law framework	II Nature of exception allowed		III Level of interest promoted			
Internal market	equity		Member State			
Competition		efficiency		undertaking	consumer	
State aid	equity	efficiency				EU
SGEI	equity	efficiency	Member State			

still further. In any event, it would be interesting to examine (again) the standards of the exceptions applied in the different realms and their (dis) similarities.

Universal service, consumer protection and citizenship

The citizenship concept is increasingly often and loosely used in the context of the public services. There appear to be three main strands. The first of these is Article 18 TFEU and access to public services as based on the *Grzelczyk* (2001) case law. This chimes with access in the Charter of Fundamental Rights of the European Union – although there it is brought under the heading of solidarity, not citizenship. The second is that of the market citizen,[27] or of consumer rights.[28] The third links citizenship to USO.[29]

One of the main future directions for EU law in this field is no doubt the interface between universal service, citizenship and consumer protection. Attentive readers will have noticed how I have made this point repeatedly without being able to give much more substance to this assertion. The reason for this is quite simply that I do not yet have sufficient background in the EU law on consumer protection or on citizenship to develop this relationship much further in a meaningful way. A thumbnail sketch of the relationship between these potentially mutually reinforcing categories could look as shown in Figure 7.1.

Also, above I have noted that there is a tension between consumer protection – including in the context of universal service (such as in energy) – and efficiency. This means that protection may be effective but also inefficient and inequitable because it may chase or price cheaper services that could have benefited less wealthy consumers out of the market. The link with citizenship is even more difficult to construe if we take it to refer not to the new and hybrid concept of 'market citizenship' but to the provisions in the Treaty that are essentially about non-discrimination.

[27] Monti, above n. 1. [28] Davies, above n. 6.
[29] Micklitz, H.-W., 'Universal services: Nucleus for a social European private law', in M. Cremona (ed.), *Market integration and public services in the European Union* (Oxford University Press, 2011), 63–102; Davies and Szyszczak, above n. 12.

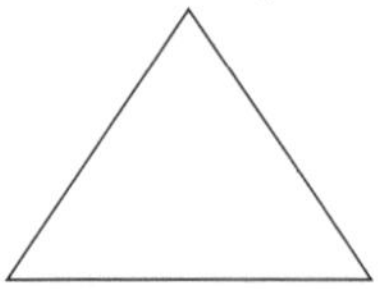

Figure 7.1 Three dimensions of the individual interest in EU law

Not all observers are equally hesitant. With regard to the above-mentioned perception of public services as a persistent irritant, we can cite Tony Prosser:

> [P]ublic services are no longer seen as an unwelcome impediment to the creation of a single market but rather as essential expressions of our citizenship rights as Europeans.[30]

These are hopeful words for which I have sympathy. Yet in the Charter of Fundamental Rights of the European Union SGEI are ranked under the solidarity provisions, not under citizenship. Moreover, so far Jo Shaw's scepticism whether EU citizenship, even if developed further, would add much legitimacy in any event seems justified.[31]

Nevertheless, it appears evident that the universality principle that underlies most public service obligations (even when imposed indirectly, at wholesale level), and especially universal service obligations, can both define and give substance to certain basic social and economic rights for individuals under EU law. Hence in my opinion it is not impossible or even implausible to link the three concepts – even though, for example, a Treaty amendment extending citizenship to this effect seems highly unlikely at present.

A regulation on SGEI?

Instead the instrument that would be most suitable for a codification of public services in their manifestation as SGEI appears to be the Regulation that can be adopted by the European Parliament and Council under Article 14 TFEU based on the ordinary legislative procedure. Of course such a text cannot take the place of the citizenship provisions in the Treaty, but comparably to the Residency Rights Directive, it could complement them.[32] The Commission

[30] T. Prosser, 'Competition law and public services: From single market to citizenship rights', *European Public Law* 11 (2005), 543–63, at 562–3.

[31] J. Shaw, 'Citizenship: Contrasting dynamics at the interface of integration and constitutionalism', in P. Craig and G. de Búrca, *The evolution of EU law*, 2nd edn (Oxford University Press, 2011), 575–609.

[32] Directive 2004/38/EC of the European Parliament and of the Council of 29 April 2004 on the right of citizens of the Union and their family members to move and reside freely within the territory of the Member States amending Regulation (EEC) No 1612/68 and repealing Directives

has so far successfully resisted all calls to draft a proposal for an SGEI Regulation. It harbours justified fears that such an instrument might escape from its control. Instead the Commission might prefer to adopt measures single-handedly based on Article 106(3) TFEU – however, this option by now seems to be limited to Decisions, and foreclosed for reasons of democratic legitimacy, as far as Directives are concerned.

In any event, it could be a useful exercise or thought experiment for future research to speculate further on what the contents of an Article 14 TFEU Regulation might be, in order to establish whether it could be worthwhile in spite of the risks involved. This would require a balance between equity and efficiency, state and market, and the different levels of government within the EU. At this point I only have some general intuitions to offer on this exercise. First, it already seems clear that if adopted, such a Regulation would in and of itself form an affirmation that public services are here to stay, at least in terms of the universality of their objectives. Second, it would be interesting to see whether it could add anything in terms of solidarity across national borders and give further substance to European citizenship. In sum, if it were likely to deliver form and substance in both respects, an Article 14 TFEU Regulation could be attractive as a contribution to the objective of constructing a European social market economy.

64/221/EEC, 68/360/EEC, 72/194/EEC, 73/148/EEC, 75/34/EEC, 75/35/EEC, 90/364/EEC, 90/365/EEC and 93/96/EEC, OJ 2004, L158/77.

Bibliography

Baldwin, R., Cave, M., and Lodge, M., *Understanding regulation: Theory, strategy and practice*, 2nd edn (Oxford University Press, 2013)

(eds.), *The Oxford handbook of regulation* (Oxford University Press, 2010)

Baquero Cruz, J., *Between competition and free movement: The economic constitutional law of the European Community* (Hart Publishing, Oxford, 2002)

'Social services of general interest and the state aid rules', in U. Neergaard et al. (eds.), *Social services of general interest in the EU* (TMC Asser Press, The Hague, 2013), 287–313

'The state action doctrine', in G. Amato, C.-D. Ehlermann and A. Komninos (eds.), *EC Competition law: A critical assessment* (Hart Publishing, Oxford, 2007), 551–90

Barnard, C., 'EU citizenship and the principle of solidarity', in M. Dougan and E. Spaventa (eds.), *Social welfare and EU law: Essays in European law* (Hart Publishing, Oxford, 2005), 157–80

The substantive law of the EU: The four freedoms, 4th edn (Oxford University Press, 2013)

'Unravelling the Services Directive', *Common Market Law Review*, 45 (2008), 323–94

Barr, N., *Economics of the welfare state*, 5th edn (Oxford University Press, 2012)

Benyon, F., 'Broadcasting and the EU consumer', in F. S. Benyon (ed.), *Services and the EU citizen* (Hart Publishing, Oxford, 2013), 75–85.

(ed.), *Services and the EU citizen* (Hart Publishing, Oxford, 2013)

Boeger, N., 'Solidarity and EC competition law', *European Law Review*, 32 (2007), 319–40

Bork, R. H., *The antitrust paradox: A policy at war with itself* (Basic Books, Chicago, 1978)

Bovis, C. H., 'The conceptual links between state aid and public procurement in the financing of services of general economic interest', in M. Krajewski, U. Neergaard and J. van de Gronden (eds.), *The changing legal framework for services of general interest in Europe, between competition and solidarity* (TMC Asser Press, The Hague, 2009), 149–70

European public procurement law, 2nd edn (Edward Elgar, Cheltenham, 2012)

Bracq, S., 'Droit communautaire matériel et qualification juridique: Le financement des obligations de service public au coeur de la tourmente', (2004) *Revue trimestrielle de droit européen*, 40 (2004), 33–70

Buendia Sierra, J. L., 'Chapter 6: Article 106 – exclusive or special rights and other anti-competitive state measures', in J. Faull and A. Nikpay (eds.), *The EU law of competition*, 3rd edn (Oxford University Press, 2014), 809–79

Exclusive rights and state monopolies under EC law: Article 86 (former Article 90) of the EC Treaty (Oxford University Press, 2000)

Buendia Sierra, J. L., and Panero Rivas, J. M., 'The *Almunia* package: State aid and services of general economic interest', in E. Szyszczak and J. W. van de Gronden (eds.), *Financing services of general economic interest: Reform and modernization* (TMC Asser Press, The Hague, 2013), 125–48

Buttigieg, E., *Competition law: Safeguarding the consumer interest. A comparative analysis of US antitrust law and EC competition law* (Kluwer Law, Alphen aan den Rijn, 2009)

Cantillon, B., Verschueren, H., and Ploscar, P. (eds.), *Social inclusion and social protection in the EU: Interactions between law and policy* (Intersentia, Antwerp, 2012)

Clarke, I., 'The role of procurement and SGEI after *Altmark*', in E. Szyszczak and J. W. van de Gronden (eds.), *Financing services of general economic interest: Reform and modernization* (TMC Asser Press, The Hague, 2013), 69–84

Craig, P., 'Integration, democracy and legitimacy', in P. Craig and G. de Búrca (eds.), *The evolution of EU law*, 2nd edn (Oxford University Press, 2011), 13–40

Cremona, M. (ed.), *Market integration and public services in the European Union* (Oxford University Press, 2011)

Cseres, K. J., *Competition policy and consumer protection* (Kluwer Law, Alphen aan den Rijn, 2005)

'The controversies of the consumer welfare standard', *Competition Law Review*, 3 (2007), 121–73

Davies, G., 'The effect of Mrs Watts' trip to France on the National Health Service', *King's Law Journal*, 18 (2007), 158–67

'What does Article 86 actually do?' in M. Krajewski, U. Neergaard and J. van de Gronden (eds.), *The changing legal framework for services of general interest in Europe: Between competition and solidarity* (TMC Asser Press, The Hague, 2009), 51–67

Davies, J., *The European consumer citizen in law and policy: Consumption and public life* (Palgrave Macmillan, London, 2011)

Davies, J., and Szyszczak, E., 'Universal service obligations: Fulfilling new generations of services of general economic interest', in E. Szyszczak et al. (eds.), *Developments in services of general interest* (TMC Asser Press, The Hague, 2011), 155–77

Dawes, A., '"Bonjour Herr Doctor": National healthcare systems, the internal market and cross-border medical care within the European Union', *Legal Issues of Economic Integration*, 33 (2006), 167–82

de Bijl, P., et al., *Universal service in banking*. TILEC report, 14 March 2006

de Búrca, G., 'The principle of proportionality and its application in EC law', (1993) *Yearbook of European Law*, 13 (1993), 105–50

(ed.), *EU law and the welfare state: In search of solidarity* (Oxford University Press, 2005)

de Búrca, G., and Weiler, J. H. H., *The worlds of European constitutionalism* (Cambridge University Press, 2011)

de Cecco, F., *State aid and the European economic constitution* (Hart Publishing, Oxford, 2013)

de Visser, M., *Network-based governance in EC law: The example of EC competition and EC communications law* (Hart Publishing, Oxford, 2009)

DG Competition, 'Non-paper on services of general economic interest and state aid', 12 November 2002

Dougan, M., 'The constitutional dimension to the case law on Union citizenship', *European Law Review*, 31 (2006), 613–41

'Expanding the frontiers of Union citizenship by dismantling the territorial boundaries of national welfare states?' in C. Barnard and O. Odudu (eds.), *The outer limits of European Union law* (Hart Publishing, Oxford, 2009), 119–66

Dougan, M., and Spaventa, E., 'Educating Rudy and the non-English patient: A double bill on residency rights under Article 18 EC', *European Law Review*, 28 (2003), 699–712

(eds.), *Social welfare and EU law: Essays in European law* (Hart Publishing, Oxford, 2005)

Drijber, B. J., and Stergiou, H., 'Public procurement law and internal market law', *Common Market Law Review*, 46 (2009), 805–46

EAGCP (antitrust subgroup), *An economic approach to Article 82*, July 2005

EAGCP (state aid subgroup), *Services of general economic interest*, June 2006

Ezrachi, A., and de Jong, K., 'Buyer power, private labels and the welfare consequences of quality erosion', *European Competition Law Review*, 33 (2012), 45–50

Faull, J., and Nikpay, A., *The EC law of competition*, 2nd edn (Oxford University Press, 2007)

The EU law of competition, 3rd edn (Oxford University Press, 2014)

Ferrara, M., *The boundaries of welfare: European integration and the new spatial politics of social protection* (Oxford University Press, 2005)

'Modest beginnings, timid progress: What's next for social Europe?' in B. Cantillon, H. Verschueren and P. Ploscar (eds.), *Social inclusion and social protection in the EU: Interactions between law and policy* (Intersentia, Antwerp, 2012), 17–40

'Towards an "open" social citizenship? The new boundaries of welfare in the European Union', in G. de Búrca (ed.), *EU law and the welfare state: In search of solidarity* (Oxford University Press, 2005), 11–38

Fiedziuk, N., 'Putting services of general economic interest up for tender: Reflections on applicable EU rules', *Common Market Law Review*, 50 (2013), 87–114

'Services of general economic interest and the Treaty of Lisbon: Opening doors to a whole new approach or maintaining the "status quo"?' *European Law Review*, 36 (2011), 226–42

'Towards a more refined economic approach to services of general economic interest', *European Public Law*, 16 (2010), 271–88

Finger, M., and Finon, D., 'From the "public service" model to the "universal service" obligation', in M. Finger and R. Künneke (eds.), *International handbook of network industries: The liberalisation of infrastructure* (Edward Elgar, Cheltenham, 2011), 54–69

Gabathuler, D., and Sauter, W., 'The allocation of scarce resources and spectrum assignment in mobile communications: The case of UMTS', in P. A. Buigues and P. Rey (eds.), *The economics of antitrust and regulation in telecommunications: Perspectives for the new European regulatory framework* (Edward Elgar, Cheltenham, 2004), 213–38

Gautier, A., and Paolini, D., 'Universal service financing in competitive postal markets: One size does not fit all', *Review of Network Economics*, 10 (2011), 1–30

Gerard, D., 'EU competition policy after Lisbon: Time to review the "state action doctrine"?' *Journal of European Competition Law and Practice*, 1 (2010), 202–10

'Protectionist threats against cross-border mergers: Unexplored avenues to strengthen the effectiveness of Article 21 ECMR', (2008) *Common Market Law Review*, 45 (2008), 987–1025

Gerber, D., 'Constitutionalising the economy: German neo-liberalism, competition law and the "new" Europe', *American Journal of Comparative Law*, 42 (1994), 24–84

Law and competition in twentieth century Europe: Protecting Prometheus (Oxford University Press, 1998)

Gideon, A., 'Higher education institutions and EU competition law', *Competition Law Review*, 8 (2012), 169–84

Habermas, J., *The crisis of the European Union: A response* (Polity Press, Cambridge, 2012)

Hancher, L., and Larouche, P., 'The coming of age of EU regulation of network industries and services of general economic interest', in P. Craig and G. de Búrca (eds.), *The evolution of EU law*, 2nd edn (Oxford University Press, 2011), 743–81

Hancher, L., and Lavrijssen, S. A. C. M., 'Networks on track: From European regulatory networks to European regulatory "network agencies"', *Legal Issues of Economic Integration*, 36 (2009), 23–55

Hancher, L., Ottervanger, T., and Slot, P. J. (eds.), *EU state aids*, 4th edn (Sweet & Maxwell, London, 2012)

Hancher, L., and Sauter, W., *EU competition and internal market law in the healthcare sector* (Oxford University Press, 2012)

'One step beyond? From *Sodemare* to *Docmorris*: The EU's freedom of establishment case law concerning healthcare', *Common Market Law Review*, 47 (2010), 117–46

'Public services and state aid', in C. Barnard and S. Peers (eds.), *European Union law* (Oxford University Press, 2014), 539–66

'This won't hurt a bit: The Commission's approach to services of general economic interest and state aid to hospitals', in E. Szyszczak and J. W. van de Gronden (eds.), *Financing services of general economic interest: Reform and modernization* (TMC Asser Press, The Hague, 2013), 249–72

Harbo, T. I., 'The function of the proportionality principle in EU law', *European Law Journal*, 16 (2010), 158–85

Harker, M., Kreutzmann, A., and Waddams, C., *Public service obligations and competition*, Final Report, February 2013, CERRE Centre for regulation in Europe

Hatzopoulos, V. G., 'Killing national health and insurance systems but healing patients? The European market for health care services after the judgments of the ECJ in *Vanbraekel* and *Peerbooms*', *Common Market Law Review*, 39 (2002), 683–729

Regulating services in the European Union (Oxford University Press, 2012)

Hay, C., and Wincott, D., *The political economy of European welfare capitalism* (Palgrave Macmillan, Basingstoke, 2012)

Hemerijck, A., *Changing welfare states* (Oxford University Press, 2013)

Hendrickx, F., 'The Services Directive and social dumping: National labour law under strain?' in U. Neergaard, R. Nielsen and L. M. Roseberry (eds.), *The Services Directive: Consequences for the welfare state and the European social model* (Djøf Publishing, Copenhagen, 2008), 243–58

Holmes, J., 'Fixing the limits of EC competition law: State action and the accommodation of the public services', *Current Legal Problems*, 57 (2004), 149–74

Hovenkamp, H., *The antitrust enterprise: Principle and execution* (Harvard University Press, Cambridge, Mass., 2005)

Jans, J., 'Proportionality revisited', *Legal Issues of Economic Integration*, 27 (2000), 239–65

Joerges, C., 'Law, economics and politics in the constitutionalisation of Europe', *Cambridge Yearbook of European Legal Studies*, 5 (2002–3), 123–50

'*Rechtsstaat* and social Europe: How a classical tension resurfaces in the European integration process', *Comparative Sociology*, 9 (2010), 65–85

Kavanagh, J., 'Financing services of general economic interest: The European Commission's economic tests', in E. Szyszczak and J. W. van de Gronden (eds.), *Financing services of general economic interest: Reform and modernization* (TMC Asser Press, The Hague, 2013), 149–59

Kliemann, A., and Stehmann, O., 'EU state aid control in the broadband sector – The 2013 broadband guidelines and recent case practice', *European State Aid Law Quarterly*, 12 (2013), 493–515

Krajewski, M., Neergaard, U., and van de Gronden, J. (eds.), *The changing framework for services of general interest in Europe: Between competition and solidarity* (TMC Asser Press, The Hague, 2009)

Larouche, P., *Competition law and regulation in European telecommunications* (Hart Publishing, Oxford, 2000)

Lavrijssen, S. A. C. M., 'The protection of non-competition interests: What role for competition authorities after Lisbon?' *European Law Review*, 35 (2010), 634–59

Lavrijssen, S. A. C. M., and Hancher, L., 'Networks of regulatory agencies in Europe', in P. Larouche and P. Cserne (eds.), *National legal systems and globalization: New role, continuing relevance* (TMC Asser Press, The Hague, 2013), 183–220

Le Grand, J., *The other invisible hand: Delivering public services through choice and competition* (Princeton University Press, 2007)

Loozen, E., 'Professional ethics and restrictions of competition', *European Law Review*, 31 (2006), 29–48

Louis, F., and Vallery, A., '*Ferring* revisited: The *Altmark* case and state financing of public service obligations', *World Competition*, 27 (2004), 53

Majone, G., *Dilemmas of European integration: The ambiguities and pitfalls of integration by stealth* (Oxford University Press, 2009)

'The rise of the regulatory state in Europe', *West European Politics*, 17 (1994), 77–101

Maletic, I., *The law and policy of harmonisation in Europe's internal market* (Edward Elgar, Cheltenham, 2013)

Manunza, E., and Berends, W. J., 'Social services of general interest and the EU public procurement rules', in U. Neergaard et al. (eds.), *Social services of general interest in the EU* (TMC Asser Press, The Hague, 2013), 347–84

Marks, G., Hooghe, L., and Blank, K., 'European integration from the 1980s: State-centric v. multi-level governance', *Journal of Common Market Studies*, 34 (1996), 341–78

Mastroianni, R., 'Public service media and market integration: A differential application of free movement and state aid rule?' in M. Cremona (ed.), *Market integration and public services in the European Union* (Oxford University Press, 2011), 149–77

McGowan, F., and Wallace, H., 'Towards a European regulatory state', *Journal of European Public Policy*, 3 (1996), 560–76

Micklitz, H.-W., 'Universal services: Nucleus for a social European private law', in M. Cremona (ed.), *Market integration and public services in the European Union* (Oxford University Press, 2011), 63–102

Micklitz, H.-W., Reich, N., and Rott, P., *Understanding EU consumer law* (Intersentia, Antwerp, 2009)

Milward, A. S., *The European rescue of the nation state*, 2nd edn (Routledge, London, 1999)

Monti, G., 'Article 81 and public policy', *Common Market Law Review*, 39 (2002), 1057–99

EC competition law (Cambridge University Press, 2007)

Monti, M., *A new strategy for the single market: At the service of Europe's economy and society*. Report to the President of the European Commission, José Manuel Barroso, 9 May 2010

Morgan, B., and Yeung, K., *An introduction to law and regulation: Text and materials* (Cambridge University Press, 2009)

Motta, M., *Competition policy, theory and practice* (Cambridge University Press, 2004)

Myklebust, J. P., and O'Malley, B., 'Netherlands: Dawn raids over "illegal" tuition fees', *University World News* issue 188, 7 September 2011

Neergaard, U., 'The concept of SSGI and the asymmetries between free movement and competition law', in U. Neergaard et al. (eds.), *Social services of general interest in the EU* (TMC Asser Press, The Hague, 2013), 205–44

'Services of general economic interest: The nature of the beast', in M. Krajewski, U. Neergaard and J. van de Gronden (eds.), *The changing framework for services of general interest in Europe: Between competition and solidarity* (TMC Asser Press, The Hague, 2009), 17–50

'Services of general (economic) interest and the Services Directive – What is left out, why and where to go?' in U. Neergaard, R. Nielsen and L. M. Roseberry (eds.), *The Services Directive: Consequences for the welfare state and the European social model* (Djøf Publishing, Copenhagen, 2008), 65–120

Neergaard, U., et al. (eds.), *Social services of general interest in the EU* (TMC Asser Press, The Hague, 2013)

Neergaard, U., Nielsen R., and Roseberry, L. M. (eds.), *The Services Directive: Consequences for the welfare state and the European social model* (Djøf Publishing, Copenhagen, 2008)

Neven, D., and Verouden, V., 'Towards a more refined economic approach in state aid control', in W. Mederer, N. Pesaresi and M. Van Hoof (eds.), *EU competition law – Volume IV: State aid* (Claeys and Casteels Publishing, Deventer, 2008)

Newdick, C., 'Citizenship, free movement and health care: Cementing individual rights by corroding social solidarity', *Common Market Law Review*, 43 (2006), 1645–68

Nicolaides, P., Kekelekis, M., and Kleis, M., *State aid and practice in the European Community: Principles and practice*, 2nd edn (Kluwer, Alphen aan den Rijn, 2008)

Nihoul, P., and Rodford, P., *EU electronic communications law: Competition and regulation in the European telecommunications market*, 2nd edn (Oxford University Press, 2011)

Nijenhuis, A., 'Electronic communications and the EU consumer', in F. S. Benyon (ed.), *Services and the EU citizen* (Hart Publishing, Oxford, 2013), 47–74

Nistor, L., *Public services and the European Union: Healthcare, health insurance and education services* (TMC Asser Press, The Hague, 2011)

Odudu, O., 'Are state-owned health-care providers undertakings subject to competition law?' *European Competition Law Review*, 32 (2011), 231–41

The boundaries of EC competition law: The scope of Article 81 (Oxford University Press, 2006)

'Economic activity as a limit to Community law', in C. Barnard and O. Odudu (eds.), *The outer limits of European Union law* (Hart Publishing, Oxford, 2009), 225–43

Ogus, A. I., *Regulation: Legal form and economic theory* (Hart Publishing, Oxford, 2004)

O'Leary, S., 'Solidarity and citizenship rights in the Charter of Fundamental Rights of the European Union', in G. de Búrca (ed.), *EU law and the welfare state: In search of solidarity* (Oxford University Press, 2005), 39–88

Oliver, D., Prosser, T., and Rawlings, R. (eds.), *The regulatory state: Constitutional implications* (Oxford University Press, 2010)

O'Loughlin, R., 'EC competition rules and free movement rules: An examination of the parallels and their furtherance by the ECJ *Wouters* Decision', *European Competition Law Review*, 23 (2003), 62–69

Page, A. C., 'Member States, public undertakings and Article 90', *European Law Review*, 7 (1982), 19–35

Pennings, F., *European social security law* (Intersentia, Antwerp, 2010)

'Inclusion and exclusion of persons and benefits in the new coordination Regulation', in M. Dougan and E. Spaventa (eds.), *Social welfare and EU law: Essays in European law* (Hart Publishing, Oxford, 2005), 241–60

Pesaresi, N., and Pilley, O., 'Retail banking, social inclusion and public service', *Competition Policy Newsletter*, 10 (2003), 1: 14–20

Poiares Maduro, M., *We the Court: The European Court of Justice and the European economic constitution* (Hart Publishing, Oxford, 1998)

Prosser, T., 'Competition law and public services: From single market to citizenship rights', *European Public Law*, 11 (2005), 543–63

The limits of competition law: Markets and public services (Oxford University Press, 2005)

'Regulation and social solidarity', *Journal of Law and Society*, 33 (2006), 364–87

'Theorising utility regulation', *Modern Law Review*, 62 (1999), 196–217

Rennuy, N., 'The emergence of a parallel system of social security coordination', *Common Market Law Review*, 50 (2013), 1221–66

Rodrigues, S., 'Towards a general EC framework instrument related to SGEI? Political considerations and legal constraints', in M. Krajewski, U. Neergaard and J. van de Gronden (eds.), *The changing framework for services of general interest in Europe: Between competition and solidarity* (TMC Asser Press, The Hague, 2009), 255–66

Ronellenfitsch, M.,'Das Altmark-Urteil des Europäischen Gerichtshofs', *Verwaltungsarchiv*, 95 (2004), 425–42

Ross, M., 'Article 16 EC and services of general interest: From derogation to obligation', *European Law Review*, 25 (2000), 22–38

'Promoting solidarity: From public services to a European model of competition', *Common Market Law Review*, 44 (2007), 1057–80

'SSGIs and solidarity: Constitutive elements of the EU's social market economy', in U. Neergaard et al. (eds.), *Social services of general interest in the EU* (TMC Asser Press, The Hague, 2013), 95–121

Rusche, T. M., and Schmidt, S., 'Transport', in E. Szyszczak and J. W. van de Gronden (eds.), *Financing services of general economic interest: Reform and modernization* (TMC Asser Press, The Hague, 2013), 217–48

Sánchez Graells, A., 'The Commission's modernisation agenda for procurement and SGEI', in E. Szyszczak and J. W. van de Gronden (eds.), *Financing services of general economic interest: Reform and modernization* (TMC Asser Press, The Hague, 2013), 161–81

Public procurement and the EU competition rules (Hart Publishing, Oxford, 2011)

Sauter, W., 'The *Altmark* package mark II: New rules for state aid and the compensation of services of general economic interest', *European Competition Law Review*, 33 (2012), 307–13

'Case T-289/03 *British United Provident Association Ltd (BUPA), BUPA Insurance Ltd and BUPA Ireland Ltd* v. *Commission* [2008] ECR II-81', *Common Market Law Review*, 46 (2009), 269–86

Competition law and industrial policy in the EU (Oxford University Press, 1997)

'Harmonization in health care: The EU Patients' Rights Directive', in B. Cantillon, H. Verschueren and P. Ploscar (eds.), *Social inclusion and social protection in the EU: Interactions between law and policy* (Intersentia, Antwerp, 2012), 105–29

'The impact of EU competition law on national healthcare systems', *European Law Review*, 38 (2013), 456–78

'Proportionality in EU law: A balancing act?' *Cambridge Yearbook of European Legal Studies*, 15 (2012–13), 439–66

'Services of general economic interest and universal service in EU law', *European Law Review*, 33 (2008), 167–92

'Squaring EU competition law and industrial policy: The case of broadband', TILEC Discussion Paper 2013/21

'Universal service obligations and the emergence of citizens' rights in European telecommunications liberalization', in M. Freedland and S. Sciarra (eds.), *Public services and citizenship in European law: Public and labour law perspectives* (Oxford University Press, 1998), 117–43

Sauter, W., and Schepel, H., *State and market in European Union law: The public and private spheres of the internal market before the EU Courts* (Cambridge University Press, 2009)

Scharpf, F. W., 'The asymmetry of European integration, or why the EU cannot be a "social market economy"', *Socio-Economic Review*, 8 (2010), 211–50

Community and autonomy: Institutions, policies and legitimacy in multilevel Europe (Campus, Frankfurt am Main, 2010)

'Der einzige Weg ist, dem EuGH nicht zu folgen', Interview in *Mitbestimmung* (2008), 7/8, 18–23

'The European social model: Coping with the challenges of diversity', *Journal of Common Market Studies*, 40 (2002), 645–70

Governing in Europe: Effective and democratic? (Oxford University Press, 1999)

'The joint-decision trap: Lessons from German federalism and European integration', *Public Administration*, 66 (1998), 239–78

Schepel, H., 'Delegation of regulatory powers to private parties under EC competition law: Towards a procedural public interest test', *Common Market Law Review*, 39 (2002), 31–51

Schweitzer, H., 'Services of general economic interest: European law's impact on the role of markets and of Member States', in M. Cremona (ed.), *Market integration and public services in the European Union* (Oxford University Press, 2011), 11–62

Senden, L., *Soft law in European Community law* (Hart Publishing, Oxford, 2004)

Shaw, J., 'Citizenship: Contrasting dynamics at the interface of integration and constitutionalism', in P. Craig and G. de Búrca, *The evolution of EU law*, 2nd edn (Oxford University Press, 2011), 575–609

Sinnaeve, A., 'State financing of public services: The Court's dilemma in the *Altmark* case', *European State Aid Law Quarterly*, 2 (2003), 351–62

Slot, P. J., 'Public distortions of competition: The importance of Article 106 TFEU and the state action doctrine', in U. Neergaard et al. (eds.), *Social services of general interest in the EU* (TMC Asser Press, The Hague, 2013), 245–62

Smith, M. P., *States of liberalisation: Redefining the public sector in integrated Europe* (SUNY Press, Albany, 2005)

Snyder, F., 'EMU – integration and differentiation: Metaphor for European Union', in P. Craig and G. de Búrca (eds.), *The evolution of EU law*, 2nd edn (Oxford University Press, 2011), 687–716

Spaak, P. H. (Spaak report), Comité intergouvernemental creé par la Conférence de Messine, *Rapport des Chefs de délégation aux Ministres des Affaires étrangères* (Brussels, 1956)

Spaventa, E., 'Seeing the wood despite the trees? On the scope of Union citizenship and its constitutional effects', *Common Market Law Review*, 45 (2008), 13–45

Streit, M. E., and Mussler, W., 'The economic constitution of the European Community: From "Rome" to "Maastricht"', *European Law Journal*, 1 (1995), 5–30

Sunstein, C. R., and Thaler, R. H., *Nudge: Improving decisions about health, wealth, and happiness* (Yale University Press, New Haven, 2008)

Szyszczak, E., 'Modernising state aid and the financing of SGEI', *Journal of European Competition Law and Practice*, 3 (2012), 332–43

The regulation of the state in competitive markets in the EU (Hart Publishing, Oxford, 2007)

(ed.), *Research handbook on European state aid law* (Edward Elgar, Cheltenham, 2011)

Szyszczak, E., et al. (eds.), *Developments in services of general interest* (TMC Asser Press, The Hague, 2011)

Szyszczak, E., and van de Gronden, J. W. (eds.), *Financing services of general economic interest: Reform and modernization* (TMC Asser Press, The Hague, 2013)

Talus, K., *EU energy law and policy: A critical account* (Oxford University Press, 2013)

Tinbergen, J., *International economic integration*, 2nd edn (Elsevier, Amsterdam, 1965)

Townley, C., *Article 81 EC and public policy* (Hart Publishing, Oxford, 2009)

van de Gronden, J. W., 'The Services Directive and services of general (economic) interest', in M. Krajewski, U. Neergaard and J. van de Gronden (eds.), *The changing legal framework for services of general interest in Europe: Between competition and solidarity* (TMC Asser Press, The Hague, 2009), 233–54

van de Gronden, J. W., and Sauter, W., 'Taking the temperature: EU competition law and health care', *Legal Issues of Economic Integration*, 38 (2011), 213–41

van der Meij, A. P., *Free movement of persons within the European Community: Cross-border access to public benefits* (Hart Publishing, Oxford, 2003)

Vedder, H., 'Of jurisdiction and justification: Why competition is good for "non-economic" goals, but may need to be restricted', *Competition Law Review*, 6 (2009), 51–75

Vedder, H., and Holwerda, M., 'The European Court's jurisprudence after *Altmark*', in E. Szyszczak and J. W. van de Gronden (eds.), *Financing services of general economic interest: Reform and modernization* (TMC Asser Press, The Hague, 2013), 53–67

Veljanowski, C., 'Economic approaches to regulation', in R. Baldwin, M. Cave and M. Lodge (eds.), *The Oxford handbook of regulation* (Oxford University Press, 2010), 17–38

Weatherill, S., *EU consumer law and policy*, 2nd edn (Edward Elgar, Cheltenham, 2013)

Wilhelmsson, T., 'Services of general interest and European private law', in C. E. F. Rickett and T. G. W. Telfer (eds.), *International perspectives on consumers' access to justice* (Cambridge University Press, 2003), 149–66

Winterstein, A., 'Nailing the jellyfish: Social security and competition law', *European Competition Law Review*, 19 (1999), 324–33

Yeung, K., 'The regulatory state', in R. Baldwin, M. Cave and M. Lodge (eds.), *The Oxford handbook of regulation* (Oxford University Press, 2010), 64–85

Index